THE TUDORS AND STUARTS

By

M. M. REESE

Formerly Head of the History Department at Wellington College

'When the people contend for their liberty, they seldom get anything by their victory but new masters.'

HALIFAX.

LONDON

EDWARD ARNOLD (PUBLISHERS) LTD.

First published 1940
Reprinted 1942, 1945, 1947, 1949, 1951, 1952, 1955, 1958, 1959, 1960, 1962, 1964, 1966, 1968, 1971

ISBN 0 7131 1354 5

By the same author
SHAKESPEARE: HIS WORLD AND HIS WORK
THE CEASE OF MAJESTY

Printed offset in Great Britian by The Camelot Press Ltd, London and Southampton

PREFACE TO THE TENTH IMPRESSION

When this book was first published in 1940, it was in the hope that it might be found useful in providing classes of young students with a common starting-point in their studies. The 'dictated note' is the bane of history teaching, as everyone connected with the business is in theory willing to agree; but in practice, with classes tending to be large and the subject seldom being allowed sufficient space in the time-table, it is not always easy to give the group that common basis of knowledge necessary before any topic can be usefully discussed. The student needs an adequate and intelligible outline of his period before a detailed study of any of its features can have any meaning for him.

This book therefore aimed to fill the wide gap between the elementary text-book and the larger, more detailed and expensive volumes in such a series as the Oxford History of England, which takes four volumes to cover the period from 1485 to 1714. It was designed primarily for history specialists in secondary schools, the intention being to stimulate them into the effort of interpretation while at the same time giving them enough solid matter to assist them in scholarships and examinations at advanced level. Experience has suggested that it can also be read with some profit both by undergraduates in the early stages of studying for degrees and by many of the stronger candidates at the ordinary level of the G.C.E.

But whoever reads it, and for whatever purpose, this book does not aim at being an end in itself. It is intended merely to help students through the opening phase of their work as specialists, and to relieve teachers of the weariness of tracing an elaborate outline. A certain amount of knowledge has necessarily been taken for granted, and to keep the book to a convenient length I have dealt only fragmentarily with Scotland, Ireland and the early history of the British Empire.

For the tenth impression the reading-list has been considerably revised and brought up to date, and for many helpful suggestions here I must gratefully acknowledge the help given to me by Mr. T. Charles-Edwards, of Ampleforth College. I have also taken the opportunity of making a small number of minor alterations and corrections in the text.

January, 1959. M. M. R.

CONTENTS

CHAP. PAGE

I HENRY VII

1. Henry's claim to the throne . . . 11
2. Henry's government 13
3. Henry's financial measures . . 18
4. Henry's foreign policy 21

II WOLSEY

1. Character of the new King . . . 26
2. The rise of Wolsey 29
3. Wolsey as Chancellor 31
4. Wolsey and the Church 33
5. Wolsey's foreign policy 37

III THE REFORMATION UNDER HENRY VIII

1. The King's 'divorce' 46
2. The breach with Rome 50
3. The definition of doctrine . . . 55
4. Scotland and France 57

IV ENCLOSURES AND POOR RELIEF IN THE SIXTEENTH AND SEVENTEENTH CENTURIES

1. The problem of enclosures . . . 60
2. The government's attitude to enclosures . 63
3. The Tudor Poor Law 70
4. The Puritan attitude to poverty . . 73

V THE REIGN OF EDWARD VI

1. Somerset as Protector 78
2. The Regency of Northumberland . . 83
3. The succession plot 86

Contents

CHAP.		PAGE
VI	THE CATHOLIC REACTION AND THE SETTLEMENT OF ELIZABETH	
	1. The Spanish marriage	88
	2. Mary's persecution	92
	3. The settlement of 1559	96
VII	ELIZABETH'S FOREIGN POLICY: SCOTLAND AND FRANCE	
	1. The danger from Scotland	102
	2. The bid for Calais	107
	3. Mary, Queen of Scots	109
VIII	THE STRUGGLE WITH SPAIN	
	1. Causes of the quarrel with Spain	118
	2. Elizabeth and the Netherlands	127
	3. War with Spain	132
IX	CATHOLIC AND PURITAN	
	1. The Counter-Reformation	141
	2. The growth of Puritanism	145
	3. The effects of Puritanism	153
X	THE INHERITANCE OF JAMES I	
	1. The character of James	158
	2. The Divine Right of Kings	163
	3. The difficulties of James's inheritance	169
XI	JAMES'S QUARRELS WITH PARLIAMENT	
	1. Puritans and Catholics	176
	2. Parliamentary opposition: the Scottish question	182
	3. Financial questions	185
XII	THE FAILURE OF JAMES'S PERSONAL GOVERNMENT	
	1. James's favourites	188
	2. James and the common law	192
	3. James's foreign policy	196
	4. James meets parliament again	199
	5. James goes to war	202

CHAP. PAGE

XIII THE BREAKDOWN OF THE CONSTITUTION
1. The character of Charles I . . . 206
2. The parliaments of 1625 and 1626 . . 208
3. The Petition of Right 212
4. The final breach with parliament . . 217

XIV CHARLES GOVERNS WITHOUT PARLIAMENT
1. Charles's financial measures . . . 221
2. Strafford and the policy of Thorough . 226
3. William Laud 231
4. The war with Scotland 236

XV THE FORMATION OF PARTIES
1. The attack on the prerogative . . 240
2. Disputes about religion 243
3. The two parties 251

XVI THE GREAT REBELLION
1. The reasons for parliament's victory . 255
2. Progress of the war 256
3. Rogues fall out 266
4. The second civil war 273

XVII THE INTERREGNUM
1. The rule of the Rump 277
2. The Barebones Parliament . . . 284
3. The experiments of the Protectorate . 286
4. Foreign affairs during the Interregnum . 293

XVIII THE RESTORATION
1. The collapse of the Protectorate . . 303
2. The Restoration settlement . . . 308
3. The Clarendon Code 314
4. The fall of Clarendon 320

XIX THE REIGN OF CHARLES II
1. The Cabal and the Treaty of Dover . 325
2. The ministry of Danby 335
3. Oates and Exclusion 339
4. The Tory triumph 344

Contents

CHAP.		PAGE
XX	The Second Revolution	
	1. '*Capax imperii nisi imperasset*' . .	350
	2. The Revolution	357
	3. The settlement	361
XXI	The Defence of the Settlement	
	1. The settlement of Great Britain . .	368
	2. 'King William's War'	372
	3. Spanish Succession	377
XXII	The Growth of Parties	
	1. Whig and Tory	386
	2. Parties under William	390
	3. The Whig war and the Tory peace	394
	4. The Tories and the succession . .	397
	Note on Enclosures in England, 1485–1607 .	404
	Lists of Contemporary Rulers	
	1. The Papacy	406
	2. The Holy Roman Empire . .	407
	3. France	407
	4. Spain	407
	5. Scotland	407
	Genealogies	
	1. The House of Tudor	408
	2. The Yorkist Claimants to the Throne .	409
	3. The English Succession	410
	4. The Spanish Succession . . .	411
	Select List for Further Reading . . .	413
	Index	419

MAPS

PAGE

Hereditary Possessions of Charles V 41

Enclosures in England, 1485–1607 67

The Elizabethan Seamen and the Maritime War with Spain 121

The Netherlands in the time of Elizabeth . . 128

England in the Great Rebellion—I 258

England in the Great Rebellion—II 259

The Colonisation of North America 331

The Netherlands in the time of William III and Marlborough 373

Western Europe at the end of the Seventeenth Century 379

THE TUDORS AND STUARTS

CHAPTER I

HENRY VII

Henry's claim to the throne; plots against him. His methods of government. Financial measures. Foreign policy.

1. *Henry's claim to the throne*

Henry VII picked up his crown on Bosworth field. A parliament hastily summoned to London declared that royal power was vested in the person of ' our now sovereign lord King Henry ' and in the heirs of his body; but that word ' now ' expressed much weariness, much cynical resignation, the fear of the English people that they might never be relieved from the wars and disorders which for so long had destroyed the country's peace. The measure of Henry's achievement is that he kept the crown which he seized from the head of a rival slain in battle; that he built a strong and orderly government out of the chaos which had overwhelmed his predecessors; and that he handed to his son a secure throne, an undisputed succession, and a brimming treasury.

In 1485 there was no reason why Henry should not have gone the way of other usurpers; why yet another rebellion should not at once have unseated him from the throne to which rebellion had brought him. His technical claim to the throne was flimsy. His great-grandfather had been steward to the Bishop of Bangor; his grandfather, Owen Tudor, clerk of the wardrobe to Henry V's French Queen. Owen Tudor took the first step in making his house famous: he won the love of his mistress, married her, and had two sons, Edmund and Jasper. Edmund married Lady Margaret Beaufort, and in their only child, Henry, flowed the royal blood of England and the royal blood of France. Henry, then, had some sort of hereditary claim, but there were many who had a better. For the Beaufort title to the throne had been barred by a royal decree of Henry IV ; if, on the other hand, this title were valid, the real heir, in a country which did not admit the Salic Law, was not Henry, but his mother. With better claim than either Beaufort or Tudor were the members of the house of York : the boy sons of Edward IV, if they were alive ; Edward, Earl of Warwick, son of the Duke of Clarence ; or the three sons of John de la Pole, Duke of Suffolk. Hereditary right was not strong on Henry's side, and he never urged it strongly. His real claim was a better one, and only a successful revolution could disturb it : he was *de facto* King. But in promptly acknowledging his title, parliament fortified his position with the sanction of legality.

But it was fifteen years before Henry could feel himself secure. The Yorkists would not allow a crown so easily won to be lightly held, and a succession of conspiracies and risings reminded Henry how unsafe was a usurper's throne. In 1486 he married Elizabeth, the daughter of Edward IV, and in his children united the White Rose with the Red. This politic gesture, of a man whose head was master of his heart, was welcomed by the mass of the people, who were weary of the endless factions which divided the country ; but it was wasted on uncompromising Yorkists, jealous of their family's honour, and the turbulent nobles of the North, who would not suffer the King's attempt to govern them. Overseas, Margaret of Burgundy, sister of Edward IV, nourished conspiracy. No pretender, no discontented plotter, appealed to her in vain ; pursuing her relentless quarrel with Henry, she cherished his enemies in England and Ireland and the courts of Europe. In 1486 Humphrey Stafford raised the West against the Tudor, and Lovell's rebellion in the North nearly captured him at York as he was celebrating the feast of St. George. A year later, a youth named Lambert Simnel, the son of an Oxford baker, claimed to be the Earl of Warwick. Henry had Warwick in the Tower, and produced his prisoner; but Simnel was crowned King in Yorkist Dublin, and came to England to try his fortune. Although Margaret of Burgundy sent 2,000 German mercenaries to his aid, he was routed at Stoke, and his noble allies, Lovell and the Earl of Lincoln, were slain. Simnel was treated with contemptuous mercy: Henry placed him in the royal kitchen, where he lived to a contented old age. But the Yorkists were not done. Perkin Warbeck, whose father was a boatman at Tournai, was coached in Paris to bear the rôle of Richard of York, the younger of the Princes murdered in the Tower. The Irish gladly crowned him King. 'I think ye will crown apes in Ireland at the last,' Henry once remarked. James IV welcomed him to Scotland, and gave him a high-born wife, and the 'little cockatrice of a King'[1] crossed the Border full of confidence. He was beaten back; and when he landed in Cornwall, in 1497, only a handful of the discontented Cornishmen would follow his standard. Warbeck joined Warwick in the Tower. Two years later, both were executed, on charges of attempting to escape and of conspiring further plots against the King. The charges may have been false, but as long as Warwick was alive, Margaret of Burgundy would find pretenders to impersonate him; and Ferdinand of Spain, anxious that the throne which his daughter was to share should be secure, convinced Henry that further mercy would be unwise. After 1499 Henry was troubled no more.

2. *Henry's government*

A man who mounts the throne with the sword in his hand, with only a flimsy title to support him, and with powerful influences intriguing to drive him out, cannot afford the luxury of basing his rule on political theories and novel constitutional experiments. Henry VII is credited with having founded something called the 'New Monarchy'. Those who read history

[1] Bacon.

backwards have compared Lancastrian ' lack of governance ' with the Tudor efficiency which followed it, and inferred that Henry VII fashioned new instruments of government and guided the constitution into new paths. If this happened, it was not done consciously. Henry was not an innovator ; rather, he was the last of the mediaeval Kings, and one of the greatest of them. He was a practical man, a usurper on an unsafe throne, and his aims were personal : to keep the crown which was his by conquest, and to hand it to his son unchallenged by any rival at home or overseas. In pursuing his own ends he served his country well ; for he established order, rid the country of the menace of the overmighty subject, kept out of foolish and costly wars, and encouraged his people in their increasingly profitable commerce. To attribute these measures to a benevolent paternalism, or to a deliberate constitutional theory, is to endow Henry with qualities which he did not possess. He was not an attractive person. He was niggardly, circumspect and cunning ; no idealism refreshed his arid, cautious mind ; the treasures of the New Learning stored his brain with political shrewdness, but left him empty of moral purpose. But had he been an idealist, chivalrous and warm-hearted, he would not have achieved what he did. His business was to rule, and he ruled. He loved order, because order preserved his throne ; he suppressed the feudal nobles, because their power was dangerous to him ; he was thrifty, because a full treasury could buy him loyal service ; he fostered trade, because subjects who are prosperous do not disturb the régime that makes them rich. To reach his objects, Henry needed to create nothing. The mediaeval constitution had worked before, and a resourceful, wealthy King could make it work again. There were laws to be obeyed if there were a government strong enough to enforce them, institutions waiting to be used by a King who knew his mind. Henry knew what he must do ; and, wrote Bacon, ' what he minded, he encompassed '.

His first task was to crush the feudal barons who in the fifteenth century had fallen on Kings impoverished, weak, and entangled in foreign wars, and had scrambled for the Crown as a prize to be kept among themselves. The barons had themselves made Henry's task easier. For the wars had weakened them ; death in battle had extinguished several noble lines ; the expense of maintaining private armies had crippled those which remained. Henry gathered the débris of civil war : he confiscated the lands of those attainted for having fought for Richard III, and resumed the estates of the dead. Ultimately, all the acquisitions made by the houses of Lancaster and York reverted to the Tudors. Henry then determined that the curse of private war should cease. An act passed in 1487 forbade the nobles to keep armies of liveried retainers ; and if they resisted, the walls of their feudal strongholds crumpled before the new weapon of artillery. The same act forbade them to tamper with justice by ' maintaining ' private suitors at their own cost and appropriating the rewards of a successful suit.

The barons found themselves thrust from their traditional place as advisers of the Crown. The aristocracy had monopolised the councils of the Lancastrian Kings. Now, weakened and discredited, they were replaced by men whom the King chose to nominate from the social class—ecclesiastics, knights and lawyers—which most eagerly supported the new dynasty. Bray, Morton, Fox, Guildford, Empson, Dudley, Poynings, the ablest of Henry's servants, were men of the middle class. They owed their loyalty to the King who had raised them, their interest was to keep the government efficient, and they did not expect rewards in estates and titles. Excepting Henry's own relatives, the Earls of Oxford, Shrewsbury and Surrey were the only nobles to hold high office during the reign ; and Oxford found to his cost that the King's regard for him did not permit him to defy the Act of Livery. The barons soon found too that the reins of local government were slipping from their hands. Beneath the great territorial families lay a class of smaller landowners, country knights and squires, who had been enriched by the growing prosperity of the age ; and their ranks were strengthened by newcomers from the towns, merchants who had taken advantage of the wars to buy the estates of the older families.

These gentry were drawn to the Tudors by a common purpose, the checking of the overmighty subject, and the restoration of effective government. On them, therefore, the Tudors laid the burdens of local administration. As officers of the shire-levy, they defended the state when it was threatened by revolution ; as Justices of the Peace, they provided the Crown with a civil service. Their work was unpaid ; they were bound to the Tudors by the ties of interest, and in the next reign their sturdy co-operation was Henry VIII's greatest strength in the House of Commons. The Justices of the Peace superseded the sheriff and the feudal organisation of the manor. They held petty and quarter sessions, and kept serious offenders for the assizes ; they had charge of local officials, such as mayors and constables ; they kept the highways in good repair, watched for the King's enemies, collected horses and supplies in emergencies, and made the King's will known by proclamations. Their administrative duties required them to control wages and prices, regulate apprenticeship and the supply of labour, supervise weights and measures, and prevent hoarding and profiteering. In the provinces they were the link between the government and the people. Tied to the Crown by a common interest, they served it more zealously and faithfully than the feudal aristocracy had ever done.

Some things, however, the gentry could not do. At best, they were only amateurs, and many of them were quite humble men ; moreover, their duties mostly sprang from custom, and few of their powers were defined by statute. When a local magnate disobeyed their commands or defied the government, they had no resources with which to answer him. In these emergencies the jurisdiction of the King's Council came to their aid. Statutes designed to check the nobility, such as the Act of Livery and Maintenance, were rarely enforceable in the courts of common law, where witnesses and juries were easily browbeaten, bribed and bullied. One of the most important features of Tudor rule was the development of the judicial activities of the Council ; and the special task of these prerogative courts was to punish offenders who were too powerful to be restrained by the processes of the common law, and to give poor suitors the justice which the ordinary courts denied them. A celebrated act in 1487 defined more precisely the judicial powers of the Court of Star Chamber. Its first duty was to keep order, and it was competent to deal with cases of livery and maintenance, riots and unlawful assemblies, bribery of jurors and witnesses, and all such attempts to disregard the law of the land. It had to deal also with immense numbers of suits which it did not itself initiate ; for its decisions were swift, its fees low, and it preferred a rough justice to the letter of the law. Henry established also a special committee, later the Court of Requests, to hear the complaints of poor men. These two courts sat in London, but there were similar courts in the distant parts of the country. The members of the household of Arthur, Prince of Wales, had extraordinary judicial powers in the Western shires ; and when he died, in 1502, this jurisdiction was incorporated into the Council of the Marches. In the Yorkist North the problem was harder, for the feudal magnates clung more tenaciously to their posts and administrative duties ; but the King's hand was often felt, and in the next reign a proper organisation was established.

In such ways Henry bent the feudal nobles to his will. By the end of his reign the aristocracy, which in the fifteenth century had made the country a playground for its private quarrels, lay broken and unrespected, with few powers and only a nominal dignity. In 1509 there was only one Duke, the Duke of Buckingham, and only one Marquis, the Marquis of Dorset, in the kingdom. It was typical of Henry's policy that he had bestowed on his second son, by the time that he was three, the following titles : Warden of the Cinque Ports, Constable of Dover Castle, Earl Marshal, Lord-Lieutenant of Ireland, and Warden of the Scottish Marches ; further, to reconcile the Yorkists, he was created Duke of York, and the King's second son has held the title ever since. Henry's purpose was plain. He gathered into his own hands several remunerative posts, and brought them under his own supervision ; they provided incomes for his children without increasing taxation ; and the necessary duties were performed more safely by deputies chosen by the King, than by irresponsible feudal magnates.

3. *Henry's financial measures*

Henry was not safe unless he was rich. If civil war were to break out on his death, a full treasury would enable his son to keep his throne. He set himself, therefore, to amass all the wealth which the resources of the constitution and the ingenuity of his advisers could offer him, and so to avoid the paralysing poverty which had brought his predecessors into so many of their misfortunes. Little of his revenue came from parliament.[1] The customary 'tenths' and 'fifteenths' were unproductive; they were difficult to collect, and were always unpopular. Henry had only six parliamentary grants during his reign. Parliament did, however, permit him, when rebellion or invasion threatened, to levy forced loans and benevolences. (In 1497 a blacksmith led 15,000 Cornishmen as far as Blackheath, to protest that the Scots were unlikely to invade Cornwall.) For the most part, Henry used other methods. The revenue from Crown lands was increased by wise administration, as well as by the seizure of forfeited estates. The feudal obligations of wardship, relief and marriage were exacted to the full; for instance, in 1504 Henry demanded grants for the knighting of his son Arthur, who had been knighted fifteen years before, and was now dead, and for the marriage of his daughter Margaret. Similarly, he enforced his rights to military service, to purveyance, and over the temporalities of vacant bishoprics and abbacies. The Crown's revenue from the customs was doubled during the reign, largely because Henry's orderly government and policy of peace, and his lavish encouragement of new enterprises, created conditions in which trade could flourish. In his passion

[1] Henry called few parliaments—only one in the last twelve years of his reign—and their sessions were brief. This of itself distinguishes him from the other Tudors, who used parliament for all their important business.

for getting, Henry was not too proud to enter the market in person. Like Edward IV, he conducted private and anonymous transactions, in wool, tin and wines, which brought him his share in the growing prosperity of his people.

After 1500, when his position was secure, he sank to baser devices. The nation's loathing of his tax-collectors, Empson and Dudley, ' the two ravening wolves ', and the legend, probably false, of Cardinal Morton's ' fork ', tell their own story. The new expedients were not illegal, but a scrupulous King, or a King whose throne was vulnerable, would not have ventured to use them.[1] Offices were sold, bishoprics were kept vacant, ecclesiastical preferment was auctioned. Above all, avarice began to taint the administration of justice. Justice, it was recognised, offered ' *magnum emolumentum* ' for the Crown. Fees grew heavier, fines more ruthless ; pardons were sold to delinquents who could afford to pay ; it was even possible to buy the King's favour in judicial proceedings. Empson and Dudley, wrote Bacon, ' being lawyers in science and privy councillors in authority, turned law and justice into wormwood rapine. . . . Justice was well administered in his [Henry's] time, save where the King was party, save also that the Council-table intermeddled too much with *meum* and *tuum*.'

By these resources Henry balanced his accounts. During his reign the revenues received by the Exchequer rose from £52,000 to £142,000 a year, and Henry was able to leave an immense fortune to his son. The King contrived to ' live of his own '. He had built his financial recovery on sources of revenue which had been available to his predecessors ; none of his expedients was new or unfamiliar. By unwearying economy, by watching always for inefficiency or corruption, and by avoiding wasteful adventures abroad, he had made the Crown financially independent ; and only in emergency, as mediaeval convention

[1] The same deterioration infected his whole character ; he sacrificed honour and dignity to the pursuit of power. When Queen Elizabeth died, he was prepared to marry Catherine of Aragon, his daughter-in-law ; or Joanna of Castile, who had become insane.

demanded, had he gone to parliament for extraordinary supplies.

While building up a fortune for himself, Henry did not neglect the prosperity of his people. His thrifty mind ' could not endure to see trade sick ',[1] and he strove to recover for English commerce the advantages which the long wars had thrown away. The navy had languished, and foreign ships carried English cargoes ; the merchants of the Hanseatic League controlled the Northern markets and the rich trade in hemp, pitch, fur, timber and corn from Russia and Scandinavia. The nationalist impulses of the age favoured a policy of insular self-assertion. An early Navigation Act restricted the wine trade with Bordeaux to English ships ; a treaty with Denmark brought English merchants into competition with the Hanse for the trade of Scandinavia and the fishing industry of Iceland ; another, with Riga, gave them access to the naval stores of the Baltic. Henry fought a tariff war with Venice over the wines of the Levant ; and, in order to press the Venetians, he entered into an agreement with Florence and set up an English staple at her port of Pisa. He granted a charter to the Merchant Adventurers, and gave them all the assistance of the state in their war against the privileges and monopolies of the Hanse. But the most important of England's commercial activities was the wool trade. The great mart for English wool was the Netherlands, where the raw product was required for manufacture. Each country depended heavily on the other, but the need of the Flemings was greater ; for, while English wool could find a market somewhere, the Flemish manufacturers were helpless without their raw materials. Henry unscrupulously exploited this helplessness, partly in the interest of the English merchants, and partly to force Philip, Count of Flanders, to abandon his automatic support of pretenders to the English throne. In 1496 the Magnus Intercursus freed the trade with Flanders of all the duties which had been imposed during the commercial struggle of recent years. Another agreement, ten years later, allowed English merchants to sell by retail, and

[1] Bacon.

released them from paying tolls in Flanders ; but these terms were so crushing to the Flemings that they were soon relaxed.

At home Henry protected new or struggling industries, such as the silk industry in London, worsted at Norwich and rope at Bridport. The object of Tudor mercantilism was to keep money in the country. Trade was ' good ' if it produced work for the people, and it was to be discouraged if it prospered the few at the expense of the many. Thus in years of good harvest, when the price was low, corn could be exported ; but when the price was high, import duties were relaxed. A high tariff excluded foreign manufactures which could be produced in England. Further, the wrath of the government fell on those who cheated the consumer, and lowered the reputation of English workmanship, by producing shoddy goods. The Council discovered that ' divers persons by subtil and undue sleights have deceivably imagined and contrived instruments of iron, with the which irons, in the most highest and secret places of their houses they strike and draw the said irons over the said fustians '. Doublets made by this process lasted for months, instead of years, ' to the great hurt of the poor commoners and serving men of this realm, to the great damage, loss and deceit of the King's true subjects, buyers and wearers of such fustian '.

4. *Henry's foreign policy*

In his dealings with foreign countries, Henry's first object, as in all his doings, was personal : he had no appetite for glorious enterprises, for defeat would have been fatal to his throne ; but a shrewd policy of marriages and alliances would oblige foreign governments to recognise his dynasty. Again, Henry's interest and his people's ran side by side. England had suffered enough from the folly of claiming the crown of France ; a long peace and light taxation were the necessary counterpart of internal order.

In the early years of his rule the courts of Europe, accustomed to rapid changes on the throne of England, disregarded Henry's respectful overtures, and found it more expedient to intrigue with his enemies. At length, his firm treatment of rebellion persuaded them that they had chosen to support the losing side. Using too the mutual mistrust between Spain and France, he was presently able to have his rights acknowledged, and his enemies expelled from the countries which had harboured them. The ambitions of Charles VIII of France gave Henry an early opportunity to show his worth as a diplomatist. Louis XI had annexed to the French Crown the provinces of Burgundy, Provence and Anjou ; Charles was now anxious to absorb into his dominions Brittany, the last of the independent provinces of France. The growing power of the French King awakened the jealousy of Ferdinand of Spain. Ferdinand's anxiety was Henry's opportunity. In 1489 he concluded the treaty of Medina del Campo with Spain, which, with only one deviation, was to guide English foreign policy for eighty years. The alliance was cemented by the betrothal of the young Prince Arthur to Catherine of Aragon, and Ferdinand's promise to pay into Henry's treasury a substantial dowry. It was all that Henry could wish. One of the most influential of the royal houses of Europe had recognised him as King of England, and welcomed him into an alliance ; the defence of Brittany would allow him to repay the generous hospitality given him during his exile ; and his people would go eagerly into a war with their hereditary enemy.

But it was not to be one of those traditional wars of conquest about which the apprentices were singing in their ballads. Henry's real object had been achieved when he had won the friendship of Spain ; if there must be a war, it should be war for profit. However, he spoke eloquently to parliament of his plans for the recovery of Gascony and Guienne ; ' France is no wilderness ', he said. He was granted a war subsidy, and with it he collected an army of 10,000, conveyed it to France, garrisoned posts that were too strong to be attacked, and sat down to wait upon events. Neither Spain nor France really wanted to fight. Charles had settled the dispute over Brittany by marrying the Duchess Anne, and was now preparing to hurl himself on Italy ;

while Ferdinand was content when he had acquired Roussillon and Cerdagne, in the Eastern Pyrenees. Thus, without having exerted himself, Henry was able to make a most favourable treaty : at Etaples, in 1492, Charles bought off the hostility of the invader by paying him 745,000 gold crowns and promising to banish Warbeck from his territories. Henry returned home well satisfied. Like Edward IV at Pecquigny, he had been well paid for doing nothing ; his people had granted him a subsidy to prosecute a war, France granted him another to remain at peace.

This was Henry's only active intervention in foreign affairs. The long struggle between France and Spain for dominion in Italy broke out in 1494, and Henry, wiser than Wolsey, stayed out of it. Each side, however, needed his goodwill. The marriage in 1496 of Joanna of Castile, daughter of Ferdinand, to Philip of Flanders, son of the Emperor Maximilian, united Spain and the Hapsburgs.[1] Charles, therefore, could not risk invasion by adding England to his enemies ; and Ferdinand had to remember that by depriving the Flemings of their supply of wool, Henry could drive them into rebellion against Philip and Joanna. Henry went quietly on his way, obliging the rulers of Europe to recognise his claim and exile his enemies. Pope Innocent VIII recognised him as King, and Henry remained on good terms with his two successors, without being tempted to meddle in Italian politics. Ferdinand's growing respect for him indicated how securely he had established himself on his throne. When Arthur died, only a few months after his marriage, no one was more anxious than Ferdinand to retain his alliance with England by marrying Catherine to Henry's second son, or even, if need be, to Henry himself. This suited Henry well enough, although it was typical of both Kings that they should haggle about the payment of another dowry. For no important family in England was neutral in the feud between Lancaster and York, and none of his four children could marry an English subject without bringing the old feud to life again. Arthur and Henry

[1] To complete the alliance, Ferdinand's son John married Maximilian's daughter Margaret ; but John died in 1497.

married Catherine of Aragon ; of his daughters, Margaret married James IV of Scotland, and after Henry was dead, Mary married Louis XII of France. The new dynasty had arrived.

Within the British Isles there were hard problems to tackle. Ireland had been restless since Henry II's conquest, and throughout the Middle Ages the Scots had been always ready to cross the Border at the bidding of the French. To Henry's mind, the best way to be at peace with the Scots was to be at peace with the French ; except for an unsuccessful invasion in 1496, they gave him no trouble during his reign. He cemented the truce by giving his daughter in marriage to their King [1] ; and it was no fault of his that in the next reign a war with France provoked the Scots to their old policy of Border warfare, and that the supporters of the Francophil Duke of Albany drove Margaret in flight back to England. Nor could any permanent settlement be found for Ireland. The most that Henry could ensure was that order should be kept. Sir Edward Poynings won some of the native barons to his side by means of statesmanship reinforced by bribery ; and he passed a law, which remained unrepealed for nearly three hundred years, that, while all statutes made by the English parliament were to be valid in Ireland, those made in the parliament at Dublin must be sanctioned by the Crown. After Poynings had been recalled, because his administration was too expensive, the scholarly but efficient Earl of Kildare ruled his brother-Irish with a strong hand ; he fought his private enemies at the King's expense, but that was the price which Henry had to pay for comparative quietness.

In more troubled times, when the attack of determined enemies was pushing the Crown of England inch by inch nearer to surrender, Francis Bacon dedicated to Prince Charles, for his guidance in the ways of government, a history of this ' peaceful, politic and rich prince . . . a wonder to wise men '. Henry Tudor ranks with Henry II and Edward I among the great Kings of the Middle Ages. He was not, as they were, an

[1] The great-grandson of the marriage united the two Crowns.

innovator ; but in making mediaeval institutions work again, he also fitted them to bear the strain of the swift, unheralded changes which followed when he was dead. For this he has been acclaimed, somewhat hastily, as the founder of a political system, as well as of a dynasty. But Henry could not look into the future. He could not foresee that his son would be the master of the Church, or that within a hundred years parliament would be an active partner in the business of government ; he could not know that economic revolution would impoverish the Crown and make it impossible for the King to live of his own. He could not even know that, as soon as he was dead, his son would shatter his peace and his delicate economy by launching a senseless war on France. Henry's work was done when he handed to his successor an undisputed crown, a flowing treasury and a government that worked. He succeeded by adapting the available means to realise his ends. He returned to the mediaeval ideal of good government and a well-ordered society, and founded his dynasty on a principle as ancient and honoured as the rule of law. But Henry lived in an age of transition : in some respects his government flowed with the currents of the changing times. It was insular ; it valued peace and prosperity before conquest and the standards of a dying chivalry ; when the manners of the Middle Ages were yielding to the dogmas of national self-sufficiency, it cherished the enterprises which made men rich ; in readiness for the coming struggle for existence, it set its own house in order.

CHAPTER II

WOLSEY

The new King. War with France. Rise of Wolsey. Wolsey as Chancellor. Wolsey and the Church. His foreign policy. His fall.

1. *Character of the new King*

There have been few more remarkable Kings than Henry VIII. He has left his mark on the history of his country not only because he was a man of outstanding abilities ; nor yet because he was stubborn and self-willed ; but because the egotism of the King, which was the driving-force of his actions, and the new and thrusting assertiveness of his people, itself a kind of egotism, urged them both in the same direction. Like his father, he was fitted for the business of governing. The greatest of his gifts was statesmanship ; it was slow to mature, but even while Wolsey held the centre of the stage, Henry was watching, and discovering through others how much might be attempted, how much might succeed. The lion slowly learned his strength ; then, in the fullness of it, he broke England's ancient bonds with Rome, grasped for the state the wealth and jurisdiction of the Church, and defied the Pope and the sovereigns of Europe to do their worst against him. With some instinctive awareness of his people's destiny, he cared for the navy and made it strong ; and when Wales and Ireland received the laws and institutions of England, and Calais was ordered to send two burgesses to the English House of Commons, the beginnings of an empire had been made. These things were not done by chance ; they were not mere incidents to Henry's pursuit of pleasure, the outcome of his wilfulness. Henry's selfishness was reckless of the pain he inflicted on others ; no hint of compassion or justice softened his masterful progress to his chosen ends ; his conscience, a pliable instrument, was too ready to identify itself with his will. But the blemishes on his character did not mar his statesmanship. He had a statesman's grasp of opportunity, the sense of what might be attempted and when to attempt it. He chose to serve him strong men, all of whom knew that he must be obeyed. He respected his opponents, and won them over by persuasion rather than by bluster and threats ; to the unconvinced and the hesitant he readily explained his motives, and taught them to believe that his interest was also theirs. Such a man was an appropriate ruler of an adolescent nation, to whose growing parochialism the world had begun to seem very frightening.

At first these powers were hidden, perhaps even from himself, by the cultural attainments of the Renaissance Prince. After his dark, unattractive father, he caught the imagination of his people. He was graceful, agile and strong ; he could hunt, joust, and play tennis with the best of his subjects ; he played the lute, the harp, and the organ, and himself composed the tunes to which he danced. From his grandmother, Lady Margaret Beaufort, he inherited his love of scholarship and scholarly men, his skill in languages and appetite for theology. The finest minds of the age adorned his court : the presence of Thomas More, Linacre, Colet, Mountjoy, Tunstall and Richard Pace brought to it, in the opinion of Erasmus, more learning than could be found in any university. For the first twenty years of his reign Henry was well content to devote himself to sport, music, and the scholarship which was the flower of English Humanism.

His first action illustrated both his ruthlessness and his instinct for making popular gestures : he sacrificed to the people's indignation his father's servants, Empson and Dudley. The cruel death of the two men who were in large measure responsible for amassing the fortune in Henry's treasury showed thus early that the servants of the Tudors could look in vain for gratitude if the state demanded their sacrifice.

Henry's vitality soon sought a more adventurous outlet than jousting and the chase. Less prudent than his father, he prepared to gamble the wealth, so carefully and so anxiously accumulated, on the elusive quest of glory. In simple piety he equipped a crusade to join Ferdinand of Spain in a war upon the infidel. Ferdinand, however, decided that there was more pressing business on hand. The French had overrun Italy, and were besieging the Pope in Bologna; and he persuaded Henry to join Spain and the Venetians in the Pope's Holy League to drive the invader out of Italy. In fact, Ferdinand's pious concern for the Papacy was a sham. His real object was to carve an Italian kingdom for his second grandson out of the territories of Milan, Venice, Genoa and Florence; and, more immediately, he wished to seize Navarre from its King, Jean d'Albret. But Henry was easily duped. He was induced to revive his ancestral claim to the crown of France, and to lend force to it by seizing Guienne. In the summer of 1512 an army under the Marquis of Dorset attacked Guipuscoa. The troops got out of hand, looted the countryside and died in hundreds of disease; finally they mutinied, and their commanders had no choice but to sail ignominiously for England. In the meantime, while the English raid diverted the attention of the French, Ferdinand had quietly seized Navarre and retired from the war. When pressed by Henry, he blandly admitted that he had made his peace with France.

With Spain and France in alliance, England was critically placed. Fortunately, the campaign of 1513 redeemed the disgrace of the previous year. Henry went in person to France at the head of a capable army; it took Thérouanne, the first English conquest in France since Joan of Arc turned the tide of war against the Duke of Bedford; and when the French came to relieve the town, a sudden panic precipitated them into the bloodless rout known as the battle of the Spurs. The capture of Tournai, the richest city north of Paris, closed the campaign.

To complete the triumphs of this notable year, the Earl of Surrey had cut to pieces an invasion from the Scots, and James IV and his nobility lay dead on the field of Flodden. But Henry was learning wisdom. The elation of victory did not urge him to further aggression. He had justified himself, but he did not propose to be again the instrument for forwarding the subtle designs of his father-in-law. As, moreover, the war had been costly, he was ready to welcome a truce. In 1514 Wolsey sealed a ' perpetual peace ' with France by marrying her King, Louis XII, to Henry's sister Mary. The marriage effectively answered the French agreement with Ferdinand and the Emperor, and suggested that the English knew how to use the weapons of diplomacy as skilfully as the weapons of war. Henry put away his dream of conquest ; the two later wars with France had different objects. He announced that ' we are well content with this island of ours ', and left to Wolsey, who was more adroit than he, the task of grappling with the treacherous diplomats of the continent.

2. *The rise of Wolsey*

Thomas Wolsey, the son of a wealthy grazier of East Anglia, was typical of the new age. At Oxford he was the ' boy bachelor ', and the quality of his intellect distinguished him from his contemporaries ; but his sweeping ambition was not content with an academic life. The path of ambition lay through the Church. Fox, the Bishop of Winchester, brought him to the notice of the government ; in 1507 he was chaplain to Henry VII, and two years later the new King's almoner. He was typical of the self-made men whom the Tudors chose to serve them. He rose to power and responsibility because he was able ; he was promoted in the Church because in this economical way the Tudors rewarded those who served them faithfully in the state. The Tudors were not afraid of ambition, for men with their way to make are good servants to those who hold the keys of power. Wolsey's conspicuous talent immediately commended him to Henry VIII, who was a fine judge of men. He became a Privy Councillor in 1511 ; he was victualler to the disastrous expedition of 1512, and in the campaign of the following year he was always at Henry's right hand ; in 1514 he negotiated the marriage and the peace. His services were soon rewarded : Henry made him Archbishop of York, Louis gave him the Bishopric of Tournai, the Pope created him a Cardinal. In his avarice he grasped more power than any English statesman has ever held. He held, at various times, the Bishoprics of Lincoln, Bath and Wells, Durham, and Winchester ; also he held, illegally, the *commendams* of Salisbury, Worcester and Llandaff, which were occupied by non-resident aliens ; and he swelled his income by receiving the temporal revenues of the Abbey of St. Albans, the richest abbey in England. So much he seized from his own country ; and if Warham had not outlived him, he would have had Canterbury as well. By the Pope he was made *legatus a latere*, and finally legate for life.

In 1515 he rose also to the highest dignity in the state, when he succeeded Warham as Lord Chancellor. As early as 1513, when he held none but ecclesiastical posts, he directed the country's foreign policy ; as Chancellor, all administration was in his hands ; and his accumulation of ecclesiastical honours gave him supreme authority in the Church, for Warham bent before the wind. In all departments of Church and state only the King was his master ; and only a strong King could have allowed a subject to gather so much power, and yet have struck him down when the hour came. But for fifteen years the Cardinal overshadowed the King. Henry liked him, respected his abilities, and drew strength from his vitality. Moreover, Wolsey was ready to busy himself with the dry details of administration, while Henry played and danced and dabbled in theology. 'Writing', Henry confessed, 'is to me somewhat tedious and painful.' So Wolsey invented new pastimes for him, encouraged him in his hobby of building a navy, and flattered his wisdom as scholar and theologian, while he reserved for his own attention the important business of the state. State documents were sent straight to him, ambassadors were more often at his palaces than at Henry's ; for, complained the Venetian Giustiniani, '*agere cum rege est nihil agere* '. He lived with the pomp and splendour of a prince ; partly because self-made men are vain, partly because his taste in fine things was exquisite, and partly because he judged that his master's honour required that the high officers of state should not be as other men. He set no limits to his pride, and sought favours of no one. His power and glory had no roots in the affection of the people, the respect of the nobility, the co-operation of parliament or Bishops ; he depended solely on the King, and when the King deserted him, there was no one —not even the Pope—to break his fall.

3. *Wolsey as Chancellor*

When Wolsey held the post, the Chancellor was more than the highest officer of the law ; so varied were his administrative duties that, in Stubbs's famous phrase, he was ' secretary of state for all departments '. Mediaeval customs were fast dying, however, and Wolsey was the last Lord Chancellor to govern the country. Primarily, the Chancellor was the keeper of the King's conscience. ' The King ', wrote Wolsey, ' ought of his royal dignity and prerogative to mitigate the rigour of the law, where conscience hath the more force ; and therefore in his princely place he hath constituted a chancellor to order for him the same.' The Chancellor's business was to administer equity : that is, to soften the severity of the common law when present circumstances had diminished the value of precedents, to supply deficiencies where no law existed, to bring the law up to date where feudal custom had languished. Necessarily the law falls behind the times, as modern developments bring problems unprovided for ; and the business of equity was to supply remedies which were beyond the reach of the common law.

Wolsey overstepped the traditional limitations of his office. In his eyes, it provided him with a mandate to supervise every detail of administration ; the Tudor monarchy responded to the needs of the people, and Wolsey as Chancellor embodied the policy of efficient government which was the monarchy's justification. 'He alone', reported Giustiniani, 'transacts the same business as that which occupies all the magistracies, offices, and councils of Venice, both civil and criminal.' The first of his duties was to enforce law and order. Here he achieved the work which Edward IV and Henry VII had begun; the nation learned that the government was master, and the Englishman's respect for the powers which rule him dates from Wolsey's administration. In Star Chamber he made his deepest impression on the public mind, and through him this court, which had existed since the middle of the fourteenth century, made its reputation as the terror of the rich and the ally of the poor. He extended its authority, said Sir Thomas Smith,[1] 'to repress the insolency of the noblemen and gentlemen of the north parts of England who . . . made their force their law'. In a single year the Earls of Surrey and Northumberland, the Marquis of Dorset, Lord Abergavenny and Lord Hastings appeared before him for offences which the common law had failed to punish. In Star Chamber he showed the magnates that there was one law which rich and poor alike must observe, and that there was in the country only one will, which must be obeyed. The most notable victim of this anti-feudal policy was the Duke of Buckingham, who went to the block in 1521 on a charge of disloyalty to the King. But Wolsey's arm reached beyond the magnates' crimes of maintenance, rioting and oppression, to the humbler crimes of humbler men: frauds, libels, forgeries, contempt of justice, and all the petty misdemeanours of the anti-social. In Star Chamber, too, he controlled the financial policy of the country, fixing prices and regulating the flow of trade in the general interest.

In the Court of Requests, another legacy from the previous reign, Wolsey heard the claims of those who were too poor to take their suits to any other court. For common law could be rigid and oppressive, and it was the government's business

[1] Secretary of State under Elizabeth, and author of a work, *De Republica Anglorum*, on the Tudor constitution.

to redress its injustices for the benefit of those who had been its victims. In this court he appointed Commissions to enquire into all enclosures made since the accession of Henry VII ; and here he heard cases of disputed wills, burglary, disagreements about marriages, trusts, assaults and maritime disputes. He did not hesitate to issue writs to bring cases from the hearing of the common law to his own courts. To meet the pressure on his jurisdiction he delegated his authority to special courts, such as the Council of the Marches, the admiralty courts or the Duke of Richmond's court in the North. Finally, he used his power as legate to invade the province of ecclesiastical jurisdiction, and to bring the trial of heresy within the competence of the state.[1] He did not define the scope of his activity, but the authority of the great seal might be used to bring within his jurisdiction any case which was not reserved by statute for the common law ; he trespassed wherever conscience could break down the system of the Middle Ages.

The resistance of the common law was tough, and Wolsey's concentration of power in Chancery did not survive him. He trusted too much, said his biographer Cavendish, to 'his own wit and wisdom' ; 'his own opinion was his law'. Conscience has too wide a latitude to serve as the foundation of justice. The Chancellor's conscience, as Selden pointed out a hundred years later, is as erratic a standard of law as the measure of the Chancellor's foot. When Wolsey had gone, and his courts felt no longer his arrogant genius and his amazing energy, the common lawyers narrowed the scope of the royal conscience. In his time, however, he served his master well. In forcing high and low to respect the law of the land he fulfilled the purpose of the Tudor monarchy.

4. *Wolsey and the Church*

Wolsey did not cause the English Reformation, but he, if anyone, had the power to postpone or avert it. When Henry VIII broke with Rome, he had the support of the English middle classes, which in their new self-consciousness and strength had

[1] Though not, of course, of the common law.

solid, but removable, grievances against the Church. Wolsey knew these grievances, because they were loudly voiced in the early days of his power ; with his unprecedented authority as Cardinal and legate, he had the means of redressing them. He chose, however, to follow a programme of reform devised by himself, modest in its scope and qualified by his own breaches of canon law ; and further to outrage the susceptibilities of laymen by the blunt intrusion of the clergy into their lives.

The laymen's complaint was the old one which had divided Henry II and Becket beyond reconciliation : that, while they were themselves subject to the criminal jurisdiction of the Church, the clergy were immune from the jurisdiction of the state. Laws passed in panic against the Lollards long ago were still on the statute-book ; they gave the Church absolute power over the lives and goods of laymen whom it chose to accuse of heresy. On the other hand, any clerk could claim benefit of clergy to protect him from the penalties of the state for offences which he committed against it. The quarrel was bitterly contested in the parliament of 1515, which debated whether it should renew an act of 1512 restricting benefit of clergy and the privileges of sanctuary. On the advice of Wolsey, the parliament was dissolved before the act had been renewed, but this victory for the Church was won at a high cost. For the uncompromising attitude of the clergy seemed to block the hope of reform. There was little chance that remedial legislation would pass the House of Lords, where the Bishops and Abbots outnumbered the temporal peers ; Convocation defended the outburst of the Abbot of Winchcombe, who in a sermon at St. Paul's asserted that the Crown had not the right to determine the limits of criminal jurisdiction ; while in the highest seat of authority, Pope Leo X had declared before the Lateran Council that the law of God forbade laymen to sit in judgment over priests. The Commons challenged these opinions, and the Londoners demonstrated against the Bishops. If jurisdiction were transferred to laymen, protested the Bishop of London, a London jury would hang a clerk, ' be he as innocent as Abel '.

To these serious grievances, the enemies of the clergy added smaller complaints of excessive fees for mortuary and probate, pluralism, non-residence, the corruption of the monasteries, and other ancient abuses. Here, then, was Wolsey's opportunity to reform. The Church could have made concessions without injuring its dignity ; if it refused to reform, more than its dignity would be lost. Wolsey, however, followed a path of his own. There should be reform, but he disagreed with the critics of the Church over the objects of reform, and the methods by which it should be carried out. He did not intend to allow any secular power to have a hand in his reformation ; and because the Commons were so bitter towards the clergy, he summoned only one parliament during the years of his supremacy. The Church must cling to its autonomy, and reform itself from within ; reformation should be undertaken by himself, and he alone should decide its scope and objects. To this end, he pressed the Pope to make him a Cardinal ; and he did not cease to apply for further enlargements of his authority until, in 1524, he was appointed legate for life.

Wolsey made poor use of his extraordinary authority. It is true that under him the Church was well administered and its rights unquestioned. He would never tolerate ignorance and lax discipline in any who served him. It is true, too, that he undertook a programme of reform which was approved by such men as More and Erasmus. He proposed to foster the spread of learning, reform monastic morals, create some new Bishoprics, and even to cancel the payment of annates to the Pope. The Humanists, with their faith in the sovereignty of reason, pointed to ignorance and superstition as the cause of the maladies which infected the Church. The root of reform was education. The lectureships which Wolsey founded at Oxford were a starting-point for a reformation along Humanist lines. His Colleges at Oxford and Ipswich were intended to furnish the Church with a regular supply of educated clergy ; and the money which he seized from his dissolution of the smaller monasteries, and from his visitations to the larger foundations, was appropriated to finance these excellent objects. This, however, was the limit of his reformation. In his courts of Arches and Audience he administered the law with his invariable thoroughness; he reformed the Augustinian, Benedictine and Dominican Orders; and after his death Henry adopted his plan to create new Bishoprics. But he neglected his important opportunities: he left untouched the serious vices of the Church, and he did nothing to harmonise its relations with the state.

In fact, the Church was more unpopular in 1529 than when the outburst of criticism had persuaded Wolsey that something must be done to reform it. Moreover, Wolsey's own arrogance had so stirred the hostility of the clergy against him that the Church, its unity broken, was powerless against the secular attack launched by the King and the Reformation Parliament. Wolsey was not a churchman by conviction. The Church was to him a means to accumulate an unprecedented store of wealth, jurisdiction and power. His own person proclaimed the very abuses against which sincere reformers protested: he never preached, and rarely said Mass; he was guilty of pluralism [1] and non-residence, he held Bishoprics *in commendam*; he lived with a mistress, and tried to have his natural son appointed Bishop of Durham at the age of eighteen; three of his dioceses he never visited, and he did not go to York until the last months of his life. His slender plans for reform were insignificant by the side of the irregularities for which he offered no apology. At the same time, his energy made the English more intimately conscious of the Church and its pretensions than they had ever been before; they felt the difference between an ecclesiastical jurisdiction remotely wielded from Rome, and a jurisdiction actively wielded in England and reinforced by the resources of Chancery and Council. The grievances of 1515 grew still more urgent when the Chancellor protected the ecclesiastical courts from the interference of the common law.

Meanwhile, as the representative of Rome, Wolsey invaded

[1] Wolsey's pluralism meant that in 1529 the lay peers outnumbered the Bishops and Abbots. Thus the House of Lords did not oppose the Reformation.

the privileges of the English clergy. The self-government of the English Church was overthrown by the ubiquitous intrusion of his legatine authority ; he prevented Warham from summoning the Convocation of Canterbury, usurped ecclesiastical patronage, robbed the Bishops of their jurisdiction and their fees, tampered with elections, and harassed the monasteries with his drastic visitations. His ruthless use of his powers as papal legate broke down the constitution of the mediaeval Church, and awakened in all Englishmen, priests and laymen alike, a hatred of papal centralisation. When Wolsey fell, and his enemies gathered about him to take their revenge, the wrath of the common lawyers blew cold beside the wrath of Bishops and Abbots, whose jurisdiction and revenues he had assaulted. Thus in the crisis of the Reformation the clergy did not oppose the action of the state ; for they preferred a King who respected their jurisdiction and their autonomy to a legate who extinguished all their privileges.

5. *Wolsey's foreign policy*

When Charles VIII invaded Italy in 1494, he started a rivalry between France and Spain for the possession of Italy which lasted for two generations. England had no concern with this quarrel. Henry VIII's intervention in it, although redeemed by the spectacular successes of 1513, had brought no advantages to compensate the money it had wasted, and Henry wisely decided that his people's interests would be better served by peace. The responsibility for the alarms and the restless diplomacy of the next fifteen years lay with Wolsey. His motives were largely selfish. The argument that he interfered in Europe in order to maintain a balance of power cannot be allowed, for his intervention usually tilted the balance even more heavily in favour of Charles V ; nor can it be urged in his defence that England's safety or advantage ever demanded the policy which he chose to adopt. He interfered for two reasons : first, his vanity pressed him to make his fame as a diplomatist, and to dictate settlements to the warring nations. It pleased him, as Giustiniani shrewdly observed, to be hailed as 'the arbiter of Christendom'. Secondly, he shaped his policy according to the needs and interests of Rome. The Popes were Italian Princes, and the fluctuations of the war in Italy awoke their concern for their temporal possessions. They could not stand aside from the war and be indifferent to it; nor were they able to give their whole-hearted support to one side or the other. French or Spanish mastery of Italy was equally distasteful to them. They were disposed, therefore, to ally themselves with the side whose position was for the moment the weaker, and to trust in these ignoble shifts to save them from complete surrender to a foreign power.

Wolsey's policy was to take the same side as the Pope. 'Our policy', said the Bishop of Durham in 1515, 'will be that of Rome.' Wolsey was the representative and the champion of the Papacy in England; from it he derived the powers which he valued most, 'my legacy . . . wherein stood all my high honour', and he determined to place the resources of himself and his country at its disposal in the embarrassments of its foreign policy. Every change in his attitude to foreign powers corresponded to a change in the attitude of Rome; and if his policy may be described as the preservation of a balance of power, it is only in so far as he assisted the Pope to maintain a balance of power in Italy. Wolsey was not disinterested; for no disappointment could extinguish his hope that one day he would be Pope himself, and he wished the inheritance of St. Peter to be worthy of him.

The 'perpetual peace' which Wolsey had negotiated in 1514 collapsed in three months. Louis XII, who was fifty-two, was unable to survive his marriage to Mary, who was seventeen; and his successor, the reckless, ambitious Francis I, refused to submit to a settlement which excluded him from the wealth and culture of Italy. In 1515 he crossed the Alps, routed the Swiss at Marignano, recovered Milan from the Sforzas, and mastered Italy as far as Naples. Wolsey was alarmed. Milan was the keystone of his policy, for the safety of the papal dominions depended on its being in friendly hands; he could not leave it in the possession of an invader who might be tempted to lead his armies southwards towards Rome. So he fell back on the feeblest resource of an island nation, and offered bribes to the other powers of Europe to induce them to dislodge the French; overriding the opposition of the rest of the Council, who saw no reason to involve England in the war. Wolsey had a poor choice of allies. Ferdinand was soon to die, and his successor had promised not to interfere unless Navarre were restored to the French. Wolsey had to depend, therefore, on the aged and impecunious Emperor Maximilian, who in 1513 had served as a private in the English army for a hundred crowns a day. In 1516 Maximilian made a feeble and unsuccessful attempt to recover Milan; then, although Wolsey offered him further bribes if he would renew his efforts, he made his peace with the French. The settlement soon became general. Charles, the new King of Spain, and Leo X had already been obliged to make agreements with Francis in order to protect their Italian territories from attack; and Wolsey, with the French faction under the Duke of Albany causing him anxiety in Scotland, was in no position to pursue a struggle which the Pope had already abandoned. On a pretence of composing their differences in order to make war upon the Turk, the powers sent representatives to London in 1518 to negotiate a general peace. As consolation for leaving Milan in the hands of the French, Wolsey was able to pledge Henry's daughter Mary to marry the infant Dauphin, and to surrender his Bishopric of Tournai for an annual pension. Although this high-sounding 'universal peace' attracted some prestige to England and himself,[1] he had to recognise that his attempt to influence events from an island remote from the sphere of action had been costly and unavailing.

In 1519 Charles of Spain succeeded his grandfather Maximilian as Holy Roman Emperor. He was master of the dominions of the House of Hapsburg, the territories of the Empire, Spain, Flanders, Naples and the Spanish conquests in South America;

[1] 'It was the best deed that ever was done for England', said the peace-loving Bishop Fox.

he had at his service the learning of Italy, the wealth of the Indies, the *tercios* of Spain, and the land-knights of Germany. So great were his resources that all Europe might soon lie at his feet. For France, encircled by the Hapsburgs and the sea, the danger was serious ; most European wars break out because the French feel themselves to be suffering from claustrophobia, and Francis I resolved that he must break through the ring which surrounded him. The Imperial election, then, quickly destroyed the peace of 1518, and it was for the smaller combatants of Europe to determine on which side they would fight. The battleground would be Italy, whose possession offered to Francis the only escape from Hapsburg encirclement, and to Charles the means of closing the gap in his communications : Milan, with its port at Genoa, was still the heart of the situation.

Both Charles and Francis eagerly sought the alliance of England. To Francis the value of the alliance would be largely negative : his rear would be safe from English raids on Picardy or Guienne. To Charles, however, England had something definite to offer : the straits of Dover were the sea-route between Spain and the Netherlands, and this route was sufficiently valuable to Charles to assure his goodwill even during the years of the breach with Rome, and to cause him to marry his son to Mary Tudor. If England must fight at all, her interests dictated an alliance with Charles ; for Charles controlled the largest market for English wool, and her King was married to a Spanish Princess. Wolsey preferred the Spanish alliance, but for different reasons. First, Charles promised to use his influence to make him Pope when Leo died ; and secondly, Leo, being a Medici, found the presence of the French in Milan and Florence odious, and was willing to help Charles to drive them out. The sumptuous meeting of Henry and Francis at the Field of Cloth of Gold was designed to allay French suspicions and to get better terms from Charles. It was a wasteful display of chivalry, at which the two Kings paraded their wealth and their courtly accomplishments ; the real business was done at an unheralded conference with Charles at Gravelines. In May,

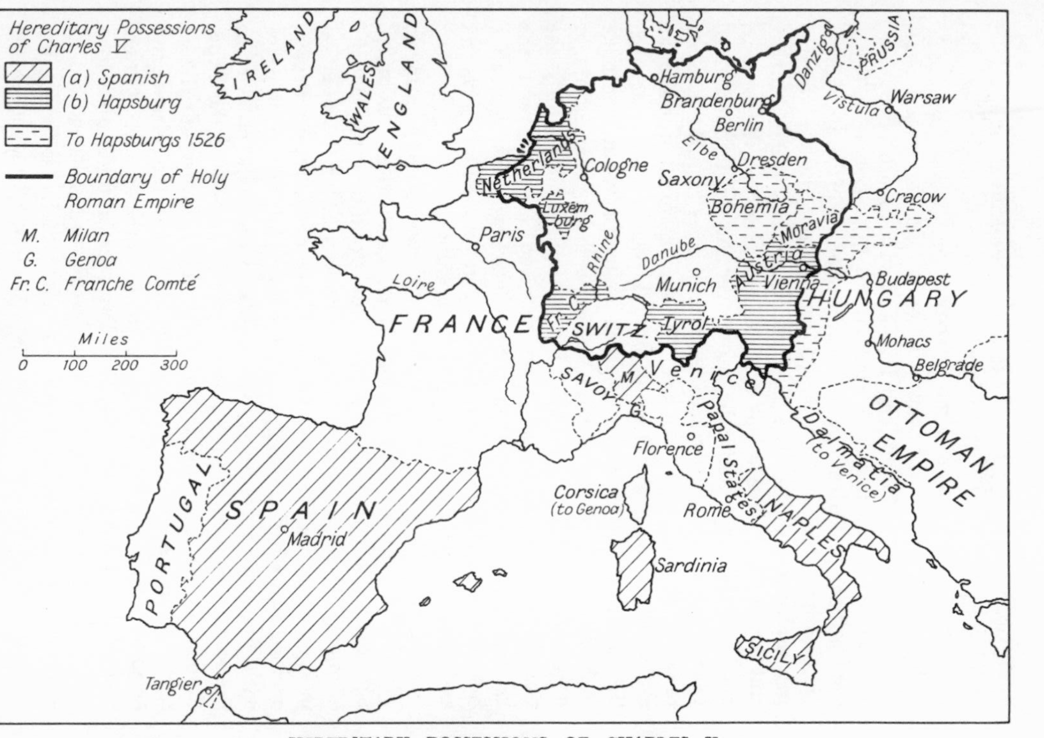

HEREDITARY POSSESSIONS OF CHARLES V.

1521, on the day on which Luther was condemned at the Diet of Worms, the Pope entered into an alliance with Charles, and in August Wolsey signed an agreement at Bruges.

The war disappointed Wolsey's hopes. In November, 1521, Charles recovered Milan, and Leo X died a month later; but, although Wolsey offered to send an English army to overawe the Cardinals, Charles procured the election of his tutor, Adrian of Tortosa. Further, England's participation in the fighting was undistinguished. The Earl of Surrey laid waste Morlaix and Artois in the barbarous spirit of the Hundred Years War, but his activities brought the Scots over the Border, and Lord Dacre, lacking material resources, was obliged to make a treaty to check their advance. In 1523 Wolsey organised an elaborate attack on France: the Duke of Suffolk was to co-operate with the Emperor's troops and a rebellion contrived by the Constable of France. Suffolk led a large and capable army, and brought it within forty miles of Paris, but his allies failed him; the Constable's treachery had been detected in time, and the Emperor's Burgundians would not advance beyond Fuentarrabia. Suffolk had neither pay nor reinforcements for a solitary advance, and a promising campaign came to nothing.

The same year brought Wolsey a further disappointment. The death of Adrian again brought the Papacy within his grasp, but again Charles failed to keep his promise: the Medici Clement VII was elected. The new Pope, viewing the situation in Italy with the keen and interested eye of an Italian Prince, decided that Charles was growing too powerful, and made peace with France. Accordingly, in 1524 England took no part in the war. Released from the hostility of England and the Pope, Francis gathered all his strength for the recovery of Milan; but at Pavia, in February, 1525, his army was annihilated, and he and his commanders fell into the hands of the enemy. Others beside Francis felt the rout at Pavia as a crushing blow. Charles's grip on Italy was now too secure to be shaken, but he was unwilling to share his prize with allies who had done nothing to help him to win it. Wolsey and the Pope had chosen the winning side, but they had abandoned it too soon to be entitled to share the spoils. Wolsey hopefully invited Charles to depose Francis and restore to Henry VIII the territories of his Plantagenet ancestors, but Charles left him, if he wished, to invade France alone. Wolsey's policy had not brought him the Papacy, and he had won no great victories to reconcile the English to a war for which they had no enthusiasm. Instead, his designs had been fruitless, and parliament and people complained of the taxes which he demanded to pay the cost of his ambitions. In 1523 he had demanded a heavy tax on land and goods, and had displeased the Commons with a hectoring speech ; and two years later he levied an ' Amicable Loan ' of a sixth of all men's property. The protests against his exactions, and the indignities inflicted on his tax-collectors, should have converted Wolsey to a policy of peace, but the further humiliations of the Papacy urged him once more to take the field in its defence.

Clement's chief danger now came from Charles. Changing sides, he joined Francis in a Holy League to recover Italy from the Spaniards, but his new alliance failed to improve his fortunes. Pescara, the Emperor's finest general, seized the Lombard towns, and in the autumn of 1526 Rome itself was rifled by Spanish and Italian troops ; a few months later, a larger imperial army, tired, hungry and mutinous, entered Rome and comprehensively sacked it. Clement was made prisoner. Wolsey could not watch these outrages without resolving to avenge them. The sack of Rome, although the blame was laid on the Lutheran troops in the imperial army, cost Charles the public opinion of Europe, and made it easier for Wolsey to force England into the war. ' This must stir the hearts of all Christian Princes ', he said, and he professed to fear for the Papacy another Babylonian Captivity. France and England declared war in January, 1528 ; and, with the great Genoese seaman Doria on their side, Wolsey was confident that they would win. For Wolsey much was at stake : if the Holy League freed Clement from his bondage to Charles, Henry could be granted his divorce, and Wolsey's legatine authority would be justified. Early successes raised false hopes. The French besieged the Spanish army in Naples, and Doria beat Charles's navy at Salerno. Then Doria changed sides, and took the command of the sea with him; he drove the French out of Genoa, and in June, 1529, the French army was once more annihilated, at Landriano; 'not a vestige of the army is left'. These events decided Clement: 'I have quite made up my mind', he said, 'to become an imperialist and live and die as such.' He made his peace with Charles at Barcelona, and Florence was restored to the Medici. Francis, too, had had enough: in an agreement with Charles at Cambrai the French consented to Hapsburg domination in Italy. Campeggio adjourned the court at Blackfriars, and Clement ordered the King's divorce to be heard at Rome.

England had contributed nothing to the war, and she was not consulted when it was brought to an end. So far had she fallen from the artificial pre-eminence to which Wolsey had raised her in 1518 and 1521. The war had caused immediate unemployment in the wool trade, and the people's distress had issued in riots; the cloth-workers of Kent planned to seize Wolsey and turn him adrift in a boat bored with holes. For Wolsey, as the French ambassador remarked, was 'the only Englishman who wishes a war with Flanders'. The people's resentment obliged him to depend on his allies and the subsidies which he paid them; and his attempt to be the arbiter of Christendom, and to direct the events of Europe from afar, finally collapsed when the combatants made a settlement without reference to his wishes.

The collapse of his foreign policy was fatal to Wolsey. For he could justify the exorbitant powers which he wielded in England only if he could persuade the Pope to do Henry's bidding. For fifteen years he had bound the country to the interests of the Papacy, only to find at the last that he had promised more than he could perform. He had promised Henry that the Pope would annul his marriage; but the policy which he had pursued had made the Pope the helpless servant of the Emperor. Charles had seen his sisters removed from the thrones of Hungary and Denmark, and he had no sentimental feelings for his aunt; but he could not tolerate English interference in Italy, and he was determined that he, and not Wolsey, should be master at Rome.

Henry had no further use for the legate of a Pope who was the chaplain of Charles V. Wolsey's enemies descended on their awaited prey. A torrent of accusation [1] swept away his dignities and his power: the nobility complained of his proud jurisdiction in Star Chamber, the clergy of the tyrannies of his authority as legate. Lawyers, courtiers, pamphleteers and merchants joined the throng which cried for his blood. He was stripped of his offices, but he was granted a handsome pension and allowed to go to his diocese of York, where, for the first time, he devoted himself to his spiritual functions. But he abused the mercy that was shown to him. For his intrigues with foreign powers he was summoned to the Tower on a charge of treason, and he died at Leicester Abbey in November, 1530, when on his way to a less merciful end.

All that he had stood for perished with him. He was the last of the ecclesiastical statesmen of mediaeval England; the dominant forces of the new age, the new instinct of patriotism, the zest for seafaring and discovery, the commercial importance of the alliance with Flanders, the growing power of the middle-class laity in parliament, escaped his notice and attention. The common law turned back the encroachments of Chancery and Star Chamber, the laity overthrew his ecclesiastical pretensions, the King, realising that his island was small and remote, returned to the isolation which better served its interests; because he despised parliament, he left no statutes to perpetuate his work. His importance in English history is that he uncovered Henry's strength. As Chancellor and legate he concentrated in himself a monopoly of jurisdiction and power which taught Henry that he might be both King and Pope.

[1] The charges included giving the King diseases; and, to exonerate Henry for his long subservience to such a villain, Wolsey was also accused of witchcraft.

CHAPTER III

THE REFORMATION UNDER HENRY VIII

The King's 'divorce'. The problem of Church and state. The breach with Rome. Attack on the monasteries. Definition of doctrine. Henry's last years: Scotland and France.

1. *The King's 'divorce'*

As the years passed by, and Catherine of Aragon still failed to bear him a son, Henry VIII became increasingly anxious about the succession. Of the six children born to him, only a daughter, Mary, survived infancy; and a King's first duty to his people was to have a son to succeed him. Matilda had been the only woman to sit on the throne of England, and civil war had followed naturally; it would follow as naturally, men felt, with the memory of the Wars of the Roses close behind them, if a woman were to succeed to the throne of the Tudors. James V of Scotland had a claim as the son of Margaret Tudor; the Dukes of Norfolk and Suffolk had claims through their wives, who were respectively daughters of Edward IV and Henry VII; the Marquis of Exeter was descended from Edward IV, Lord Montague from the Duke of Clarence.[1] The number of claimants reflected the number of factions which might arise to challenge Mary's crown. If the King did not have a son, the dynasty might be overthrown, and the work of Henry VII dissolve into anarchy.

The welfare of the nation demanded that, since she had failed in her duty as Queen, Catherine of Aragon should be

[1] His descent from Edward III had been the underlying cause of the execution of the Duke of Buckingham in 1521.

removed ; and the issue might in the long run have proved simpler if there had not been plausible moral arguments to reinforce those of expediency. Catherine had been married to Henry's brother Arthur ; and since the book of Leviticus forbade a man to take in marriage his brother's widow, Pope Julius II had been asked to provide a special dispensation for her to marry Henry. Many had challenged the validity of the dispensation when Julius granted it. Events seemed to justify their scruples. For in an age of faith it was possible to read in the unprecedented mortality of Henry's children the evidence of God's displeasure with his marriage. Henry himself was convinced that he had broken God's law, and there is no need to question his good faith when he discovered that he had harboured a ' perpetual scruple ' about his marriage. He vowed that, if he were given a son, he would head a crusade against the Turks. For her part, Catherine shared his misgivings ; and she believed that the blood of the Earl of Warwick, shed at her father's bidding before she came to England, was a further cause of her afflictions.

The quarrel with Rome, therefore, was not rooted in Henry's infatuation for Anne Boleyn. Henry's wooing was urgent and tempestuous, and Anne yielded to it in 1529, four years before his marriage was annulled. But this did not solve his more serious problem : the succession was not safe unless his son were born in wedlock. He had already a natural son, to whom he had given the significantly Tudor titles of Duke of Richmond and Somerset ; and there is little doubt that Henry intended, if he had no legitimate son, to nominate him to the succession in preference to Mary. But he could not feel that his dynasty was secure unless his marriage with Catherine were annulled—a divorce was insufficient, for Catholics do not recognise divorce—and he were indisputably married to Anne. The bigamy hopefully recommended by the harassed Clement did not serve his purpose.

Henry had first contemplated ridding himself of Catherine in 1514, when his fury with Ferdinand for betraying him in the

French war inclined him to rid himself of all things Spanish, including his Queen. In 1527 he instructed Wolsey to cause the Pope to annul the marriage. Wolsey did not object to the divorce, and he wasted no sympathy on Catherine ; but he had two reasons for wishing to dissuade Henry from his intention to marry Anne Boleyn. First, he wished to cement his anti-imperial alliance with France by marrying Henry to Renée, the deformed sister of the King ; and, secondly, Anne, the ' night-crow ', represented the anti-clerical interests which were seeking to overthrow him. His first task, however, was to secure the divorce which Henry had demanded. His own authority, and with it the authority of the Pope in England, depended on his success ; and he was anxious for the case to be settled by the Pope before Henry was tempted to take the law into his own hands. Embarrassed by the presence of the imperial armies in Italy, Clement sought to evade the responsibility. In vain he implored Catherine to cut the knot by withdrawing into a nunnery ; he was obliged at length to send Campeggio to England to hear Henry's claims. The collapse of the Holy League in 1529 clinched the issue : the court was adjourned, and the hearing was called to Rome. Suffolk broke out at Blackfriars : ' I see the old said saw is true, that never Cardinal or legate did good in England.' Wolsey fell, and in his ruin dragged down the Papacy which had abdicated all its powers to him, and at the last had failed him.

Henry, then, had to make his own way out of his difficulties ; and the bitter controversies of 1515 had taught him where to look for his allies. The divorce was not the cause of the English Reformation, but it brought to a head the grievances which Tudor England bore the Church. More, Colet and Erasmus had disturbed its fat slumbers by the scorn they poured on ecclesiastics who fell short of their professions ; and abroad, Luther had shaken the foundations of its authority by asserting the priesthood of all believers. But such things had happened before : Wycliffe had attacked the corruption of the clergy and uttered doctrines which they had forcefully condemned. The Church had been unpopular before: the Statutes of Provisors and Praemunire, and, less formally, the violence done by the people to the Pope's representatives, had expressed the anti-clericalism of the age which rejected Wycliffe's theology. At the beginning of the fifteenth century there were all the elements necessary for a split with Rome: the Papacy had debased itself before the Kings of France at Avignon; the nation had shown its hostility to the Church's wealth, jurisdiction and temporal powers; Wycliffe and the Lollards pointed the way to spiritual reformation. But the Kings of the House of Lancaster sat insecurely on their thrones, and their weakness drew them closer to the Church; with their new powers of persecution the clergy took new life.

Henry VIII in 1529 had no such need of the Church; rather, since it ventured to oppose him, he needed to be master of it. There was no dispute about doctrine; Henry never changed the opinions about Luther which in 1521 had made him Defender of the Faith. Nor, when he began his attack, did he intend to cut England adrift from Rome; he was driven to that when the Pope would not heed his threats. His quarrel was the climax of the long struggle between Church and state. In nationalist England there was no room for the mediaeval Church. The clergy were an independent corporation in the community, owing their first allegiance to a foreign master, paying dues to him and seeking his judgment as the final court of appeal. The canon law which they administered was made without the King's assent. In a hundred different ways they wielded authority over the people with which the secular government could not interfere, baptising them, marrying them, administering the sacraments, arbitrating questions of wills and inheritance, caring for the sick, distributing charity among the poor. Holding too the keys of everlasting life, the Church could dominate the minds and consciences of men, and extract from them a loyalty and service which were often withheld from the King. These powers were no longer compatible with the development of England. The growth of national self-consciousness, of which the monarchy was the symbol and the power, made demands on men's loyalty which they could not reconcile with their loyalty to the universal Church. With or without Luther, with or without Anne Boleyn, Henry must sooner or later have joined issue with the Church, and have made with it, as the Kings of France and Spain had already done, some agreement by which it should no longer impede his sovereignty. The day was past when men might allow their consciences to distinguish between the things which were Caesar's and the things which were God's.

The Church was unable to withstand the King's attack. The downfall of the feudal aristocracy, the other bulwark of mediaeval society, had left it vulnerable to its enemies. The laity resented its immunities and its power over heretics,[1] and were casting greedy eyes on its wealth; the Humanists' mockery of its sloth, its miracles and relics, had exposed it to the people's ridicule; Wolsey's excessive pride had divided it against itself. The nation was ready to follow Henry's lead. It disliked the divorce, sympathising with Catherine, hating Anne, and fearing that the quarrel with the Emperor would harm the wool trade; but its pride would not consent to see the affairs of the King settled by the issue of French and Hapsburg rivalry in Italy. When Charles and Francis petitioned the Pope to forbid the English parliament to discuss the divorce, they could not have done better service to Henry's cause.

2. *The breach with Rome*

The Long Parliament of the Reformation was summoned in November, 1529, to redress 'the enormities of the clergy'. Henry played his cards skilfully. He put the people into a good humour by attacking abuses which he knew to be unpopular, and by making small reforms which saved their pockets. The English Reformation opened with no statement of doctrine, but with an attack on clerical fees. Parliament's first business was to remove mortuary and probate fees, restrict the rights of

[1] Nor did the laity welcome the Church's ban on usury and excessive profits.

sanctuary and set limits to pluralism and non-residence. Then it was adjourned for more than a year, while Henry tested the resistance of the clergy. All who had recognised Wolsey's legatine authority had been technically guilty of a breach of Praemunire, and on this head the King extracted a fine of £118,000 from the Convocations of York and Canterbury. Further to expiate an offence of which all had been guilty, the clergy recognised Henry to be 'singular protector, only and supreme lord, and, so far as the law of Christ allows, also Supreme Head of the English Church'. Meanwhile, English envoys had been at the foremost universities of Europe, seeking the opinions of the canon lawyers on the lawfulness of the King's divorce. Most of the verdicts were in his favour. Thus, with the canon law at his back, the laity clearly ready to plunder the Church's privileges, and the clergy themselves not daring to resist, Henry had prepared the ground for his battle with the Pope. It was still not his object to separate the English Church from Rome; like all rulers, he was fundamentally conservative, and he would not recklessly embark on a revolution. His purpose was to show the Pope his strength, and to force from him a satisfactory settlement of his demands. The Annates Act of 1532 was a piece of elaborate blackmail. It forbade the payment to Rome of annates, the first-fruits of the revenues of new Bishops. Henry deplored to the Pope the 'importunity' of his subjects in passing the bill, and delayed his own assent to it in order to give Clement time to reconsider his attitude. In the same year parliament passed laws which further restricted benefit of clergy and the powers of the ecclesiastical courts; and the clergy completed their submission to the King when Convocation undertook to offer its existing laws to the King's approval, and to pass no further legislation without his consent.

Clement's refusal to be coerced brought matters to a head. In November, 1532, he forbade Henry to separate himself from Catherine and take a new wife, and Henry answered him with flat defiance. 1533 was the critical year. In January Anne was pregnant, and Henry secretly married her; in May Cranmer, hastily appointed Archbishop of Canterbury in succession to Warham, proclaimed in a court at Dunstable that Julius's dispensation had been unlawful, and that Henry and Catherine had never been husband and wife. Thus restored to his innocence, Henry had Anne crowned in Westminster Abbey in June, and in September Elizabeth was born at Greenwich. Since the Pope condemned all these proceedings, it only remained to strip him of all his authority in England. The Act in Restraint of Appeals was the first constitutional breach with Rome. But it was more than that. Its terms revealed that the English Church, although released from its dependence on the Pope, had found a new master in the King, whose authority was proclaimed henceforth to embrace all jurisdictions, both spiritual and temporal. The Church's power was to be restricted by the laws of the land as decreed by the King and his parliament. A single blow had broken the supremacy of the Pope and brought the government of the Church into the hands of the King.

The legislation of 1534 swept away the vestiges of the Pope's authority. All dues hitherto paid to Rome, including Peter's Pence, were to be paid to the Crown; abbeys and religious houses exempt from episcopal control were brought under the jurisdiction of Chancery; and provision was made for the election of Bishops by royal authority alone. A Heresy Act deprived the Church of the initiative in prosecutions. The Act of Supremacy registered Henry's claim to the revenues and jurisdictions which had previously belonged to the Church. One step had still to be taken, for Henry had not lost sight of the purpose which had started him on the road to supremacy: a statute vested the succession in the heirs of Anne Boleyn. Henry's work was done. As Convocation meekly declared, 'the Bishop of Rome has no more authority in England than any other foreign Bishop'.

A Church which had been stripped of its power could scarcely hope to be left in possession of its property and wealth. The attack on the monasteries was the necessary and expected gesture of a government anxious to complete what it had begun. The wealth of the monasteries was alone sufficient to tempt the King and his advisers to destroy them, and the scorn which the Humanists had poured on them suggested that their existence was no longer justified. In addition, as the last stronghold of the old ideas, they were the least national element in the country. Thomas Cromwell, lately a servant of Wolsey, had carried out the King's policy during the critical years of change ; he was rewarded by his appointment as Vicar-General, to exercise on the King's behalf all the rights attached to the Supreme Head of the Church. As Vicar-General he conducted an investigation of the monasteries. It was the mission of the visitors to find fault, and the Black Book, in which they set forth the results of their enquiry, contained formidable evidence of corruption and evil living. These conclusions need not be taken too seriously, for by their nature they were a record of what was bad in the monasteries, and not of what was good and worth preserving ; they did, however, provide the government with plausible grounds for dissolving 376 lesser monasteries whose income was less than £200 a year. Three years later, in 1539, the greater houses followed them into destruction ; and the suppression of the mendicant orders and the Knights of St. John completed the overthrow of the institutions which might still acknowledge the authority of the Pope. Their immense wealth and estates [1] passed to the Crown. Henry created six new Bishoprics and founded a few schools, and later in his reign he established five Regius Professorships at the Universities. Otherwise, the opportunity to do good was wasted. The wealth of the monasteries was not devoted to any national or charitable purposes. Instead, it was used in part to relieve the financial difficulties of the Crown, and in part to lull the nation into accepting the changes which Henry had made. The sale of monastic lands and their tithes was a simple way to reward the service of the loyal and to stifle the discontent of those who murmured ; by its means Henry created a new aristocracy with a vested interest in the Reformation and pledged to resist all attempts to undo his work.

[1] An eighth of the cultivated areas of England.

This served his immediate ends, but he would have been wiser to have clung to what he had seized; for it was this Reformation aristocracy, rich when the Crown was poor, which a hundred years later challenged the prerogative of the Stuarts.

These changes were not made without opposition. James V contemplated an invasion, the feudal aristocracy in the North were restive, and the various claimants to the throne grew strong in hope. But Henry had a short way with those who openly resisted him. He executed the Nun of Kent, whose ravings, delivered in epileptic trances, or, as some preferred to believe, with the inspiration of Heaven, prophesied God's vengeance on all who forwarded the divorce. A savage act passed in 1534 brought into the category of treason words spoken against the King, and even the refusal to answer leading questions. In 1535 the Carthusian priors of London died as traitors because they would not admit Henry to be their Supreme Head. In the same year the government struck down Thomas More, the ex-Chancellor, and Fisher, Bishop of Rochester, the only Bishop who had consistently opposed its measures. They died because they would not take the required oath to the succession, and because their consciences told them that Henry was not, and could not be, the Head of the Church. A rising in Lincolnshire developed in 1537 into the Pilgrimage of Grace, the only serious rebellion during the reign; it was defeated by treachery and punished with murderous cruelty. Henry was master of his realm. He would be in danger only if Charles and Francis settled their endless quarrel and combined to attack him. Henry had little cause to fear invasion, but he took his precautions. In 1533, on the pretext of a dispute with his merchants, he closed the staple at Calais; the immediate distress in Flanders convinced Englishmen that the Emperor could not afford to make war on them. Again, in 1538, when Charles and Francis paused in their strife, Henry took steps to counter their alliance. He allowed Cromwell to open negotiations with the Lutheran Princes of Germany, and promised the Flemings that for seven years they should pay the same duties as English merchants ; and as a dreadful example to pretenders, he spilled the last drops of royal blood in England : Lord Montague, the Marquis of Exeter and the aged Countess of Salisbury went to the block. His measures were effective. There was no invasion ; Spain and France resumed their quarrel ; successive Popes vainly excommunicated Henry, deprived him of his crown, and raged against the ' unprofitable island '. As Luther remarked, ' Junker Harry meant to be God, and to do as pleased himself '. Parliament had allowed him to break with Rome, master the Church, make his own definition of treason, marry as he pleased, dispose of his wives and alter the succession at his whim ; it had cancelled his debts and given to his proclamations the force of law ; the country had remained loyal to him through excommunication, rebellion and the fear of invasion. The birth of a son in 1537 filled the cup of Henry's triumph, and persuaded him that God approved of what he had done.

3. *The definition of doctrine*

The Church had found a new master, but its doctrines remained unaltered. To be a Lutheran was as serious an offence as to deny the King's supremacy, and the new Head of the Church considered it his duty to draw up articles of faith which should counter the spread of heresy and promote in his subjects a desirable ' unity and concord in opinion '. The Ten Articles, prepared in 1536 by the King's own hand, were intended ' to establish Christian quietness and unity ' by re-stating the orthodox dogmas of the Catholic Church ; and the ' Institution of a Christian Man ', or Bishops' Book, of the following year merely supplemented the Ten Articles where they had been vague or defective. In 1539 the Anglican Church passed its first act of uniformity. The Act of Six Articles was an uncompromising assertion of Catholic doctrine ; it was carried in the full tide of the Catholic reaction against the Lutheran tendencies to which Cromwell had tempted Henry when there was fear of an invasion. Norfolk and the Catholic party reached the height of their influence when Henry put away Anne of Cleves, the unbeautiful seal of a Protestant alliance for which there was no longer any need, sent Cromwell to his death, and married his fifth wife, the Catholic Catherine Howard.

But Henry and the Catholics were fighting a losing battle. Henry was a sincere believer in the old faith, and he did not wish to change it ; but, since he had destroyed the body of the Roman Church in England, he strove in vain to preserve the breath which had animated it. His attempt to keep alive the faith and doctrine of the Middle Ages, with himself in the place of the Pope, depended only on the force of his own personality, and was certain in the long run to fail. He had made drastic changes, and even he was unable to draw an arbitrary line at which change must cease. A party strong at court and among the Bishops favoured the new opinions, and wished to relax the strict orthodoxy of the English Church ; Cromwell, Henry's Vicar-General, and Cranmer, his Archbishop, were its leaders. Although Henry himself made no concessions to the new faith, and in the King's Book of 1543 once more declared his unimpeachable Catholicism, the tendencies of his later years prepared the way for the doctrinal revolution which followed his death. The reformers won their greatest victory when an English version of the Bible was issued in 1539, and when Cranmer made an English translation of the Litany. For the essence of Luther's teaching was that Christians should draw their inspiration, not from the teachings of the Church, but from God's word as revealed in the scriptures ; and once the scriptures were available for Englishmen to read in their own tongue, reformation could not be stayed.[1] Other slight changes led, although perhaps unconsciously, in the same direction. Even the Ten Articles had ordered worshippers not to believe that ' ceremonies have power to remit sin ' ; subsequent proclamations regulated the number of saints' days, because they interfered with harvest-work, provided an English

[1] It was found impossible to enforce the Six Articles. ' They continued in force,' said Cranmer, ' little above the space of one year.'

Bible for every Church in the land, and ordered the destruction of shrines and the removal of relics. The influence of the Catholics waned after the fall of Catherine Howard, and in the last months of his life Henry instructed Cranmer to convert the Mass into a Communion service. Most significant of all were the preparations which he made for the reign of his son. Henry's failing health made it probable that Edward would begin his reign as a minor, and Henry decided to place him in the care largely of Protestants. His tutors were Protestants ; Gardiner, the most stoutly Catholic of the Bishops, was omitted from the Regency Council. Finally, the attack made on the reactionary Howards at the close of the reign showed that Henry feared their behaviour when he was dead. Surrey was attainted of treason in 1546, and Norfolk lay under sentence of death on the night when Henry died himself. With Henry dead and the Howards disgraced, the reformers had the future in their hands.

4. *Scotland and France*

His victory over the Pope went to Henry's head. As the range of his egotism broadened and sought its limits, he could not be content until the whole of the British Isles acknowledged his supremacy. Of Wales he was already master ; Irish and Scots should admit him as master too. He was the first English King to assume the title of King of Ireland ; he imposed on the Irish the English system of land tenure, English justice and the English tongue ; he forced them to renounce the Pope and accept himself as their ecclesiastical Head ; and as the corollary of his supremacy, he seized the wealth of their monasteries and plundered their shrines. As his deputy, Anthony St. Leger ruled with strength and judgment, and under him the Irish lived quietly ; but to the discontents which had made Ireland always difficult to govern, Henry had added the poison of religious differences. The native Irish resisted the Reformation, and remained loyal to the Pope ; and through Ireland, England's Catholic enemies would always be able to strike and wound.

Then Henry turned to Scotland. He found it intolerable to his dignity that there should flourish in Scotland a powerful French party, led by Mary of Guise, the Queen, and Cardinal Beaton, the Archbishop of St. Andrews ; further, James V had for ten years been threatening to invade England to restore the authority of the Pope. Confident that France's duel with the Emperor would deprive the Scots of their traditional ally, Henry determined to punish their importunity ; reviving the ancient claim of the English Crown to suzerainty, he declared the Scots to be rebels, and ordered Norfolk over the Border to teach them a lesson. The news of Henry's crushing victory at Solway Moss broke James's heart, and left his week-old daughter Mary as ruler of his kingdom. Henry now had the opportunity to gain his objects by statesmanship and peace : the Scots were willing to betroth Mary to Edward, and with that Henry should have been content. He refused, however, to abandon his claim to their homage, and even to their crown. Parliament pronounced that ' the late pretensed King of Scots ' had been a usurper, and that the time was ' apt and propice ' for Henry to recover the crown that was rightly his. This folly was fatal to Henry's more sober purposes. Stiffened by encouragement and material assistance from Francis, the Scots broke off negotiations with England, and planned to marry their Queen to a Valois Prince.

Henry's ambition had thus not only bungled a statesmanlike plan for uniting England with Scotland ; it had now driven the Scots to seek a marriage which might put England in serious danger. To prevent it, he was obliged to declare war on France. The last years of his reign were occupied with war on two fronts. The Earl of Hertford took Edinburgh and burnt it, and in 1545 he ravaged the Lowlands, destroying the harvests and sacking towns and villages. But the French war went ill. Boulogne was captured, but in 1545 the country was invaded at two points : the Scots crossed the Border and defeated the northern levies at Ancrum Moor ; while a French fleet, after cruising in the Solent, landed forces on the Isle of Wight. Disease, the habitual enemy of navies, came to Henry's rescue, and the French withdrew ;

and the murder of Beaton, not without Henry's connivance, weakened their hold on Scotland. Henry made peace with France, but when he died he was preparing a fresh campaign to compel the Scots to marry Mary to his son.

In his last years Henry was not an attractive figure. His imperious nature had fed on success, and would not suffer opposition. His treatment of the Scots, whom he was too proud to conciliate and too weak to subdue, showed how far arrogance had obscured his judgment. But his hold on his people persisted to the end. When invasion was threatened in 1539, and again during the more serious alarms of 1545, there was no hint of rebellion inside the country. The people rallied to protect their King, with no thought of criticising his policy. The despotism of the Tudors rested ultimately on the consent of the nation, since their only armed force was a hundred yeomen of the guard; in the emergencies of rebellion or invasion, they were at the mercy of their subjects. When Henry appealed to his people, they always responded. In 1545 they paid without a murmur the exceptionally heavy loans and subsidies which he exacted for the defence of the nation; and 'if this be not sufficient', said the commons of Surrey, 'His Grace shall have more'. His rule was always harsh, and at the end his passion was his only law. The English consented to it because the political doctrines of the age taught that the King must be strong; and the system which Henry had built up was strong enough to stand the test of a Regency, the reign of a zealous, unpractical Queen, the coming of new faiths, and the assault of a counter-revolution.

CHAPTER IV

ENCLOSURES AND POOR RELIEF IN THE SIXTEENTH AND SEVENTEENTH CENTURIES

The problem of enclosures. Policy of the government. Its failure. Tudor schemes for poor relief. Poor relief after 1660. The Puritan view of poverty.

1. *The problem of enclosures*

In the Middle Ages agriculture was carried on by the ' open field ' system. Each tenant of the manor had his own strips of the huge fields to cultivate for himself, his share of the common to graze his beasts, and his share of the forests for firewood. His strips of arable land were scattered all over the fields, and were divided from those of his neighbours, not by fences, but by balks of turf ; thus a bird's-eye view of mediaeval England showed, not the chessboard pattern of to-day, but vast stretches of ploughland extending from the manor-house. The agrarian revolution began when enterprising landlords, finding that pasture was more profitable than tillage, decided to abandon corn-growing and use their lands for keeping sheep ; and, to define the limits of their property, *enclosed* their fields with hedges and fences.

The enclosing movement was not a novelty of the sixteenth century : strips of arable land were consolidated at Gorleston in the reign of Henry III, and as the manorial system gradually broke up, the waste land of the manor was occupied and enclosed. After the Black Death labour was scarce, and therefore dear ; and the great advantage of sheep-farming, from the landlord's point of view, was that one or two shepherds could care for hundreds of sheep. Moreover, it was profitable: 'the foot of the sheep turns sand into gold', drawing wealth from soil that was too barren to be cultivated. English wool fetched good prices in the markets of Flanders, and with the growth of woollen manufactures at home, the English clothiers called for a steady flow of raw material. Sheep-farming, then, offered larger and more certain rewards than tillage, wherein the land had been exhausted by constant use, and the crops were at the mercy of the weather and lazy or quarrelsome neighbours. Its drawback was that, in order to secure lands for pasture, landlords enclosed the common wastes, where their tenants grazed their cattle, and then the arable strips, where they grew their meagre supply of food. The yeomen were driven from the land by the raising of their rents, and heavy fines for the renewal of leases; and, often, by naked eviction. Only a few of them could hope to be employed as shepherds; the rest, excluded from learning a trade by the jealousy of the guilds, took to the roads and the charity of the monasteries. Thus the wide outcry against enclosure for sheep-farming rested on two deep-seated objections. First, 'the decay of tillage' imperilled the nation's supply of corn; for the encloser 'desireth nothing but grass in his grounds'. Secondly, the 'depopulation' which it caused drove honest yeomen into becoming rogues and vagabonds. Discontent expressed itself in pamphlets and broadsides, and found its way into literature. 'Sheep have become devourers of men', wrote Thomas More in *Utopia*; '. . . they unpeople villages and towns.' 'God gave the earth to men to inhabit, and not unto sheep and wild deer', complained William Tyndale; and Latimer's sermons denounced the 'step-lords . . . unnatural lords', on whose lands, 'where have been a great many householders and inhabitants, there is but a shepherd and his dog'. The monks were no less covetous than the lay landlords. They 'leave no ground for tillage', complained More; 'they enclose all in pastures; they throw down houses; they pluck down towns, and leave nothing standing but only the church to make of it a sheepcote'.

Neither the grievance nor the lamentation was new. In 1414

a petition from Chesterton, in Cambridgeshire, protested that only a barn now stood where formerly had been a thriving agricultural community; and the same year brought a similar complaint from Darleton and Ragenell, in Nottinghamshire. 'The chief destruction of towns and decay of houses', wrote John Hales, 'was before the beginning of the reign of Henry VII.' English wool was already famous in the fifteenth century. What made the problem so grave in the Tudor period was the new attitude to the ownership of property. Enclosure was an aspect of the change from a collective economy to individual enterprise; and the transition had almost as many victims as the new system when it was established. The economy of the Middle Ages had echoed the words of the Book of Proverbs: 'Give me neither riches nor poverty, but enough for my sustenance.' Its aim was subsistence, to hold economic activity in its place as the servant, not the master, of civilisation. The ethics of society condemned the usurer, the trader who charged more than the just price for his goods, the speculator who 'buys in order that he may sell dearer'. The ownership of property was sublimated into an ethic of service: the man who prospered was expected to come to the aid of the man whose crops the storms had ruined, and not to exploit his misfortunes by lending him money at interest. Precept might outrun performance, but mediaeval doctrine had no place for economic enterprise which did not aim at the good of society as a whole. But the Renaissance and the Reformation, following the swift economic development of the fifteenth century, brought a message of individual expediency. In Tudor England a change took place in the psychology of ownership. Abandoning the mediaeval belief that property carried obligations to society, landowners argued that they might do as they pleased with their own, and rejected as unwarranted interference the efforts of the government to recall them to their duties. The flourishing men of commerce who invested their profits in land were insensitive to the call of responsibility. Ignorant of the old bond between the landlord and his tenant, they were deaf to the rebukes of the government, the imprecations of the preachers, and the cries of the evicted. As the feudal manor disappeared, men began to invest their capital in land for what return it would bring them. Their avaricious temper made impossible the government's task of checking the spread of enclosure.

2. *The government's attitude to enclosures*

Except when Northumberland was Regent, the attitude of the Tudors to enclosure did not waver : enclosure was a social evil to be condemned, prevented and punished. Many landlords enclosed their land in order to increase its yield of crops, thus ridding themselves of slovenly neighbours and finding it possible to rest the soil every three years ; this sort of enclosure was not to be condemned, for it provided both food and labour. The wrath of the government and the people fell on those selfish landlords who enclosed their estates to make parks for their own use, and on ' the great sheep-masters ' who enclosed for pasture, to the decay of agriculture and the impoverishment of their tenants. The government had several reasons for taking the side of the yeoman against his master. It inherited the mediaeval view of society as a living organism, a body which could not be well if any of its members was sick ; it opposed, therefore, those covetous men whose prosperity was founded on the misfortunes of the poor. Their concern, too, was partly patriotic. For the yeoman was the backbone of the nation, the mainstay of its economy and the strength of its armies ; whereas, ' shepherds be but poor archers '. The Tudors were further influenced by practical motives. Enclosures caused discontent, and discontent sometimes issued in risings which were troublesome to suppress ; the government was not yet well equipped to deal with social disorder. Again, the Tudors were concerned for their revenues : for when farms were broken up and disappeared, the property was not re-assessed, and the revenue due from it was lost. Lastly, although the widespread condemnation of sheep-farming was probably sound, it was based in part on a miscalculation of cause and effect. In the first half of the sixteenth century prices steadily rose, in the second half they soared. The economic thought of the time was unable to find the real explanation : prices rose because the circulation of gold and silver from the mines of South America cheapened the value of money ; and the government's miserable expedient of debasing the coinage [1] aggravated the disease which it sought to relieve. Sheep-farming was the natural scapegoat of economic ignorance. It was an important cause of social dislocation, but it was blamed beyond its responsibility.

The policy of the Crown was first defined in the reign of Edward IV. The Yorkists depended on the middle classes, the Lancastrians on the great landed families. The Yorkist judges, Bryan and Danby, had, therefore, a powerful motive for their decision in this reign that evicted tenants had a legal case against their lords ; they ruled that tenants should be protected if they could prove that the lord had broken the ' reign of custom '. The first measure in the Tudor period was an act of 1488, which restricted the size of farms in the Isle of Wight, on the ground that the recent depopulation had made the island ' open and ready to the hands of the King's enemies '. A year later the government passed a general act in restraint of sheep-farming, and thereafter Star Chamber and the Court of Requests were busy punishing breaches of the law. Wolsey set up a commission in 1517, to investigate all enclosure undertaken since 1488, and offenders suffered heavily in his courts. But it was soon clear that the Tudors were failing in their policy of protecting the tenants. The Crown and the Council were playing a lone hand. In this respect the Tudors' strength was their weakness. For the country gentry, on whom they relied for passing legislation in parliament and for seeing, as magistrates, that it was obeyed, were in this matter the offenders on whom the government's hand would have fallen. The steady repetition during the sixteenth century of statutes, orders, proclamations and commissions, gave the measure of the government's failure to

[1] The currency was debased five times between 1527 and 1551

achieve its objects. Parliament was unwilling to prohibit enclosure by legislation. ' It is hard ', ran the *Complaint of Roderik Mors*, ' to have these ills redressed by Parliament, because it pricketh them chiefly which be chosen to be burgesses.' ' The ears of our great sheep-masters do hang at the doors of this House ', protested a member in 1601. Legislation which did find its way through parliament was half-heartedly administered by the Justices of the Peace, and there were subtle ways of evading it. A law in 1534 forbade any man to own more than 2,000 sheep ; so the landlords, ' to colour the multitude of their sheep, father them on their children, kinsfolk and friends ', and, ploughing a single furrow across a field, reported it as land under the plough. ' Let the preacher preach till his tongue be worn to the stump,' complained Latimer, ' nothing is amended ' ; in spite of the government's orders, said Hales, the offenders ' returned to their old vomit '. The dissolution of the monasteries brought land into the possession of urban capitalists, who treated it as a commodity to be bought and sold at a profit, in defiance of the criticisms of such as Hales, who protested that ' it is not lawful for a man to do what he lists with his own ; but every man must use what he hath to the utmost benefit of his country '. To put the land again under the plough was one of the objects of the Pilgrimage of Grace.

A spirited attempt to resist the evil was made by Protector Somerset. ' Maugre the devil, private profit, self-love, money and such-like the devil's instruments, it shall go forward ' ; for the realm ' must be defended against the enemy with force of men and the multitude of true subjects, not with flocks of sheep and droves of beasts '. But his commission was obstructed and his orders disregarded. In 1549 the rebels who followed Ket from Norfolk indicated the nature of their principal grievances by killing and eating 20,000 sheep. Somerset sympathised with their sufferings, and was willing to confer with them and consider remedies ; but Somerset was overthrown for being thus ready to betray the interests of his class, and for three years England endured a government which hastened enclosures as a matter of policy. Northumberland represented the landowning classes, and conceded their right to make what profit they might from their property, unimpeded by thoughts of the common welfare. Enclosing for pasture was made legal ; and opposition to profiteering was stifled by a measure which made it a felony for twelve men, and treason for forty, to meet to consider means to raise their wages, lower prices or destroy enclosures.

The government of Elizabeth vigorously resumed the traditional policy of the Tudors, and supplemented it by trying to employ in manufactures those for whom no work could be found on the land. An act in 1563 confirmed the legislation 'for maintenance of husbandry and tillage' passed under Henry VII and Henry VIII, and ordered that all land which had been four years under the plough since 1528 should be 'kept in tillage for ever'. Enclosures were denounced from the pulpit, judges on circuit were ordered to see that the laws were enforced, the Council of the North and the Wardens of the Marches were bidden to 'look after and redress all wrongful taking of commons, decay of husbandry and oppression of the poor'. But the complaints which flowed into the Privy Council from all parts of the country revealed that the government's conscientious activity was unavailing. 'These enclosures', said Philip Stubbs in 1583, 'be the causes why rich men eat up poor men as beasts do grass. . . . They take in and enclose commons, moors, heaths, and other common pastures, whereout the poor commonalty were wont to have all their forage and feeding for their cattle, and (which is more) corn for themselves to live upon.' There were serious disturbances, and a rising in Oxfordshire, when in 1593 parliament was induced by the persuasions of the sheep-masters, reinforced by Bacon's ignorance of economics, to repeal the act of 1563. The trouble spread even to the Scottish Border, where it was particularly important to keep the people in a good humour. In 1598, therefore, the government reverted to its former policy, and ordered farm-houses to be rebuilt and pasture to be restored to tillage. A debate in

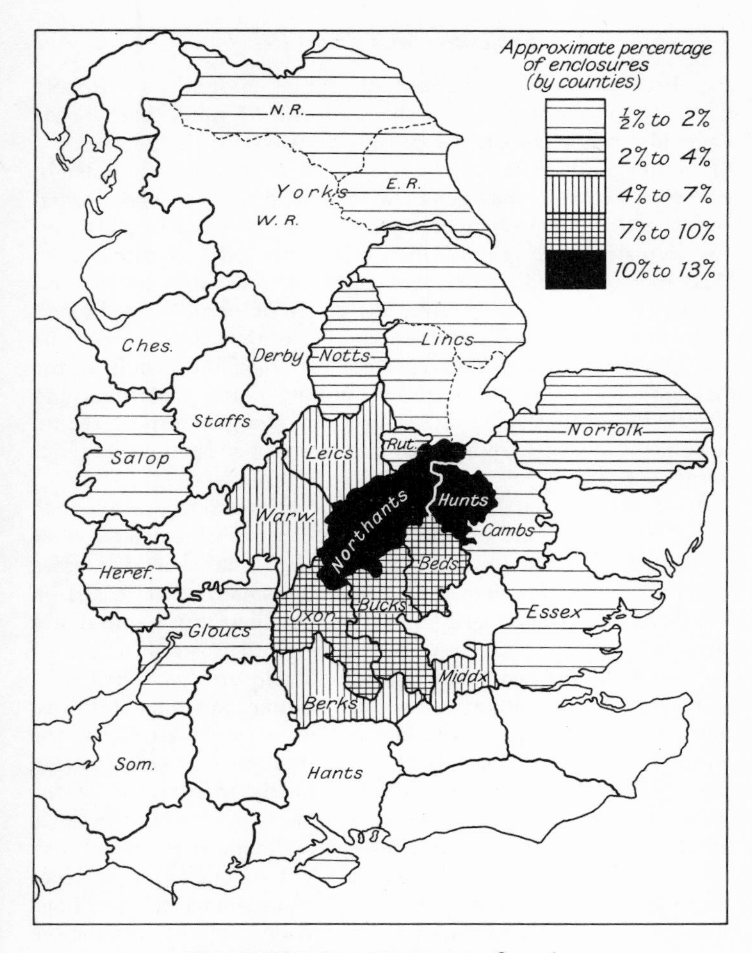

ENCLOSURES IN ENGLAND, 1485–1607

After E. F. Gay (*Quarterly Journal of Economics*, vol. XVII) by permission of the Harvard University Press. See also the note on page 404

Elizabeth's last parliament showed conflicting opinions. Robert Cecil defended the policy of the Tudors: 'I think that whosoever doth not maintain the plough destroys this kingdom. . . . If we debar tillage we give scope to the depopulator.' Raleigh, however, voiced the business man's plea for unrestricted industry: 'The Hollander, which never soweth corn, hath by his industry such plenty that will serve other nations. . . . And therefore I think the best course is to set it at liberty and leave every man free, which is the desire of a true Englishman.' Raleigh's arguments failed to convince the House, and the statutes of 1598 were not repealed. In 1607 the people of the Midland counties rose in revolt, pulling down enclosures and destroying property. To placate them, the government set up a commission of enquiry, but discontent persisted throughout James's reign.

Modern research has revealed that between 1455 and 1607 only 2·76 per cent. of the cultivated areas of England were enclosed. In face of the unceasing lamentation which arose from the poor, this figure is surprisingly small. It is based on evidence that is necessarily defective, but there can be no doubt at the end of the sixteenth century England was still a land of open fields and common wastes. Enclosure provoked discontent because, although its total volume was small, it was, like Mary's burnings, concentrated in a single area. In the nine Midland counties which were the great wheat-growing areas of England, it is probable that nearly 10 per cent. of the land was enclosed; and distress was more severely felt because in these areas there was little alternative employment to absorb the evicted labourers. 'I complain not of enclosure in Kent or Essex,' wrote a contemporary, 'where they have other callings and trades to maintain their country by, or of places near the sea or City, but of enclosure in the inland countries which takes away tillage, the only trade general they have to live on.' In these districts the disappearance of a whole village through enclosure created a problem for which there was no immediate remedy.

Change of policy after 1640

The personal government of Charles I breathed a new vigour into the administration of the law, and enclosure and depopulation were punished with heavy fines ; but thereafter a new spirit was abroad. The constitutional defeat of the Crown in 1641 brought power to the classes which had offended most gravely against the social legislation of the Tudors. Even the government of the Protectorate was swift to defend property against riots, and after the Restoration the ruling classes placed no obstacles in the path of self-interest. A few pamphleteers uttered the traditional protests of the previous century, and the echo of their voices can still be heard in *The Deserted Village* ; but their complaints went unheeded by a generation which held changed opinions about agriculture and the ownership of land. The dangers of sheep-farming now seemed less formidable, since, in spite of it, the country was growing enough corn to keep the price low, and in good years to provide a surplus for export. Enclosure for arable, and a general improvement in the science of farming, had blunted the most serious of the criticisms urged against pasturage. Further, the expansion of industry and trade after the Restoration provided work for labourers evicted from the land. Thus sheep-farming provoked fewer complaints, and the new vogue in economic thought defended the right of the landlord to have a good conscience in putting his property to the best advantage. The familiar doctrine of the free trader made itself heard, that the promptings of self-interest would most readily procure the good of the community. ' Liberty for every man to enjoy his lands in severalty and enclosure ', urged Samuel Fortrey in 1663, would be ' one of the greatest improvements this nation is capable of '. A spreading determination to organise the natural resources of the nation and employ them to the best advantage, was the prelude to the imperialism and economic aggressiveness of the eighteenth century ; and a society based on self-interest and economic freedom was not long in forgetting its obligations to the poor.

3. *The Tudor Poor Law*

In the sixteenth century the English government had to face for the first time the problem of unemployment. The charity and alms of the Church had sufficed to meet the rare and inconsiderable unemployment of the Middle Ages, and to care for the poor when they were sick; the policy of the Crown was expressed, as under Edward III, in enactments that men must either work or go to prison.[1] Such a policy is doubtless adequate when there is work to be had, but the sixteenth century could not dismiss the problem so easily. Thousands of labourers, the helpless victims of enclosure, took to the roads because there was nothing else for them to do; artisans, debarred from work by the exclusiveness of the guilds, were forced to join them. Even the merits of Tudor government had their social disadvantages. For the Statute of Livery threw out of work the armed retainers whose mediaeval profession had been civil war, and the Tudors did not fight enough wars to give them regular service abroad. The dissolution of the monasteries and the chantries not only deprived beggars of their charity, but drove a huge body of monks to swell the army of labourers, artisans, soldiers, friars, pilgrims, professional invalids and touting scholars, which infested the roads and was the terror of lonely farm-houses. Vagabondage became a profession, with laws and an idiom of its own, and there was only Dogberry to deal with it. Beggars broke into houses, pillaged sties and roosts, robbed markets and made their homes in barns. Autolycus cozening the shepherd on his way to market with a full purse was a figure whom all Elizabethans could recognise. Shakespeare might give Falstaff and his rogues the colours of romance—'Diana's foresters, gentlemen of the shade and minions of the moon'—but vagabondage was the symptom of a deep social disorder. The extraordinary career of Mary Frith, who ruled the underworld of Stuart London, revealed the perfection of technique attained by those who were forced to prey on a society

[1] Cf. St. Paul: 'if any would not work, neither should he eat.' (*Thessalonians* iii. 10).

which could not give them honest work. The beggars roamed the country, speaking the ' canting ' tongue, each accompanied by his doxy, devising ingenious swindles to practise on society. There were pedlars, tinkers, knife-grinders, minstrels, fencers, actors, jugglers, fortune-tellers, palmists, conjurers ; Abraham men, like Mad Tom in *King Lear*, who feigned madness ; Clapperdogens, like Bardolph, who picked his nose with spear-grass to make it bleed, with bandaged eyes, foaming mouths and running sores to betray the incautious into an ill-rewarded mercy.

The problem of the ' masterless ' soon became too grave to be solved by indiscriminate barbarism. Vagrants were whipped, put in the stocks, and sent back to their own parishes ; fortune-tellers were burned as witches, beggars were hanged for the smallest theft. These measures were insufficient. The beggars met their deaths without complaint, and the abuses continued. Tudor England did not shrink from its responsibilities : local initiative backed the efforts of the Crown to show society's willingness to share its burdens. Slowly and painfully the sixteenth century overcame its fear-inspired repugnance towards beggars, and realised that not all of them were poor through their own fault. The distinction was first made in an act in 1531, which provided that, while the able-bodied, the ' sturdy beggars ', should be whipped and sent home ' to labour as true men should do ', the impotent poor might obtain from Justices of the Peace a licence to beg. Five years later another act took a great step forwards by organising the official provision of relief for the poor ; the state assumed the social duties of the Church which it had lately mastered and was about to plunder. The sturdy beggar was still to be punished ; but the impotent were to be kept, and the industrious and willing to be provided with work. Churchwardens were ordered to make collections on Sundays, and fines were imposed on parishes whose contributions fell short of the expected sum. Except that it did not levy compulsory taxation, this act of 1536 contained all the features of the more famous Elizabethan Poor Law. It recognised that the poor fell into three categories: the sick and impotent, who required hospitals and outdoor relief; the wilful vagrant, who should be punished; and the industrious poor, for whom the state presently provided a technical education and materials for work.

Henceforth the chief difficulty was financial. Charity had been for so long the province of the Church that men did not incline readily to making contributions at the behest of the state. Here the example of the large cities, such as London, Norwich, Coventry and York, which organised the relief of their poor, was of service to the government; the appeal to charity failing to produce good results, poor relief had finally to be made compulsory. Since men of 'froward and wilful mind' declined to respond to the 'gentle exhortation' of the Bishops, an act in 1563 ordered that they should be handed over to the magistrates and forced to pay their contributions to the parish fund. This was the beginning of compulsory assessment for poor relief. The Statute of Apprentices in the same year sought to solve the problem of rural unemployment by commanding all able-bodied persons to work in the fields, unless they could prove that they had other employment. It further insisted on long contracts, and set up a system of wage assessment which recognised that there should be different rates in different parts of the country; so as to 'yield to the hired person, both in time of scarcity and in time of plenty, a convenient proportion of wages'. In 1572 a compulsory rate was levied on all, and officials were ordered to assess and collect it in each parish; and in 1576 all cities were obliged to provide a store of wool, hemp, flax and other materials, so that the industrious poor might be set to work and paid for their labour. At the same time, the punishment of rogues and beggars was made more severe. The act of 1572 ordered them 'to be grievously whipped and burned through the gristle of the right ear with a hot iron of the compass of an inch about'; and in 1576 Bridewells, or houses of correction, were set up to discipline them for honest work. The famous statute of 1598, which was confirmed in 1601, summarised the Tudors' contribution to the relief of the poor. By compulsory taxation of the people, the aged and the impotent were to be supported, the industrious taught a trade and given means to exercise it, the idle and vicious to be punished and set to better ways; finally, the children of paupers were to be apprenticed to a master.[1] For the first time, the English people undertook a corporate responsibility; and the system which was thus fashioned out of the needs and experience of two generations was, with few modifications, the basis of poor relief in England until the Amendment Act of 1834.[2]

4. *The Puritan attitude to poverty*

The effectiveness of the Tudor Poor Law, as of the condemnation of enclosures, depended on the consciences of the local officials who were trusted to administer it. These officials, being themselves men of wealth, were naturally tempted to evade their burdens, and were reluctant to make themselves unpopular by a too zealous administration of the law. The parish overseers, therefore, were more disposed to save the purses of their wealthy neighbours than anxious to see that the needy were granted the proper relief which the government intended them to receive. Parishes took what steps they could to limit their responsibilities. Thus couples newly married were sometimes forbidden to live in their village, lest their children should burden the rates; and people hitherto self-supporting were thereby turned into vagrants, because they could not find a parish to support them. Under James I the gentry were largely successful in evading their obligations, and, except during the years of dearth between 1621 and 1623, the Poor Law was not vigorously administered. The personal government of Charles, however, displayed a social conscience which was the despair of its enemies. The Privy Council set

[1] In times of scarcity the government enforced measures to provide cheap corn for the poor.

[2] Although poor relief was thus administered by the state, there was also much private and voluntary charity.

up a commission to ' quicken ' the Justices of the Peace and execute the poor laws, which ' in most places of this kingdom are little regarded '. For ten years the commissioners bestirred local authorities into a grudging activity, provided a regular supply of cheap corn, reprimanded defaulters, and severely punished farmers who took advantage of scarcity to charge high prices for their wheat. The King and his Council showed a care for the destitute seldom equalled before the twentieth century.

The civil war brought fresh burdens to the poor which the revolutionary governments were unable, and to some extent unwilling, to relieve. The fighting dislocated trade and laid waste the land ; crops were seized to victual the armies ; parliament's excise raised the prices of necessaries ; and charitable institutions were less able to perform their work of relief. Although the citizens of London voluntarily formed a Corporation for the Poor, little was done during the Commonwealth to relieve distress ; the men of property who broke up the settlements of the Diggers showed small concern for the sufferings of the poor, and the Protector, who did much to make the people moral, was less actively moved to consider their material well-being. There was no improvement after the Restoration. The weakening of the prerogative had destroyed the machinery by which the government had been able to stimulate local effort. The poor laws remained on the statute-book, but their enforcement depended on the initiative of each parish ; and the new ruling classes were inspired to perform their duties only when they had occasion to be afraid of riots. Their want of public spirit was soon expressed in the Law of Settlement, which they passed in 1662. Parishes had always been unwilling to bear the charges of poor people not born within their boundaries, and the authorities of London and Westminster in particular were burdened with the poor who drifted to the capital from all parts of the country. The new law stated, therefore, that overseers had the power of removing to their places of ' legal settlement ' all who might become chargeable on the rates. Although it was later modified, and although its administration was haphazard, the law had unfortunate results. The poor had no freedom to move about in search of labour, and expectant mothers were chivvied from parish to parish lest their children should be a charge on the rates. A more statesmanlike solution of a real problem would have been to organise a group of parishes, instead of the single parish, as the unit of poor relief.

The fundamental explanation of the new indifference to the sufferings of the poor lay in the triumph of Puritanism, which was only driven below the surface, and not destroyed, by the Clarendon Code. Puritan teaching on economics differed from the Catholic teaching which had inspired the social policy of the Crown until 1640. 'There is a kind of natural unaptness in the Popish religion to business', wrote a Restoration pamphleteer. Whereas the Crown had striven to uphold an ordered and graded society, and a fair distribution of wealth, the Puritan faith was rooted in an individualism which broke down restrictions. It exalted the profitable qualities of sobriety and thrift among the highest of human virtues; Puritans, wrote Sir William Petty, were 'thinking, sober and patient men, and such as believe that labour and industry is their duty towards God'. A man could best serve God by labouring in his vineyard and diligently using the talents which God had given him; his faith should issue in works. 'At the day of Doom men shall be judged according to their fruits. It will not be said then, Did you believe? but, Were you doers, or talkers only?'[1] The cobbler busy at his last was surer of salvation than the monk and the friar, who 'live only to themselves and to their formal devotion'; 'for his is a calling of God, and theirs is none'.[2] Sloth, therefore, rather than avarice, was the greatest enemy of the spiritual life. For 'God hath commanded you', warned Baxter, 'some way or other to labour for your daily bread.' 'He that hath lent you talents hath also said, "Occupy till I come."'[2]

[1] Bunyan, *Pilgrim's Progress.*
[2] Rev. Richard Steele, *The Tradesman's Calling.*

The Puritan ethic of thrift achieved a revolution in economic thought. It broke down the fetters which had restrained the accumulation of profit, for it gave moral and religious sanction to the Englishman's commercial energies. Trade, proclaimed a member of the Long Parliament, was ' the fairest mistress in the world ', and Charles II found that his people did not spare themselves to woo her, and at the same time to acquit themselves piously in the sight of God. Excluded from public life by the Clarendon Code, the Dissenters threw their energies into shop-keeping and commerce. Under their influence—and all the big cities were predominantly Puritan—the making of money become almost a moral duty, the token of a well-spent life. This thriftiness, together with the religious sanction by which it was dignified, was the foundation of eighteenth-century imperialism, and of the qualities which made possible the Industrial Revolution.[1] So far, perhaps, it was admirable; but other, less attractive qualities were born of it: in particular, a deliberate indifference to the predicament of the poor. Convinced that a man won the struggle of life by the strength of his character, and not by the aid of helping circumstances, the Puritan saw in poverty, not a misfortune calling for his pity, but a moral failing which he should condemn.[2] The new type of landowner, eager to free his high estate of its ancient obligations, found the arguments of the Puritans convenient to his purpose. Baxter, who was neither avaricious nor cruel, defended enclosure on the ground that workers serving an employer would undergo a moral discipline which the self-supporting yeoman missed. The poor, then, were no longer society's victims, to whom society owed a debt; they were to be blamed for their own ' idle, irregular and wicked courses ',[3] by which they had brought distress upon themselves. Society was seen as a sort of joint-stock enterprise, in which men's rights corresponded to their investments; those who had no stake in it could not claim to

[1] All the great iron-masters of the eighteenth century were Non-conformists.

[2] So in 1697 paupers were required to wear badges. [3] Steele.

take anything from it. To help the poor was no longer an act of mercy, but the crime of pampering the degenerate and idle; the true charity was to reform their souls (which was inexpensive), whereas the Poor Law kept wages artificially high. In his pamphlet *Giving Alms no Charity*, Defoe naïvely denounced the 'luxury, pride and sloth' of the wage-earning classes; and a tract published in 1714 proclaimed that the existence of the poor was necessary to civilisation. For the poor 'have nothing to stir them up to be serviceable but their wants, which it is prudence to relieve, but folly to cure. . . . To make society happy, it is necessary that great numbers should be wretched as well as poor.'[1] With these sentiments abroad, the administration of the Poor Law at the close of the seventeenth century laid most emphasis on repression. Even Locke, in a report to the Board of Trade, stressed the vice and idleness of the poor, and recommended that they be treated with severity. Newly constructed workhouses gave the poor time to reflect on the error of their ways, but did nothing to make them better citizens.

[1] Mandeville, *Fable of the Bees*.

CHAPTER V

THE REIGN OF EDWARD VI

Somerset. The progress of Protestantism. Northumberland. Cranmer's Prayer Books.

1. *Somerset as Protector*

The will of Henry VIII appointed for the minority of his son a Council of sixteen Regents, of whom he intended that none should have precedence over the others. As soon as he was dead, however, Edward Seymour, Earl of Hertford, who was the uncle of the young King, persuaded the Council to nominate him as Lord Protector, and took the title of Duke of Somerset. Somerset was not the right man to govern the country. In many ways he was generous and enlightened: he pitied the poor, and was anxious to relieve their misfortunes; he rightly desired to bring Scotland under the authority of the English Crown; and, although he was himself 'well-disposed to pious doctrine', and 'abominated the fond inventions of the Papists', he was prepared to allow the people to believe what they pleased without being persecuted. But he did not combine enlightened aims with statesmanlike means. Awareness of his liberal outlook gave him a warm conceit of himself, and in his self-conscious idealism he took little account of the opinions and interests of those with whom he had to work. Yet he had not the practical ability to carry his plans to success. His self-confidence blinded him to the impression which others had of him, and his idealism was tarnished by surprising inconsistencies: he was greedy, destructive and high-handed. Finally, even his virtues were inappropriate to the time in which he lived. The new aristocracy which the Tudors had created did not appreciate his dreams of social justice ; the age demanded stronger government than he was disposed or able to provide ; and a policy of religious toleration was approved neither by the Catholics nor by the reformers.

Henry VIII had striven to ban ' diversity of opinions ' in the Church of which he was the Head ; but when Somerset relaxed the strictness of his rule, the way was open for the apostles of the New Learning freely to spread their doctrines among the people. Parliament repealed the more severe of Henry's measures : his Treason Act, the Statute of Proclamations, and the Act of the Six Articles ; it also repealed the old Lollard statute, *De Haeretico Comburendo*, and no longer insisted that the Mass be celebrated in Latin. Archbishop Cranmer was known to have eaten meat in Lent ; the laity were allowed to take Communion in both kinds ; the clergy were given permission to marry. It was clear that the Church had come under a more lenient hand. The measures of the previous reign were withdrawn because ' as in tempest or winter one course and garment is convenient, in calm or warm weather a more liberal race or lighter garment both may and ought to be followed and used '. The day of battle was past, the royal supremacy was assured ; in a more peaceful atmosphere men might breathe the air of freedom.

The reformers did not waste their opportunity. Protestant zealots, hitherto restrained by their wholesome fear of Henry, poured into the country from abroad ; not Lutherans only, but the apostles of a harsher creed, the envoys sent by Calvin from Geneva. During Edward's short reign foreign divines and foreign congregations won a remarkable hold on England. The Italian Peter Martyr was a Professor of Divinity at Oxford, Martin Bucer at Cambridge, although he could speak no English ; John à Lasco, a fugitive from Poland, was pastor of the foreign community in London ; the German Paul Fagius was Reader in Hebrew at Cambridge ; there were congregations of French-speaking Walloons at Canterbury and Glastonbury. This foreign invasion had a permanent effect on the English Church. It destroyed the insular settlement which Henry had created and sought to maintain, and brought England into the stream of controversy which had already made its course through the continent. The English fell to debating the doctrine of grace, the validity of the Eucharist, and similar questions of theology, on which Henry had ordered them to live in ' unity and concord '. ' Transubstantiation, I think, is now exploded ', wrote Peter Martyr late in 1548. The English Church had a brief age of theological debate, when all men were free to advance their opinions without fear of political penalties.

But it was not long before Somerset and Cranmer, and the more moderate leaders of the Protestant movement, began to be alarmed by the swift and violent changes which the extreme reformers were eager to introduce. In 1547 the hand of the government had fallen on the chantries and religious institutions of the guilds, and appropriated their endowments, on the ground that they were nurseries of superstition. (Some of the ecclesiastical property seized during this reign was devoted to education, usually in the form of a restoration of previous endowments. Those schools which acknowledge Edward VI as their founder were the schools which his ministers did not finally destroy.) The dissolution of the chantries was greeted as ' the last dish of the last course ; after chantries, as after cheese, nothing is to be expected '. But it inspired a widespread and comprehensive attack on images, in which the iconoclasm which sprang from conviction was indistinguishable from a more secular iconoclasm which saw profit in the looting of churches. With the object of checking this destructive irreverence, and of setting limits to the doctrinal changes which the advanced reformers were attempting to make, the government drew up the first uniform service-book of the English Church ; and parliament, in accepting it, passed in 1549 an Act of Uniformity to compel its use. This Prayer Book was the work of Cranmer. It bore the mark, not only of his perfect command of the English language, but of his inborn love of compromise. Cranmer was not a zealot; in Henry's reign his mind had moved slowly in the direction of doctrinal reform, but he rejected the harshness and dogmatic certainty of the continental creeds. Because he was not a fighter, and because his beliefs did not harden into an infallibility which would admit no alternatives, he chose to tread that middle path of compromise which led to the settlement of Elizabeth. When Elizabeth and her ministers had to make their difficult choice between the old faith and the new, they had Cranmer's moderation to guide them on a course which otherwise they might not have known how to take. The Prayer Book of 1549, therefore, was conservative and embracing; the Catholic Tunstall and the Puritan Hooper could each conform to it. The form of worship which it prescribed did not strain the regulations of the King's Book of 1543, nor did it vex the consciences of the ardent reformers from Switzerland. In 1549 the practice of the English Church differed in only three respects from the practice decreed by Henry VIII: for the sake of simplicity of worship, images had been destroyed; the clergy were allowed to marry; and the cup was administered to the laity at Communion.

The middle course which Somerset and Cranmer attempted to steer outraged the conservative temper of the people. When the new service-book was introduced at Whitsuntide, 1549, the men of Cornwall and Devon arose to demand a return to the immemorial practices of the Church. The overthrow of the religious houses had brought the land into the possession of the worst type of landlord; and now the profanation of images, and the new Liturgy, had taken away symbols that had been full of reverent associations for rural folk. The new services were 'like a Christmas game'. The rebels asked for the Mass, the Six Articles, and the restoration of the monasteries. They were defeated, but their resistance was fierce; and the government's use of foreign mercenaries seemed to the West-countrymen to be typical of the alien ungodliness that was taking hold of the land.

The Western revolt was the beginning of Somerset's fall. Ket's rebellion in East Anglia next turned against him the sympathies of the landowning classes. For Ket did not rise against religious change, which was welcome in the radical Eastern counties; he rose to protest against enclosures, low wages and the high price of corn. The rebellion was not immediately crushed, because Somerset sympathised with its objects. He had set his heart on checking the spread of enclosure, and therefore he was prepared to come to terms with the rebels; he even offered them a free pardon, and agreed to discuss their grievances, if they would disperse. This generosity did not please the members of the Council, whose interest as landlords it injured, and the rebellion was crushed by the Earl of Warwick, assisted by German and Italian mercenaries, at the battle of Mousehold Heath. Under Warwick's leadership, the Council turned angrily on Somerset. His sympathy with the poor was dangerous to men of property. His opposition to sheep-farming encouraged the poor to riot; and he held a Court of Requests in his own house, to which he encouraged them to bring their complaints. He had further alarmed the nobility by ordering the execution of his brother, Lord Seymour of Sudeley, the Lord High Admiral. Seymour was clearly a traitor: 'a man', declared Latimer, 'furthest from the fear of God that ever I heard or knew of in England'. Although he was Admiral, he made a secret compact with the Channel pirates; he issued his own debased coinage: and finally he collected armed retainers and began to plot the overthrow of the government. But even a traitor is entitled to a fair trial; and Somerset dealt high-handedly with him, sending him to the scaffold before he had made his defence. What Somerset had done once he might do again; he had that idealistic sort of arrogance which, convinced that its cause is just, is contemptuous of the forms of legality. There were some uneasy consciences in the Council, and Warwick and his followers determined to bring Somerset's authority to an end. In October, 1549, he was deprived of his office and sent to the Tower, and in 1552 he was executed on charges manufactured by the new rulers of England. The poor lamented the end of the 'good Duke', and dipped handkerchiefs in his blood.

Admiration of Somerset's aims must be qualified by criticism of his methods. A doctrinaire idealist was not the man to govern Tudor England; and he failed to achieve his objects, either because they were themselves inappropriate to the time, or because he blundered in their execution. His social policy provoked disturbances with which the government scarcely had the resources to deal. His toleration released the disintegrating energies of headstrong reformers who tried to force the English Church to logical, but unwelcome, extremes. Finally, his attempt to attach Scotland to the English Crown drove the Scots into the arms of the French. He desired a united country, 'having the sea for wall, and mutual love for its garrison'; and, sensibly enough, he revived Henry's plan of marrying Edward to Mary. But, again like Henry, he did not realise that union must depend on the unforced consent of the Scots. He crossed the Border in the full panoply of war and routed the Scots at Pinkie. The victory was fatal to him; this rough manner of wooing enraged the Scots, and Mary was hurried to France and betrothed to the Dauphin. Somerset was content with the laurels of the victor, and abandoned the policy which he had tried so clumsily to carry out.

2. *The Regency of Northumberland*

Somerset's authority was seized by John Dudley, Earl of Warwick, who in 1551 suppressed Tunstall's see of Durham and made from its estates the Dukedom of Northumberland. He was the son of Edmund Dudley, Henry VII's tax-gatherer, and he possessed in full measure those vices of greed and acquisitiveness with which his father was less reasonably charged. During the years when he was at the head of the Council of Regency—he did not take Somerset's title of Protector—the country was governed in the narrow interests of the landowning class. No thought of patriotism, or even of Somerset's misdirected idealism, came to relieve his dreary, oppressive selfishness. Except that he claimed to be a sincere Protestant, he did not do even lip-service to any higher motive than personal ambition. He neglected the common obligations of the government. He debased the coinage, until the shilling contained only three-pennyworth of silver ; he legalised enclosure, and punished as treason any concerted attempt by its victims to protest against it ; he starved the navy, which had been Henry's pride, withdrew the English garrisons from Scotland, allowed the French to buy back Boulogne, and neglected the scanty force which was clinging to Calais. Henry's fears for the succession had been justified. Here again was the overmighty subject, secure in his pride and master of the government ; and under him the country fell again into lawlessness and chaos. To protect his authority, Northumberland persuaded parliament to revive most of the vicious provisions of Henry's Treason Act, but he did not feel himself safe unless he was attended by a bodyguard of foreign mercenaries.

In the story of the Reformation Northumberland's Regency is important because his calculated acquisitiveness led him to permit the further advance of the Protestant religion. He had two reasons for deciding to continue the religious policy of the Protectorate. If he had declared in favour of the old religion, he would have been obliged to admit Norfolk and the Catholics to some share of his authority ; and, secondly, Protestantism offered him the prospect of plunder. At once, then, he announced his zeal for the new faith, and the reformers acclaimed him as ' that most faithful and intrepid soldier of Jesus Christ ', worthy to be compared, in his pious enthusiasm for religion, with Moses and Joshua of former times. The first measure of his first parliament was an act for the removal of images, ' images of stone, timber, alabaster or earth, carved or painted '. In its anxiety to remove all that might tempt the people to superstition, the government laid its hands on ' all the jewels of gold and silver, as crosses, candlesticks, chalices, and all other gold and silver and ready money . . . and all copes and vestments of cloth of gold, cloth of silver, and cloth of tissue '. Bells, proclaimed by the revolutionaries of another age to be ' trinkets of the eternal Father ', were destroyed ; the lead was even torn from the roofs of churches, to be melted down. Churches were used as stables, livings were presented to grooms and gamekeepers, while their masters appropriated the revenues.

While the rulers treated religion as a means to serve their greed, there were many who looked on these changes with sincere approval. The self-interest of courtiers is no index of the feelings of the people ; while most Englishmen deplored and hated Northumberland's vandalism, the creeds of Luther and Calvin gripped the minds of some with a strength of purpose which persecution was to be unable to shake. John Knox, banished from Scotland and dwelling in the North of England, acclaimed Northumberland's policy as the fruit of a godly mind ; and such divines as Ridley and Hooper, who was reluctant to become a Bishop because he was required to wear obnoxious vestments at his consecration, moved much farther from the old faith than Cranmer was prepared to go. Cranmer had watched these changes with an uneasy heart, and in 1552 he was called upon to sanction them in a revision of the Prayer Book. The comprehensiveness of the first Book, which allowed the Communion service to be regarded as a modified form of the Mass, did not satisfy the Swiss reformers, who treated the ceremony of the Eucharist as purely commemorative. The second Prayer Book of Edward VI defined more precisely those points of doctrine which the first Book had deliberately left vague ; and, under the growing influence of continental theologians, defined them in favour of Swiss ideas.[1] The term ' minister ' took the place of ' priest ', and ' table ' of ' altar ' ; the doctrine of transubstantiation was rejected, and a special Rubric was inserted to accommodate the scruples of Knox, who protested that it was idolatrous to kneel when receiving the bread and wine. The second Act of Uniformity, unlike the first, compelled laymen to accept the new service, on penalty of excommunication ; it was, therefore, the first of the long series of acts obliging Englishmen to go to Church and to participate in the form of worship which the state prescribed. But Cranmer and the more conscientious

[1] Zwinglian. rather than Calvinist.

reformers could not be satisfied with this policy of continually introducing by royal command religious changes for which the minds of the people had not been prepared. Martin Bucer warned the King of the danger of 'taking away by force false worship from your people without sufficient preliminary instruction', and to counter the forces that were only destructive, Cranmer laboured to reform the canon law and to provide the new national Church with a uniform statement of dogma. Much as the canon law needed to be overhauled, his *Reformatio Legum Ecclesiasticarum* was rejected by a secular government because it proposed that the clergy should exercise their full mediaeval jurisdiction. Cranmer had to be content with the Forty-two Articles of Religion, which were sanctioned by the Council in 1553. He hoped that they would lead the people into the 'concord and quietness in religion' which was his dearest aim. The articles were liberal in scope. Although they condemned the more serious errors of the Catholic Church, they asserted free will, as well as Luther's doctrine of justification by faith, and tactfully omitted to define good works. They were Cranmer's last attempt to guide the English people along the *via media* which he had chosen for himself.

3. *The succession plot*

The confused changes of Edward's short reign were halted in 1553 by the death of the King. Although he was not yet sixteen, he had already shown the Tudor gifts of learning, statesmanship and ruthlessness; it is not possible to surmise what course English history would have taken had he lived to develop a will and a policy of his own. For Northumberland, his death was fatal; even though his health had for so long been delicate that Northumberland had made his preparations to meet the event. Henry VIII's will declared that if Edward died without issue, he should be succeeded by Mary and Elizabeth. Northumberland had made it his business to acquire a personal ascendancy over Edward, and he urged that, if Mary were allowed to be Queen, the Protestant faith would be undone and the old religion restored. The appeal to his piety persuaded Edward. He declared his half-sisters to be illegitimate—this had been done before—and left the Crown by will to the Protestant Lady Jane Grey, who was the grand-daughter of Henry's sister Mary by her marriage to the Duke of Suffolk. With Lady Jane on the throne, Northumberland's influence would be secure ; for he had already taken the precaution of marrying her to his son, Lord Guildford Dudley.

His disillusion came swiftly. Edward died on July 6th, and on August 3rd Mary entered London in triumph, with the enthusiastic support of the Protestant population of East Anglia. Northumberland tried to save himself by recanting. When he knew that his cause was lost, he proclaimed Mary to be Queen ; and in a further hope of winning her forgiveness, he declared that at heart he was a Catholic, and always had been so. These shifts did not save him, and with two followers he went to the scaffold. The unopposed accession of Mary vindicated Tudor methods of government. The people welcomed her, though she was the Spanish daughter of a Spanish mother ; the Protestants of Norfolk helped her to her throne, though they knew her to be a Catholic ; for she was a Tudor, and Tudor rule meant orderly and pacific government. The people chose to abide by the will of Henry VIII, and rejected the reign of adventurers, profiteers, and European zealots. All the conditions were present for fifteenth-century anarchy and civil war ; but the people, drilled into law-abidingness by the first two Tudors, preferred to be loyal to tradition and the hereditary succession. The collapse of Northumberland's conspiracy paid a tribute to the Tudor ' despotism ', by showing that sixteenth-century England endorsed it and found it to be necessary.

CHAPTER VI

THE CATHOLIC REACTION AND THE SETTLEMENT OF ELIZABETH

The Spanish marriage. The restoration of Catholicism. Mary's persecution. The difficulties of Elizabeth. The settlement of 1559.

1. *The Spanish marriage*

History is unsympathetic to failures. The reputation of Mary Tudor has suffered the fate of those who fight for losing causes, and posterity at least owes her the service of reconsidering her actions in the light of the faith which she inherited and for which she struggled with all her heart. She was the most honest and the least ruthless of Tudor sovereigns. Her court and her government were uncorrupt; she refused to debase the coinage, and toiled to pay the crushing debts which the Regents had left her; she tried to help the poor; she cared for the country's welfare, and deeply felt the humiliation when Calais was lost. Moreover, she was compassionate towards the men who had wounded her mother and burdened her own childhood with years of indignity and suffering. By nature pitiful and magnanimous, she forgave most of the rebels who plotted against her throne; no sixteenth-century ruler was more generous to traitors. But her mind and spirit dwelt in the past. In the misery of her childhood she was consoled only by her unswerving faith in her religion. She cared more for her people's souls than for their bodily estate, and she believed that their souls would be safer in the keeping of the priests of a foreign Church than of the zealous ministers whom her brother had appointed. Her Spanish confessors had taught her that it was her sacred mission to lead her subjects again into the charge of the Universal Church. The inexorable demands of her mission made her deaf to the counsels of expediency, and turned her natural clemency into a pitiless indifference to human suffering. She persecuted heretics, while she pardoned traitors, because in her sight offences against the state were trivial by the side of offences against the Church. Her beliefs were, in the best sense, mediaeval; and this alone was enough to condemn her rule to failure in sixteenth-century England.

Change was gradual at first. The first parliament of the reign repealed all the ecclesiastical legislation of Edward VI, and restored 'divine service as used in England in the last year of Henry VIII's day'. The Prayer Book was suppressed, and the Mass was celebrated once more in Latin; the Catholic Bishops—Gardiner of Winchester, Bonner of London, Tunstall, Heath of Worcester, Day of Chichester—were released from prison and restored to their duties; Norfolk and Courtenay received back their estates; and, while the foreign preachers and their allies hastened from the country, several of the Protestant Bishops were arrested, ostensibly on the ground of having assisted Northumberland's treason. Had she been content with these conservative changes, Mary would have retained the popular support which had brought her to her throne. After the chaos and misgovernment of the minority, the mass of the people cried for the strong rule of 'good King Harry's' day, and desired nothing better than to order their religion as he had left it. Although some had accepted the new religion in simple piety, and were strong enough in their faith to die for it, the recent changes had been too swift and confused, and too obviously inspired by material concerns, to take root among the people. The nation was still Catholic; it still desired the Latin Mass and the sacraments and the ceremonies of the old religion. But it did not desire to return to Rome; it insisted that Mary, like her father, should be the Supreme Head of a Catholic but national Church.

Mary, however, did not read the signs. She lacked the Tudor flair for estimating public opinion; further, she was fighting for wider issues than the independence of a secular, state-controlled Church. Thus she did not take warning from the things which her parliament refused to do. It refused to restore the ecclesiastical property which had passed into secular hands, to declare that Henry had been lawfully married to Catherine of Aragon, to repeal Henry's ecclesiastical legislation as well as his son's, or to exclude Princess Elizabeth from the succession. Above all, Mary would not be guided by her people in the choice of a husband. Gardiner, whom she had appointed to be her Chancellor, joined with Council and parliament in advising her to marry Edward Courtenay, Earl of Devon, great-grandson of Edward IV, or Reginald Pole, a descendant of the Duke of Clarence. National sentiment demanded that she should choose her husband from among her own people, but Mary had other plans. Her principal adviser was Simon Renard, the ambassador of the Empire, and from him she learned that Charles V wished her to marry his son Philip, heir to the throne of Spain. For Charles the match offered important dynastic advantages : the English navy and the Spanish army could master the world. Mary saw it with different eyes : with the King of Spain to share her throne, she could carry through her cherished plan of forcing her people, whether they wished it or no, back to their old allegiance to the Pope.

She still would not be warned when the project of the marriage drove the English into revolt. Union with Spain revived for them all the things which they had grown to hate : Rome and the domination of an alien Church, the Inquisition, the rule of priests, and the prospect of fighting endless wars in Hapsburg interests. A conspiracy was organised to depose Mary and set Elizabeth and Courtenay on her throne, Risings in the Midlands and the West broke down, but Sir Thomas Wyatt led the Kentishmen on London. Mary was Tudor enough to make a spirited speech to the citizens of London, and they rallied to defend her Crown ; Wyatt's men were trapped at Ludgate, and the conspiracy was broken. Wyatt and about a hundred of his followers were put to death, and Mary was obliged to execute Lady Jane

Grey and her husband, who were innocent of any crime and any guilty intention ; and if she had listened to Renard, she would have executed Elizabeth and Courtenay too, and not have released them from the Tower after a short imprisonment. Then she pressed on with her plans. Fearing the ' naughty and disordered behaviour ' of her subjects, she charged them in a proclamation to use Philip and his train with ' courtesy, friendly and gentle entertainment, without ministering towards them any manner of cause of strife or contention ' ; but when Philip came to England, he wore a shirt of mail and had his own cook to prepare his food. He was married to Mary in Winchester Cathedral in July, 1554. They were acclaimed as ' King and Queen of England, France, Naples, Jerusalem, and Ireland, Defenders of the Faith, Princes of Spain and Sicily, Archdukes of Austria, Dukes of Milan, Burgundy and Brabant, Counts of Hapsburg, Flanders and the Tyrol '. Council and parliament did all in their power to rob the match of its disastrous effects. They refused to crown Philip as King of England ; the marriage treaty stipulated that Mary was to control England's politics and handle its revenues ; that no foreigner should hold command in the army or navy ; that England should not be drawn into purely Spanish wars ; and that a son of the marriage should rule in England, Burgundy and the Netherlands, but not in Spain. The marriage answered the betrothal of Mary Stuart to the French Dauphin, and served the interest of the all-important trade with Flanders ; but when all had been said in its favour, the English felt it to be humiliating and dangerous, tying the country ' to the tails of the Spanish galleons, like cockles floating on the sea '. It undid the labours of the Tudors to make England independent of continental ties. Marriage was the weapon with which the Hapsburgs were wont to conquer ; might they not master England and reduce her to the servile status of the Netherlands ? Mary had made England an unwilling accomplice in Spanish designs ; and the partnership was even to be one-sided, for Spain refused to admit English merchants to the lucrative commerce of South America.

2. *Mary's persecution*

In November, 1554, Mary summoned her third parliament and the work of conversion began in earnest. So far, the Catholic reaction had made little headway. The measures of the previous reign had been repealed, and about a fifth of the clergy had been deprived, most of them because they were married. Charles V had advised Mary, through Renard, to go slowly, for he had feared that a too drastic programme of reform would provoke the whole country into revolt against the marriage before it had been accomplished. To that end he had kept the zealous Pole out of England until Philip was safely married. But in the winter of 1554 Pole arrived, with the authority of papal legate, to receive England back into the arms of the Mother Church. It is unsafe to speak of ' packed ' parliaments in Tudor times, for the electors often showed themselves to be uncompromisingly independent of the wishes alike of the government and the magnates; but Mary's third parliament was more amenable to her wishes than either of its predecessors had been. Once satisfied that the monastery lands were not to be taken from them,[1] the members readily endorsed the government's policy. Having reversed the attainder against Pole which had been carried under Henry VIII, they besought his forgiveness for the country's backsliding, and asked to be reconciled with Rome. Although England had ' declined from the unity of Christ's Church ', Pole had come ' to call us home again into the right way from whence we have all this long while wandered and strayed abroad '. Pole solemnly absolved them from the sin of schism, and they hastened to complete the work of reaction. They revived the old statute *De Haeretico Comburendo*, and repealed, with certain exceptions, all the anti-Roman legislation passed in England since the twentieth year of the reign of Henry VIII. They were willing enough to repeal the Act of Supremacy, and to restore the Bishops and the canon law to their old

[1] Those who held the estates of the Church might ' without scruple of conscience enjoy them, without impeachment or trouble by pretence of any General Council, canon or ecclesiastical law '.

authority, but they haggled over the provisions which concerned finance. Not only did they refuse to restore the Church property which had been appropriated ; they retained the measures passed in 1529 against probate and mortuary fees, and surrendered annates to the Pope only after a warm struggle. The Queen restored the ecclesiastical property which was still in the possession of the Crown, but her example was not followed by her people ; of all the dissolved monasteries only Westminster, Sion, Smithfield, and Greenwich were restored to life.

Catholic orthodoxy was now clearly defined by the law, and the persecution of heretics began. The responsibility for it must lie with Mary herself and Cardinal Pole ; and, to a smaller extent, with Gardiner. Philip and Renard cannot be made to shoulder the blame, or even to share it. They wished to pacify the country, and reconcile it to the Spanish marriage and Spanish policy ; knowing that persecution would inflame the passions which they were most anxious to calm, they counselled Mary to be moderate. Nor did the persecution mask any motives of political ambition or material greed. It had no other purpose than to rescue English souls from heresy. Pole and the Queen were sure that their sacred work could be done in no other way ; and Gardiner, repenting that he had once assisted his master to repudiate Rome, was willing to adopt the methods he had seen Henry use so successfully. The Protestant martyrs did not die in vain, and there were few of them that had no memorial. The moving pen of a skilled reporter has told of their sufferings, and in the colourful and harrowing pages of the *Book of Martyrs* they have received the honour which was the due of their quiet, uplifting courage. It is from their persecutors that due honour has been withheld. Mary's motives were as pure as theirs ; and if the weapon which she used was ugly and mistaken, her father had used it before her, and rulers of every faith were using it wherever she turned. Miguel Servetus, whom Calvin burned at Champel in 1553, was the first Protestant martyr slain by Protestant intolerance ; and at Augsburg in 1555 the powers of Europe agreed to the principle to which Mary appealed, that each ruler might establish his own religion within his territories. Finally, it must be remembered that, when Mary began her work, she did not foresee how far it would lead her. Prompted by Gardiner, she did as her father and Cromwell had done: she did not fear to strike at the most eminent of her enemies, in the hope that their fate would melt the resolution of humbler men. To the same purpose, every martyr was given the opportunity to recant. In recent years men had changed their faiths so easily and so often, that Mary was unprepared for the stubbornness of the men who resisted her. There can be little doubt that if the first victims had been men of weaker grain, and had recanted as the government implored and wanted them to do, Mary would have achieved her purpose almost without shedding blood.

The first man to die was John Rogers, Canon of St. Paul's, the author of *Matthew's Bible*. He stretched his hands in the flame 'as if it was cold water', and 'died as quietly as a child in his bed'. Hooper was burned in a slow fire at Gloucester, with his pardon before his eyes; Ferrar of St. David's died at Carmarthen, and Latimer and Ridley at Oxford. The courage of these men carried the day. They removed from the new religion the disgrace with which the mercenary policy of Northumberland had stained it, and showed that 'if Protestants did not know how to govern, they knew how to die': their example sanctified their cause, and condemned Mary's policy to fail. Gardiner died at the end of 1555, and Philip left the country, but the useless suffering went on. Cranmer was burned in the following March, cheating the government at the last of a public recantation of his heresy, and with Pole installed at Canterbury, the fires of Smithfield burned still more fiercely. During the reign about three hundred people were sacrificed, some sixty of them being women. Most of the victims dwelt in the areas round the main roads between London and the ports; only forty-four came from outside East Anglia and the Home Counties, and only two from north of the Humber. Mary knew that she was failing, but her creed would not allow her to relent; the persecution ceased only when she died.

Religion was not Mary's only failure. She failed to bear a child who would carry on her work; she failed to hold the affection of the husband to whom she was devoted. When he realised that she would not give him a son, Philip callously deserted her and went abroad; and Renard, now accepting the Princess Elizabeth as heir to the throne, schemed to marry her to the Catholic Duke of Savoy. But the final tragedy of Mary's life was still to come: in the last year of her reign the dutiful daughter of Rome saw her country at war with the Pope. The Spanish marriage was to blame. Cardinal Caraffa, who had become Pope Paul IV, was an ardent Neapolitan; and although he was a sincere and pious churchman, his secular ambitions hindered his pursuit of religious ends. He tried to use the resources of the Papacy to drive the Spaniards out of Naples; and in his quarrel with Philip he sought, and readily obtained, the help of France. Mary's conscience was torn between her duty to the Pope and her duty to her husband. The worldly interest prevailed, and England entered the war on the side of Spain; and the Pope retaliated by depriving Pole of his authority as legate. The war justified all the forebodings which had possessed the people since the odious Spanish alliance had been made. The country was distracted by bad harvests and epidemics; parliament responded half-heartedly to the Queen's appeals for subsidies; and foreign bankers would not charge less than 14 per cent. on loans. England could not bear her part in the war; she could not even defend what was already hers. When the Governor of Calais asked in despair for men and money, Mary wrote to assure him that 'no attack on Calais was intended'. Before her letter arrived, the Duke of Guise appeared before the walls with 25,000 men. In January, 1558, Calais surrendered, and Guisnes a fortnight later. In fact Calais was well lost. It was an obsolete survival of mediaeval wars and mediaeval hopes. As long as it was held, the rulers of England were tempted to undertake absurd and unpractical campaigns to extend their dominions in France; nor, since the development of new trade-routes, was it any longer so valuable as a staple. But these considerations did not mitigate the humiliation of the country, and the Queen felt it as keenly as any of her subjects. It was the crowning misfortune of her reign. A few months later she died, in the knowledge that she had failed in the mission to which she had dedicated all her powers and all her energies. In the imperishable words with which Castellio had rebuked Calvin : ' to burn a man alive does not defend a doctrine but slays a man '. Like the Inquisition and like Alva's Council of Blood, the fires of Smithfield had nourished the heresies which they sought to destroy. Mary's short reign was decisive in the history of the English Church : it proved that persecution for conscience's sake was alien to the English, and was hated by them as the business of priests and foreigners. After her day no Englishman was burned for his religion. Both Catholics and Puritans would die for their beliefs, but always the government would insist that their offence was treason against the state.

3. *The settlement of 1559*

The great reign of Elizabeth I opened in dismal circumstances. England was ' ragged and torn with misgovernment ' ; it was tied to the interests of a foreign power ; the treasury was empty in the face of debts of over a quarter of a million pounds, most of them burdened with a ' biting ' interest. The Privy Council lamented to see ' the realm disordered, all things dear, the French bestriding the realm, one foot in Scotland and one foot in Calais, certain enemies and no certain friends '. But the first problem of the new government was to contrive a settlement of religion. For nearly twelve years there had been confusion, as the people changed their faith in obedience to the varying whims of their rulers ; Elizabeth's achievement was to draw up a settlement that was too comprehensive in its terms to give offence, and, by identifying it with good government and national independence, to make it the basis of a distinctive Anglican Church.

Elizabeth and her advisers could not merely restore the past.

Although most of the people would have preferred to return to the personal and arbitrary settlement made by Henry VIII, too much had happened since his death for this to be possible. The Protestant missionaries who had invaded the country under Edward VI had left indelible marks behind them ; Mary checked the swing to reform, and drove the nation too hard in the opposite direction. In this confusion the old landmarks of 1547 were uprooted, and it would have been folly to try to put them back. Elizabeth could not ignore the last twelve years ; she must either favour one of the two extremes, or pick her way between them. Her character fitted her for the political responsibilities of her task. The cast of her mind was secular ; she cared only for the nation, and not at all for conscience. The dangers of her youth, when any indiscretion might have brought her to the scaffold, had taught her to repress or discipline her emotions ; and the natural bent of her Renaissance mind inclined her to despise idealism and strong passions. Men's consciences were safe in her keeping, for she ' would make no windows into their souls '. Her only concern was to settle the religious quarrels which vexed the country, so that her people could live together in unity and peace, and in the strength which is born of them.[1]

At first she may have been tempted to adopt a moderate form of Catholicism. The people had resisted Mary's policy because they had associated it with Spanish and clerical tyranny ; but at heart they were predominantly Catholic, and tradition would reconcile them to the old Burgundian alliance. Further, if the Pope could be persuaded to declare Elizabeth legitimate, the claims of Mary Stuart, and all other Catholic pretenders to the throne, would be silenced. The Protestants were not strong enough to threaten her crown, and had no serious candidate in whom to invest their claims. Lastly, a Catholic England would be safe from the attack of France and Spain and the menace of the Counter-Reformation. But Eliza-

[1] She declared that her aim was ' to secure and unite the people of the realm in one uniform order to the glory of God and to general tranquillity '.

beth rejected the counsels of safety; she had a braver rôle to play. She was Anne Boleyn's daughter, and from her birth she had been the symbol of Henry's breach with Rome; her proud sense of England's independence, as well as of the political rights of secular sovereigns, found subjection to the Pope to be intolerable. Like her father thirty years before, she stood for independence and an English Church controlled by Englishmen; in defiance of Catherine of Aragon's daughter, the champion of a foreign Church and foreign interference.

She began cautiously; her position was too weak for her to do otherwise. Preaching at Mary's funeral, the Bishop of Winchester likened Henry VIII to Uzziah, and warned Elizabeth against becoming Head of the Church. '*Laudavi mortuos magis quam viventes; sed feliciorem utroque iudicavi qui necdum natus est.*' For his importunity he was ordered to keep his house, but he was not otherwise molested. A proclamation in the first month of the reign forbade 'the breach, alteration or changes of any order and usage presently established'. Bonner and the Catholic Bishops went about their duties, and the Spaniard de Feria reported that the new government was showing no inclinations towards revenge. Each man could interpret for himself the significance of the enigmatic 'etc.' which followed the Queen's titles on public documents. But in small ways Elizabeth made plain what she intended. Most of her Councillors were men with Protestant sympathies; some heretics were released from prison, and the 'wolves' of Geneva and Frankfort were heard again in the pulpits. On Christmas Day, when the Bishop of Carlisle insisted on elevating the Host, the Queen left the service. The Mass was not celebrated at her coronation, and she objected that the sacred oil 'was grease and smelled ill'. At the opening of parliament she shouted to the Abbot and monks of Westminster, who approached her with lighted tapers, 'Away with those torches. We can see well enough.'

In these trifling incidents Elizabeth felt her way, and when parliament assembled, in January, 1559, the government had a religious programme ready to put before it. It was already clear that the settlement would have to be the work of the state, for the Church refused to purify itself by its own organs : meeting in the same month, Convocation declared uncompromisingly in favour of transubstantiation, the Mass, and the supremacy of Rome. Parliament agreed readily enough that tenths and annates should again be paid to the Crown ; but three months of vehement controversy, which included a colloquy in Westminster Hall, were needed before it would accept the government's measures to change the forms of religion. Three drafts of the Act of Supremacy were made before parliament would pass it into law. In its final form it revived the ecclesiastical legislation of Henry VIII, and asserted that all clergy and holders of offices under the Crown must take an oath [1] recognising the Queen as ' the only Supreme Governor of this realm, as well in all spiritual and ecclesiastical things or causes as temporal '. The Act of Uniformity prescribed a single form of worship, based on the Prayer Book of 1552, and imposed a fine of a shilling on all who refused to attend church on Sundays and holy days. These two vital statutes of Elizabeth's reformation passed the House of Lords only because Pole had been remiss in appointing Bishops. Five sees were vacant when Mary died, and by a remarkable coincidence Pole and four other Bishops died before the end of the year. Thus the spiritual opposition to the Crown's policy was considerably weakened ; even so, two of Mary's Bishops had to be put in prison, and the Act of Uniformity passed the Lords by only three votes. Elizabeth's religious settlement was imposed on the nation by the will of the government ; the leaders of the Church were hostile to it, and parliament, at best, was lukewarm in its favour.

The government did all that was possible to accommodate the Catholics. Offensive phrases which referred to the ' detestable enormities ' of the Bishop of Rome were removed from the Litany ; vestments were retained, and the Queen showed, by

[1] In 1563 the oath was administered also to lawyers, schoolmasters, and members of parliament, and the penalties for refusing it were made more severe.

her preference for ' crosses and candles ', that she at least was out of sympathy with the new fashion of stripping the service bare of ceremonial. Moreover, by accepting the title of Supreme Governor, she abandoned the power, which had been implicit in her father's title, to perform spiritual acts in her own person. To accommodate all consciences on the question of the Eucharist, the Black Rubric of 1552 was omitted from the Prayer Book, the Real Presence was nowhere specifically denied, and to the Zwinglian wording of 1552 was added the Catholic wording of 1549. The settlement was administered in the conciliatory spirit in which it had been framed. Only one Bishop, Kitchin of Llandaff, and few of the deans would take the oath of supremacy, but not more than two hundred of the lower clergy refused it. If Mary's clergy seemed to be pusillanimous, they were entitled to wonder whether this settlement would last any longer than those which had gone before it. But as the years passed, the Catholics discovered that, if they did not make plots, they had only the shilling fines to fear. Many found an English Bible and English services acceptable to them, and they were able to develop a compromise between outward conformity and inward belief which satisfied all but the most vigorous consciences.

The government had made a framework for a national religion, and it was the task of the Elizabethan divines to inspire the people with reverence and sincerity of belief. Elizabeth chose as her Archbishop Matthew Parker, a learned, scholarly man, who had been brought up in the Renaissance faith in education and reason. He ' reverenced monarchy, loved decency and order, and nothing shocked him so much as violent enthusiasm '. The drastic innovations of the more democratic brands of Protestantism horrified him, and he was distressed to find the English Church barren of doctrine or discipline. Vandalism had broken out again on Mary's death, the clergy were ignorant or indifferent, and the people, bewildered by constant change, were losing their faith. Parker's task was to root English Protestantism in something deeper than superficial conformity to a settlement imposed from above. A proclamation in 1560 protected ecclesiastical property from irreverent pillage; and two years later Parker issued a Book of Homilies which avoided questions of doctrine, but laid down precepts for seemly behaviour and a proper reverence. The Church received a formal body of doctrine in 1563, when Convocation sanctioned the Thirty-nine Articles which Parker, omitting the tendencies towards Zwinglianism, had based on the Articles of 1553; but they were not accepted by the Queen and parliament until 1571, when the bull of excommunication had made the breach with Rome irreparable. Parker's labours were complicated by the demands of the political situation, and by the Queen's personal indifference to doctrine, but he had his reward. His reasonableness and love of order stamped the English Church with a character of its own, and raised it above the level of political compromise.[1]

But this lay in the future. In 1559 the makeshift settlement had still to prove itself. Like the settlement of 1689, it clothed itself with the passing of time in virtues which at first it did not possess. At first its merits were negative: while few men liked it, few could find in it principles which they were unable to accept. It accommodated all but the extremists of both parties, and even for them there was no terror. But in the last instance the success of the settlement was bound up with the success of the reign; it survived because Elizabeth held to her precarious throne and grew in the respect and admiration of her people. It came to be associated in men's minds with the rising tide of prosperity; with honest money, low taxes, and a peaceful, orderly, and unoppressive government. At length it grew to mean more than this: it was the symbol of English independence, a native compromise drawn midway between 'the two infallibilities of Rome and Geneva', which the people would defend against foreign attack. It was not so much a test of religion as a test of loyalty; and that is why, in an England proudly aware of the obligations of patriotism, there were more Protestants in 1603 than there had been in 1558.

[1] What the Church of England came to mean to its finest sons may be read in the exquisite poetry of George Herbert.

CHAPTER VII

ELIZABETH'S FOREIGN POLICY: SCOTLAND AND FRANCE

The situation in 1559. Defeat of the French in Scotland. Intervention in France. Mary in Scotland. Her deposition and flight. The problem of Mary.

1. *The danger from Scotland*

Elizabeth's foreign policy was dictated by the same motives which had inspired her settlement of religion. Throughout her long reign the threat of foreign domination was never far away: at first the House of Guise, already all-powerful in Scotland and France, sought to bring England into the alliance which they controlled; and later the heretic Queen seemed to stand alone in the path of the Counter-Reformation and the overwhelming strength of Hapsburg Spain. In these dangers Elizabeth did not falter. Her methods may have been unheroic: she procrastinated, changed her mind, betrayed her allies, left her ministers ill rewarded for their service; she was parsimonious, unenterprising, and inconstant, tacking before the shifting winds of necessity; but all her doings bore witness to her inflexible purpose, that England should be free. She was 'mere English',[1] and no foreigner should have power in her land.

Since her purpose was to preserve her country's independence, she could not, by the nature of her mission, take long views. The clue to her policy must be sought rather in the schemes and ambitions of the powers with which she had to deal, since their

[1] 'She is very much wedded to her people' reported de Feria, 'and thinks as they do.'

policy shaped hers. Elizabeth never took the initiative. The more aggressive of her ministers often implored her to do something decisive: to give a lead to the Huguenots, to accept the sovereignty of the Netherlands, to identify herself openly with the Protestant Lords of Scotland, even to come to open war with Spain. But she shrank from decisions, from taking steps which she could not retrace; she would not commit herself to policies or alliances which might impede her freedom of action. She would use any instruments that chance or diplomacy might offer her, the religious passions of Knox or rebellions in France and Holland, but she used them for her purposes, and had no time to spare to serve theirs. War she hated with all the strength of her thrifty mind; its false glories did not deceive her, and she avoided it for as long as she could. Her shifts and hesitations had an unswerving object: 'to teach still peace to grow', to gain time while her religious settlement took root, and her people learned to be Englishmen before they were Catholics; so that when war came, if come it must, they would stand united to meet it. Watchfulness, therefore, rather than consistency, was the essence of her policy; but it would be rash to see in her opportunism only the shifts and subterfuges of an unreliable and vacillating mind. Elizabeth put her trust in something surer than a feckless policy of 'wait and see'. She was not a fool who tamed Mary Stuart and refused to be duped by William of Orange; who bore always the love and loyalty of her seamen; who chose such men as Cecil and Walsingham, Parker and Whitgift, Gresham and Jewel, to do her service.

A woman who wore a crown started with every prejudice aroused against her. The reign of Mary had borne out the melancholy predictions which men had made, and her sister came to the throne in an atmosphere of masculine contempt. Government was a man's business; courts were made to revolve round Kings, not Queens. Her ministers waited for her to marry and until then they proposed themselves to deliberate those grave matters which were 'too much for a woman's knowledge'. A husband, as Philip of Spain deferentially reminded her, would 'relieve her of those labours which are only fit for men'. But Elizabeth intended differently. In the first months of her reign she refused to marry Philip. More, she said she would never marry; she told the Spanish ambassador that 'she yearns to be a nun and to pass her time in a cell praying'. At first these protestations were impatiently attributed to a woman's modesty; but as time made it clear that she meant what she said, her councillors and parliaments grew ever more importunate in loud-voiced insistence that she change her mind. The Tudor dynasty depended on her single life; beyond her lay civil war and the dread of foreign invasion. Thus it was her duty to marry and secure the succession. Elizabeth knew better than her critics. Her virginity became the symbol of that national independence which it was her mission to defend. If she married a foreign Prince, she bound herself and her people to serve his interests. She might marry one of her subjects: the Earl of Arundel and Sir William Pickering were put forward as representatives of the older aristocracy. But if she married at all, she threw away her strongest weapon. The Queen of England was the best marriage in Europe: unmarried, she kept all Europe hopeful and expectant, unwilling to fight against her if they might conquer her by wooing; married, she lost her power. Early in her reign she had to master her personal feelings. She was deeply attached to Lord Robert Dudley, the dark, handsome son of the Duke of Northumberland; and when his wife died, he was free to marry her. Whatever her private impulses were, she suppressed them in her duty to her people. Her sex, which should have been her weakness, she turned into her greatest strength.

At the start of the reign the outlook was black enough. In particular, England's safety was threatened by the ambitions of the House of Guise. Coming from Lorraine in the time of Francis I, the Guises had won honour and confidence at the court of France; a Duke of Guise had recovered Calais from England; he, and his son after him, were to be the champions of the Catholic cause in the endless wars of religion. Moreover, Mary of Guise, the widow of James V, was Regent of Scotland during the minority of her daughter Mary; under her shrewd leadership the French party in Scotland had recovered the authority which they had lost when Beaton was murdered. In 1558 Mary Stuart, who had been thrown into the arms of the French by Somerset's unwisdom ten years before, married the Dauphin; a year later, she was sitting with him on the throne of France. Mary, now just seventeen years old, was in her own right Queen of Scotland; by marriage, Queen of France; and, by her descent from Margaret Tudor, heir to the throne of England. To Catholics, repudiating Elizabeth as a bastard and a heretic, she was rightful Queen already. No one could mistake the danger in which England lay: the Guises, with France and Scotland already in their hands, believed that Mary had only to advance her claim for all the Catholics of England to rise and drive Elizabeth from her throne. The 'auld alliance' had never seemed so threatening.

At the same moment, Elizabeth rejected the overtures of Spain: she refused to marry Philip, although he offered to help her to recover Calais. She lost both Calais and a suitor, for Philip took his offers elsewhere. He made peace with France at Cateau-Cambrésis, and married Elizabeth of Valois, a daughter of Henry II; and Elizabeth had to abandon Calais, in spite of a face-saving clause in the treaty that in eight years it should revert to England. But more was involved in the treaty than the possession of Calais. During the very months in which Elizabeth was fashioning her religious settlement, and leading her people back to the path of heresy, the two great Catholic powers had composed their differences, and were free, if they wished, to punish the English for their bold impiety. Elizabeth, however, judged this danger for what it was worth. Philip was a pious man, but he valued Spain's national interests more highly than his religion; and those interests would not permit him to invade England in the cause of the Guises and Mary Stuart. Elizabeth did not need to marry him to be sure of his help if the Guises should attempt to bring England, as well as Scotland and France, into their control.

Elizabeth had allies elsewhere. There was a party in Scotland with interests akin to hers : to break the power of the Catholic Franco-Scottish alliance, defy the Pope, and establish a Protestant national Church. In Scotland the Reformation, lacking the restraint of Henry VIII, had moved faster than in England. The rigorous creed of Calvin was congenial to the Scottish temperament, and even from his exile Knox had inspired the people to detest the heathen idolatries of the French. At the same time, the members of the nobility, with their eyes on the loot of the churches, organised themselves as the Lords of the Congregation of Christ Jesus, and took a covenant to drive out the Regent and her French adherents, and correct the hateful errors of the Romish faith. Rebellion broke out against the government. Hearkening to the clear call of his trumpet, Knox's ' rascal multitude ' fell upon the images which they detested ; at Perth, Scone, Stirling, St. Andrews and Edinburgh churches and Abbeys succumbed to the assaults of militant Calvinism. ' Burn the nests ', cried Knox, ' and the rooks will fly.'

Here was Elizabeth's opportunity. Knox and the Congregation were rebels, and she hated rebels ; but their aims were her aims, and she must help them to succeed. From Gresham at Brussels she learned that the Spaniards in the Netherlands had no money to spare for an invasion ; and from Throckmorton in Paris she heard that religious dissension was growing, and that the French had trouble enough of their own. Gresham raised loans from the Antwerp bankers, and sent her weapons and ammunition, some of which he seized from Philip's arsenal at Malines. Confident that France and Spain were unable to interfere, Elizabeth sent an army to aid the rebels, and ordered Admiral Winter to sail to the Forth and ' impeach ' the French in any way he could. Her intervention turned the scale. Although the English soldiers bungled their attack on the fortress of Leith, Winter's ships intimidated the French into surrender. The Regent was dying, and the French accepted the terms on which the rebels insisted. By the Treaty of Edinburgh, signed in July, 1560, they agreed to evacuate Scotland, and to hand over the government to a committee of twelve ; and Mary and her husband removed from their arms the insignia of England and Ireland. When the news arrived that the Spaniards had been terribly defeated by the Moors at Tripoli, Elizabeth could be secure in her triumph. She was able, Gresham boasted, to 'make the proudest prince in all Christendom to stoop and yield unto that noble carcass of hers '. But she knew where to stop. She had gained her ends, and she refused to bind herself to the Protestant nobles by paying them pensions and marrying the Earl of Arran. For the first time an English army had entered Scotland in peace and left it with the goodwill of the inhabitants ; the Protestants shared her aims, and she did not propose to pay them pensions for being of the same mind as herself. Moreover, Arran was heir to the throne if Mary died childless ; to marry him would involve Elizabeth in dynastic claims to the Scottish throne, and turn against herself the patriotic spirit which had just ejected the French. Before the end of the year Francis II was dead, and Mary was no longer Queen of France. The first crisis of the reign was over.

2. *The bid for Calais*

To strengthen her position, Elizabeth sought to win more allies abroad. Reports from Paris encouraged her to believe that she could embarrass the Guises, and prevent their contriving their revenge in Scotland, by assisting the Huguenots to rebel. France was on the threshold of a generation of civil war. Calvinism had laid its grip on the middle classes, and in France, even as elsewhere, there were nobles who found in the cause of religion an excuse to challenge the government. Like fifteenth-century England, France was to know the curse of the overmighty subject. The nobles divided themselves into factions and wrestled for power ; and the government, since it was too weak to rule, was obliged to supplicate and soothe. For the House of

Valois was dying out. Henry II had left four sons: the first, Francis II, Mary's husband, died in 1560; Charles IX reigned until 1574; Henry III was assassinated in 1589; and the fourth, the Duke of Alençon, died in 1584. All died without children, and the Valois line was extinct. Throughout the thirty years in which these worthless people trifled on the throne, the policy of the Crown was the policy of their mother, Catherine de Medici, who died only a few months before the last of her sons. Catherine herself was a shrewd, scheming woman, with something of Elizabeth's hatred of war and of the ideals for which men were disposed to fight. But she was a tenacious mother. During all those years she laboured with unwavering vigilance and courage to protect the rights and interests of her unlovable brood. Her object was peace, because war distracted the country; and when fighting broke out in France, she did not rest until she had balanced the scales between the contesting parties, and persuaded them to lay down their arms. Such a policy was a confession of weakness: the government tried to maintain a balance of power between warring factions which it was too feeble to suppress. To save herself from Guise and the Catholics, to rescue her son from the influence of Coligny and the Huguenots, Catherine bribed, pleaded, intrigued, assassinated, and even planned a wholesale murder; but the persistence of the civil wars showed how little authority she and her sons commanded.

In 1562 the wars were just beginning, and Elizabeth hoped to turn them to her advantage. Her motives were not, as the Spanish ambassador wrongly interpreted them, aggressive; she was attacking in order the better to defend, to protect herself by securing allies. In September, 1562, she made a secret treaty with the Huguenots: she would help them with men and money, and in return she should receive Calais when the rebellion had succeeded; meanwhile, the English might occupy Le Havre as a security. The agreement recalled the intervention of mediaeval Kings in the strife of Burgundians and Armagnacs. But the enterprise was not a success. Catherine managed to persuade both sides to respond to the call of patriotism; after some inconclusive fighting, they settled their differences and turned on the invader. After a heroic defence the Earl of Warwick was forced to surrender Le Havre and leave the country. Worse, Elizabeth had to submit to humiliating terms. She threatened to ban French wines from England, to starve the people of coal, to harass their fishing, even to bombard their coasts ; but she could not bluff them into restoring Calais. By her invasion she had forfeited all right to it, and it was finally lost to England.

Elizabeth had blundered, but she learned from her mistake ; she did not again provoke French patriotism by an open declaration of war. Moreover, the next few years offered her a more effective means to counteract the influence of the Guises. As the religious wars dragged on, a party grew up in France in support of the Queen-Mother's policy of order and appeasement ; and the goodwill of these *Politiques* was a surer foundation on which to build than the ambitions of the Huguenots. Within ten years Elizabeth was able to make a defensive alliance with the French government. Meanwhile, the failure of 1562–3 had no disastrous results, and there was this to be said in favour of the treaty with the Huguenots : the bid to recover Calais, although it was not Elizabeth's primary object, stressed the contrast between her policy and her sister's. As a patriotic gesture, it was opportune, for it showed that she was sensitive to the traditional interests of her people.

3. *Mary, Queen of Scots*

The death of Francis II was a serious blow to the ambitions of the Guises, for their protégée Mary Stuart was no longer Queen of France ; so far, Elizabeth could rejoice in it. But it also reopened the problem of French influence in Scotland, for it meant that Mary must at length return to rule over her own people ; and it seemed, as the Earl hastened to point out, that Elizabeth would have been wiser to have married Arran and, by claiming the Scottish throne, to have prevented Mary's return.

Mary came to Scotland in the summer of 1561. She was a Stuart, with all the qualities of her ill-fated House. Her heart was stronger than her head: she loved heroic deeds, and was eager to perform them; by her charm she could win men to serve her with devotion; but her emotions ran away with her will and intellect, and blinded her to the consequences of the courses which they drove her to pursue. From the first her task called for the delicacy and tact of an experienced diplomat. She came from the culture and gaiety of the court of France to a land which she found cold and depressing; where the nobles were intent upon the greedy pursuit of gain, where earnest ministers preached before her their interminable sermons, and where the people offended her eyes with their dirty, uncouth, heretical habits. Knox received her with unchristian mistrust, and made ready to blow again upon his trumpet. Finding in her 'an indurate heart against God and His truth', he had her presented with a huge Bible, and the godly advised her of their prejudices by burning before her eyes effigies of Korah, Dathan and Abiram, whose sin had been idolatry. But Mary began her reign with statesmanlike discretion. She was affable and tolerant; she showed no missionary enthusiasm, and did not threaten those who were fat with Protestant plunder; she chose her advisers from men of all shades of religious and political opinion. Knox was saddened by her moderation. He could find no cause for offence, except that Mass was celebrated at Holyrood, and that her ladies wore tassels on their skirts, and spent the night in fiddling and dancing. For, as he mournfully complained, the 'fire-edge' of Protestant zeal was burning low. Elizabeth had angered the Scots because she would neither pay them pensions nor marry Arran; and if Mary would be content to rule wisely, and leave them in possession of their loot, they were prepared to transfer their allegiance from Elizabeth to her.

But Mary's undoing was her desire to succeed to the crown of England, from which the Treaty of Edinburgh had totally excluded her. As the first Stuart pretender to the English throne, she sent Maitland of Lethington, the most resourceful of her ministers, to London to press her claim.[1] But Elizabeth would have none of it ; indeed, she would not appoint a successor at all. During the years when she had herself been heiress to a throne, she had learned of the temptations which ambitious men lay in a successor's path. ' It is hard to bind princes ', she said, ' when hope is offered of a kingdom. . . . Do you think I could love my own winding-sheet ? ' To declare Mary to be her successor would offer the Catholics of both countries too strong a motive to conspire her death. In 1562 she was dangerously ill with smallpox, and the country braced itself for civil war ; but when she recovered, she was still adamant.

Mary then attempted to force her hand by marrying ' powerfully '. Ever since her first husband had died, a press of suitors had been seeking a match which was no less important than any which Elizabeth might make. Philip's son Don Carlos, Charles IX of France, the Austrian Archduke Charles, the Huguenot leader Condé, had all put forward their claims. Elizabeth tried to distract these suitors from their purpose by hinting that she might marry any of them herself, but this comedy could not be played for ever. Mary would presently find a husband, and, whoever he might be, the marriage must endanger England's safety. Elizabeth did her best to force on her a husband who would be innocuous : she raised her favourite Dudley to the Earldom of Leicester, and recommended him to Mary. It was a desperate throw, and Mary was not to be deceived. She would marry Leicester only if Elizabeth would promise her the succession, and on this matter Elizabeth would not relent.

The outcome fulfilled Elizabeth's gloomiest fears. Mary decided to marry her cousin Henry Stuart, Earl of Darnley. Darnley was the grandson of the Earl of Angus, the second husband of Margaret Tudor ; he had, therefore, a claim in his own right to the thrones of England and Scotland, and his marriage to Mary united the two branches of the descendants

[1] To earn Elizabeth's gratitude, Mary did not act when England intervened in France in 1562.

of Margaret. The choice of Darnley, in preference to a foreign Prince, indicated that Mary was aiming seriously at the English throne ; for, with his powerful connections in both countries, he was a man whom the Scottish and English Catholics could support without doing injury to their patriotism or to their scruples about a legitimate succession. Elizabeth protested, and the Scottish Protestants organised a rebellion, but it was in vain. The Pope removed ' the impediment of blood ', and in 1565 Mary and Darnley were married ; a year later a son was born to them, the future James I of England. The Commons expressed the alarm which filled all loyal Englishmen : unless Elizabeth married, or appointed her successor, she was no better than a parricide. The Queen's reply showed that her spirit had not failed her. She was not to be rebuked by men who treated serious matters ' like a lot of inexperienced schoolboys ', and she did not intend to declare her policy ' to a knot of hare-brains '.

The game was in Mary's hands, but the defects in her character mastered her restraint. Infatuated with Darnley, she threw aside the caution which hitherto had reconciled the Scots to her rule. To Philip and the Pope she applied for assistance in the religious crusade to which, she said, her conscience now impelled her ; she confiscated the lands of those who had been involved in the recent rising ; the English ambassador was dismissed from Edinburgh ; preparations were made to coerce the Scots by foreign arms back into the Catholic faith. It was a hopeless quest. John Knox knew his duty, the Protestant nobles knew where their interest lay. The rebels began, with Darnley's connivance, by murdering David Rizzio, Mary's Italian secretary, and thereafter Mary delivered herself into their hands. Her infatuation for Darnley had quickly burnt itself out. His part in Rizzio's murder was more than she could forgive, and even the birth of their son could not bring them together ; early in 1567 the house where he was lying ill was destroyed by an explosion, and his body was found strangled in the grounds. Many men in Scotland had cause to hate Darnley and to wish him dead ;

but if Mary's implication in the crime cannot be proved legally, her actions after the murder proclaimed her moral guilt. As her passion for Darnley waned, she had fallen in love with the Earl of Bothwell, the most dashing and the least scrupulous of the Scottish nobles ; and public opinion pointed to Bothwell as the murderer and Mary as his accomplice. Had Mary declared her innocence on her word as a Queen, and ordered an honest and open enquiry into Darnley's death, she could have cleared her name of a guilt in which few men wanted to believe. Instead, she had Bothwell acquitted in a packed and terrorised court which his accuser did not dare to attend ; created him Duke of Orkney ; and three months after Darnley's death, and only twelve days after he had divorced his former wife, she married him with the rites of the Protestant Church.

The Scots could stand no more. If Mary had not instigated the murder, she had taken the part of the man whom everyone held responsible for it ; and, to marry him, she had shamelessly abandoned the principles and rites of the Church for which she had lately professed such zeal. In June, 1567, within a month of her marriage, she surrendered to the rebels at Carberry Hill ; and, since she refused to renounce Bothwell, who had fled abroad, she was forced to abdicate her throne. The infant James was crowned at Stirling, and the country was governed by a council of Protestant lords under the Earl of Murray. The rule of the Regency, however, was harsh and uncongenial ; the Catholics began to repent of their hasty action, and to wish to give their Queen another chance, for she might, as the Bishop of Ross declared, have sinned under the malignant spell of witchcraft. The Hamiltons favoured her cause, and in the spring of 1568 she escaped from Lochleven Castle and called her subjects to her banner. Her hopes died swiftly. Murray routed her troops at Langside, and she rode across the Border to throw herself on the mercy of her cousin of England.

Her coming presented Elizabeth with the most difficult decision of her reign. Elizabeth's attitude to the recent events in Scotland had bewildered and distressed her ministers. At first she had been willing to do all in her power to embarrass Mary, and it was with her knowledge and approval that the nobles had risen to murder Rizzio. But Mary's deposition was another matter. Elizabeth was always tender for the rights and safety of sovereigns, and she could not condone a rebellion which might put unhealthy ideas into the minds of her own subjects. The Scots, she declared, ' have no warrant nor authority by the law of God or man to be as superiors over their prince and sovereign '. Abandoning her old alliance with the Scottish Protestants, she instructed her envoys to baulk the Regency and to intrigue to have Mary released from Lochleven. Mary made her appeal, therefore, confident that Elizabeth would use all the resources of England to restore her to her throne.

Elizabeth's problem was extraordinarily difficult. It was one thing to denounce the rebels for their impious conduct ; but to go to war with them, with the object of restoring Mary, was not to be contemplated. On the other hand, to deliver her to Murray, and the death which the Scots demanded, would be merciless and impolitic. She could not be allowed to go abroad, to plead her cause at foreign courts and perhaps to persuade the French to intervene again in the affairs of Scotland ; nor, with her dangerous claim to the succession, could she be allowed to move freely about England inciting the Catholics to rebellion. Fearing to adopt any of these dangerous courses, Elizabeth decided to solve the problem by keeping Mary for the present under observation in England ; and to provide herself with a pretext for a course which she had neither legal nor moral right to pursue, she declared that she would arbitrate in the quarrel between Mary and her subjects. Both parties were summoned to plead their case before an English tribunal, which sat first at York and later at Westminster. Murray produced the famous Casket Letters, which were supposed to prove Mary's complicity in the murder of Darnley. But it was not Elizabeth's purpose to have Mary's name irretrievably blackened ; if her guilt were proved, she must be handed over to Murray and the Scots. Accordingly, Elizabeth made use of the Scottish verdict of ' not proven '. In January, 1569, she pronounced an equivocal verdict : that, while Murray and his party had done nothing which impaired their honour as loyal subjects of their Queen, no crime had been ' sufficiently proven ' against Mary. It was a subtle, if unconvincing, escape from an impossible dilemma. It safeguarded the present, for enough had been urged against Mary to give Elizabeth a moral right to detain her ; and it left the way open for renewed negotiations in a more settled future. Elizabeth intended to keep Mary in England until the memory of her crimes had faded and the passion of the Scots had cooled ; and then to restore her to her throne on terms which, by fettering her freedom of action, should be acceptable to her Protestant subjects.

This plan was never put into action, for the fate of Mary ceased to be the private concern of Elizabeth and the Scots. These were dangerous years for Elizabeth. England was drifting into hostility to Spain ; Alva's persecution seemed to be crushing the resistance of the Netherlands ; two overwhelming defeats in 1569 threatened the independence of the French Huguenots. At home, the Catholic and feudal nobility were discontented, and Philip's over-zealous ambassador, de Spes, was nourishing their discontent into conspiracy ; and even some of the loyal ministers, Leicester among them, were deploring the drift from Spain and seeking to alter the trend of the nation's policy. In this dangerous hour Elizabeth's enemies gathered round Mary. De Spes tried to involve the English Catholics, Alva, and the Pope in a plot to set her on the throne ; his plans broke down, because Alva was not impressed by the statistics which he collected, or by the hopes which he founded on them, but he had sown dissatisfaction which grew into revolt. The Northern Rebellion of 1569 was badly mismanaged. Its aims were confused, its leaders suspicious and irresolute ; Norfolk, the figurehead of the revolt, broke down and surrendered to the government. The Earls of Westmorland and Northumberland abandoned their men when the royal army approached, and fled into Scotland ; and Dacre's rising in the following year was crushed by Hunsdon on the banks of the

Gelt. Cowardice, divided aims and mutual jealousy wrecked a movement which under efficient leadership might have involved the country in civil war; Elizabeth punished the rebels with ruthless severity, and England was never again to be troubled by feudal rebellion.

But the underlying object of the rising might still be achieved by different hands. The rebels had intended to release Mary, marry her to the Duke of Norfolk, the leader of the English Catholics, and put her on Elizabeth's throne. Two attempts on her behalf had failed, but others might succeed; and the Ridolfi plot of 1571 resumed the long series of Spanish efforts to seize or assassinate Elizabeth, and hand her crown to Mary. These conspiracies obliged Elizabeth to revise her intentions. In the changed circumstances it was impossible to think of restoring Mary to Scotland, even if the Scots would consent to have her. But what was to be done with her? The English had no doubt: she was guilty of treason, and she should die. The Commons demanded the blood of 'the monstrous and huge dragon' who had conspired against the safety of the realm; Convocation complained that she 'hath heaped up together all the sins of the licentious sons of David', and echoed the demands of parliament. But Elizabeth shrank from signing the death-warrant of a sister-Queen. To appease the bloodthirsty clamour of her people, she gave them the head of Norfolk, who went to the block in 1572; but she would not give them Mary. Partly from policy, partly from mercy, and partly from sheer weakness, she kept Mary in captivity but spared her life; and for fifteen more years Mary was to be a constant danger to the life of her captor, the centre of foreign conspiracies against the safety of England. Elizabeth's motives are unfathomable, but she may have been wiser than her critics. They saw only the immediate danger to the state: since she would neither marry nor name her successor, the Queen's life was the only protection from civil war. As long as Mary lived, the Catholics and the Spaniards had a clear motive for conspiring Elizabeth's death. Elizabeth endured with amazing courage an ordeal that broke the nerve of Oliver Cromwell : the threat of assassination was always hanging over her. For she believed, in defiance of her ministers and her parliaments, that Mary alive could in some ways serve English interests better than Mary dead. In the first place, political murder is a weapon which is often turned on him who wields it ; a martyred Mary was likely to breed worse dangers than a slightly futile dowager weaving plots with furtive foreign agents. Secondly, she might always be used with advantage against Elizabeth's other enemies. If the Scots grew turbulent, a threat to restore Mary would sober them ; she might be released to nourish faction in the court of France ; above all, she was an obstacle to the ambitions of Spain. As long as she was alive, Philip had misgivings as he plotted against England and Elizabeth ; for she, rather than the Hapsburgs, would profit by his success. In Elizabeth's forbearance there was wisdom, as well as courage and mercy.

CHAPTER VIII

THE STRUGGLE WITH SPAIN

Causes of the quarrel with Spain. Elizabeth I and the Netherlands. The Armada and the last years of the war.

1. *Causes of the quarrel with Spain*

The traditional policy of England, which only Wolsey had been incautious enough to neglect, was to remain on good terms with the master of Flanders. The plea of the old 'Burgundian alliance' had been urged by Mary Tudor in defence of her marriage to Philip; and, disastrous as that marriage turned out to be, it was with confidence that in 1558 Philip sought to renew the alliance by offering his hand to Elizabeth. Elizabeth rejected him, and he found his bride in France, but common fear of the Guises bound England and the Hapsburgs in the close compact of a common interest. In the early years of her reign Philip did Elizabeth many valuable services: his ambassador watched over her safety at home; at Cateau-Cambrésis he tried to persuade the French to restore Calais to England; and when the wrath of Europe was stirred against the heretic Queen, he delayed the vengeance of Rome during the perilous years when the settlement of 1559 was taking root. In 1560 his orders detained at Brussels a papal envoy who was on his way to make trouble for Elizabeth, and at Trent he and his brother Ferdinand resisted the entreaties of Catholic refugees who were imploring the Pope to be revenged on the heretic. In taking Elizabeth under his protection Philip was consulting no interests but his own; he did not wish to see Mary Stuart on the throne of England. Elizabeth showed small gratitude for these services, for she knew the motives which inspired them; but for the first ten years of her reign she did not openly depart from the traditional foreign policy of her country.

There were, however, two reasons why the old alliance with Burgundy must break down, and Elizabeth's early harmony of interest with Philip change to hostility and war. The first of these was the growing economic rivalry between the two countries: the commercial ambitions of the English were operating unfairly on Flemish merchants in the old world, and conflicting with the Spanish and Portuguese monopoly in the new. In Europe, the mercantilist policy of the government was poisoning good relations with Flanders. It raised the duties on articles imported from Flanders, and prohibited the import of some goods altogether; the carrying trade was restricted to English ships; and Flemish merchants were required to spend the proceeds of their sales on English goods before they left the country. The Spanish government naturally retaliated, and the flow of trade between England and Flanders was blocked by a rising wall of tariffs; in 1563 many English merchants abandoned Antwerp and carried their goods to Emden.

The conflict in the new world was much more serious. By the Bull of Alexander VI the Spaniards and the Portuguese claimed a prescriptive right to the treasure and commerce of America and the islands of the Caribbean. Their monopoly cramped the enterprise of English merchants, who began to enquire by what right the Pope had partitioned the earth and bestowed kingdoms. The Portuguese preserves had been invaded before Elizabeth came to the throne: William Hawkins of Plymouth ventured to the coast of Guinea and across the Atlantic to Brazil, and, after his example, fleets sailed almost every year to West Africa in search of ivory, gold and pepper. In 1562 his son John challenged the monopoly of Spain. The rapid disappearance of the aboriginal population had put the Spanish planters in America in such need of slave labour that they were ready to defy their government and buy it from an English interloper. So Hawkins descended on the African coast, kidnapped the helpless natives, and carried them over the Atlantic to the Spanish colonies. His enterprise was illegal and immoral, but it was successful; and when he sailed again, the Queen and her courtiers lent him ships and shared in his profits. In 1567 he set out for a third time on a traffic which was becoming a regular feature of the country's commercial activity. This time, however, he was unfortunate. A Spanish fleet found him in the harbour of San Juan d'Ulloa, where he had put in to refit his ships; and in violation of their promised word, the Spaniards set upon him and drove him out of the harbour with heavy losses. This incident, with the bad feeling which it bred on both sides, put an end to peaceful trade with Spain; whatever the policy of their governments might be, henceforth the merchants were at war. The next few years were years of danger: the Northern Rebellion, the Bull of excommunication, and the Ridolfi plot, created an emergency in which every available ship was needed in home waters. Thus it was not until 1572 that Francis Drake sailed to the Indies to avenge the treachery which had robbed and humiliated Hawkins four years before. At Nombre de Dios, on the Isthmus of Panama, he seized the treasure of the Peruvian mines as it was brought overland on mules to the harbour; and from a high tree in the heart of Darien the Cimarron Indians showed him the Pacific, fresh seas to conquer in the future. What Drake had done, others attempted in the years which followed. The greed and spirit of England's seamen would make no truce with Spain until they were admitted to the rich commerce of the Caribbean. When, moreover, the Spaniards began to treat as heretics the merchants and sailors who fell into their hands, commercial interest became a religious crusade. Hawkins and Drake urged the government to change its policy: to abandon the Burgundian alliance and the trade with Flanders, and seek the richer prizes which were to be had from marauding overseas. The more adventurous of the courtiers, such as Leicester, Walsingham and Hatton, who shared in the enormous dividends of piracy, echoed the counsels of the seamen; but the Queen, although she too

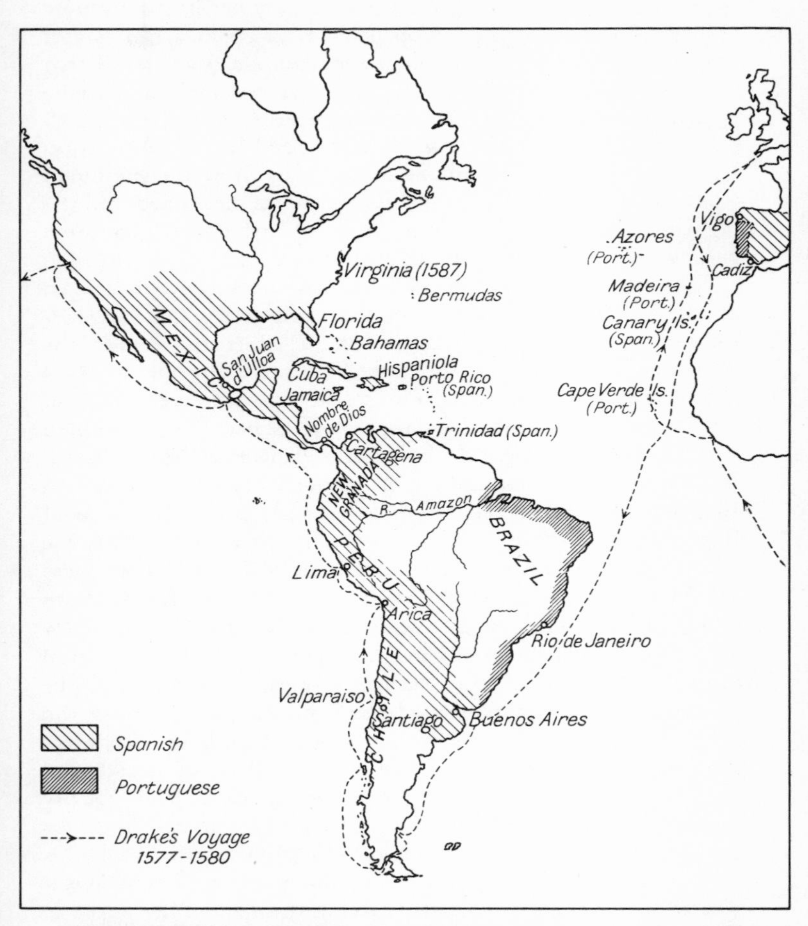

THE ELIZABETHAN SEAMEN AND THE MARITIME WAR WITH SPAIN

shared in the plunder, and was anxious to lay her hands on more of it, was too cautious to risk open war with Spain. Her pirates had her blessing, but to Philip's complaints she answered that their doings were beyond her control. It was the seamen who finally brought Philip to his knees, and forced him to launch his great Armada in a despairing bid to end their deadly work. By cutting its communications at sea, they drew the life-blood of the Spanish Empire ; for its existence depended on the regular flow of treasure from America, which all too often poured into the pockets of English courtiers.

The second cause of the breach with Spain was religious. All Englishmen knew that over the horizon lay the Counter-Reformation ; sooner or later Rome's effort to recover the allegiance of heretics would bring Catholic Europe to their shores. So far, it was true, Philip had stayed the vengeance of the Pope ; for a time Hapsburg interests had obliged him to support Elizabeth against the greater danger of Mary Stuart. But this situation was not permanent : Mary as a prisoner in England was less formidable to Spain than Mary as Queen of Scotland and France. Philip soon came to recognise that the success of Spain rested upon the success of Rome. For it was the Pope who had granted him America and the Indies, from which he drew his wealth ; whereas the Reformation stood for all the forces which sapped his strength : nationalism, political unrest, and economic aggression. It meant the revolt in the Netherlands and the unlicensed attack on his possessions in the New World. Hapsburg interests marched with the Counter-Reformation, and Philip became the spearhead of its attack.

The interests of England were equally clear, and equally capable of being masked by the loftier pretexts of religion : for England to be safe, the Reformation must survive. Elizabeth's secular mind had no place for religious idealism, but where it existed in others she could make it the instrument of her purpose. The object of her policy, therefore, was to aid the Protestant cause wherever it was threatened ; and in particular, to prevent Philip from mastering the Netherlands and using it as a base from which to launch an attack on England. The seventeen provinces of the Netherlands, which were the northern outpost of Philip's Empire, had mostly been acquired by the Dukes of Burgundy in the fifteenth century, and had passed to the Hapsburgs when Mary of Burgundy married the Emperor Maximilian. The provinces had submitted to the rule of Charles V, although he had taxed them heavily and persecuted the reformed religion, because he was a Fleming by birth. But Philip they hated : they found him clumsy and heavy-handed, neglectful of their privileges and contemptuous of their habits and their language. He left the Netherlands in 1559, never to return ; and the provinces soon realised that their prosperity was to be taxed to finance Hapsburg ambitions, their liberties suppressed in conformity with Philip's notions of the respect due to monarchs, and, in the Calvinist districts of the North, their religion persecuted in the cause of Catholic unity. The Regency at Brussels was harassed by protests against taxes, the Inquisition, the presence of Spanish soldiers, the Spanish monopoly of remunerative offices ; and it was the policy of the English government, not to challenge Philip's sovereignty in the Netherlands, but to increase the difficulties of the Regency, in order that the provinces should not be made to serve Spain's dynastic ambitions.

When Elizabeth began, therefore, to stimulate disorders in the Netherlands, and to encourage refugees to settle among her people and teach them their industries, Philip was driven to retaliate. His weapon lay ready to his hand : the English Catholics were only waiting for a lead, and they would rise for Mary, Queen of Scots. At the same time, Philip decided to take strong action in the Netherlands. In 1567 he sent the Duke of Alva, a fine soldier and a resourceful statesman, to reduce the provinces to order and obedience ; and in the following year Don Gueran de Spes arrived to open the Spanish offensive in England.

The old alliance was breaking fast. Before the end of 1568 Elizabeth offered further provocation to Philip. A fleet, carrying money lent by the bankers of Genoa to pay Alva's troops in the Netherlands, put in at Plymouth and Southampton to seek refuge from the Channel pirates. To avenge the disgrace in the harbour of San Juan d'Ulloa, Elizabeth claimed that the money might as well be lent to her as to Philip, and appropriated the sum of 800,000 ducats. Alva retaliated by seizing the goods of English merchants in the Netherlands ; the English government in its turn seized the Flemish goods that were in England, and trade between the two countries came to a standstill ; the City of London was obliged to send its fleet to Hamburg. This quarrel stimulated the missionary zeal of de Spes. He intrigued with the Catholic nobility to put Mary on the throne, and with Philip and Alva to bring England to her knees by imposing an economic blockade. But his plans failed to mature. He viewed too optimistically the strength and resources of the nobles, and he underrated his opponents : the Northern Rebellion collapsed. Meanwhile, the English were successfully evading the economic blockade. English goods were passed into Europe through the friendly ports of La Rochelle and Hamburg, and imports came to England in the ships of Venice and Ragusa. De Spes tried in vain to stop the leakages in his system ; he discovered, like Napoleon in another age, that to place an effective embargo on English trade he must be master of every port in Europe. Moreover, his restless plotting received no encouragement from Alva. Alva was too shrewd a statesman to launch Spain on a war which she could not afford, and he was less readily impressed than de Spes by the high hopes of a handful of English intriguers ; he knew, too, that their trade with England was vital to the prosperity of the Netherlands, and therefore to his task of appeasing them. Thus he attempted to moderate the enthusiasm of de Spes, and, for the present at least, to settle the causes of dispute between Philip and Elizabeth.

Elizabeth too was seeking a way out of her difficulties. In 1570 the Bull of excommunication released her Catholic subjects from their allegiance ; and the Ridolfi plot in the following years, another fruit of the indefatigable labours of de Spes, warned her again of the danger in which she stood. In this crisis she turned again to France; not, this time, to the Huguenot rebels, but to the government. For Catherine de Medici had as good cause as Elizabeth to fear the advancing tide of the Counter-Reformation; with Catholicism, and the Hapsburgs, triumphant in England, Scotland and the Netherlands, France would be surrounded and almost isolated. Not until the Ethiopian were white, men said, would an Englishman learn to love a Frenchman, but a common fear of Hapsburg designs brought Catherine and Elizabeth into a defensive alliance. The French wished to cement the alliance by marrying Elizabeth to the Duke of Anjou, the heir to the throne. Elizabeth extricated herself from this embarrassing proposal by declaring that her faith forbade her to marry a Catholic, and the news of Spain's great victory over the Turks at Lepanto put an end to haggling over details. A treaty was signed at Blois in April, 1572: each government undertook to defend the other from attack, even from an invasion made in the name of religion; and an English staple was to be established in France, to balance the loss of the Netherlands market. None of the clauses of the treaty ever operated, but Elizabeth had strengthened her position: at a time when Spain was plotting to set Mary on the English throne, she had contrived that Mary's cause should not be supported by the French as well; and her union with the Queen-Mother and the moderate party in France was in later years to frustrate the designs of Philip and the Catholic League.

For the moment, however, the alliance was shattered by the Massacre of St. Bartholomew. Events had moved too fast for Catherine. Yielding to the persuasions of Coligny, the Huguenot leader, she had consented to a plan to drive the Spaniards from the Netherlands and divide the provinces between France and the successful rebels. In England, Walsingham and the war-party were urging Elizabeth to join in the war and take her share of the spoils. The capture of Brill by the Dutch pirates launched the rebellion; the Netherlands rose against Alva and summoned

England and France to their aid. But neither Catherine nor Elizabeth had the temperament to take decisive action. Elizabeth drew back, for she did not wish to see France in possession of the Netherlands; and Catherine, realising that Coligny's influence had imperilled her precious balance of power, determined to be rid of him. On the night of St. Bartholomew [1] the Huguenot leaders, who had gathered in Paris for the wedding of Henry of Navarre to Catherine's daughter, were murdered in their beds. All over the country Catholic mobs fell on the Huguenots; the Pope struck a medal to celebrate their triumphant doings, and welcomed Catherine through a sea of blood to the side of the Counter-Reformation.

Catherine had done more than she intended. Elizabeth and her court, dressed in black, listened to the French ambassador's explanation that the massacre had been an 'accident'. The French alliance was too valuable to be thrown away on a question of religious principle, and Elizabeth was willing enough to accept Catherine's apologies; the Duke of Alençon was offered as a husband, and in 1575 the Treaty of Blois was formally renewed. But a more immediate result of the massacre was a truce with Spain. Alva advised Philip to take advantage of the temporary coldness between England and France, and make his peace with Elizabeth, at least until he had mastered the Netherlands. The shock of the massacre had prepared the English to accept a settlement with Spain, and the merchants had long been anxious to resume their trade with Flanders. Therefore a series of agreements in 1573 and the two following years assessed the losses on the property confiscated in 1568, and removed all obstacles to the trade between England and the Netherlands. For her part, Elizabeth promised to exclude the Dutch rebels from her ports. Her differences with Spain had been temporarily adjusted; and as a token of the happier relations between the two countries, a Spanish fleet which put in at English harbours in the autumn of 1575 was cordially received by the people.

[1] In 1572.

2. *Elizabeth I and the Netherlands*

It seemed that Elizabeth might be able to look forward to a more settled future. She had reached an understanding with Spain ; Requescens, the new Regent of the Netherlands, was less active and less ruthless than Alva ; Mary was in close captivity, and the French had renounced her cause ; English intervention had crushed unrest among the Scots, and by 1573 the Protestant Earl of Morton had established his authority as Regent. But there could be no foundation for a long-lived optimism. The men of Elizabethan England lived always so close to danger that they learned to pick their steps with the caution of those who know that the ground may crumble under their feet. As long as the Queen was unmarried, and as long as she would not name her successor, the threat of invasion and civil war lay over England.

The truce with Spain was quickly broken, for Elizabeth could not resist the temptation to tamper with the Netherlands. She knew that the peace which she so earnestly desired could not be achieved permanently until the political struggle in the Netherlands had been settled. She had her own solution of the problem : she did not dispute Philip's sovereignty in the provinces, for she did not wish to see rebels victorious over their lawful master, or the French in possession of Antwerp. But she did not wish Philip's authority to be so complete that the Netherlands could be used as a base for the Counter-Reformation, or English cloth excluded from Flanders, which was still its principal market on the continent. Her policy, therefore, as it had been with Mary in Scotland, was to urge Philip to govern with a liberal hand ; to admit the native nobility to office and to respect the ancient privileges of the people. If Philip would do as she bade him, she was ready to help him, for she had no love for the Dutch rebels, who were pirates and Calvinists ; indeed, when William of Orange menaced English commerce by attempting to blockade the Scheldt, she assured him that she would ' bend all her forces to the assistance of the King of

THE NETHERLANDS IN THE TIME OF ELIZABETH

Spain '. Her solution failed, however, because neither Philip nor Orange would compromise ; Philip was determined to force all seventeen of the provinces to bow to his will, Orange to unite them in a free, self-governing kingdom. So the struggle dragged on, and for another ten years Elizabeth pursued her bewildering course between bluster and concession, shiftless hesitation and telling intervention.

When Don John of Austria came to the Netherlands in 1576, Spain resumed her aggressive policy towards England. Under the milder rule of Requescens the rebels had been growing in strength ; and when the unpaid Spanish soldiers broke out and destroyed the city of Antwerp, the seventeen provinces, Calvinist and Catholic alike, sank their differences and united to recover their liberties. Crowned with the laurels of Lepanto, Don John came to restore them to their obedience ; and when he had mastered the Netherlands, he would sail across the Channel, free Mary from captivity, and reign with her on the throne of the heretic. Elizabeth took steps to defend herself. She declined Orange's invitation to join him in the conquest of the provinces, but she sent him unofficial help ; and when the arrogant Mendoza came to threaten her with the consequences of her intervention, she answered threat with threat. In 1577 Drake set out on his voyage round the world. He found his way to the Pacific, where only Spanish ships were wont to sail ; and from Valparaiso he swept onwards to Santiago and Lima, sacking towns, plundering ships and sinking Philip's peaceful craft. In 1580 he returned to England laden with priceless cargoes, and the Queen went to Deptford and knighted ' the master thief of the unknown world ' on the deck of the *Golden Hind*.

Meanwhile, dark clouds were gathering over the Netherlands. Philip had sent to the assistance of Don John the finest of his captains, Alexander Farnese, Duke of Parma.[1] By crushing victories at Gembloux, Louvain, Tirlemont and Aerschot,

[1] Don John died before the end of 1578, and Parma was governor of the Netherlands until 1592.

Parma dissolved the flimsy union of the provinces, and brought the Catholic, French-speaking provinces of the South permanently under the authority of Spain. The resistance of the Netherlands now depended on the spirit of William of Orange and the seven Calvinist provinces of the North; and, having been so often disappointed by Elizabeth's vacillations, the Dutch appealed in their extremity to France. In August, 1578, the Duke of Anjou [1] took the title of 'Defender of Belgian Liberties against Spanish Tyranny'. 'The only remedy left to us', moaned Walsingham, 'is prayer.' In English eyes the sovereignty of France in the Netherlands was as unwelcome as the sovereignty of Spain, and Elizabeth had to struggle to avert the consequences of a disaster which, in the opinion of her ministers, a firmer attitude by England would have been able to prevent. The French government was, as usual, wavering between two contrary policies. The Guises, burying their old quarrel with Spain, were seeking to crush the Huguenots with Spanish help, and then to make the Netherlands a client-state of the Counter-Reformation; Anjou, on the other hand, hoped to save the Protestant cause by marrying Elizabeth, and, with English help, to build for himself a kingdom in the Netherlands.

The growing harmony between Guise and Hapsburg was alarming enough, but Anjou's designs on the Netherlands were a more pressing danger. Elizabeth found herself in a delicate position: she wished to keep alive the resistance of the Netherlands to Spain, but the French must not be allowed to reap the glory and the advantage of it. She had already subsidised John Casimir, son of the Elector Palatine, to embarrass the rulers of France and Spain by indiscriminate demonstrations on behalf of the Huguenots and the Dutch; but she had a more effective weapon to use, which had not failed her yet. Substantially, Anjou had revived Coligny's policy of 1572, to seize the Netherlands from Spain and bring them under the protection of France. To check him, Elizabeth for the last time put her virginity at

[1] Formerly the Duke of Alençon. He took the title of Anjou when his brother became King.

the service of England. It was a sorry comedy. She was twenty-one years older than Anjou; he was a feckless, ugly person, disfigured by the marks of smallpox and a swollen, bulbous nose; but in order to preserve her necessary control over French policy in the Netherlands, she had to convince the cynical, suspicious French that her intentions were serious. She had to gather the advantages of a wife, without allowing herself to be led to the altar. In 1580 Philip annexed the crown of Portugal, and the French alliance became still more precious to her; and as it became more precious, its possible results in the Netherlands were more dangerous. Elizabeth played her part with unfaltering skill. 'The Queen doth not attend to other matters,' wrote Mendoza, 'but only to be together with the Duke from morning to noon. . . . I cannot tell what a devil they do.' She played her part so well that even her ministers, who knew her best, began to believe that she might be serious. The common people publicly expressed their alarm. John Stubbs of Norfolk wrote of 'The Gaping Gulph into which England is like to fall by reason of this marriage, if the Lord forbid not the banns by letting her see the sin and punishment thereof'. The Queen would not stand criticism, and Stubbs was condemned to lose his hand; and as the executioner 'clapped the hissing hot iron on the raw stump, till it fizzed like a rasher of bacon, the fellow set up an eldritch screech', but with his other hand waved his hat in the air, crying 'God save the Queen, and confound all evil counsellors'. Elizabeth did not mean to marry Anjou, but she could not allow ill-informed criticism to imperil her delicate diplomacy; and it was diplomacy which triumphantly achieved its objects. Her influence over Anjou enabled her to counter the Catholic designs of the Guises, and to concentrate the energies of the French on resisting Philip in the Netherlands and the Azores. At the same time she was able to ensure that his rôle of protector of Belgian liberties did not conflict with English interests; his obligations as a suitor distracted him from his personal ambitions in the Netherlands. Thus, although the rebels awaited him 'not otherwise than the Hebrews awaited the coming of the Messiah', he bungled his mission in the Netherlands. The Dutch could not supply him with men or equipment, Henry III was too jealous, and too frightened of the Guises, to give official sanction to his expedition, and Parma's infantry was too strong for him. He lost heart, and diverted himself with sports, pastimes and wooing, while the Spaniards conquered valuable territory. Finally, in 1583, his exasperated troops broke loose in Antwerp, as the Spaniards had done seven years before, and he was obliged to withdraw in disgrace. In the following year he died.

3. *War with Spain*

In 1585 Elizabeth was forced into the open at last. Through long and anxious days she and her Treasurer Burghley, her devoted servant for forty years, had striven, against the angry protests of the Council, the seamen, the Huguenots, the Dutch, to avoid the wasteful horrors of war. So far they had succeeded: England was still safe and still at peace. Crisis had followed crisis, and for the Queen and her ministers they had been years of unceasing emergency; but among the people, often unaware of the dangers which distracted their rulers, the years of peace and orderly government had healed old wounds and borne confidence for the future. Elizabeth had put her faith in time, and her unheroic indecisions had their reward: the England which rose united to resist the Armada was not the divided, impoverished England of 1558.

Elizabeth was forced into war because the Duke of Anjou and William of Orange both died in 1584. The death of Anjou left the childless Henry III as the last survivor of the Valois line; and his heir, now that Anjou was dead, was the Huguenot Henry of Navarre, the head of the House of Bourbon. The country immediately plunged, therefore, into what might be known as the War of French Succession, and the fate of the Counter-Reformation depended on the result of it. While the

Queen-Mother despairingly plotted and entreated, and the last of the Valois, bedecked with rings and perfumes, surrendered himself to his *mignons*, France became the battlefield of Catholic and Spanish ambition. By the secret Treaty of Joinville Philip and the Guises pledged themselves to enforce the decrees of the Council of Trent, and to offer the throne to Navarre's uncle, the Cardinal of Bourbon, who had remained a Catholic. If the Catholic League succeeded in excluding Navarre from his crown, and the Cardinal were to sit on the throne as the puppet of Philip and the Guises, the resistance of the Netherlands would inevitably be broken ; and with the whole of the western coast of Europe in his hands, Philip would be able to launch a crushing attack on England.

Meanwhile, Parma was marching on his inexorable way, 'invading deeper and deeper into the land', and drawing nearer to Antwerp, which was his goal. At this critical hour the assassin's bullet deprived the rebels of their leader : in July, 1584, William the Silent was shot at Delft by a fanatic who wished to earn the reward which Philip had offered four years before. Dendermonde and Ghent fell to Parma in the autumn, and he was able to cut the communications between Antwerp and the cities of Brabant and Flanders ; if he defeated the rebels, he would be free to join the Catholic League in France. Elizabeth wrote furiously to Henry III, to wake him to the dangers which were closing upon him : 'For the love of God rouse yourself from this too long sleep.' But Henry would do nothing ; the time was past when Elizabeth could be saved by the efforts of others. Moreover, the Catholic coalition was again threatening Britain itself. Spanish troops had taken part in a papal attack on Ireland ; in Scotland, Esmé Stuart, an envoy of the Guises, had overthrown the Earl of Morton and won the young King's confidence ; and at home, Francis Throckmorton had confessed on the rack the details of a plot against the Queen organised by Philip and the Guises. The government took firm measures : many Catholics were arrested and imprisoned, and Mendoza, Philip's ambassador, was expelled from the country.

The Council drew up a voluntary Bond of Association to protect the Queen's life. Its signatories pledged themselves to prevent the succession of any person in whose interest a plot should be made against Elizabeth, and to pursue that person to the death. Early in 1585 Walsingham's spies unearthed another conspiracy to murder the Queen, and the Association was legalised by parliament. Thus did Protestant England try to protect itself from Mary.

In 1585 Elizabeth went to war. Her task was to stiffen the resistance in the Netherlands and France of the two Protestant minorities which still defied the Catholic alliance. Navarre appeared to be strong enough to hold his own, for he was supported by the powerful influence of the *Politiques*, who refused to see France dominated by the Hapsburgs. But in the Netherlands the rebels were desperate. The fall of Antwerp in August, 1585, finally stirred Elizabeth to action: before the end of the year the Earl of Leicester set out for the Netherlands with 6,000 infantry and 1,000 horse. Elizabeth was to hold Flushing, Brill and the fort of Rammekens as cautionary towns, until the Dutch had refunded the expenses of the expedition. The expedition was not a success. Leicester's pride irritated the Dutch, his extravagance infuriated his mistress. Further, he accepted the title of 'His Excellency the Governor and Captain-General of the United Provinces'. 'I am utterly at squares with this childish dealing', wrote Elizabeth; for she still wished to recognise Spanish sovereignty in the provinces, in the vain hope of negotiating a peace on the basis of the surrender of the cautionary towns. Her constant negotiations caused the Dutch to doubt her sincerity, and made Leicester's task impossible. However, the English force won a little renown by some isolated achievements. It took Axel and Doesburg, and in a heroic hour at Zutphen it checked the great Parma himself; and the moral effect of its presence in the Netherlands stimulated the rebels as much as a series of victories.

Meanwhile, Drake was showing Philip what English seamen could do. In May, 1585, Philip had unwisely given instructions that all enemy shipping lying in Spanish ports was to be seized; accordingly, some English corn ships were seized in Bilbao, and several hundred English sailors were imprisoned. Drake's voyage of reprisal was organised, in the usual way, by a joint-stock company, but it was in effect the first national enterprise launched by England against Spain. Setting out with thirty ships and 2,300 men, Drake began his work of destruction by sacking Vigo; then, in order to weaken the communications between Spain and her colonies, he sacked and burnt Santiago and the chief towns in the Cape Verde Islands; and in the Indies themselves he captured San Domingo and Cartagena, the two largest and strongest cities in the Spanish Main, and held them both to ransom. Although he failed to find the treasure-fleet, he sailed home in 1586 laden with glory and plunder. Drake's remarkable exploit filled Europe with amazement. At home and in her colonies Spain had been plundered and held to ransom, and she had been unable to stir in her defence; the moral damage done to her outweighed the plunder which Drake had seized, for the bankers refused her any further credit, and Philip could not equip his armies. Philip was as cautious as Elizabeth herself, and as slow to adopt the courses which necessity dictated; but he could not any longer postpone the day when he should gather his strength to strike a final and annihilating blow at England. England, it was now clear to him, was the rock against which the Counter-Reformation had so often hurled itself and fallen back. Until he had defeated England, he could not call himself master of the rebellious provinces in the Netherlands, whose resistance had been stiffened by English troops and English gold; and he could not be safe from the impious seamen who scorned his threats and drained the wealth by which his empire lived.

Before the Armada sailed, the long duel between Elizabeth and Mary Stuart ended in tragedy. Walsingham's spies and informers snared Mary to her doom. She was enticed into a conspiracy formed by Anthony Babington, a young courtier, to assassinate Elizabeth and welcome the Spaniards into England.

When all was ready, the conspirators were seized, and compelled by torture to confess their guilt. By the terms of the Bond of Association Mary's life was forfeit. A special commission tried her and unanimously found her guilty; Star Chamber and parliament confirmed its decision; it only remained for the Queen to order the sentence to be carried out. Elizabeth could not nerve herself to take the irrevocable step. When parliament pressed her for a decision, she bade them accept 'an answer-answerless', and asked them to find 'some other way'. But parliament wished for no other way, and at length Elizabeth signed the warrant and entrusted it to her secretary, Davison. In February, 1587, Mary died in the hall of Fotheringay Castle. Europe shrieked its horrified protests. If Mary had been quietly strangled in her prison, Elizabeth's fellow-sovereigns would have accepted her explanation that the disaster had been an accident; but when an anointed Queen was formally tried and brought to a traitor's block, the courts of Europe were obliged, in self-defence, to cry out against the unhallowed deed. Elizabeth stilled their protests by finding a scapegoat. Davison, she said, had acted without her instructions; he was fined, deprived of his office, and put in the Tower. It was ruthless, but necessary; Elizabeth could not afford at this time to have a quarrel with Scotland. Eighteen months later, when the Armada had come and gone, Davison was freed; his fine was remitted, and he received his secretary's emoluments until his death. In his way he had served the state, and he had his reward.

Mary's death made Philip's task more straightforward. The English Catholics could expect little from the Protestant James, and they were now likely, Philip believed, to welcome himself as a candidate for the English throne. He claimed it because Mary had formally bequeathed it to him, and because he was descended through both his parents from John of Gaunt. But the Armada did not sail in 1587. Drake set out on another of his semi-official expeditions, this time to prevent the concentration of the Spanish fleet, and to seize the gold which should finance it. Thousands of tons of shipping and huge stores of supplies were sunk in Cadiz harbour; Drake patrolled the Spanish coast, and not a ship dared to move. When he was confident that the Armada would not be able to leave in 1587, he sailed home, bringing with him the *San Felipe*, the largest of the Portuguese galleons.

Drake intended to be back again in 1588, to spread fresh terror and destruction among the Spanish navy. But the habit of years was too strong with Elizabeth; in the early part of the year she was again trying to delay the inevitable. She ordered Drake to stay at home, lest his raids should impede her negotiations with Parma. The Armada, sped on its way by the devoted prayers of a whole nation, put to sea at the end of May. His ablest admiral had just died, and Philip appointed as its commander the Duke of Medina Sidonia, a 'sweet, meek man', who knew nothing of the sea. 'I possess neither aptitude, ability, health, nor fortune for the expedition', he complained; but the proud Spanish nobles would not serve under anyone less august. The Armada's object was to make contact with Parma, and to land his infantry on the shores of England. If Parma's men had landed, they would have annihilated the inexpert levies to whom the Queen spoke such brave words at Tilbury. But the Armada never reached them. In nine days of fighting it was broken, and scattered in confusion before the Protestant winds; 53 ships out of 130 dragged themselves back to Spain. The English seamen were disappointed with the result of the battle. Thirty years of fighting had taught them that they could beat the Spaniards as they pleased. But Philip had assembled a more formidable armament than they had expected, and they had allowed nearly half of it to escape them. To the landsman, however, it seemed that only a miracle had saved him. In the words which they chose to commemorate their salvation, *Flavit Deus et dissipati sunt*, the English expressed their humble thanks to the Providence which had looked with favour on their religion.

The defeat of the Armada did not put England out of danger. Philip's direct attack had failed, but the ultimate success of his designs depended on his campaigns in France and the Netherlands. If Navarre and the Dutch were beaten, a new Armada would sail from Antwerp or Brittany, and eventually it must force a landing. Elizabeth, therefore, could not afford to relax her watchfulness: Spain must still be harassed overseas, and the Huguenots and the Dutch must still be assisted in their struggle with Parma. But Elizabeth and Burghley did not allow the defeat of the Armada to turn their heads: they would not, as the seamen and the younger generation of courtiers demanded, take the initiative in a flamboyant war of conquest against the Spanish Empire. They put their trust in the defensive policy which had served them in the past, and they knew their business better than the restless adventurers who criticised their half-measures and hesitations. For the government had neither the men nor the money to fight on the grand scale which commended itself to the eager spirit of Sir Walter Raleigh. Tudor England had no regular army; its expeditions were recruited from the gaols and from the compulsory enlistment of labourers and vagabonds. Further, the Crown had to live on a much smaller income than the Kings of France and Spain. Until 1588, Elizabeth's revenue from all sources averaged about £250,000 a year; in the last fifteen years of her reign parliament made more liberal grants, and the revenue from the customs rose as trade expanded, but her income was still under half a million. Out of this she had to meet the expenses of administration, pay her servants, maintain the traditional splendour of her court, bribe her Protestant allies—and fight her wars. Her poverty explains the hesitations of her policy. It is beside the point to call her mean; she refused to undertake wars which she could not afford to fight to the end, and this was common sense. Her thrift served her well: in the years of crisis her credit was better than Philip's, who owned the wealth of the Indies.

In 1589, therefore, Elizabeth resumed her policy of casual and intermittent intervention, in the hope that the situation would eventually right itself, as it had so often done before. She sent an army to France in 1589, and another in 1591 which remained there for four years. Its object was to guard the French coast, so as to keep the vital ports out of the hands of the Spaniards; thus it gave little actual help to Navarre, and earned no place in his gratitude. Meanwhile, Navarre's powers of leadership were guiding him out of his difficulties. He won two great victories over the League, at Arques and Ivry; the Cardinal of Bourbon died in 1590, and the Catholics could offer no better claimant than Philip himself, or his children by Elizabeth of Valois; finally, in 1593, Navarre won the moderate Catholics to his side by cynically adopting their religion. The armies of the League melted away, and the French, weary of a generation of civil war, accepted Henry as their King. France's war with Spain ended too. In 1598, the year in which Philip died, Spain made the Treaty of Vervins with Henry, who did not hesitate to abandon his Protestant allies for the sake of the peace which his people sorely needed. But his withdrawal, although it caused Elizabeth to exclaim against his ingratitude, did not imperil the Protestant cause. For the Dutch also had virtually won their independence from Spain. In the anxious years after the Armada Elizabeth maintained a small army in the Netherlands, under Sir Francis Vere, from which she withdrew soldiers for the French wars as the rebels' cause steadily improved. Philip weakened Parma's control by twice requiring him to take his forces to the aid of the Catholic League in France; and in 1592 Parma died, weary of the long struggle which he had so often brought to the verge of victory. At the same time, the Dutch found a soldier of their own, in Maurice of Nassau, son of William the Silent. The tide of war turned in their favour, and early in 1597 Maurice won a crushing victory at Turnhout, which finally set the Dutch Republic on its feet. The war lingered on until 1604, but Spain's authority in the seven Northern provinces was at an end.

With little concrete help from England, Philip's ambitions in France and Holland had been successfully obstructed; but the war on the sea, from which so much was hoped, brought disaster and disillusion. Although naval exploits against Spain were financed by joint-stock companies, and were expected to reward investors for their outlay, the government was discouraged by the failure of Drake's attempt in 1589 to place the pretender Don Antonio on the throne of Portugal. Henceforth, the equipment of naval expeditions was once more left to individual enterprise. But the Spaniards had learned several lessons from their conquerors: they began to fortify their harbours, to protect their communications, and to build ships which were better suited for long voyages and Atlantic fighting. The defeat of the Armada was the beginning, rather than the end, of Spanish sea-power; whereas the English, over-confident because of their easy successes in the past, equipped their expeditions carelessly, and were more anxious to lay their hands on plunder than to paralyse Spain by occupying the vital points on her trade-routes. The English had their triumphs, notably Essex's raid on Cadiz in 1596, which obliged Philip to repudiate his debts; but the Spanish treasure-fleet was now so well guarded, and the cities of the Caribbean were so much more strongly defended, that several of the expeditions of the 1590s barely paid their expenses. Moreover, the Spaniards were now growing bold enough to retaliate. In 1595 four of their ships landed on the coast of Cornwall; in each of the two following years Philip prepared an Armada which was broken by storms rather than by the efforts of the English, and in 1601 the Spaniards landed a force in rebellious Ireland. Thus neither side was able to strike a decisive blow; and although the pirates of both countries continued their private warfare in many waters, their governments gradually abandoned the hope of forcing their enemies into submission. Philip's last advice to his son was to make peace with England; and in 1604 James I, whose spirit was not adventurous, brought the useless war to an end.

CHAPTER IX

CATHOLIC AND PURITAN

The Counter-Reformation. The policy of the government. Rise and aims of Puritanism. Repression of the Puritans. Hooker and the Church of England.

1. *The Counter-Reformation*

In 1570, weary of delay and the hesitations of its secular allies, the Papacy pronounced 'the Sentence Declaratory against Elizabeth, the pretended Queen of England, and those heretics adhering to her'; whereby she, and all who shared her impieties, 'incurred the Sentence of Anathema, and are cut off from the unity of the Body of Christ'. The blow had been certain to fall. At the Council of Trent the Catholic Church had set its house in order: it had purged itself of the abuses which had degraded its honour, but it had refused to compromise with the plausible doctrines of heretics. Now, with the Inquisition to punish its enemies, and the militant order of Jesuits to carry its message among unbelievers, it had launched its great attack against those nations which resisted its dominion.

The Bull of excommunication seriously threatened the safety of Elizabeth's government. Just as her religious settlement, as a part of her wise and thrifty administration, was beginning to take root among a people weary of religious differences, the Bull released her Catholic subjects from their political allegiance. Until 1570 there was peace in England; except when the situation was critical, the Catholics were not molested. But to the conscientious Catholic, the excommunication of his Queen was an ultimatum: it ordered him, in the name of his religion, to rebel. Although the Bull did not arrive until the rising of the Northern Earls had been defeated, it was a threat which the government could not ignore; Ridolfi's conspiracy showed at once that the allies of Mary and Philip were eager to respond to the lead which Rome had given them. Bishop Jewel voiced the patriot's protest against the Pope who acted 'as if the coasts and ends of the earth were in his hands, or as if no prince in the world might rule without his sufferance'; and parliament met in 1571 to support with strenuous enthusiasm the government's measures to protect the safety of the state. It was declared to be high treason to affirm that Elizabeth was not, or ought not to be, Queen; or that she was a heretic, schismatic, or usurper. The Act emphasised that the Pope's bid to recover the English Catholics was an attempt to destroy their natural allegiance, to create sedition, and to plot the overthrow of the realm. Thus, in the cause of the sovereignty of the secular state, it placed the designs of the Pope on a footing with the intrigues of de Spes and other agents of King Philip; and it laid on the English Catholics the intolerable burden of reconciling the claims of a spiritual master whose sway recognised no boundaries, with those of a sovereign who interpreted as treason their obedience to any authority beyond her shores.

Catholic resistance to the government was stimulated by missionary effort from overseas. In 1568 William Allen, himself a refugee from England, set up at Douai a college for the education of Englishmen who had fled abroad rather than accept the Anglican settlement of 1559. The piety and enthusiasm of these refugees persuaded Allen that he might be able to launch from Douai a mission to revive the Catholic faith in England. Young men of respectable family, between the ages of fourteen and twenty-five, were trained to dedicate their lives to the noble purpose of recovering their fatherland from the grip of heresy. On entering the college, the novice vowed that in God's good time he would 'return to England for the salvation of souls'. For seven years he submitted himself to a stern discipline of mind and body, to fit him to endure the dangers of his task; and to fix his mind on that sacrifice which might be the crowning glory of his life, the walls of his cell were hung with pictures of the torture-chamber and the scaffold. The seminary priests began their work in England in 1574. Contemptuous of intrigue or political objects, they devoted their lives to the conversion of souls; and the ruthless treatment they received from the government, which professed to regard them as the spies and emissaries of Spain, only strengthened the courage with which they trod the path that led to Tyburn. Persecution seemed to give a stimulus to their dangerous calling. Students flocked to Douai, and to similar colleges which were founded at Rome, Valladolid and Seville, and trained themselves to take the places of their brethren whose lives were claimed by the government.

The same lofty motives inspired the Jesuit mission, which descended on England in the summer of 1580. Its leader, Edmund Campion, was among the greatest of the Elizabethans. 'We are dead men to the world,' he exclaimed on the scaffold; 'we travelled only for souls.' The Jesuits were forbidden to speak against the Queen, to lend themselves to conspiracy, or to correspond with Rome on political subjects: their mission was to 'cry alarm spiritual against foul vice and proud ignorance'. But they, like the seminary priests from Douai, were compromised in the eyes of Englishmen by the plotting of men less noble than themselves. The government was unable, even it had been willing, to distinguish between Catholics who conspired against the state, and those who dedicated themselves to the conversion of men's souls. In particular, the aims of the Jesuits were prejudiced by the indiscretion of Pope Gregory XIII. Gregory was a sincere and vigorous fighter, but his methods were inconsistent; he lowered himself to criminal undertakings which degraded his cause and frustrated the work of those who served him. At the same time as he launched the Jesuit mission on England, he confounded its success by patronising an ill-conceived Spanish attack on Ireland; and he contradicted its professed motives by assuring the English Catholics that political assassination was not a sin, and promising a plenary indulgence to any who should undertake ' so glorious a work ' as the murder of ' that guilty woman of England '. Unfortunately, many of his followers were too ready to avail themselves of the unscrupulous weapons which he placed in their hands. Robert Parsons, Campion's associate in the Jesuit mission, was a man of action; his adventurous mind was eager for quicker and more substantial results than patient conversion could achieve. Thus he tired of the restraints which the nature of his mission imposed on him, and, after he had been driven in flight from England, he was the backbone of every plot which Elizabeth's enemies developed to rob her of her throne. Men like Parsons, who followed too closely the instructions of their master, soiled the cause which Campion and the seminary priests had ennobled. They cast aside the moral weapon, the only one which the best Catholics would use, and sank to violence and conspiracy. As a result of their efforts, the cause of Catholicism was for more than a hundred years identified with intrigue and assassination.

In the campaign of repression with which the government sought to protect the Queen and her people, the innocent inevitably suffered with the guilty. Catholics who had lived in peace for twenty years were forced, after 1581, to pay the enormous fine of £20 a month if they stayed away from church, and 100 marks if they attended Mass; and if they could not pay their fines, the Crown was empowered to ' seize and enjoy ' two-thirds of their estates. It was treason to seek to break down the allegiance of the Queen's subjects; and an act in 1585 attempted finally to clear the country of missionaries, by ordering all ' jesuits, seminary priests, and other priests ' to leave England within forty days, on pain of death for high treason. In these measures the modern state came to grips with the mediaeval Church; and in an age when men had not learned to make a convenient separation between politics and religion, neither side would admit or desire a compromise. The Counter-Reformation jeopardised not merely the Anglican settlement, but the safety and independence of Tudor England. The government, therefore, could argue with justice that the conflict was political; and that the men who suffered at its hands did so, not because they upheld the doctrines of Rome, but because they were guilty of treason and sedition. The victims, on the other hand, believed that they were dying the death of martyrs ; and in this conflict of principle lay the tragic futility of their sacrifice. He who was loyal to the state had to accept the Anglican settlement ; and he who was loyal to Rome had to accept the Bull which declared Elizabeth to be a deposed heretic. Both sides adopted means which degraded the principles for which they fought. Many of the Catholics became little better than common conspirators ; and the servants of the government acknowledged no scruple in their efforts to rid the country of their enemies. Judges and juries were biased, and convictions were based on the evidence of spies and informers ; torture was used to extract from suspects, not only a confession of their crimes, but the opinions which they held on such matters as the Pope's power to excommunicate the Queen. In these proceedings the tribunals of the state availed themselves of the practices which they condemned in the Spanish Inquisition. It may be argued, however, that such practices were the only safeguard against men who used political assassination as a normal and legitimate weapon ; and, to the credit of Elizabeth's government, it never shed blood if a less drastic penalty could be found. Fewer than two hundred Catholics actually died on the scaffold during twenty years of repression ; as far as possible, the state was content to fine, imprison or banish those who challenged its authority.

2. *The growth of Puritanism*

In the hour of crisis the English Catholics set their country before their religion, and flocked to join the bands of levies which mustered in 1588 to resist the Spanish invasion. The internal problems which harassed the government at that anxious time were provoked by dissidents within the Anglican Church itself. From the first, the settlement of 1559 had failed to satisfy those more ardent Protestants who wished to breathe into the national

Church a purer and more vigorcus spirit than that of a state-controlled institution. The settlement was Laodicean. It was loose and accommodating, and it was careful to avoid all pretence to infallibility; as such, it served the purpose for which it had been framed. But it could not aspire to gratify the spiritual thirst of those who, in the time of Edward VI, had tasted the bitter waters of Geneva. As soon as Mary Tudor was dead, the voices of Calvinist preachers were again raised in the pulpits; the influx of refugees from France and the Netherlands quickened the movement which they had begun; and within a few years of Elizabeth's accession, a growing and vocal party had arisen in the Church to criticise the settlement which she had made, the secular spirit in which it had been drawn up, and the evil which it was doing to the spiritual life of the nation.

The Anglican Church founded its position on a claim to historical continuity. It argued that in the fourth and fifth centuries, before it ruled over all Christendom, the Church of Rome had been a true Church; and that the Reformation, having purged it of the mediaeval errors and superstitions with which it was encumbered, had restored the one true and Catholic Church to its primitive vigour and purity. These contentions did not satisfy the extremists. They wished to carry the Reformation to its logical end; on the ground that it was incomplete until it had been freed of the Roman hierarchy and ceremonial. The Church should be ordered according to the word of God, as revealed in the scriptures and in Christ's message to His apostles. From their desire to purify the English Church of the abuses which still darkened it, these zealots won the name of Puritans. They began their campaign by attacking the ancient offences of pluralism and simony, of which the clergy were still flagrantly guilty; and by seeking to strip the services of the rites and ceremonies which they chose to regard as the 'dregs of Popery'. As early as 1559 they disputed the royal Injunctions which prescribed certain vestments for the use of the clergy. To wear a surplice was to put on the 'livery of

Antichrist'; and their consciences were similarly outraged by the use of organs in churches, the ring in marriage, the sign of the cross at baptism, kneeling at communion, and all such outward symbols of inward grace. 'The service of God', they complained, 'is grievously abused by piping with organs; singing, ringing, and trowling of psalms from one side to another; with the squeaking of chanting choristers, disguised . . . in white surplices . . . imitating the fashion and manner of Antichrist the Pope . . . with his other rabble of miscreants and chantings.' The churching of women was an obnoxious practice 'which smelleth of the Jewish purification'. The resistance to all kinds of formalism was so powerful that a petition to Convocation in 1563, to do away with 'the rags of Rome', was defeated by only a single proxy vote. But for the wishes of the Queen herself, who clung to her crosses and candles, and for the need to preserve the unity of the Church against the Counter-Reformation, the Elizabethan settlement would have been modified in its early years. For the reforming movement was strongly supported by the clergy themselves. As only one of the Bishops had been able to accommodate his conscience to the new régime, Elizabeth had been obliged to appoint a new hierarchy; and of necessity she had chosen her Bishops from that party in the Church which was out of sympathy with the policy of Mary.[1] Many of these Bishops, therefore, looked with favour on the Puritan claims, and found much in the Church that was 'barely tolerable'. 'The only thing left to our choice', said the Bishop of Durham, 'is whether we will bear these things or break the peace of the Church.' But the government would make no concession to Puritan scruples, and in 1566 Archbishop Parker issued the *Book of Advertisements*, to insist on uniformity in public worship. When forty London clergy refused to obey, and were suspended and deprived, the Puritans had made the first split in the English Church.

The quarrel over vestments, which even the Puritans admitted to be 'things indifferent', soon deepened into something more

[1] Many of them had been in exile during Mary's reign.

serious: an attack on the very organisation of the Church. The peculiar contribution of Cambridge to the history of Great Britain is that the cry for 'parity' was first heard within its walls.[1] Dr. Thomas Cartwright, a Fellow of Trinity College, gave a new impetus to the Puritan movement, by asserting that the Church of England, no less than the Church of Rome, was in conflict with the spirit and organisation of primitive Christianity. He was the first Puritan to derive the discipline and administration of the Church, as well as its doctrine, from the word of the scriptures. Bishops, he said, should relinquish their administrative authority, and devote themselves to their apostolic functions of preaching and teaching; and all the ministers of the Church should be elected by the congregations. The dispute over ceremonies fell into the background, for Cartwright had robbed the Anglican Church of the appeal to historical precedent on which it had founded its doctrine and organisation. The Puritans eagerly took up the cry for 'parity': 'Bishops must be unlorded. All ministers must be equal.'

The demand for parity, or equality, shook the fabric of Tudor government; for if there were a parity in the Church, men would soon be wanting a parity in the state. The King of France had already found Calvinism to be 'the religion of insurrection'; and Elizabeth agreed that Calvinists were 'criminals, whose desire it is to destroy allegiance to princes'. A creed so 'dangerous to kingly rule' could not be tolerated, and the Queen resolved to use all the majesty and resources of the state to close the widening schism in the Protestant ranks. But she was to find the Puritans tough opponents. Their movement was aggressive, for they were determined to force the national Church to take notice of their opinions; and they were as intolerant as the government itself of the opinions of other people. Further, they had powerful support in high places: not only in parliament, but at court and in the Council itself. Leicester was a patron

[1] Most of the Puritan leaders were Cambridge men: Travers, Browne, Barrow, Walsingham, Greenwood, Penry, Udall. So were many of the Bishops with Calvinist leanings: Pilkington, Young, Cox, Horne, Sandys, Grindal.

of Cartwright ; Burghley appointed Walter Travers, Cartwright's collaborator, to be tutor of his children ; Walsingham, Knollys, and Sir Walter Mildmay, Chancellor of the Exchequer, inspired parliamentary efforts to modify the Prayer Book. The Puritans carried the quarrel to parliament in 1571, arguing that, since the Crown was deaf to all persuasion, parliament had the power to alter the settlement which it had itself helped to make. A bill to reform the Prayer Book was introduced into the Commons by Walter Strickland, ' a grave and ancient man of great zeal ' ; and in the Protestant enthusiasm which the papal Bull had provoked, many spoke eloquently in its favour. The Prayer Book was denounced as ' an unperfect book, culled and picked out of that Popish dunghill, the Mass-book, full of abominations '. The uncompromising temper of the Puritans was expressed by Peter Wentworth, who was a relative of Walsingham. When Parker asked them to bow to the authority of the Bishops and the Council, Wentworth bluntly replied : ' We will pass nothing before we understand what it is, for that were but to make you Popes. Make you Popes who list . . . we will make you none.' Elizabeth was obliged to take drastic measures. In 1572 she forbade parliament to debate any bills touching religion, unless they had first been ' considered and liked by the clergy '. There followed a serious conflict over the rights and privileges of the members. The Queen carried the day, but the struggle was so bitter that henceforth she was reluctant to face parliament. In 1574 Cartwright was forced to leave the country, but not before he had issued a translation of Travers's *Ecclesiasticae Disciplinae Explicatio*, which became the classical exposition of Protestant nonconformity.

As soon as it had muzzled the opposition in parliament, the government had to meet a fresh outbreak of Puritan activity. The clergy of many dioceses took to holding ' Prophesyings '. The first of these meetings was held at Northampton in 1573 ; they were regular meetings, to which laymen were sometimes admitted, to study the scriptures and improve morality and discipline. Archbishop Grindal, who was Parker's successor at

Canterbury, approved of these exercises, because they stimulated the zeal, intelligence and learning of the clergy. He disliked the admission of laymen, who might be too ignorant to understand what was being said, and be filled with rebellious and schismatic thoughts ; but he wished the Prophesyings to continue, in the hope that Puritan zeal and morality might fortify the Church with a much-needed discipline. The Queen, however, regarded them as a veiled defiance of the royal prerogative, and she was afraid to permit a free discussion of religious matters. She ordered Grindal to suppress the Prophesyings ; and when he refused, she suspended him from the performance of his duties. On his death, in 1583, she appointed an Archbishop of whose integrity she could be certain. As Master of Trinity, John Whitgift had defended his University against Cartwright, and, as Archbishop, he was ready to protect the state from the evil doctrines which Cartwright had spread. The question, to his mind, as to the Queen's, was not whether the Puritans were right, but whether it stood ' with godly and Christian wisdom ' to attempt to reconstruct the national Church in the hour of danger. He brought into action the full coercive power of the state to force the Puritans to submit to the Queen's doctrines of expediency. The Six Articles of 1583 compelled the clergy to acknowledge the ecclesiastical supremacy of the Crown, and to admit that the Prayer Book and the Thirty-Nine Articles contained nothing contrary to the word of God. Two hundred clergy refused to accept the Articles, and were suspended. The Church of England had taken its stand on infallibility, and Whitgift was determined to enforce its decrees : in the Court of High Commission, which after 1583 became a regular part of the machinery of ecclesiastical administration, he called to his aid the resources of the prerogative. The proceedings of the court were swift and secret, and it was not hampered by the formalities of the common law ; it savoured, as Burghley objected, of the Roman Inquisition. But, with parliament and the magistrates strongly Puritan in sympathy, the Crown had to choose its own weapons in the struggle against the spread of Puritanism.

Whitgift's policy persuaded some Puritans that, since they could not reform the national Church, their only remedy was to break away from it. A separatist movement gathered momentum in the Eastern counties, under the leadership of Henry Barrow and Robert Browne. They held that the only basis of a Christian Church was the free congregation, and that the close connection between Church and state, which was upheld by orthodox Presbyterians, as well as by Anglicans, had no warrant in the word of God. Having no patience with the royal supremacy, these Congregationalists, or Independent Puritans, determined to achieve their desired reformation in their own way, and by their own efforts. They inspired the seven anonymous Martin Marprelate Tracts, whose appearance in 1588–9 embarrassed the government by their ribald attacks on the Bishops and the organisation of the Established Church. 'Anti-Martinists' joined issue in a battle of pamphlets, but until the government detected the secret press and punished the supposed offenders, the scurrilous jocularity of the contest undermined men's traditional reverence for the Bishops and the ecclesiastical order. The government made a final attempt to crush the Puritans. The Presbyterian leaders were imprisoned; Udall, the supposed author of the Tracts, died in prison; and three leaders of the separatist movement were executed for sedition. A Conventicle Act was passed in 1593, which punished with exile, and even death, those who refused to go to church, or attended unauthorised conventicles. This ruthlessness, coupled with a general reaction against the obvious political dangers of the democratic system of the Independents, temporarily broke the back of the Puritan resistance. But the Puritans were not crushed. If the scriptures were the authentic word of God, they must point the way to a truer order of ecclesiastical discipline than any settlement fashioned by men. No action of the government could convince the Puritans that they were wrong. They remained fundamentally irreconcilable; and if Elizabeth would yield them nothing, a Prince who had been reared in the bleak piety of Presbyterian Scotland might prove to be more generous.

Elizabeth's victory over the Puritans cost her dear. Her dealings with them, as with all her enemies, were opportunist; in defending her religious settlement, which was founded on expediency, she made no attempt to understand the motives of those who rejected it. The demand for a 'preaching' ministry voiced one of the strongest psychological needs of the age; and if Elizabeth had allowed the Prophesying movement to develop the capacity and intelligence of the clergy, the Church might have retained the loyalty of those whom Whitgift chose to oppress. But she saw only the political dangers of Presbyterianism and Independency; of their emotional background she took no account. Thus she sought to protect herself by a policy of repression which ultimately narrowed the basis of the nation's respect for the monarchy. Her repression stimulated nonconformity, rather than crushed it; and, what was more serious, she lost the goodwill of parliament. For the Puritans, like the Catholics, were torn between conscience and their duty to the state. In the last instance, men who ordered their lives on the principle of undeviating obedience to the word of God reluctantly found themselves obliged to defy their earthly sovereign. As Tristram Pistor reminded the Commons, 'This cause is God's. The rest are all but terrene; yea, trifles in comparison. . . . "Seek ye first the Kingdom of God and all things shall be added unto you."'

Elizabeth miscalculated if she thought to break men of this temper by secular compulsion. Many of her subjects believed that their Queen was in error; that, as a preacher told her to her face, she was 'an untamed heifer, that would not be ruled by God's people, but obstructed His discipline'. Her obstinacy discredited her office in their sight. Moreover, she broke off her father's alliance with parliament against the Church, and joined the Crown with the Church in obstructing parliament's desire to have the Prayer Book altered. This policy was fatal to the Crown. For the Puritans, finding that the path of religious reform by means of parliament was blocked by the prerogative's championship of the Church, were forced to concentrate their attack on the prerogative itself. The creed of the triumphant in God became the creed of an oppressed nation. From the propaganda organised by the Puritans, the men who were to resist the Crown in the next reign learned the technique of effective parliamentary action. Further, the unpopularity of High Commission threw the common lawyers into opposition by the side of religious malcontents and frustrated parliamentarians. Before James came to the throne, Elizabeth had attached the Crown to an out-of-date religious settlement, and committed it to the policy of 'No Bishop, no King'. The Church and the prerogative were branded as enemies to the individual conscience and the common law.

The discontent of the Puritans threw a shadow over the closing years of the century. The nation was disappointed by the failure of the naval enterprises against Spain; a host of demobilised soldiers and sailors reawakened the old fear of vagabonds; a serious rebellion in Ireland caused the government much anxiety, and drove home the lesson of the Spanish war by emphasising the essential weakness of the Elizabethan state. The Earl of Essex, the Queen's favourite, put himself at the head of a band of discontented courtiers, and tried to raise the City against her 'evil counsellors'. Finally, the Crown's authority was assailed in parliament itself. In 1597 there were outspoken criticisms of the monopolies with which the Queen rewarded her favoured servants, and in 1601 the protests could no longer be ignored. The aged Queen made the last of her great gestures to her people, and in a moving scene promised to mend her ways. For some years it had been clear that James VI of Scotland was the only successor to the throne whom the English ruling classes would be willing to accept; and it was a restless and dissatisfied nation which prepared to greet him in 1603.

3. *The effects of Puritanism*

The core of the Puritan's creed was his assurance of salvation. Since the tragedy in the Garden of Eden, sinful man had been doomed to destruction ; but God had been persuaded by the sacrifice of His Son, who took upon His shoulders the burden of human sin, to reprieve some of His erring creatures and take them into the Kingdom of Heaven. These elect of God, who were born in His grace, could not lose it ; as surely as those who were born without it could not receive it. The Puritan was of the elect, and he sought by piety and good works to prove his fitness for his exalted calling ; but, although his creed strengthened and purified the moral life of the nation, much was lost when Puritanism laid its grip upon the land.

In the first place, a faith which was based upon the word of God necessarily issued in confusion. Without a Church to guide him by the accumulated wisdom of past centuries, each man must interpret the scriptures in his own way. The only logical deduction from this principle was to admit complete freedom of conscience ; but only the Independents, of all the Puritan sects, were consistent enough to champion toleration. The others struggled to establish in England a system as rigid and exclusive as Anglicanism. Secondly, Puritanism was not a religion of love. For all his professed attachment to the word of God, the Puritan drew his inspiration rather from the conceptions of Paul than from the teachings of Christ. Christ was important to him as part of the machinery by which he was saved, and for having added to the penalties of Hebraic Christianity the terror of eternal punishment ; with that gospel of love which was the central message of the New Testament, he saw no need to concern himself, for it had no bearing on the all-important matter of salvation. His business was to be good, not to be charitable. Belief in a personal God injures a community's moral life when that God is, like Jupiter, compound of human weakness, or, like Jehovah, a fiat-flinging lord of wrath ; but Puritanism showed the dangers of belief in a transcendental God whose standards were unattainable by fallible mankind. Since only grace availed to save a man, and the elect were destined to be saved from the hour of their birth, a good life in this world was not necessarily to be rewarded in the next. Mammon, on the other hand, was a master whose rewards were tangible and sure ; and one of the worst results of Puritan thinking was the stern pursuit, unsoftened by Christian compassion, of the prizes of material endeavour.

Finally, the Puritan thought ill of mankind. For it was the essence of Calvinist doctrine that man was born in sin and born to damnation. In the words of Calvin himself, he was *ordure*, filth ; his earthly doings were like the scrambling of rats in the straw ; there was no good in him, except where God had planted it in the memory of His Son. As Calvin's faithful preachers carried his message to the world, men's souls grew heavy with the sense of guilt. As it was written in the Book of Proverbs, 'I know that in me, that is, in my flesh, dwelleth no good thing'. The chill of self-contempt numbed even Shakespeare's spirit : his later plays are haunted by an almost neurotic hatred of man's natural instincts. If 'Merrie England' ever existed outside a sentimental cult, the Puritans destroyed it. They denounced the maypoles and the dances of the countryside ; their attack on music and the theatre and dress drained life of colour ; ultimately, they were hostile to culture. Their deep sense of man's unworthiness taught them that all recreation was sensual indulgence. Bunyan revealed that as a child of ten he could not cast off the burden of sin ; and the sins which weighed him down were his love of hockey and dancing on the village green, and his passion for bell-ringing.

Puritanism, then, has much to answer for. Its adherents were materialist, harsh and unloving ; they did not always apply logically their acceptance of the word of God ; their consciousness of sin blighted the healthy development of the mind. But there has never existed so powerful an instrument for arousing and changing the spirit of a nation. The official Church was Laodicean, the government took refuge in unadventurous expediency ; the English Reformation had not borne its Luther. So far, the English Reformation had been the work of the rulers ; in Puritanism the people wrought their own Reformation, and ultimately forced their rulers to accept it, and stamped it for ever on the English character. In the study of the Bible, which the invention of printing had brought to every home, each man found his own faith and his own Church. The vandalism of Henry VIII stimulated this private study, by diffusing the monastic spirit among the nation ; the matchless harmonies of the Authorised Version were soon to enrich it. No secular compromise could stand in the way of the passions which it stirred.

There was much in the spirit of Elizabethan England which needed to be changed. For all their brilliance, their abundant versatility, their thirst for knowledge and adventure, the Elizabethans were adolescent and immature ; they travelled widely over life's surface, but they did not probe its depths. The difference between Shakespeare and Milton, or between Jonson and Bunyan, is the gulf which divided an England exuberant with the culture of the Renaissance from an England made Puritan. For even Shakespeare was limited by his age. His heroes were not cast in the mould of Greek tragedy ; he created no saints and no fanatics, no characters who dedicated their lives to the service of a faith or an ideal. His bad men were stagey Renaissance villains : Iago, Edmund, Iachimo, who learned their wickedness from the pages of Machiavelli. His heroes might touch the depths of suffering, but they never rose to the heights of human conduct. The splendour of Shakespearean tragedy lies in their weakness, not in their strength ; they were the sport, not of the gods, but of men and themselves.

There was point, too, in the Puritan criticisms of dress and fashion. Just as they luxuriated in euphuistic prose, and allowed Shakespeare and Bacon to spend their strength in literary conceits, so the Elizabethans lavished their energy on gaiety and amusement. Every year travellers brought word of some new fashion from abroad, and English society became the mirror of foreign influences ; people endured the discomfort of ruffs, and farthingales, and tight breeches in which it was impossible to stoop, for no better reason than that fashion was an exacting mistress. The Elizabethans lacked discrimination and refinement. They had the vices—extravagance, ostentation, an uncritical love of novelty —of people who have not really grown up. In these weaknesses Puritanism was a tonic to the English mind. The Puritan was grave, sober and reflective ; he thought of the morrow, beyond the pleasures of to-day. It was not just a coincidence that the Puritans taught the English to build an empire. The Elizabethans, impulsive, eager for quick results, were bad colonisers ; if a settlement did not yield gold and immediate profits, they abandoned it. It was the Puritan refugees who showed that a colony could grow rich by the patient labour of those who dwelt in it.

The final service of Puritanism was to provoke the defenders of the national Church to take account of their position. In 1594 appeared the first volumes of Richard Hooker's *Laws of Ecclesiastical Polity* : a last plea for unity, a last noble assertion of the mediaeval doctrine that Church and state are one. The scriptures, said Hooker, served the purpose of revealing the divine way of salvation, which could not be apparent to reason alone. But where the scriptures were silent, the Church had the power, like any other society, to make laws for its well-being, and to ordain what form of polity it pleased, provided it did not violate the spirit of God's word. 'In these things whereof the Scriptures appointeth no certainty, the use of the people of God or the ordinances of our fathers must serve for a law.' He appealed to the Puritans to revere tradition, 'the wisdom which is learned by tract of time', to restrain their zeal for an imagined perfection before it disrupted the peace and order of the Church ; for 'to bear a tolerable sore is better than to venture on so dangerous a remedy'. The way to tranquillity was by stability. The Puritans were deaf to Hooker's message of peace ; but his plea for reason and tradition, which found an answer in the sweetness of George Herbert's life at Bemerton, gave a philosophy and a dignity to the Church in whose defence Charles Stuart was to lay down his life.

CHAPTER X

THE INHERITANCE OF JAMES I

Character and policy of James. His theory of the Divine Right of Kings. History and importance of the theory. The difficulties of James's inheritance : finance ; temper of parliament ; religion ; foreign policy.

1. *The character of James*

No King of England has ever come to the throne with more confidence than James I in his fitness to occupy it. In Scotland, which was notoriously difficult to govern, he had boldly asserted his authority. Most of the Regents who had ruled during his minority had died violent deaths ; and James had himself been threatened by the intrigues of the Catholic faction, who wished to put Mary back on her throne and restore the ancient faith. But by skilfully playing off his enemies against each other, he had managed to make the influence of the Crown very real : the grasping and anti-social nobility had been obliged to bow to the authority of the Privy Council, and the Calvinist clergy to suffer the unwelcome tutelage of the bishops.

James was encouraged by his success in practical statesmanship to generalise his experience in a handbook on monarchy. His *Basilicon Doron*, which he wrote for the instruction of his son Henry, laid down high principles for the conduct of Kings towards God and men. James advised his son on the food he should eat, the clothes he should wear, the counsellors he should choose to guide him ; and added a timely warning on the responsibilities of kingship : ' the highest bench is sliddriest to sit upon '. But James did not feel that Scotland was worthy of his talents. He longed to display his kingcraft before a larger audience. The whole of Europe should be his chessboard, and he would move the pawns at his pleasure; the princes and statesmen of many lands should gather at the court of Solomon and seek his judgment. He was impatient for Elizabeth to die, and grumbled that she would 'continue as long as sun and moon'. For England would be worthy of him, and he of England. In this prosperous land, whose streets were paved with golden promise, the stage was set for Solomon to make his entrance. England was a fine place, and all the better for having James of Scotland as her King.

In May, 1603, the new King entered London. His subjects gathered curiously in the streets to see him. Accustomed to the regal ways of Elizabeth, they found his appearance unkingly. Nature had been ungenerous to James: his head was too large for his body, and his tongue was too large for his head; wide, goggling eyes stared loosely at men until the vacant scrutiny embarrassed them; rickety legs scarcely supported the clumsy body, and James had to lean on the shoulders of those who walked at his side. Rizzio had been murdered before his mother's eyes, and James was born with an incurable horror of cold steel. Even to perform the traditional ceremony of knighthood made him tremble. Scottish assassination plots had driven him to strange and undignified precautions: he slept behind a thick mattress, and wore padded clothes, 'his breeches in great pleats and full stuffed'. He was hot-tempered and emotional; his interest was quickly engaged, but he was incapable of persistence or steadiness of purpose. Above all, he was vain. He liked to be admired, and as a King he could insist upon it. 'Let me never apprehend that ye disdain my form and undervalue my quality', was his warning to Somerset, and Somerset was rash to ignore it.

This was not the equipment of Solomon. James had many good qualities, but they could not balance his fatal want of dignity. The contrast between him and Elizabeth told heavily against him. Elizabeth had been aloof and terrible. When the Commons approached her with a grievance, the fear of her displeasure outweighed their sense of injustice. Even when she was shamelessly flirting with Leicester or Anjou, or filling the air with masculine curses, she was still dignified ; the Tudors were majestic even in their follies. But James had no majesty in his person. He appeared too often among his people, engaged too readily in controversy with them, was too easily excited ; and excitement emphasised his impediment, so that his Scots speech grew blurred and inarticulate. When Elizabeth addressed her subjects, she spoke in stirring English, with attachment and condescension perfectly blended. James was all too familiar. He would be, he said, 'the great schoolmaster of the whole land'. He likened the Commons to a cow that was trying to cut off her own tail ; the tail being himself, the ordained of God. He complained of criticism in the Commons, where 'our fame and actions have been tossed like tennis balls among them'. To urge that England and Scotland be united under a single government, he used this curious figure of speech :

> I am the husband and all the whole Isle is my wife. I hope, therefore, that no man will be so unreasonable as to think that I, that am a Christian King under the Gospel, should be the Polygamist and husband to two wives.

These homely similes were no doubt appropriate : they suitably illustrated the point which the King was anxious to make. But their very homeliness, linked with James's shambling gait and slobbering tongue, were out of harmony with his claim to an inviolable majesty. Englishmen could better understand, and more easily respect, a King who bluntly swore.

James was a fine scholar : an expert theologian, a keen and witty debater ; 'translucent with logic', says Carlyle, 'radiant with wit, with ready ingenuity, and prismatic play of colours' ; with a gift for 'conclusive speculation'. But his learning was dangerously near to pedantry. It had not that irresponsibility which saved Renaissance wit from growing tedious. James had a way of lecturing his subjects which irritated them, and blinded them to the strength of his intellect. Moreover, his wisdom was of the head only, not of the heart. There were odd and primitive flaws in it: so intelligent a man had no need to be superstitiously afraid of witches and tobacco. His brain was quick, but his sympathies were sluggish. He could see his adversary's point in an argument, but he could not understand temperaments that were different from his own. The Puritans who came to him with nice points of doctrine, the country squires who stubbornly mistrusted his friendliness with Spain, the lawyers who held him within the boundaries of their unfamiliar statutes, were men whom he could not understand, and would not bother to understand. In England he fell foul of traditions and prejudices which he had not known to exist. Conscience, narrow patriotism, a finicky respect for the laws, he lumped together as wrong-headedness and factious opposition. He closed his mind to ideas that were outside the circle of his own intellectual musings, and fatally disregarded the harm which they could do him.

James has done most hurt to his reputation by his reliance, during the last fourteen years of his life, on young and attractive favourites. While Robert Cecil was alive, all was well: James consulted the ministers of the previous reign, and often took their advice. But in 1612 Cecil died, and thereafter James gave his confidence to two young men who had neither birth nor fortune, and only moderate abilities: Robert Carr, a penniless laird from Teviotdale, who became Earl of Somerset; and George Villiers, the son of a Leicestershire squire, who was the notorious Duke of Buckingham. Men who had known Leicester and Essex were well enough accustomed to court favourites, but Elizabeth had seldom allowed her private affections to direct her public policy. James made no such distinction; the favourite's whim was his master's law. Experienced statesmen took their orders from Somerset and Buckingham, and did them homage for favours expected or received. Somerset rewarded

James by involving himself in an odious scandal, and the unpopularity of Buckingham wrecked five successive parliaments.

James's infatuation for these men is understandable. It was less discreditable, and less fatal to him, than his failure to see the point of view of men who differed from him. For James had had an abnormal life. Before he was two he had lost both his parents: his father had been murdered, his mother gone to her long captivity in England. He was brought up by uncouth nobles and dour, suspicious clergymen; men who used him for their political purposes, who lectured at him, jostled him, pulled at his sleeve. James was starved of affection; and, not unnaturally, he grew up disliking hard and practical men of the world. His Queen, Anne of Denmark, was a coarse, unsentimental woman, who failed to give him the affection which he had always been denied. So he turned to these specious, handsome young men, with their social grace and abundant charm. When he was still a boy, James had caused Elizabeth great anxiety by his sudden affection for Esmé Stuart, Duke of Lennox. Lennox was sent by the Duke of Guise to convert James and the Scots to Catholicism and restore Mary. He was the first person to flatter James; and James responded so readily that the Protestant lords grew alarmed and drove Lennox out of the country. With the English favourites James had the same sort of intimacy. The relationship was thought offensive; also it was pathetic, and politically it was disastrous. Although he was always poor, James lavished gifts on his friends, and gave costly pageants in their honour. As gout and disease crippled him in mind and body, he depended on them more than ever. Their confident vitality stimulated him. His delight in Buckingham was unrestrained. 'Christ had his John,' he declared, 'and I have my George.'

James then was very human; and he had not the tact and dignity which alone might have reconciled his subjects to his shortcomings. Even in his virtues he was slightly comic: it was his misfortune to make ridiculous everything that he touched. When, therefore, he claimed the mantle of divinity, he wore it incongruously.

2. *The Divine Right of Kings*

James had pronounced and uncompromising views on the sanctity of his office. His writings proclaimed, and his actions constantly asserted, that Kings were fettered by no laws made by men; their responsibility was to God, and to Him alone. The theory that the ruler had made a contract with his subjects, and might be deposed by them if he broke it, had no sanction. But the office of King was directly established by God, and Kings were His anointed servants, above the criticism of man.

James had already set forth his opinions in *The Trew Law of Free Monarchies*, which he had written in Scotland and published anonymously. By reference to Scripture, in particular to the coronation of Saul and to Samuel's words on the divine ordination of kingly rule; to the practice of Scotland, where the King was supreme in law and administration; and to the law of nature, in the relationship of father and son or of head and body, James argued that Kings should have supreme authority over all men. Although 'a good King will frame all his actions according to the law; yet he is not bound thereto but of his goodwill and for good example to his subjects'. If a King governed badly, that did not justify his subjects in rising against him; for 'the wickedness of the King can never make them that are ordained to be judged by him to become his judges'. Anarchy and armed rebellion were worse evils than tyranny. Peoples that were cursed with a tyrannous ruler should meekly throw themselves on his mercy, or pray for the intercession of God; or humbly reflect that their sufferings might be punishment for the evildoing of their ancestors. Kings were God's 'vice-gerents on earth, and so adorned and furnished with some sparkles of the Divinity'. The only restraint on their wilfulness was the knowledge that, if they failed in their trust, they would suffer torment hereafter.

James's new subjects were soon acquainted with these exalted views. He informed his first parliament that their ancient and boasted privileges were theirs by the grace of his ancestors and himself, not of right. As the reign proceeded his claims grew ever prouder. 'Kings are justly called Gods', he told parliament in 1609; 'for they exercise a manner of resemblance of Divine power upon earth. For if you will consider the attributes of God, you shall see how they agree in the person of a King.' Again, in the following year: 'Kings are not only God's lieutenants upon earth, but even by God Himself they are called Gods.' The fullest expression of James's views was contained in his speech to the Star Chamber in 1616. 'That which concerns the mystery of the King's power is not lawful to be disputed; for that is to wade into the weakness of princes, and to take away the mystical reverence that belongs to them that sit on the throne of God. . . . As it is atheism and blasphemy to dispute what God can do, so it is presumption and high contempt in a subject to dispute what a King can do, or to say that a King cannot do this or that.'

At first sight such words seem extravagant and ridiculous, particularly on the lips of a man as fallible as James. But the theory of the Divine Right of Kings has a place in the history of government, and when James formulated it his worst offence was that he was being out-of-date and rather tactless. The theory took shape during the mediaeval controversy between Pope and Emperor. When they were seeking to reduce the Holy Roman Emperors to the level of other Kings, the Popes turned to Scripture for arguments to justify their temporal claims. They found their justification in Christ's charge to Peter; and the unity of mediaeval Christendom was based on the divine institution of a single power that was sovereign over the thoughts and actions of all Christian men. Unity was the soul of government. The *plenitudo potestatis* of Rome was challenged by the Emperor and his controversialists. Marsiglio of Padua, William of Ockham, Dante in *De Monarchia*, argued that the secular power of princes was also ordained by God; and, like the Pope, they turned to Scripture for their arguments. It was written in the Book of Proverbs that 'by me kings reign and princes decree justice'; Jesus was ready to render to

Caesar the things that were Caesar's ; Jesus had submitted to the authority of Pilate. Thus Kings would admit the authority of the Pope in things spiritual, but they would not allow that authority to weaken the allegiance of their subjects to themselves.

The importance of this controversy was more than academic. Against the Pope's insistence on the unity of Christendom the Emperor urged the unity of the secular state. The successful rulers of the Middle Ages were those who made laws and were strong enough to enforce them ; to enforce them not merely on the overmighty baron, but on self-willed churchmen too. To such Kings as Henry II of England the pretensions of the clergy were intolerable. After years of feudal anarchy Henry succeeded in bringing the nobles within the restraint of the royal justice, which was swift, cheap and available to all men. Then he found that the clergy, encouraged by the Archbishop, would not submit to his jurisdiction, because they did not recognise him as their sovereign ; their allegiance was to the Pope overseas. During the Middle Ages this struggle was fought out everywhere, between Kings who claimed to be masters of all men who lived within their boundaries, and Popes who claimed the allegiance of all Christian souls.

The theory of Divine Right, therefore, served the state in two ways : first, it defied the sovereignty of the Pope, whose temporal ambitions often made him a dangerous rival in the political field ; and secondly, it bound the community by stronger ties than those of feudal obligation. The fabric of feudalism easily crumbled into anarchy ; where the King was first among equals, and the only sanction of government was the will of the strong, peace and order could not flourish, except by accident. The cure for anarchy was to make obedience a religious duty, and to exalt the community, personified by its ruler, above the interest of individuals. Thus Divine Right took shape. The office of monarchy was divinely ordained ; the principle of hereditary succession was indefeasible (for there must not be a war of inheritance every time a King died) ; Kings rendered the account of their stewardship to God alone, and He was their only judge; and lastly, it pleased God that subjects should not resist their rulers.

The events of the sixteenth century gave the theory a new importance and new tasks to perform. For when the Kings and Princes of Europe threw off their allegiance to the Pope, they found at hand a theory that would justify their proceedings and retain for them the obedience of their people. The Church of Rome fought a long counter-attack, but Divine Right defeated it. Kings asserted that the divine institution of the secular power entitled them to establish what religion they pleased within their borders, and to drive out those who refused them obedience. The new national consciousness of the peoples of Europe supported their claim. The Pope became an anarchist, an intruding foreigner, who sought to break down the unity which gave nations their strength. His followers were executed as traitors to the common weal, while Kings took advantage of this patriotic enthusiasm to make themselves more powerful than they had ever been before. They threw off the shackles of feudal custom and successfully defied the rival sovereignty of the Church; and their subjects, glad to be protected from feudal disorder and an Italian master, readily supported them. From the Reformation was born absolute monarchy and the nation-state.

The British Isles stood outside the long struggle between Emperor and Pope, and mediaeval England had no need of Divine Right. In Saxon times the King had been elected by the Witan, and he held his throne on condition that his conduct was acceptable. The long series of Charters wrung from Norman and Angevin Kings showed that the tradition was not dead; and in the fourteenth century the English showed how jealously they guarded their ancient privileges by depriving two Kings of their thrones. The fate of Richard II, who was deposed in 1399, came upon him because English constitutional theory was unsympathetic to despotism. Richard was the first King of England to speak the language of Divine Right. He declared that the laws were in his own mouth, '*et aliquotiens in pectore suo*'. He flouted the barons, the traditional advisers of the Crown, compelled parliament to abdicate its powers to a Council of Eighteen, and used his dispensing power to evade laws that thwarted his purpose; for statutes made by man could not stand against the law which was the breath of God. Richard was swept from his throne, and his outraged people took the opportunity to impose humiliating restrictions on his Lancastrian successors. Thus ended the bid of a mediaeval King to break from the fetters of law and custom, and rule '*solutus legibus*' as his fancy led him. The English view of kingship, and its necessary limitations, was summarised at the close of the Middle Ages by Sir John Fortescue, Chancellor to Henry VI. The King's authority in England was tempered by the common law. If he broke it, or tried to replace it by the law of his own inclination, he was removed. The right to resist unlawful despotism had thrust deep roots into the soil of England.

But in emergency the state must be strong; and in the long emergency of the sixteenth century the English for the time abandoned their traditional jealousy of the Crown, and submitted to what the eyes of foreign observers regarded as a despotism. When Henry VIII was bold enough to cut through the bonds which for nearly a thousand years had held England to Rome, he exposed himself to the vengeance of the Catholic world. The country approved his action, if not his motives, and prepared to resist the forces which he and they had unloosed. A state which was divided against itself could not have defeated the Counter-Reformation, with the might of Spain to lead it. The English therefore united themselves behind their rulers, and submitted to actions which they had resisted in the past and in the future would resist again. With the Queen excommunicated, and foreigners urging her subjects to plot her death, it was no time to weigh the niceties of constitutional procedure; the people must unite to defeat the enemy who was within the gates. With the Pope instructing all true Catholics that their only obedience was to him, it must be made clear to all who dwelt in the realm of England that their sacred loyalty was to the Queen, and to none other. Like the Church, the state was sanctioned by the word of God, and the narrower loyalty must in the last instance exclude the wider one. The statesmen of England did not hesitate to use the arguments which continental Protestants were using in the same cause of national unity. Marsiglio's *Defensor Pacis* was translated in 1535, although his chapters on the restraint of bad princes were omitted as 'not pertaining to this realm of England'. Bishop Gardiner's book *On True Obedience* attributed the power of the King to God's ordinance; Latimer's sermons, the works of the Elizabethan bishops, Shakespeare's plays, bear witness that Tudor England regarded monarchy as an office more than human. The fifth commandment applied to Kings as well as fathers, for the King was the father of his people. Jewel, who was Elizabeth's Bishop of Salisbury, wrote that 'our common teaching is that we ought so to obey princes as sent of God, and that whoso withstandeth them withstandeth God's ordinance'; thus obedience was the due of princes and magistrates, even 'though they be very wicked'. The famous words of the Bishop of Carlisle (in *Richard II*, IV. i.) forbade 'subject and inferior breath' to speak treason against 'the figure of God's majesty'. Hamlet dared not lay hands on God's anointed servant, although he was a murderer.

Two generations of crisis had made the English think differently about their Kings; and when James expressed the theories which posterity has condemned, he was claiming no more than many were partly willing to concede. Sir Walter Raleigh believed that monarchy was the best 'regiment' because it resembled the sovereign government of God; the universities and the Bishops whole-heartedly preached non-resistance; and Francis Bacon, the finest intellect of the age, specifically approved of James's book, and insisted that in the interests of the commonwealth the King might rise above the law. If James and his supporters were wrong, it was because they had not read the signs; for the times were changing.

3. *The difficulties of James's inheritance*

When James came to the throne, Crown and people were falling out of harmony. The years between 1529 and 1588 had been years of strain and constant danger. The fear of invasion from abroad and of rebellion at home had driven the government to take desperate measures for the public safety, and had blunted the criticism of those who might have protested that the letter of the law was being strained. Superficially examined, the government of the Tudors might have seemed to be a despotism. Royal proclamation created laws that were never sanctioned by parliament; the Crown had authority to suspend or alter existing statutes; by his prerogative the King was able to regulate the flow of trade, the growth of industry and the right of public speech. The government could arrest whom it pleased, detain them without trial, and extract their evidence by means of torture. Various forms of imposition enabled it to levy taxation which parliament had not voted. The old claims of parliamentary privilege were invalid against an executive which tampered with the elections, created new constituencies, suppressed unwelcome debate, and threw troublesome members into the Tower. The Council and its offshoots tried offenders by processes unknown to the common law. Parliaments sat, or did not sit, at the royal pleasure; judges were removed from the bench if their verdicts conflicted with the government's policy. In short, the Crown used its discretionary powers to put reason of state above the iota of the law. The rights of the individual were surrendered to the public interest.

This harsh and oppressive picture of Tudor rule is softened by two vital considerations: that the nation not only consented to this exercise of arbitrary powers, but co-operated in it. The essence of Tudor government was co-operation, a unique partnership between Crown and subjects, who shared not only their dangers but their achievements. The Tudors had neither soldiers nor money. Their policy must necessarily have failed if parliament had not expressed its approval in legislation, and the Justices of the Peace in their loyal service in the countryside. The unpaid servants of the Crown, members of parliament and magistrates, shared with the Tudors and their official servants in the making of modern England. From the long and anxious crisis emerged a nation in the fine strength of early manhood. The hour of danger was past, but it had awakened qualities in the English character which in earlier ages had lain dormant. The Merchant Adventurers had wrested the trade of Northern Europe from the Hanseatic League ; English chartered companies traded at the court of Ivan the Terrible, and sent their cargoes to the East Indies and the Levant ; English fishermen set up a flourishing industry in home waters ; explorers gave their lives to the vanishing dream of a northern passage to the Indies ; seamen defied the ban of the Pope and the vengeance of the Inquisition to filch the commerce of Spanish America ; Englishmen rose to be princes of Persia, served as jewellers to the great Akbar at Delhi, and organised the navy of Japan. At home, London was already an important money market ; English cloth was carried as far as Novgorod, Constantinople, Cairo and Bengal ; sheep-farming, which cast some into poverty, enriched the productivity of the nation as a whole ; Protestant refugees from abroad brought their characteristic thriftiness, and new industries in which to exercise it. The spacious manor-houses which the Elizabethans built for themselves reflected alike their prosperity and their superb taste ; and the very solidity of these houses bore witness that the men who built them knew that the future was on their side. Tudor Englishmen were no less adventurous in the kingdom of the mind. The seed which More and Colet planted while the English Renaissance was yet young, matured into the lyric poetry of Wyatt and Surrey and the rich harvest of Elizabethan achievement.

It was this very confidence that was fatal to James. Men of this calibre would suffer no needless despotism, and James was soon to learn that, whatever his brethren on the continent had been able to make of it, in England Divine Right was only a temporary device to force into a proper obedience those who pleaded the scruples of their conscience to serve masters of their own choosing. James ascended the throne in an ominous calm. Mary Stuart was dead, the pride of Spain was beaten, the Dutch, old clients of the English Crown, were virtually independent; the union of the Crowns freed England from the menace of Border raids, and the Irish rebellion was soon to be crushed. There were no serious rivals to the throne to rally men to the service of the reigning King; only the Catholics might seriously threaten the new dynasty, and the perverse foreigner was disposed to relieve Catholics of their burdens. Thus in the fifteen years since the Armada the English aristocracy had had time to realise that the authority of the Crown in many ways conflicted with their interests and hampered the development of their class. Their years of co-operation in the business of government had sharpened their resources and quickened their sense of responsibility. In crisis they had fought by the side of the Crown in a common cause; but under the surface there had always been conflicts of policy and interest which indicated that in more settled times the Crown and its more powerful subjects would take divergent courses.

Shrewd observers must have seen how the wind was blowing, for the 'nineties were uneasy years. 'All the fabric of my reign, little by little, is beginning to fail,' Elizabeth told the King of France. The struggle over monopolies was the climax of a decade when tempers were often on edge, and finance was not parliament's only grievance. The members persisted in discussing religion, in defiance of the Queen's orders; and they claimed with growing bitterness the privileges which attached to them as members. It was a decade of economic difficulties, aggravated by severe outbreaks of plague and by a series of bad harvests from 1592 to 1596. The shortage of food brought a swift rise in prices and even the half-hearted prosecution of the war against Spain put an unprecedentedly heavy strain on the Crown's finances. The Tudor partnership was breaking up when Elizabeth preferred to stint and economise, rather than meet a parliament which would attack her religious settlement, urge her to fix the succession, criticise her financial expedients, and harass her with talk of their privileges. Her prerogative, she said, was 'the fairest flower in her garden'; to which her Commons replied, 'God send the Prerogative touch not our liberty'.

The same critical temper which obstructed the Crown's government of the Church and its harmonious working with parliament, also found fault with the nation's foreign policy. The Queen and her advisers wished to enjoy the peace which they had won. They were old, and they had had their fill of adventure; moreover, piracy was less profitable than it had been, and there was no money to fight a large war. But the younger generation were restless. The spirit of the age urged them to adventure, and they longed to flesh their swords. Thus there was at court a war-party, with Raleigh as its spokesman, which pestered the government to drive the Spaniards from their empire, rescue the natives from superstition, and make fresh markets accessible for English merchants. The government had no sympathy with such irresponsible schemes, and Burghley reminded his critics that 'a realm gaineth more by one year's peace than by ten years of war'. But the dispute went deep; it disclosed a fundamental difference of outlook. The intermittent expeditions of these years were haphazard and ill-organised, because the government had no appetite for aggression, and private investors were soon discouraged when they found that they were running financial risks for no certain reward. The war-party blamed the government for its apathy and its neglected opportunities. Here again the Crown was beginning to lose touch with the aspirations of its subjects.

James then was unlucky in his time and in his inheritance. He cannot fairly be blamed for many of the misfortunes that befell him. He inherited a parliament which was growing more uncompromising in its attitude to the Crown, and a latent opposition to the religious settlement which his predecessors had made. All the issues on which he fell foul of his parliaments —religion, finance, foreign policy, parliamentary privilege—had been sources of gathering bitterness in the years before he came to his throne. While the Queen was alive, the opposition held their hand, and did not press their grievances too far. For she was old, and she had served England well ; and she could still, if need be, awe them with that astonishing blend of majesty and graciousness which marked her dealings with her people. But there were those who dared to whisper that they would be glad when she was dead ; and let her successor beware, if he were not a man of tact.

James was not a man of tact ; and when he rashly began to try conclusions with his subjects, it was revealed to him how completely he was in their hands. The worst feature of his unprincely inheritance was an empty Treasury. The Irish rebellion had broken Elizabeth's precarious economy, and she bequeathed to James nothing better than £200 and some three thousand dresses. Even in the last years of her reign, her total revenue was under half a million pounds, of which about a quarter came from parliamentary grants. The plain truth was that the Crown's income was inadequate for the expanding needs of government. Parliament was never generous with subsidies ; 'when the sheep was to be shorn', the Queen had complained, 'there was much cry but little wool'. There was no machinery for assessing incomes, and wealthy men sent in dishonest returns, and were taxed, as Raleigh confessed, on 'not a hundredth part of our wealth'. The taxpayer still believed that in normal times the King should 'live of his own'.

By the end of the sixteenth century this sound mediaeval maxim was profoundly unfair to the Crown. On the one hand, the government had incurred new responsibilities, and with them new expenses ; on the other, the fall in the value of money had depreciated the value of the Crown's hereditary revenues. No figures can be exact, but it has been estimated that what in 1500 had cost £1 could not be bought at the close of the century for less than £4. Henry VIII and the Regent Northumberland had debased the coinage, and the Spaniards had flooded Europe with silver from the mines of Peru; and in 1600 the value of money was still falling. Merchants could accommodate themselves to the changing values, and landlords could raise their rents; but the Crown had depended for hundreds of years on a fixed income from its hereditary estates, and this could not be increased. Thus in an age of rising wages and rising prices, the biggest employer and purchaser in the land relied on an income that had not been adapted to the changed circumstances. The expenses of government, even in time of peace, required more money than the Crown possessed; and while the King was relatively poorer, the tide of Tudor prosperity was carrying his subjects to a wealth which they had never known before. The King might share the benefits of this prosperity if he could increase the customs duties, but parliament mistrusted all financial expedients which it could not control. Elizabeth had twice dared to equip the navy by purveyance, which her predecessors had agreed to abandon; but she had been brought to a stop when she tried to solve her difficulties by granting monopolies. Although the Crown might ease its embarrassment by selling its estates, and scattering offices and titles among those who would bid highly enough for them, in fact it could not carry on the government of the country without summoning parliament and humbly asking for funds. Parliament's control of the purse had never been such a deadly weapon as economic change had made it by 1603. For Divine Right could not live without bread.

James's task, therefore, was not an easy one, and he was the worst man in the world to be called on to perform it. The Tudors had made parliament a partner in the business of government; a junior partner only, with set and limited work to do, but a partner none the less. As the members grew in wealth and importance, they felt that the subordinate position which they had consented to occupy during the time of crisis should be exchanged for one of constitutional equality with the Crown.

This change had to take place. The work of administration was becoming too much for one man and a small body of councillors ; and the wealth and responsibility of the landed oligarchy fitted them to share in the central government of the country. Under a tactful King this necessary transition might have been arranged without bitterness, and certainly without bloodshed. James had the wrong gifts. As he reminded his first parliament, 'we are an old and experienced King'. Practical experience had shaped his theories and formed his ways of thought ; his belief in the divine sanctions of his office prepared him to expect unquestioning obedience ; his pedantic certainty made him impatient of criticism or guidance. He was the last man to preside satisfactorily over an age of transition.

Because this was the character of the new King, seventeenth-century history took the course of bitterness, anarchy and murder, before it settled that the aristocracy and the wealthy middle class should deprive the Crown of its sovereignty. The result of the struggle was inevitable. The victors had the balance of economic power on their side, although they called it liberty. When James refused to admit them to a fuller partnership with himself, they used their power to make his position impossible. If the Stuarts trod the path of tyranny, it was because their enemies barred the traditional ways of government. Equally, if the Stuarts had not clung to theories of government that in England were obsolete, their enemies would not have been driven to anarchy as a means of securing their ends. The Stuarts had the harder task, for it is never easy for a ruler to sign away his interests ; the men who preached freedom might have been more forbearing. In most of the issues which divided him from his parliament, James was intellectually and morally in the right ;[1] but the question of right dwindled before the question of power. Timidity and a fundamental common sense kept James from pressing his beliefs beyond the boundaries of compromise ; but his son, who was inflexible, had to die.

[1] He defined his aims as 'one worship of God, one Kingdom entirely governed, one uniformity of law'.

CHAPTER XI

JAMES'S QUARRELS WITH PARLIAMENT

The Puritans : Millenary Petition, Hampton Court Conference, the Authorised Version ; Gunpowder Plot. Early opposition from parliament. The Scottish question. Financial problems : Bate's case, the Great Contract.

1. *Puritans and Catholics*

The new reign opened eventfully. Before 1603 was out, James had hanged without trial a pickpocket who was found in the press at Newark, received a petition from the Puritan clergy, and survived two conspiracies against his throne. To men who remembered the anxious days of Elizabeth these plots were trifling. The Bye Plot, engineered by a Catholic named Watson, was a plan to kidnap the King and blackmail him into remedying the grievances of his captors ; it was betrayed to the Council by the Jesuits. The Main Plot was more serious, because its aims were more drastic and the conspirators were more eminent men. They planned to set on the throne Lady Arabella Stuart, who was descended from Margaret Tudor and the Earl of Angus ; and Cobham, who betrayed his fellow-conspirators, declared that Raleigh was implicated. Certainly Raleigh did not love the new régime : for opposing its foreign policy he had been deprived of several of his offices. But opposition is not necessarily treason, and the evidence against him was vague and conflicting. The government was blundering and hesitant. After an unsatisfactory enquiry Raleigh was put in the Tower, and others were executed or imprisoned. Three of the plotters were condemned to die, and brought to the scaffold, where they were told that the King had reprieved them. James hoped to show that Solomon could be both terrible and merciful, but his handling of the case brought him no honour.

The Puritans had won no sympathy from Elizabeth and her advisers, but they reasonably hoped that the new King, who had been brought up by Presbyterians, would be more accommodating. The Millenary Petition, which they presented to him on his way to London, contained the moderate demands of orthodox Puritanism. They required, they said, ' not a disorderly innovation, but a due and godly reformation ' of those elements in the English liturgy which still savoured of Rome. They asked that the surplice be not ' urged ' on ministers ; that the sign of the cross in baptism, the ring as a symbol of marriage, bowing to the altar, and other gestures of idolatry, should no longer be compulsory ; that the music played in churches be ' moderated to better edification ' ; that the Sabbath be observed according to the Fourth Commandment ; that the ' longsomeness ' of the service be curtailed, to give more time for sermons ; that the altar be kept ' tablewise ' in the middle of the church, and not covered and railed at the east end, ' pageanted about, like a dreadful idol,' as Milton was to say. These demands were familiar, and probably they carried the support of a large body of Englishmen. Reform was sought, but only of ' things indifferent ' ; and the necessary changes in the Prayer Book would be slight. The Millenary Petition asked no more than that clergymen and their congregations should be allowed to follow their own preferences in the externals of their worship.

James might have ignored the Petition, or quietly refused it ; or, as Bacon advised, he might have conceded some of its demands. Unhappily, he took none of these courses. The occasion offered rich opportunities which he could not bring himself to ignore ; his imagination took wings, and he saw himself, like some dignitary of Rome, as arbiter of a theological disputation. He would summon both parties to his presence, and their spokesmen would muster their arguments ; when they had done, he would weigh the decision and give his verdict.

In 1604 the disputants assembled at Hampton Court: for the established Church, Whitgift and eight of the Bishops; for the Puritans, Reynolds, Knewstubs, and other divines. After the spokesmen of the established Church had stated their case, James prepared to hear the Puritans. They repeated their demand for the modification of ceremonial; then they asked that articles be added to the liturgy to express their doctrines of grace and pre-destination, and that permission be given for 'prophesyings' to be resumed. What answer James would have made to these requests will never be known, for an unfortunate misunderstanding shattered the hope of a friendly settlement. During his speech Reynolds used the word 'presbytery'. Hearing it, James was 'somewhat stirred'; and hastily and incorrectly he chose to infer that the English Puritans were asking him to assent to a Presbyterian organisation after the model of Scotland. His verdict was not the calm judgment of Solomon, but a fretful denunciation of those who threatened the safety of the Prince by striving after a parity. 'Stay, I pray you, for one seven years before you demand that of me: and if then you find me pursy and fat, and my wind-pipes stuffed, I will perhaps hearken to you.' He accused Reynolds of challenging his supremacy in the Church. For Presbytery 'as well agreeth with a monarchy as God and the devil. Then Jack, and Tom, and Will, and Dick shall meet, and at their pleasures censure me and my council and all our proceedings. . . . No Bishop, no King, as before I said.' He insisted that there should be 'one doctrine and one discipline, one religion in substance and in ceremony', and closed the conference with a threat to punish the Puritans for their effrontery. 'If this be all that they have to say, I shall make them conform themselves, or I will harry them out of the land, or else do worse.'

A jubilant Bishop was persuaded that 'his majesty spake by the instinct of the spirit of God', and Lord Chancellor Ellesmere decided that at last he appreciated the truth of the saying, '*Rex est mixta persona cum sacerdote*'. But James had made a bad mistake. He was wrong to identify the men who presented and defended the Millenary Petition, with the rugged, uncompromising Presbyterians of Scotland. The fate of the Marprelate pamphleteers, and the effective vigilance of the government, had abated the first flush of Puritan ardour, and the inspiration of Hooker and Andrewes was breathing new life into Anglicanism. English Puritanism, therefore, was less powerful, in parliament and at the court and the universities, than when Elizabeth had first been troubled by its blunt opposition to her settlement. In 1603 its spirit was moderate and accommodating, and James might, without risk to his security, have made concessions in 'things indifferent'. Instead, his hastiness reopened a quarrel which wise statesmanship might have settled, and made of religion a grievance to which all his enemies would rally. For the King was head of the Church, and only the exercise of his prerogative could change its rules and organisation. Since James was adamant, and would permit no change, he obliged the religious extremists to find fresh tactics: realising that petitions did not achieve their ends, they began a constitutional attack on the prerogative, with the object of transferring the Crown's ecclesiastical supremacy to parliament. The members of the House of Commons were, for the most part, only lukewarm in their Puritanism; but the discontented among them were eager to add the dissatisfaction of sincere Puritans to the roll of grievances with which, they assured James, his people were afflicted. 'Religion is the touchstone of all actions,' said Sir John Eliot; 'and what rests not on this centre can have no perfection or assurance.' John Hampden, who had both eyes always on the main chance, confessed that 'if it were not for this reiterated cry about religion', the Commons 'could never be certain of keeping the people on their side'. In keeping religious discontent in the forefront of their complaints, the Commons were on safe ground; and when the Crown's foreign policy, and the indiscretions of Arminian churchmen, seemed to place Protestantism in real danger, they could proudly boast that their foresight had been justified.

By his unwisdom in treating the Puritans as a sect conspiring against his authority, James thus made them more dangerous than they would have been if he had conceded some of their demands: he allowed an alliance to be formed between the political and the religious opponents of his prerogative, and gave them a common purpose in weakening it. From James's point of view, 'No Bishop, no King' was a shrewd analysis of the situation, but it was his attitude which gave the alliance of Puritans and Commons its strength; the counter-alliance, inherited from Elizabeth, of Crown, Council and Bishops could not avail against it.

Unaware of the dangerous path he was treading, James went on to fulfil his threats against the Puritans. 'I have peppered them soundly', he wrote of the Hampton Court Conference. A proclamation in July, 1604, declared that 'what untractable men do not perform upon admonition they must be compelled unto by authority'; and Convocation passed canons which defined the Anglican creed, just as the Catholic position had been defined at the Council of Trent. But the zeal of Bancroft, the new Archbishop of Canterbury, was not satisfied with definition: he required the clergy to take an oath that the existing Prayer Book was not contrary to the Word of God. This caused the first serious schism in the English Church. About sixty Puritan clergy, who could make no compromise with their conscience, refused the oath, and were deprived of their livings. Bancroft's measures were less stringent than those which Elizabeth had taken against the Puritans, but they came at an unfortunate time. Realising that they had nothing to gain from the Crown, the Puritans became bellicose again; and their lay allies resisted the government's attempt to define the articles of their faith. The cause of the 'silenced brethren' was taken up in parliament, and the demands of the Millenary Petition were defended by men who would not have been moved to take interest in it if James had quietly disregarded it.

Before the Hampton Court Conference was dissolved, the Bishops decided to undertake a new translation of the Bible.

King James's Bible, the Authorised Version of 1611, is the greatest achievement of the English people. It was prepared by forty-seven scholars, who based their work on the translation made by William Tyndale in 1525. The matchless beauty of its rhythms has preserved for later ages the perfection of the English language at the peak of its development. Its language was the language of the people,[1] not of learned men; its images are concrete, its phrases homely and uncomplicated; its dignity is in simplicity.

A year after James had thus wounded the religious feelings of a large section of his people, his Catholic subjects conspired against his life, his authority and his Church. The story of Gunpowder Plot has been told too often. A group of Catholic gentlemen, most of them from Shakespeare's country by the Avon, planned to blow up the Houses when the King opened parliament; and in the following chaos to seize the organs of government and rouse the dormant strength of English Catholicism. They were betrayed, and their plot was dignified by the heroism of those who suffered for it; and not least of that soldier of fortune, the Yorkshireman Guido Fawkes, who undertook to fire the fuse, and refused to buy his own life by selling his friends.

Catesby and his accomplices gravely injured the cause they had hoped to serve. As a whole the English Catholics had been living peacefully. Their conduct in 1588 had proved their loyalty, and most of them asked only to be forgotten. Persecution had languished, except where an over-zealous magistrate drove priests from their hiding-places in old manor-houses and punished covert celebrations of the Mass; in normal times the fines for recusancy totalled little more than £1,000 a year. Given a moderate temper on both sides, the wound might gradually have healed. But there were intransigent men among the Catholics, successors of Robert Parsons, whose loud-voiced indiscretion poisoned it and kept it open. They boasted of their determination to rise against the heretics and overthrow them, and looked for the day when once again 'faggots should

[1] Over 90 per cent. of the words used were of English derivation.

be dear '. This unreasonableness, no less than the vigour of a too ardent Protestantism, kept the penal laws on the statute-book. James had been disposed to tolerate the Catholics, but his ministers restrained him ; and Watson's foolish conspiracy, which was in part the outcome of disappointed hopes, gave substance to their mistrust. Gunpowder Plot was an attempt to reverse the whole position by a single blow. If it had succeeded, as it could have done, England might have become Catholic again ; and in the west and north, where feudalism still lingered, the change would have been welcomed. Its failure was fatal to reconciliation. James's generous plans for freedom of conscience were changed to ' utter detestation ' ; the ' good and provident laws ' against Catholic worship were reimposed, and for more than a dozen years they were rigorously enforced all over the country. Recusants were forbidden to practise law or medicine, or to hold military or civil posts under the government. Moreover, the enemies of the Catholics had been given a weapon which they knew how to use : two hundred years later the cry of ' No Popery ' was still strong enough to overthrow a ministry.

If the Catholics suffered for the Gunpowder Plot, so, ultimately, did its intended victim. James did not, as Elizabeth would have done, use this attack on his life to appeal to the affection of his subjects. In a few years, as he jeopardised the Protestant interest in his pursuit of the dangerous favours of Spain, they were to say that he was little better than a Catholic himself. Already Catholicism meant the Inquisition and the fires of Smithfield ; now it meant conspiracy and assassination as well. The first result of the Englishman's renewed mistrust of all things Catholic was to be the frustration of James's schemes for European peace.

2. *Parliamentary opposition : the Scottish question*

James's first parliament, which sat from 1604 until 1611, immediately challenged both the theory and the practice of his government. The members came to Westminster already displeased with the King's attitude at Hampton Court and Bancroft's campaign against obstinate Puritans, and they were quick to assert their rights. The Ccurt of Chancery had annulled the election for Buckinghamshire of Sir Francis Goodwin, who was an outlaw. When the Commons pleaded privilege, James informed them that they 'derived all matters of privilege' from the grace and condescension of the Crown, and 'desired and commanded . . . as an absolute King' that they do his bidding; although eventually he admitted their right to be judges of disputed elections.

Other disputes quickly followed over purveyance, wardships, and the favour shown to Scotsmen; and the Commons won a further victory when a member named Shirley, who was imprisoned in the Fleet as a debtor, was finally allowed to take his seat. So tender were the members on the question of their privileges that in June, 1604, they presented to James the Form of Apology and Satisfaction. Although it was written in words of deep respect, the Apology was in part a lecture to the foreign King on the ways of the English constitution, and in part an expression of the growing disharmony between legislature and executive. It asserted parliament's traditional rights of free elections, free speech and freedom from arrest, and declared that these privileges were of right, and not of grace. James was reminded that 'the prerogative of princes may easily and do daily grow; the privileges of the subject are for the most part at an everlasting stand'. Further, although the King was head of the Church, he had no power to 'alter religion' without the sanction of his parliament, which had approved all the changes made by Henry VIII.

Thus early King and parliament joined battle, and the division between them was fundamental. The Apology, for all its polite language, bluntly defied James's theory of kingship: while James denied the power of law or custom to restrain his authority, parliament asserted the mediaeval principle that the King was bound by the laws and the will of his people. 'The voice of the people, in the things of their knowledge, is said to be as the voice of God.' The sturdy, bigoted, independent country gentlemen who came to Westminster when the King summoned parliament, knew little enough of the difficulties of government. Their administrative experience was limited to the running of their own estates, to interviewing bailiffs, assessing the poor-rate, and condemning poachers. They were ignorant of foreign affairs, and they never realised how much the government cost to run. They were parochial in their opinions, and mistrustful of courtiers and councillors. But they knew their strength. Both as members of the Commons and as Justices of the Peace they had been indispensable to the Tudors, and they insisted on playing their part as rulers of the nation. They were jealous of the ancient privileges of parliament, but James was not wise enough to learn from their early defiance that he must defer to them. He complained petulantly of their 'curiosity, from morning to evening, to find fault with my propositions', thus treating as personal insults the first stirrings of national resentment.

He was soon to find himself thwarted again, in his plan to bring England and Scotland under a single administration. A royal commission, which had the support of Bacon, recommended that trade between the two countries be unrestricted; that '*post-nati*', Scots born after James's accession, be naturalised *de facto*; and that a measure be passed to naturalise '*pre-nati*'. James enthusiastically supported these recommendations, wishing to bring all his subjects under one law and one religion, but parliament argued against so dangerous a precedent. For if a Spanish prince were to marry an English princess, and succeed to the English throne, the English might find themselves naturalised as Spanish citizens. This far-fetched concern for the national welfare concealed baser motives. English men of business feared Scottish competition in their trade, English courtiers feared that Scots would usurp their offices, and the common lawyers mistrusted the intricacies of Scottish law. All that James could save from a plan which would have benefited both countries was a decision of the judges, in the case of

Robert Colvill who was born in Edinburgh in 1605, that '*post-nati*' were English citizens. English parliamentarians had not yet discovered that the Scots were their 'brothers'.

3. *Financial questions*

In all his doings James was handicapped by the Crown's poverty. 'This eating canker of want' ate away the Divine Right of Kings, for it put the Stuarts at the mercy of their enemies. The Commons were content to reiterate the ancient but now impracticable dogma that 'the King should live of his own', and were more concerned that he should not overstep his rights, than that he should have sufficient resources to carry on the business of government. James was undoubtedly extravagant, and his sense of the dignity of his office would not let him humble himself by presenting parliament with a frank statement of his economic difficulties. Thus, through ignorance and indifference, parliament kept him short of money, and attacked all sources of revenue which had not the sanction of feudal legality or parliamentary statute.

In his embarrassment James turned to the Lord Treasurer, Robert Cecil, now Earl of Salisbury. Salisbury did what he could to curb James's congenital improvidence, and to reduce the debt and the yearly deficit by finding fresh sources of revenue. The decision of the judges in the case of John Bate seemed to make available a regular flow of non-parliamentary taxation. In an attempt to share in the benefits of expanding trade, the Crown imposed by prerogative additional duties on various commodities imported from abroad, and in 1606 Bate refused to pay a duty on currants. There was no statute to forbid the levying of indirect taxes without consent of parliament, and the Court of Exchequer decided in favour of the King; declaring that the ports were 'the gates of the King', and that duties levied there were at his discretion. The decision was sound law and sound economics, for the regulation of trade was in the hands of the King, and industry could not be protected unless he had power to revise the tariff. When, however, in 1608 Salisbury issued a revised Book of Rates, his object was not to protect industry, but to swell the income of the Crown. The increased duties were on luxuries and foreign manufactures, and Salisbury had sought the approval of the City merchants before imposing them. But to parliament, unconcerned for the moment with legal or economic propriety, they were a source of revenue which might make James independent of their control, and a gage of battle which they were happy to accept.

The last sessions of James's first parliament were stormy. The Crown had lost the delicate art, so invaluable to the Tudors, of controlling sessions and directing the course of debate. Its supporters in the Commons were no match for the leaders of the opposition, and its best men were in the Lords because the King needed the money which they were prepared to pay for their titles. The common lawyers were at issue with James's theories of sovereignty, the merchants were clamorous against the new impositions, the Puritan members referred again to the plight of their 'silenced brethren'. The whole House joined in indignation to chastise Dr. John Cowell, the Master of Trinity Hall, who in a dictionary of legal terms had ventured to assert that the King 'is above the law by his sovereign power', and might, if he pleased, set aside the laws. Parliament therefore was in no mood to accept the Great Contract, by which Salisbury sought to make James finally solvent. By impositions, sales of property, and various unwelcome economies, he had reduced the Crown's debts by two-thirds. He now asked for a grant of £600,000 to pay off outstanding debts and found a reserve fund; in return for which the Crown would commute its revenues from purveyance and feudal dues for an annual sum of £200,000, and consent to the regulation of impositions by statute. These proposals were never carried. James was soon asking for more than £200,000, while the Commons were reluctant to concede as much. During several heated debates the Commons quoted statutes of Edward I against the levying of impositions, questioned the rights of the prerogative, complained of High Commission and pluralist Bishops, and asserted their ancient privileges when James bade them keep to the matter at hand. Wearily James prorogued parliament, and early in 1611 he dissolved it. A great opportunity had been missed: not, perhaps, of making James finally solvent, for he was too thriftless ever to live within his means; but of bringing Crown and parliament to some agreement in finance, and of persuading parliament to acknowledge that in the modern world mediaeval maxims of finance no longer applied.

James dissolved his first parliament with a sense of injury. 'All that spite and malice durst do to disgrace and infame us hath been used. To be short, this Lower House, by their behaviour have periled and annoyed our health, wounded our reputation, emboldened all ill-natured people, encroached upon many of our privileges and plagued our purse with their delays'. The steady hostility of the Commons lends some colour to the theory, advanced by James and his son as the only explanation of disloyalty which they could not understand, that certain prominent members were determined from the start to embroil King and parliament: to use the King's financial weakness to frustrate the executive, and so to force the Crown to share the fruits as well as the responsibilities of government. The Stuarts never realised where they stood. Clinging to their mystical notions of kingship, they did not make those gestures of reconciliation and concession which would have softened the harshness of their failure. As the rift widened, exasperation led both sides to press their principles beyond what was reasonable or expedient, and to do less than justice to those of their opponents. The leaders of the popular party insisted too much on their mission to uphold law and liberty; while the Crown was too ready to treat as merely factious the attempt of the common lawyers to restrain the prerogative, and of the Commons to take their share in the administration of the country. In the bitterness of the struggle much was lost that should have been preserved. The union with Scotland was not the only beneficial scheme to be sacrificed to the constitutional quarrel.

CHAPTER XII

THE FAILURE OF JAMES'S PERSONAL GOVERNMENT

James's favourites. His conflict with the common law. His foreign policy: the Thirty Years War, the Spanish marriage. His third and fourth parliaments.

1. *James's favourites*

The death of Salisbury in 1612 deprived James of an experienced and reliable counsellor, who had striven to keep his master's debts in control and to find some basis of agreement between Crown and parliament. Henry, Prince of Wales, died in the same year. The death of these two men left its imprint on the rest of the reign. For Salisbury was wise in the ways of the Tudor constitution, and would not have allowed James to irritate the country by ruling for ten years with only one parliament; and Henry, 'the English Marcellus', who was credited with all the virtues which his father lacked, would have restrained him from the courses which brought Crown and court into dishonour. Henry loved horses, admired the enterprises of Henry of Navarre, was firm for the Protestant faith, and hated to see Raleigh's fierce energy burning itself out in a prison. These qualities endeared him to the patriotic party, and indeed to the country at large, and would have made him a more suitable King than his diffident, bookish brother. Had he lived to enter upon his inheritance, he would have postponed the English revolution by eagerly making war on Spain.

Freed from the cautious advice of Salisbury and the often expressed contempt of his son, James sought the counsel of men whom his people hated. First among these was Don Diego Sarmiento de Acuna, Count of Gondomar, who arrived in England in 1613 as the envoy of Spain. For nearly ten years James chose to consult this Spaniard in preference to his English ministers, and was guided by him to make decisions in foreign policy which branded the government with the stigma of Catholicism. Gondomar knew his man. The way to James's confidence was to flatter him; and Gondomar deliberately blundered when he spoke in Latin, and suffered himself to be corrected by the King. James, according to the Venetian ambassador, was 'accustomed to be as liberal to his favourites with his secrets as with his riches', and there was little that Gondomar did not get to know. His influence on James was shaken neither by the assaults of the Londoners on his residence and his person, nor by the clamour of ministers and Commons against his dangerous counsels.

James had English advisers too, but they were not men in whom the nation felt confidence. Robert Carr came from Teviotdale to be a page at court. Attracting the King's attention, he rose to rank and wealth on estates confiscated from Raleigh, and in 1613 was made Earl of Somerset. A scandal involving divorce and murder brought him low. The affair was unfortunately typical of the squalor and corruption of James's court, and the disgrace of the servant tainted the name of the master who delighted to honour him.

No sooner had Somerset fallen than George Villiers stormed his way into the King's affection, brushing aside the competition of a candidate of the Howards whose face was daily beautified 'with posset curd'. Villiers was a more dangerous man than Somerset because he meddled more deeply in affairs of state. Winning the heart of the son as well as the father, he was for ten years the virtual ruler of England, and as long as he ruled, there could be no harmony between Crown and parliament. James was fascinated by his speciousness, his handsome figure and his charming ways. He made him Duke of Buckingham, and called him Steenie, after that Stephen whose face was like an angel's ; resolving, said Sir Henry Wotton, ' to make him a Masterpiece '. Buckingham was not altogether unworthy of the favours he received. Many men more incompetent and more dishonest than he have held positions of trust and commanded the applause of their own and later generations. He was brave, resourceful and intelligent. At a time when the business of government was impeded by blundering, peculation and factious rivalries, he showed administrative abilities out of the ordinary. His long record of failure was extenuated by circumstances in which no one could have succeeded. Indeed, his service would have been less disastrous to the Stuarts had he been less gifted, and therefore less certain that he must ultimately vindicate himself. He had all the defects of the man who is less thorough than spectacular. As Clarendon noted, he was so eminent in the state that no one dared to advise him frankly or to point out the dangers which lay in his path. The King was too much infatuated to be critical, and when he offered his faltering advice, it was not heeded. Buckingham too often launched his enterprises with inadequate preparation ; and when they failed, he optimistically embarked on something fresh, careless of the consequences to his master or himself. In the last analysis, life was a game. Too often the welfare of the state turned on the gambler's throw.

Between 1611 and 1621 James called only one parliament. His first parliament's unrelenting criticism made him unwilling to call another if he could avoid it, and he preferred to govern through the prerogative and the extensive machinery of the Council. In this Gondomar supported him, knowing that the Commons were hostile to Spain and suspicious of James's Spanish sympathies. But in thus deciding to do without parliament, James departed from the theory and practice of the Tudor constitution, and also opposed the advice of the best of his servants. The strong men among the supporters of the Stuarts—Salisbury, Bacon, Cranfield, Wentworth, even Buckingham—were never afraid to face parliament ; for they were confident that they could hold it in its rightful place in the constitution, as the instrument of legislation and supply, and the forum of public opinion on the questions of the day. Events betrayed their confidence. They were unable to assert their will over an assembly which took on the rôle of critic and administrative rival, and the executive temporarily lost its necessary authority over the legislature.

The parliament which sat for a few weeks in 1614 left James more soured than before. He summoned it because Bacon, who still hoped to find the Commons in reasonable mood, recommended it as the best solution of his financial difficulties. For the only time during his reign he made an attempt to tamper with the elections. Certain magnates undertook to procure the election of men favourable to the government. But the efforts of these 'Undertakers' were clumsy and unsuccessful, their candidates being generally rejected by the voters; and the old leaders, Phelips, Hakewill and Sandys, were reinforced by young and vigorous members such as Wentworth, Eliot and Pym. The Commons refused to take the customary Communion at the Abbey, 'for fear of copes and wafer-cakes'. They went instead to St. Margaret's, and took the sacraments in a body so as to detect recusants among their number. This uncompromising and suspicious attitude was maintained throughout the session. Sir Ralph Winwood, the government's leader in the Commons, was simple and inexperienced, and his meek demand for subsidies was scarcely heard among the din of grievances and protests. Irritated by a stream of complaints, about impositions, Scotsmen, courtiers, monopolies, 'Undertakers' and 'silenced brethren', James sought the goodwill of Gondomar, and dissolved the Addled Parliament.

His financial shifts during the next few years were at first unsuccessful. An appeal for a patriotic gift realised almost nothing, and Coke's vigilance scotched an attempt to raise a benevolence. By 1618 the debt had reached £900,000 and there was a deficit on the year of £137,000. James was only saved from having to throw himself again on the mercy of parliament, by the financial skill of Lionel Cranfield, a London merchant, who had entered the royal service. Ably backed by Buckingham, Cranfield undertook drastic reforms of household and public expenditure. His keen, precise mind saved the Crown thousands of pounds by economies in the wardrobe, the navy and other expenses. In 1619 receipts balanced expenditure. Cranfield was rewarded with the Treasurership and the Earldom of Middlesex, and the government seemed to be facing a more settled future.

But financial stability was bought at a price. The monopolies and impositions which maintained it were unpopular with merchants who had to pay them, and with constitutionalists who challenged their lawfulness; and Cranfield's economies had made enemies of those whose pensions and sinecures had suddenly vanished. When a crisis in foreign affairs brought parliament together again, much was to be heard about these grievances. James was secure only so long as he could avoid meeting parliament.

2. *James and the common law*

Meanwhile, James was facing attack from another direction. Until 1714 judges held office during the King's pleasure; they could be dismissed if their verdicts did not satisfy the government, and mostly this was a sufficient reason why they should do what was expected of them. In James's reign, however, the impartial administration of the common law had as its champion one of the stoutest fighters in English history.

Sir Edward Coke, formerly Speaker of the House of Commons, was appointed Attorney-General in 1594, and Chief Justice of Common Pleas in 1606. The law was Coke's fetish, the idol of his worship; 'the golden met-wand and measure' of the propriety of all actions. By the test of the statute-book and centuries of legal precedents, he found that he could not approve of the actions and theories of the King. James's theory of monarchy was unknown to English law. He was straining the prerogative beyond its legal boundaries and seeking to treat the judges as mere delegates of his will. In this emergency Coke knew how to act. He was the Crown's servant, but he would not tarnish his ideal by making any truce with political expediency. To his mind, the Bench should be the independent arbiter between the Crown and its subjects; the law was not the instrument of the prerogative, but the immovable boundary which marked its limits. Against the supple wisdom of Solomon he pitted the cold letter of the law.

His truculent obstinacy defeated the King on several fields of battle. When James and Bancroft sought to assert the judicial independence of the ecclesiastical courts, Coke successfully denied the Crown's claim to decide whether cases should be tried by common or canon law. In 1608 he denied the King's authority to hear cases in person. In 1610 James referred to the judges parliament's complaint that he had made use of proclamations to create offences unknown to the law. (He had irritated business interests by prohibiting by proclamation the manufacture of starch, and any further building in London.) Coke did not hesitate. 'The King hath no prerogative but that which the law allows him', and parliament had repealed the special concession made to Henry VIII. In 1615 he denied the jurisdiction of commissioners appointed to reform abuses in the navy. Two years later he complained of the King's attempt to intimidate the judges by requesting them to give their opinions on a certain case individually and privately. 'Such particular and auricular takings of opinion' made it harder for them to give their honest opinions; and Coke alone gave the answer which the Crown did not wish to hear. In 1616 he strained James's patience too far. James had granted Bishop Neile a living *in commendam*, and his right to do this was being challenged in law. James required that, as his prerogative was being called in question, the judges should consult with him before giving their verdicts. For prerogative 'is no subject for the tongue of a lawyer, nor is it lawful to be disputed'. Alone of the judges Coke defied the King's claim of *raison d'état*, and was deprived of his offices for his 'perpetual turbulent carriage'.

His career did not end here. He had himself elected to

parliament in 1621, and was promptly imprisoned for his continued resistance to the prerogative. But he managed the impeachment of his lifelong enemy Bacon, and crowned his work by being prominent among the framers of the Petition of Right, by which the prerogative was at length brought within statutory limits.

It is easy to make too much of Coke's continued championship of the liberty of the subject; the theories of his great enemy expose the many limitations of his outlook. Coke reverenced the law as it stood, to the tittle of its technicalities. He thought to safeguard liberty by constant reference to precedents. But the judgments of the past may be unjust in the present; a rigid adherence to the standards of other ages may hinder the development of a community. Coke's arguments were often pedantic and artificial. His mania for precedents led him to quote against the Stuarts statutes passed in other reigns for other purposes, and to submit their actions to the test of superannuated feudal charters. It was he who manufactured the importance of Magna Carta. Shakespeare wrote a play about King John and did not mention it; certainly it had small bearing on seventeenth-century problems. In short, Coke required a government confronted with the complexities of modern administration to conform to feudal notions of finance, and constitutional maxims that were pleasing to Bracton and Sir John Fortescue.

Coke let his mind dwell in ages when men had seen no reason to question the supremacy of the law. The citizen of the twentieth century, in democratic countries at least, also considers that the law is supreme, and expects his rulers for general purposes to abide by it. But he would not hesitate to deny that in an emergency, such as a war or a general strike, the government may suspend the laws and take what measures the public safety demands. *Salus populi suprema lex.* Moreover, he would admit the effective right of the government to decide when such an emergency exists. This was the issue between Coke and Bacon. The Reformation had changed men's outlook, and in particular it had given a new importance to the state. Kings claimed a divine sanction for their office because the safety of their people often demanded it ; they claimed too the exercise of sovereignty, the right to overstep the law in the public interest, to deny justice to the individual for the welfare of all. If Coke understood this point of view, he would have none of it. Nothing should usurp the rule of law ; and this may mean the rule of lawyers, who alone can unravel it. He fell back on the ritualistic mumbo-jumbo of his faith : 'Magna Carta is such a fellow that he will have no sovereign.'

While Coke buried his head in the barren sands of precedent, Bacon's brilliant, sinuous mind sought arguments to defend paternal monarchy. His ideal, and Strafford's after him, was that a vigorous monarchy, furnished with wise counsellors, should rule benevolently for the common good of all its subjects ; that parliament should vote supplies and make the laws ; and that in emergencies, of whose existence it was the judge, the Crown should be permitted to rise above the law and act as a sovereign power. Where the laws obstructed this ideal, they must be reformed ; and the judges were the lions who supported Solomon's throne, 'but lions under the throne, being circumspect that they do not check or oppose any points of sovereignty'.

Neither Coke nor Bacon solved the problems of the age. While Coke's theories of government were obsolete, Bacon's were rather a philosophic idealisation of the Tudor past than a guide to the present. Coke's denial of sovereignty led to the Petition of Right, a piece of administrative nihilism which made impossible government according to the Tudor formula of the Crown-in-Parliament. When the popular party had destroyed the instruments of conciliar government, and had begun to build for themselves, they automatically proclaimed the sovereignty of parliament. By 1642 Coke would have been a royalist. Bacon, on the other hand, rightly asserted that in the modern state there must be a sovereign power ; but he was wrong in believing that parliament would consent to keep to its subordinate place in the constitution. His balance of constitutional powers was out of date. But he made an even worse mistake in thinking that the mediaeval idea of a government conducted in the interests of all classes was any longer possible in a country whose political character had been altered by economic revolution. His biography of Henry VII, which he wrote as a text-book on monarchy for Prince Charles, was an echo from a vanished world.

3. *James's foreign policy*

James practised peace; partly because he could not afford war, partly because violence horrified him, and partly from an intelligent awareness that peace best suited England's interests. As far then as events were within his control, he strove to keep, not merely England, but the whole of Europe at peace; and when war at length broke out, he attempted from his tiny corner of Europe to mediate between Protestant and Catholic, and by the marriage of a boy and a girl to still the clash of arms. Like all his projects, James's foreign policy was conceived in grandeur, but it faltered in execution, and tailed off in humiliating failure. England had nothing to gain by war, by spendthrift raids on the continent or privateering in the Caribbean; nor, even when the Thirty Years War was at its height, had she anything to lose by peace. By the standards of morality and commonsense, James was right. Yet his foreign policy rounded off the failure of his reign: it confirmed his people's mistrust of his House, and enabled parliament to put forward revolutionary demands for the control of his ministers, his policy and his expenditure.

In 1604 James brought to a close the long and unsatisfactory war with Spain. The peace revived the traditional alliance with Burgundy, and was welcomed by the merchants, whose commerce had been roughly handled by pirates. The government refused to give way on the point that was vital: it would not admit that English trade with America was illegal. For several years there were no threats to the country's peace. The Dutch had won their independence from Spain; James was on good terms with Henry of Navarre, and looked with favour on Sully's lofty, but nebulous designs for a universal peace. When there was a succession dispute in the Duchies of Cleves and Juliers, James joined France, Holland and the Lutherans of Germany in a Protestant League, and enjoyed himself in the satisfying rôle of mediator. The better to play his part as Protestant champion, he married his daughter Elizabeth to Frederick, Elector Palatine. Indeed, so elated was he by his success and his high reputation that in 1613 he contemplated becoming Czar of Russia; but Michael Romanov was elected instead.

So far James might seem to have redeemed his failures at home by his successes in a wider field; but the same man could not be both the champion of Protestantism and the friend of Spain. As early as 1604 he had contemplated the marriage of his son to a Spanish princess, and for twenty years he clung to the scheme, undeterred by the example of Mary Tudor or the outspoken disapproval of his subjects. The scheme made little headway while Prince Henry was alive. Henry was more sensitive than most Stuarts to the gusts of public opinion, and he uncompromisingly declared that no two religions should lie in his bed. Charles, however, was dutifully prepared to accept a bride of his father's choosing. With Gondomar's subtle prompting, James soon persuaded himself that nothing would please the King of Spain better than to marry his daughter to a Prince of heretic England.

Whatever the absolute merits of the plan, James should never have allowed himself to entertain it. Rightly or wrongly, the English regarded Spain as Catholicism incarnate. Their horror at the Gunpowder Plot, and their insistence that he maintain the rigour of the penal laws, should have convinced him that they were in no temper to come to terms with the old religion. The sacrifice of Raleigh in 1618 gave immediate point to their hatred of Gondomar and his designs. To appease the war-party, Raleigh was released from prison to go in search of gold in the Orinoco. James told Gondomar where he was going, and promised that he should die if he violated Spain's neutrality. The expedition was wretchedly equipped. Warned to expect him, the Spaniards attacked his ships, and Raleigh returned to die on the old charge of treason. His long imprisonment and his ignoble death have won for him the sympathy of posterity, but even invested with a martyr's halo he is an unattractive figure. His proud intransigence presented the government with an awkward problem, and probably James chose the best way of solving it ; and at the end he gave Raleigh a gambler's chance to save himself. A government which desires peace at home and abroad cannot afford to keep at large men who are expressly contemptuous of peaceful ways.

The outbreak of the Thirty Years War shattered James's security. In 1618 the Bohemians rose against their Hapsburg masters, and offered their throne to James's son-in-law, the Elector Palatine. Against the advice of everyone whom he chose to consult, including James, he accepted it ; and within a few months the Emperor's troops had not only driven him from Bohemia, but had overrun his Electoral territories, and in the name of the Counter-Reformation were threatening the Protestantism of Northern Europe.

English opinion was undisturbed by Frederick's loss of the crown of Bohemia, for to most Englishmen Bohemia was a place off whose coasts seamen might reasonably be wrecked. But the concerted action of the Emperor's troops with the Spanish armies from the Netherlands seemed to make the safety of the Palatinate a token of the safety of Protestantism everywhere. The great Hapsburg offensive, which was to carry the Counter-Reformation to the shores of the North Sea and the Baltic, had begun. To James's natural anxiety for his daughter was added his alarm for 'the state of religion through all Christendom, which almost wholly, under God, rests now upon my shoulders'. He exaggerated his responsibility, just as he exaggerated the power of his diplomacy, unsupported either by armies or by the co-operation of his subjects, to restrain Hapsburg ambition.

He had a plan (so much could not be said for his critics): Prince Charles should marry the Spanish Infanta, and for her dowry she should bring the Palatinate, which James would restore to his contrite son-in-law. With the bone of contention removed, fighting would cease. The plan had the advantage that the solution it proposed was a peaceful one; and if James could have stifled the Thirty Years War at its beginning, all Europe would still be in his debt. For two conspicuous reasons, however, it was not practicable. First, the English had not abated their dislike of the Spanish marriage, and that James should urge it when Protestantism was in actual danger quickened their mistrust of the government's policy. In deference to Gondomar, the penal laws were relaxed in 1619, and they were not enforced again until 1640 [1]; it seemed to be further evidence of Spain's hold over the King's mind. Secondly, the Spaniards were unable, even had they really been willing, to fulfil their side of the bargain. For the Palatinate was in the hands of the Emperor, and they could not be expected to wrest it from him by force. They politely regretted that 'we have a maxim of state that the King of Spain must not fight against the Emperor'. For the present, however, it suited Spain to delude James that his hope might be fulfilled, and it was not until 1623 that he realised that he had been deceived. For four years, during which firm intervention from England might have been decisive, nothing emerged from the English government but diplomacy and words and unrealisable conditions of peace; while the unpopularity of the marriage scheme drove the majority of Englishmen to the Puritan side in politics.

4. *James meets parliament again*

By 1621 the situation had grown so serious that James was obliged to summon his third parliament. He did not anticipate that this parliament would obstruct his policy. The Elector's plight had excited widespread alarm in the country (although attempts to raise loans or gifts for his assistance had been unsuccessful), and it was expected that domestic grievances would be shelved while the Protestant religion was in danger. The duty of parliament when war threatened was to vote the

[1] Except for a few months in 1626.

supplies which the government needed for its military and diplomatic effectiveness. But James was too sanguine. What in fact this parliament did was to refuse adequate supplies, condemn the government's policy, and advance claims to seize the administration and execute measures of its own. So far from forgetting their grievances, the members made use of the foreign crisis to batter the prerogative. Between 1621 and 1629 the shadow of the continental war hung over English politics. Its obligation to shape a foreign policy put the Crown at the mercy of the Commons, who welcomed the country's disgrace abroad since it enabled them to make revolutionary demands at home.

When the government asked for half a million pounds for war expenses, the Commons voted £160,000, and turned to the question of monopolies. Two of the worst offenders, Mitchell and Mompesson, fled in alarm, and in their absence were impeached without a hearing. Having tasted blood, the Commons struck at higher game. A committee under Sir Robert Phelips had detected certain malpractices in Chancery, and in particular had discovered that Lord Chancellor Bacon had sometimes accepted presents from litigants before their suit had been judged. Bacon was known to be the champion of the prerogative against the common law, and Coke urged the Commons to bring him low. Bacon had not the stuff of a fighter. He admitted his guilt—in the free and easy morality of the day his crime was a common one—and implored his peers 'to be merciful unto a broken reed'. James remitted the fine and imprisonment to which he was sentenced, but he was deprived of all his offices and his seat in the Lords. These were the first cases of impeachment since the middle of the fifteenth century; in Tudor times unpopular ministers were removed by Act of Attainder. The revival of the mediaeval weapon showed that the Commons were determined that the Crown's servants should also be acceptable to themselves.

Before they would consider foreign policy, parliament had another hue and cry to follow. An elderly barrister named Floyd, imprisoned in the Fleet as a debtor, had been heard to speak disrespectfully of Frederick and Elizabeth. He was brought before the Commons—unconstitutionally, for the Commons was not a court of law—and sentenced to the pillory and a fine of £1,000. The Lords improved the occasion by increasing the fine to £5,000 ; Floyd was to ride through the City holding the tail of his horse ; he was to be whipped, and hot bacon was to be applied to his wounds between the lashes ; and then he was to be imprisoned for life. The ferocity with which both Houses pursued Floyd was a way of expressing criticism of James's foreign policy. By his conduct of the case John Pym made his parliamentary reputation.

The Commons' advice on foreign affairs attempted to reverse the policy of the King. They asked him to seek a Protestant marriage for his son, and to declare war on Spain ; and instead of the military intervention in Germany which the situation demanded, they were in favour of an Elizabethan war of piracy, 'to enrich ourselves as well as to defend our right and ourselves'. The Palatinate was to be recovered by a naval enterprise in the Caribbean. These counsels were a constitutional affront to the Crown, for royal marriages and foreign policy undoubtedly lay within the prerogative, and were outside the province of the Commons. James refused to listen to the advice, and strove to silence the authors of it. He was met by an angry clamour about the privilege of free speech, and in December, 1621, the Commons entered in their Journals a Protestation about their rights. The Protestation was the first constitutional split between Crown and parliament. The Commons demanded of right that all 'arduous and urgent affairs' in the realm should be referred to them ; and since they controlled supply, and could refuse to finance policies which they disliked, they were in effect claiming to direct the administration of the country. This, as James objected when he tore the protest from the Journals, was 'an usurpation that the majesty of a King can by no means endure'. In the following month he dissolved parliament, complaining that 'some fiery and popular spirits' had ventured 'to argue and debate publicly of matters far above their reach '. Parliament had challenged the Crown's right to powers which hitherto had belonged without question to the authority of the prerogative.

5. *James goes to war*

Disregarding parliament's criticisms, James went ahead with his own solution of his son-in-law's difficulties : he pressed on negotiations for the Spanish marriage. In 1623 Charles, accompanied by Buckingham, went to Madrid to do his own wooing. Bearing the transparent pseudonyms of Tom and John Smith, they set out, thought James, like ' dear adventurous knights to be put in a new romanso '. Their quest was a failure. Their long bluff called at last, the Spaniards said that the Pope's permission must be obtained, and that Charles must first declare himself a Catholic. While these objections were being discussed, Englishmen and Spaniards fell out. The English were distressed by the stiff etiquette which surrounded the Infanta, and took to disparaging the pride, the customs and the accommodation of their hosts. For their part, the Spaniards were amazed by Buckingham's insolent informality, and concluded that they would rather put the Infanta down a well than entrust her to such a man. When Verney lost his temper and struck a priest, it was time for the suitors to come home. They returned humiliated and angry, demanding vengeance ; and found themselves welcomed amid bells and bonfires as returning heroes. The nation was overjoyed that the heir to the throne had returned safe and unmarried, for the Infanta might have accomplished what the Armada had failed to do, and made England Catholic again. Alarm had put the people in an ugly temper. When the collapse of a house in which they were worshipping killed nearly a hundred Catholics, the Londoners stood by and cheered, and would not help the injured ; and the Bishop of London refused a Christian burial to the dead.

Charles and Buckingham demanded war as the only reply to the indignities they had undergone. James, who was crippled by disease, could refuse them nothing, and at last consented to abandon the peace which he had cherished for so many years. Parliament was summoned in 1624, and asked to finance the very war which it had demanded at its last meeting. Although this was the only Stuart parliament which endorsed the general programme which the Crown laid before it, it was still determined to prescribe how the war should be fought. James was too weary to resist any further, and he sought its advice on matters which previously he had refused to allow it to discuss. As the beginning of a sound policy, the penal laws must be enforced. For its wartime offensive, parliament proposed to garrison England and Ireland, provision a fleet and make an alliance with the Dutch. For this programme the Commons voted £300,000, about a fourth of what was necessary; and, being unwilling to trust the Crown to spend the money for purposes of which they approved, they nominated treasurers to supervise war expenditure. The government's plan for a land war in Europe was rejected. The defence of the Palatinate, said Sir Francis Seymour, was not 'fit for the consideration of the House in regard of the infinite charge'. Their enthusiasm for the Protestant cause was not to involve them in undue expenditure.

James meekly allowed the Commons to dictate to him, and even consented to the overthrow of his most efficient servant. Middlesex brought the wrath of the Commons about his head by objecting to the war on the ground of expense. Charles and Buckingham, still smarting under insult, joined the clamour against him, and supported the Commons in demanding his impeachment. James gave in, but warned Charles that he would have his bellyful of impeachments: 'you are making a rod with which you will be scourged yourself'. The Commons were not yet done. Claiming to act as 'inquisitors general of the grievances of the kingdom', they followed up their victories by raising once more the question of monopolies. A law passed in 1624 declaring all monopolies to be void was the first statutory attack on the prerogative since the Wars of the Roses ended.

In 1624 England went to war. Impressment mustered Shakespeare's ' discarded, unjust serving-men, younger sons to younger brothers, revolted tapsters and ostlers trade-fallen ; the cankers of a calm world and long peace '. The force was put under the command of Mansfeld, a wandering soldier of fortune. The money allotted to it was spent before it embarked from Dover, and there was no more to be had ; for Buckingham was negotiating a French marriage for Charles, and since he was afraid to face parliament's criticisms, there was no autumn session in 1624. The expedition set out with no objective. James shrank from making an actual breach with Spain, and would not let it assist the Dutch campaign against Spinola ; and Louis XIII forbade it to pass through French territory into Europe. Finally it sailed to Flushing in January, 1625. By March 9,000 men had died of hunger and disease, and 3,000 stragglers either slunk back to England or entered the service of the Dutch.

In the middle of this humiliation James died. He had failed to convince the English that his theories of government were right, and Salisbury, Bacon and Middlesex, the ablest of his ministers, had failed to preserve the system of the Tudors. In place of the Tudor division of power, two groups were struggling for political supremacy : the Crown, the Privy Council, the prerogative courts and the Bishops were ranged against the Commons, the lawyers and the Puritans. One side took its sanction from the Divine Right of Kings, the other from mediaeval theories of a limited monarchy and the supremacy of the law. The Lords took neither one side nor the other. They were the most conservative element in the nation, and guarded the constitution against encroachment from either side. First the Crown and then the Commons seemed to present the greater danger, and the Lords wavered between the two. In 1625 they were displeased with the Crown, for James had cheapened the prestige of the peerage by his reckless grants to favourites and his sale of titles to fill his treasury.[1] They resented, too, being ousted

[1] In 1603 there were fifty-nine lay peers, of whom only eight had received their titles in the reign of Elizabeth. James created sixty new titles in twenty-two years.

from their traditional privilege of advising the Crown by upstarts like Buckingham and Middlesex. But wise statesmanship, wiser than Charles or Buckingham knew how to provide, could always recover their allegiance. The growing radicalism of the Commons was soon to drive them to the defence of the constitution, and in 1642 they were to perish with it.

CHAPTER XIII

THE BREAKDOWN OF THE CONSTITUTION

Character of Charles I. Failure of his first two parliaments. Failure of his foreign policy. The Petition of Right.

1. *The character of Charles I*

Charles was not intended to be King. Born a second son, he was brought up for the Church, and, had Henry lived, he might well have been Archbishop of Canterbury. He was studious, cultured and retiring, with more of the qualities of a scholar than a statesman. His more accomplished brother, whom he worshipped, teased him for his backwardness, for he could not speak until he was five, nor walk until he was seven. These early deformities accompanied him into manhood. He always walked with a limp, and an impediment in his speech made him hesitant and inarticulate. He was always, he said, 'unfit for much speaking', and this explains much of the haughtiness for which he was reproached. In fact, he was diffident; he was reluctant to enter upon discussions, because he could not properly express his thoughts. These defects apart, Charles was a gifted man. His bearing was graceful, his mind fastidious. He drove from his court the squalor and cheap immoralities of his father's day, and in place of drunkards and wantons he welcomed painters, poets and men of learning. No English King has had a finer taste in painting, and until his victorious enemies broke it up, his collection of pictures was the best in Europe. Many of his subjects who were debarred by their religion from any appreciation of culture held it against him that he was a connoisseur. A Puritan pamphleteer complained of 'Nonesuch Charles squandering away millions of pounds on braveries and vanities, on old rotten pictures and broken-nosed marbles'. Those who knew Charles best loved him most, and these men have paid tribute to his qualities as a husband, a father and a friend; while the course of his life enabled him to show the whole world his personal courage and his loyalty to the things which he valued.

As a King, Charles had faults which were aggravated by the time and difficulties of his inheritance. Like his father, he believed in the mystical inspiration of his office. Although he talked about it less, he felt it more deeply. To James, Divine Right was largely an intellectual conception; to Charles, it was a question of faith, as deeply rooted as his belief in his Church. 'I must avow that I owe the account of my actions to God alone'. He died in the faith in which he had lived: he said on the scaffold, 'a subject and a sovereign are clean different things'. He inherited a prerogative and a Church; he must hand them to his successor unblemished and intact as he received them. This was the plain motive of Charles's doings. Unfortunately, it led him into the duplicity, the tendency to 'squiborate', which hampered his dealings with his subjects. Religious mystics are notorious for being unwilling to explain themselves to the uninitiated, or even to treat them with ordinary fairness. Charles was a political mystic. His lofty sense of his mission taught him that he need not explain his courses to those who had no part in the mystery of kingship. Therefore he did not scruple to deceive them. He was not obliged to keep troth with bad men; and those who obstructed him stood revealed as bad men. He need not keep troth with any subject, for King and subjects moved on different planes. As late as 1645, when his people were at war against his conceptions of government, he still hoped to bring them back to a sense of the true relationship between themselves and him. He wrote to his Secretary of State that if 'you would put them in mind that they were arrant rebels and that their end must be damnation, ruin, and infamy, except they repented . . . it might do good'.

Charles's other failings grew from that conception of his office which committed him to deliberate insincerity. He was distant and aloof. The Venetian who reported that ' this King is so constituted that he never obliges anyone, either by word or deed ', may have been exaggerating, but he was expressing the common opinion. The defect in his speech combined with the loftiness of his position to make him reserved and unapproachable. He had too the common failing of the Stuarts, of having no insight into the feelings of his people ; blindly convinced of the integrity of his purpose, he could not realise what interpretation the average man might put upon his actions. At the last, even his virtues were fatal to him. James's loquaciousness and earthy good humour had spared him the worst consequences of his mistakes ; he surrendered before the last ditch was reached. But Charles was too stubborn to compromise. Because he would not yield to base men and base designs, he had to be broken by their superior strength.

2. *The Parliaments of 1625 and 1626*

Before he met his first parliament, in June, 1625, Charles had taken two steps that were to be disastrous for him : he had undertaken to continue the war against Spain, and he had married. The marriage, negotiated for him by Buckingham, was with Henrietta Maria, daughter of Henry IV of France. A secret treaty provided that she should be allowed to maintain a Catholic household ; and that the English government should be lenient towards Catholics, and should lend help to the King of France against his enemies. It was not surprising that Buckingham was unwilling to meet the Commons while he was arranging this match. Henrietta Maria, like the Infanta, was a Catholic ; and this alone damned the marriage in the sight of the English people. As if that were not enough, the government had committed itself to a policy of toleration which it would not be allowed to carry out ; and to oppose the enemies of Louis XIII, although they might well be Huguenots. The marriage turned out to be fatal to the Stuarts in two generations: to Charles I because it tainted his court with Popery; and to his sons because it bound them to France when Louis XIV was thought to be England's greatest enemy.

The collapse of Mansfeld's expedition did not quench Charles's ardour for a war which he felt to be just. He immediately promised a subsidy of £30,000 a month to his uncle, Christian IV of Denmark, and a force of 6,000 men to the Dutch. Once more, he should have paused and reasoned. The Crown had found it impossible to live in time of peace without levying taxes which irritated parliament; the attempt to wage a war had already given the Commons an opportunity to dictate terms. Charles could not hope to hold his own when he voluntarily undertook an expensive foreign policy. His conscience, however, obliged him to support the Protestant cause; and Buckingham, who had been intoxicated by his sudden popularity when he returned from Madrid, was confident that he could persuade parliament to vote the necessary funds.

Parliament greeted the new King with a loyal address, congratulating him on the happy omen that he had succeeded at the age of twenty-five; for that was the age at which King Hezekiah had ascended his throne. The Crown's spokesmen in the Commons were nonentities, and they could not induce the members to vote more than the beggarly sum of £140,000. 'There is a necessity', said Sir Nathaniel Rich, 'to look into the King's estate, how it may subsist of itself.' Phelips, who had once been so clamorous against Spain that James had sent him to cool his passion in the Tower, now led the opposition to the vote of war subsidies. The members wanted to know why Mansfeld's expedition had failed, why they had not been summoned before it set out, and why ships had been promised for use against the Huguenots in La Rochelle. If the war was to be continued, they must supervise the expenditure of supply; meanwhile, the best assurance of the nation's safety was to suppress the Catholics at home, and this was not being done. As an example of sentiments which alarmed their patriotism they denounced Montagu's *Appello Caesarem*, a book which blended Popish tendencies in religion with absolutism in politics. Finally, they proved their mistrust of the government by proposing to grant the King the right to collect tunnage and poundage, which had been granted to his predecessors for the whole of their reigns, for one year only. Charles, who had refused to give parliament any details of the foreign policy it was asked to finance, dissolved it in August.

Having seen that the Commons were not disposed to vote money even for objects of which they had formerly professed to approve, Charles should now have made peace. He decided, however, to keep his word to his allies, and show his people that he could win great victories without their help. When English arms had achieved triumphs at which Europe marvelled, then, Buckingham argued, the penitent Commons would no longer be deaf to appeals. For Buckingham, success was always just round the corner.

The government decided to revive the glories of Drake, by a raid on Cadiz. An armada was prepared, consisting of men-of-war, merchantmen and colliers, and put under the command of Viscount Wimbledon, who had some reputation as a soldier but none as a seaman. The ships were manned by felons and vagabonds collected by the press-gang; the food was so foul that dogs passed it by; the stores were defective, the sails rotten; much of the ammunition would not fit the rusted muskets. Wimbledon set out with no definite orders and his authority impaired by a council of war; pirates in the Channel delayed his start; the merchantmen and colliers had no enthusiasm for the business, and the ships contributed by the Dutch were equally half-hearted. The attack on Cadiz collapsed in drunkenness and disorder, and Wimbledon, having sought in vain to redeem himself by finding the treasure-fleet from Mexico, discovered that his ships were unfit to remain at sea any longer. He had no more food for his men, and on the way home they died in hundreds. Buckingham has been made to bear the responsibility for this disaster. As Lord High Admiral he was responsible for the arrangements, but it is difficult to see that anyone in his place could have done better. All the expeditions sent out under Elizabeth had bad food and indifferent equipment; it was a commonplace that a large number of the crew would die of disease and starvation. Further, several Elizabethan expeditions, even though Drake or Hawkins had led them, had fared as badly. Buckingham had no money for expensive equipment, and money voted to the navy during James's reign had been embezzled by the men who were loudest in their criticism of the disaster. Finally, in twenty years of peace the English had lost the habit of war, and the men on whom the government was forced to rely were of necessity untrained and inexperienced. The real case against Buckingham is that knowing how weak his resources were, he still chose to gamble against hopeless odds.

In 1626 Charles called his second parliament without the expected victory to strengthen his bargaining. Hoping to put the Commons in a good temper, he enforced the penal laws, despite his contradictory promises to France; and he deprived them of their most active leaders by appointing six of them to be sheriffs. These devices did not avail him. The Commons continued to suspect the court of Popery, and they found a new, more dangerous leader in Sir John Eliot, a vigorous, unimaginative man, whose stream of words was endless. They would not consider supply until they had aired their grievances: the past must be explained, before the future would be provided for. Eliot had been in Plymouth when Wimbledon's expedition crawled in, and he was eloquent about the condition of the ships and the sufferings of the men. Soon the Commons followed up his hint that the country's disasters were to be attributed to 'those we trust', and made a direct attack on Buckingham, 'the moth of all goodness', by preparing his impeachment. Eliot and Digges, the managers of the impeachment, were imprisoned, and Charles protested and threatened. The Lords took the side of the Commons against him, for he had violated their privileges by putting Lord Arundel in the Tower and trying to prevent the Earl of Bristol from taking his seat. Both Houses refused to do business until he released his prisoners. Finally, to save Buckingham, he dissolved the parliament, sending the angry members to their homes in mind of the one unchallenged power which he still held over them : 'Remember that parliaments are altogether in my power for their calling, sitting and dissolution ; therefore, as I find the fruits of them good or evil, they are to continue or not to be.'

3. *The Petition of Right*

Although two parliaments had obstructed his policy, stormed his prerogative and attacked his friend, Charles resumed his efforts to fight a war unaided. To add to his difficulties, he and Buckingham had now quarrelled with France. The causes of the war into which they drifted were trivial, and a little statesmanship and discretion would have mended them. The French complained that the marriage treaty was not being fulfilled, and objected because the Queen's French attendants, who had behaved outrageously since they landed, had been expelled from England. On the other hand, Buckingham was displeased because Richelieu refused to come into the open against Spain and join in the English expeditions ; and Louis would not recognise Charles as official protector of the French Huguenots. More urgent than these diplomatic vexations was the rivalry between French and English seamen. Disputes about contraband, piracy and the seizure of merchant shipping, had already come to blows. Instead of attempting to settle these differences, Charles and Buckingham made them sufficient ground for going to war with the nation which was potentially their best ally against the Hapsburgs.

In the summer of 1627 the government went to war with its new enemy. Buckingham's attempt to seize the island of Rhé, in the harbour of La Rochelle, had all the handicaps which normally paralysed Stuart expeditions. Buckingham himself showed courage and military resource, but his half-hearted, disorganised followers shrank before the French attack. He withdrew with heavy losses, and forty English flags hung in Notre Dame. Patriots bewailed 'the greatest and shamefullest overthrow since the loss of Normandy'. 'Since England was England', said Denzil Holles, 'she received not so dishonourable a blow.' A small force sent to help the King of Denmark was cut off and surrounded at Stade, on the Elbe; and when Denbigh again took the fleet to La Rochelle in the following year, Richelieu's new fortifications so impressed him that he sailed home without venturing to test their strength.

Even an unsuccessful war has to be paid for, and in 1627 the government used drastic methods. Troops were levied from the counties; the maritime districts were forced to supply ships or ship-money; tunnage and poundage were levied by prerogative. Finally, 'resolving in a common danger to rely upon a common care and affection', Charles demanded a forced loan equivalent to five subsidies, or £350,000. Although the clergy preached on the impropriety of resisting the King, many of the gentry refused to pay, and about eighty were imprisoned by order of the Crown. In a test-case brought by Sir Thomas Darnel and other knights, the King's Bench ruled that men so imprisoned might not be granted bail. To house his troops, Charles billeted them on private persons; and to keep them in some sort of order, he was obliged to issue commissions of martial law, which involved summary jurisdiction over soldiers and civilians alike. By such measures as these the whole nation was made to suffer for the failure of Crown and parliament to come to terms.

About a million pounds were raised in 1627, but this did not meet Charles's commitments. Being unwilling to risk any more illegal expedients, he met parliament again, in March, 1628; by which time yet another grievance had come to a head. The country was growing alarmed for the safety of religion; not only in Europe, where the Protestant cause was at its darkest, but at home in England, where a thinly veiled Popery seemed to be stalking the high places of Church and state. A new stimulus had lately been given to Anglicanism by the doctrines of James Hermanzoon, or Arminius, Professor of Theology at Leyden. Arminius preached in Holland the doctrines which Hooker and Lancelot Andrewes had made the basis of the creed of the Church of England. Rejecting the Calvinist belief in a foreordained grace, he taught that man was a self-determining agent; that Christ had died for all men, and that each individual was free to receive or reject the salvation that was offered to him. Holland was an inhospitable place for such beliefs; Oldenbarneveldt was murdered for holding them, and Grotius put in prison. The Synod of Dort, which was held in 1619, condemned Arminianism as heresy, and decided in favour of the belief that God damned most of His children before they were born.

The tradition of the English Church was more sympathetic to Arminianism. For Arminius held that, although the Bible was the infallible guide of human action, the usages and the accumulated wisdom of the Church helped the worshipper to approach his God. Images and music stirred his reverence, the priest in the authority of his office broke down barriers. The Church and its organisation, which God had sanctioned, were inseparable from true religion.

These doctrines were echoed by the Anglican clergy in their growing struggle with the Puritans. To many Englishmen, however, the Arminian belief in the priesthood and the ceremonious enrichment of the service was but the new disguise in which the Scarlet Woman made war on their innocence: 'an Arminian is the spawn of a Papist'. The French Queen and her courtiers flaunted their Popery, and thousands of Catholics went unmolested because the government had again ceased to enforce the salutary laws for their restraint. Men saw danger, too, in the readiness of High Churchmen to defend the King. The political alliance which James had defined in the words 'No Bishop, no King' had tightened as the position of both Crown and Bishops had deteriorated. In their fear that a Puritan 'parity' threatened their safety, the Anglican clergy looked to the King, their constitutional sovereign, to defend them; and in return they protected him from their pulpits when the same rebelliousness showed itself in the state. By its nature, Arminianism could not be a popular movement, commanding support in parliament and nation. It appealed only to an educated minority, who knew that the Puritans would crush them if they could; so they made common cause with the King, who had the same enemies. Montagu had already appealed to Caesar: '*Domine Imperator, defende me gladio, et ego te defendam calamo.*' Bishop Laud had addressed the parliament of 1626 on the need for unity in the state, and urged them in the name of God to obey the King. The more critical the situation became, the more indiscreet were the High Churchmen. Dr. Sibthorpe, preaching before the judges, stretched the doctrine of Apostolic Obedience to include payment of the King's forced loan. 'If a Prince impose an immoderate, yea, an unjust tax, yet the subject . . . is bound in conscience to submit.' Dr. Manwaring taught that 'all the significations of a royal pleasure are . . . in the nature and force of a command', even when Kings 'command flatly against the law of God'. Such indiscretion injured both parties of the alliance, and seemed to justify the suspicion that the clergy were encouraging the King to bind his people under tyranny and deliver them to the servitude of Rome. Arminians were not Papists, and Charles was not a continental tyrant; but his undoubted preference for those elements in the English Church that were nearest to Rome convinced the Commons, when they met, that here was another matter over which they would do well to be vigilant. The Commons as a whole were not actively Puritan; and when they consorted with Puritanism, they did so because the tendencies of the court seemed to be bearing out the accusations of those religious extremists who believed that the farther a man moved from Rome, the nearer he was to God.

In opening parliament Charles made a plea for co-operation, than which 'nothing could be more pleasing unto me'. Having considered the suggestion of Pym that they should lament the distress of Protestantism by ordering a general fast, the Commons decided to postpone their attack on Buckingham, and petition the King against the recent abuses of the prerogative. If the King made a favourable reply, subsidies might be voted as he asked. Accordingly they submitted to him the four resolutions known as the Petition of Right, protesting against the levying of 'any gift, loan, benevolence, tax, or such like charge', without the consent of parliament; arbitrary imprisonment without cause shown; billeting of soldiers on private persons; and the issue of commissions of martial law. To soften the blow, the Lords had suggested the addition of a saving clause, 'to leave entire that sovereign power wherewith your Majesty is entrusted for the protection, safety, and happiness of your people'. Coke and Eliot, however, would not admit that such a power existed. 'No saving in this kind . . . can be other than destructive to our work', Eliot reminded the Commons; and Coke objected that 'sovereign power is no parliamentary word'. If the King were admitted to have discretionary authority to rise above the law, the battle would be lost.

So the Petition of Right was framed on the basis of 'thou shalt not'. So far as it went, it was admirable, and the grievances it remedied were real. In his difficulties, the King had stretched the prerogative too far, and 1627 was an unpleasant year. He might well have argued, however, that parliament had driven him to these undesirable measures, by refusing to help him to wage a war for which the nation had formerly been enthusiastic. The defect of the Petition of Right was that, outside its particular provisions, it settled nothing; it brought Crown and parliament to a constitutional stalemate. By restraining the action of the prerogative, it forbade the King to wage war unless the Commons approved of it, and prevented him from silencing his critics. But the constitutional ideas of Coke and Eliot came to a stop when they had successfully curbed the prerogative. Until parliament claimed to initiate policy and carry it out, until supreme authority in the state passed from Crown to Commons, there could be no executive action in England. The Commons in 1628 were in the position of the Constituent Assembly of

1791 in France: they had blunted the Crown's executive power, and put nothing in its place. In the eighteenth century, when their sovereignty was admitted, the Commons carried out measures which they had obstructed when they were attempted by the Stuarts. They united England and Scotland; they reformed the mediaeval system of taxation, and provided the government with money sufficient for its needs; and they armed the nation for a policy of deliberate and self-seeking aggression. Such measures were clearly necessary to the nation's efficiency; but they were equally necessary in 1625. The Stuarts were less anxious to be tyrants than to be efficient, and with this object they tried to reform the machinery of government where it was defective. The Commons affected to see in this policy a threat to their liberty, and they impeded the Crown by emphasising the defects in the constitution. The result was the chaos of 1627. But the Petition of Right offered no solution; and there could be no solution until the Commons claimed the sovereignty which they denied to the Crown.

4. *The final breach with parliament*

Charles sought to evade the Petition when it was sent up to him. He delayed, consulted the judges and looked round for expedients; but at length, in June, 1628, he gave his assent as to a private bill, thus giving the resolutions the effect of a statute. Although he was voted the promised subsidies, his acceptance of the Petition was not, as he had hoped, the beginning of better relations between himself and parliament. For while he had been hesitating about his decision, the Commons had busied themselves with other grievances. Coke revived the attack on Buckingham, and rallied the members to the chase: 'this man is the grievance of grievances. Let us set down the causes of all our disasters, and all will reflect upon him.' They inveighed against Arminians, and started to impeach Manwaring. Finally, they denied the King's right to levy tunnage and poundage, on the ground that the Petition of Right had forbidden it. Charles angrily replied that he had confirmed old liberties, not granted new ones. The difference between the wording of the clause in the Petition and the wording of the Tunnage and Poundage Act of 1641 (which forbade any ' subsidy, custom, impost, or charge whatsoever ') shows that the Commons' claim was unfounded. Realising that as fast as he made concessions, the Commons thrust new demands upon him, Charles prorogued parliament before the end of the month.

The unaccommodating temper of the Commons brought Thomas Wentworth to the side of the Crown. Hitherto the Crown had regarded him as a dangerous enemy ; he had been pricked as a sheriff in 1626, and he had gone to prison for resisting the forced loan. But his opposition had always been constructive. He had resisted only when the government resorted to illegalities, and he had always sought a compromise between Crown and parliament. Thus in 1621 he opposed the vicious attack on Floyd, and urged the Commons to face the foreign danger by granting adequate subsidies ; in 1624 he defended Middlesex, and again demanded subsidies. He deserted the parliamentary leaders because they were claiming for parliament a more exalted place in the constitution than he wished it to occupy. He wished it to perform its Tudor function of offering criticism when criticism was necessary : when, for instance, an irresponsible minister like Buckingham was directing foreign policy ; but his orderly mind hated to see the quarrel between King and parliament issuing in anarchy at home and dishonour abroad. The session of 1628 revealed that the more ruthless members of the Commons did not intend to compose the quarrel. Moreover, the unsubtle Eliot was so excitable that no wound would heal unless he were restrained. In the cause of good government, therefore, Wentworth changed sides. Now that the Petition of Right would necessarily sober Buckingham's dizzy foreign policy, more was to be hoped from the Crown than from parliament.

A few weeks later Buckingham was stabbed at Portsmouth by John Felton, a naval lieutenant, Puritan, unpaid and unpromoted.

The man was gloomy and unbalanced, and repented of what he had done; but the people hailed him as their deliverer, and cheered Buckingham's body to its grave. In September Buckingham's policy perished too. In his place, the Earl of Lindsey led the fleet again to La Rochelle, and watched the town surrender to Richelieu. Without his friend to inspire them, Charles undertook no more enterprises abroad.

'The grievance of grievances' was gone; the government could hope to find the Commons more reasonable when they met for the spring session of 1629. But reasonableness was no part of their programme. They were angry with Wentworth, and they concentrated their new attack on two sources of complaint: that Popery and Arminianism were spreading, to the scandal and danger of the nation; and that the King was still collecting customs duties to which he was not entitled. One of their number, John Rolle, had forfeited his goods for refusing to pay tunnage and poundage, and they asserted that the privileges of parliament obliged the government to restore the goods; which amounted to a claim that privilege exempted all members from paying their taxes. Then they fell to complaining about the favour shown to High Churchmen: Montagu, for instance, had lately been made a Bishop. Buckingham's death had not dispersed the accumulated discontent of years. In fact, parliament found a new scapegoat: the Treasurer Weston, 'in whose person, I fear', said Eliot, 'is contracted all the evil that we do suffer'.

Charles was weary of parliaments: 'They are of the nature of cats, they ever grow cursed with age'. Seeing that co-operation was remoter than ever, he ordered an adjournment. Eliot, whom a parliamentary session, with its opportunities for oratory, excited out of his reason, proclaimed that parliament had the right to decide when it should be adjourned. A ridiculous scene followed. Locking the doors against the King's servants, the members held the protesting Speaker in his chair, so that he should not dissolve their meeting: 'God's wounds, you shall sit until we please to rise.' Then amid shouting and brawling they carried by acclamation three resolutions which Eliot put before them : ' whosoever shall bring in innovation of religion ', or extend the sway of Popery or Arminianism, ' shall be reputed a capital enemy to this kingdom and commonwealth ' ; that it was similar treason in any subject to advise the King to levy tunnage and poundage ; and that anyone who paid these duties, if the King should levy them, was ' a betrayer of the liberties of England '. Then the Speaker was permitted to rise.

The Commons had overreached themselves. On March 10th, 1629, Charles dissolved them for their ' undutiful and seditious carriage '. Several members were thrown into prison, Strode and Valentine remaining there until 1640, and Eliot until the discomforts of confinement killed him in 1632. The cautious Rudyerd had warned his colleagues against driving the King beyond endurance : ' let it be our Masterpiece so to carry our business as we keep Parliaments on foot '. It was not only that Charles could not forgive the insult put upon the Speaker, who was his servant ; he was by now convinced that no good could come of his calling parliaments. He believed that a few seditious men were poisoning the minds of the members and frustrating his government. Defending his decision to dispense with parliament in the future, he complained of ' some few vipers ' who cast ' this mist of undutifulness ' over ' the sincerer and better part of the House ' ; and the parliamentarian D'Ewes supported him, saying that ' divers fiery spirits in the House of Commons were very faulty, and cannot be excused '. The Lords, alienated by Eliot's impetuous irresponsibility, shared the King's disgust with the Commons. Thus exactly a hundred years after the meeting of the Reformation Parliament had inaugurated the Tudor system of government, Charles admitted that the old methods would no longer work. In claiming to direct his policy and dominate his ministers, the Commons had overstepped the place appointed for them and encroached upon the undoubted rights of the prerogative. Henceforth he would rule without seeking their co-operation or advice.

CHAPTER XIV

CHARLES GOVERNS WITHOUT PARLIAMENT

Financial measures of the government: ship-money. Laud. Policy of Thorough. The war with Scotland.

1. *Charles's financial measures*

Charles issued a proclamation in which he justified his policy and appealed to the country's sympathy against the reckless and intemperate opposition of the Commons. 'That we may appear to the world in the truth and sincerity of our actions', he pointed out that, while he and his ministers had pursued a foreign policy which the nation had demanded, the Commons had disgraced England and betrayed the Protestant cause; that they had blamed Buckingham for all the misfortunes of the time, but had not abated their opposition when Buckingham was dead; that they had voted little enough money anyhow, and had diminished the value of the grants they had made, by encouraging the assessors to report falsely on men's incomes. He referred to the revolutionary conspiracy which had created confusion 'to abate the powers of our Crown', and to the treacherous men who 'under pretence of liberty and freedom of speech . . . take liberty . . . to erect an universal over-swaying power to themselves'. Finally, let his subjects thank God for 'the great peace and quietness which every man enjoyeth under his own vine and fig-tree'.

On grounds both of law and policy the King's arguments were sound, and the customary description of these eleven years of non-parliamentary government as a 'despotism' is valueless.

The Council and its organs provided a sufficient machinery for peace-time government which should never violate the letter of the law. Death soon removed Coke from the field of battle, and the judges, consulted on the legality, not on the policy, of the government's actions, gave a series of decisions which in law were unimpeachable. Nor were the Crown's objects merely selfish. It proposed to use conciliar government to promote the well-being of all classes, to purify finance, to prevent further humiliations by equipping an efficient navy, and, by means of the royal supremacy in the Church, to suppress controversy and compel a general reverence for the traditional usages of Christianity. Clarendon has testified to its success. While the continent of Europe was torn by a long and destructive war, 'this kingdom and all his majesty's dominions . . . enjoyed the greatest calm, and the fullest measure of felicity, that any people in any age, for so long time together, have been blessed with; to the wonder and envy of all the parts of Christendom. . . The kingdoms we now lament were alone looked upon as the garden of the world.'

The government's most urgent problem was finance. Although peace was made at once with France and Spain, the Crown's hereditary revenues could not meet the expenses of administration, which were over £600,000. To provide the balance—until 1635, revenue came within £20,000 of expenditure, and thereafter there was a surplus—various devices were adopted. The sale of offices, pensions and grants of land, the constant resource of the needy Stuarts, continued as before. Weston, the Treasurer, was thrifty in his master's interest; his economies in the household and his check on fraud saved money at the cost of his own popularity. The government shared in the prosperity of trade by levying tunnage and poundage; the merchants protested, but, faced with the alternatives of paying the duties or losing their trade, they quickly gave in. In 1638 the revenue from the customs was £127,000, and this was the mainstay of the Crown's financial system.

Certain other devices were less productive, and at the same

time less defensible. There was on the statute-book an old law of Edward I, that every freeholder with land worth £20 a year should become a knight, or compound for his refusal. Taught by his opponents that the laws of bygone ages sometimes made effective weapons in the present, Charles imposed this obligation on all freeholders whose land was valued above £40 a year. Similarly, the Crown revived its ancient jurisdiction over the forests. The limits of the royal forests had been fixed by a perambulation in 1297. This was now ignored, and private owners had to compensate the Crown for the encroachments of their ancestors on the Forests of Dean, Epping, Waltham, Rockingham, and the New Forest. Seventeen villages were added to the Forest of Dean; the area of Rockingham Forest was enlarged from six square miles to sixty; the whole of Essex, except for one hundred, was declared to be forest. The irritation of rural proprietors outweighed the slender financial benefits. As Clarendon explained, the burden 'lighted most upon people of quality and honour, who thought themselves above ordinary oppressions, and therefore like to remember it with more sharpness'. The same men had another grievance in the heavy fines imposed upon them for enclosure and depopulation.

So far the weight of the Crown's financial measures fell most severely on those best able to pay. For a generation or more the gentry and merchants of England had escaped paying the taxes that were due from them, and there was essential justice in their being called upon to make their contribution towards the expenses of government. When, however, the Crown found a loophole in the law of 1624 and revived monopolies, the bulk of the burden fell on the consumer. The act did not forbid the issue of monopolies to companies. Corporations were formed, therefore, to receive, in return for an annual payment to the Crown, the sole right to manufacture particular commodities, which came to include soap, wine, salt, starch and coal. These new monopolies alienated the trading classes from the Crown, and made the poor man pay more heavily for his necessaries. There was point in the eloquent complaint made by a member of the Long Parliament, that monopolies were 'like the frogs of Egypt . . . they sup in our cup, they dip in our dish, they sit by our fire ; we find them in the dye-vat, wash-bowl, and powdering-tub '.

The decision taken by the King and his advisers in 1633, to levy ship-money in the following year, sprang not from financial necessity, but from the serious and admitted needs of the navy. With Europe still at war, the country's sea-borne trade was harassed by combatants and pirates, from whom it was too weak to claim redress. Turks, corsairs from the Barbary coast, and marauders from Dunkirk, swept the Channel. The Dutch were so contemptuous of the rights of English fishermen that they landed on the East Coast to dry their nets on the beach. Merchant shipping was at the mercy of the pirates, who even dared to swoop down on the coastal towns and kidnap the inhabitants. The source of the decay of English seamanship was the tired incompetence of Lord Howard of Effingham, who, as Earl of Nottingham, was Lord High Admiral for many years ; and the systematic corruption of his treasurer, Sir Robert Mansell, and his other subordinates. James had enquired into the state of the navy, but Mansell was influential enough to blanket his investigations. Buckingham and Middlesex were not so easy to shake off, and in a few years they doubled the number of ships, at the same time halving naval expenditure. This was the measure of Mansell's corruption. The disgrace of the war years showed that Buckingham's reforms had not gone far enough, and Charles now determined to make his navy efficient. He did this of his own free will. Had his aims been merely selfish, he could have left the coast towns to provide their flimsy defences, and abandoned merchants and fishermen to the pirates and the Dutch. He preferred, however, in the interests of national prestige, to enforce the claims of Selden's *Mare Clausum*,[1] and assert England's authority in the

[1] A pamphlet published in 1635 in reply to the *Mare Liberum* of Grotius. It asserted that the sea could be treated as private property.

narrow seas. Apart from a loan appropriated for the fortifications of Berwick, every penny levied by ship-money was spent on the navy.

The first levy was on maritime districts only, but in 1635 it was extended to the whole kingdom. Another general levy in the following year suggested that the government had found a means to impose a permanent tax on the whole kingdom, and a caucus of the opposition, which met regularly at Broughton, the home of Lord Saye and Sele, decided to fight a test-case. The case was heard in 1637, the year in which Captain Rainborough vindicated the government's policy by rescuing over three hundred Englishmen from the corsairs of Sallee. John Hampden, a wealthy landowner of Buckinghamshire, objected to paying the tax of twenty shillings for which he was assessed. Only two of the judges condemned ship-money as illegal,[1] and seven of them decided that the King had a right to call on the service of his subjects in time of danger, and that he had the sole right, without recourse to parliament, of decreeing when an emergency existed. The verdict of the judges alarmed the nation, for there was a prospect that the government might impose unlimited taxation on a plea of emergency that the judges would always support. One of the judges, Finch, had boldly asserted that to the King's right and power of defending the kingdom 'no act of parliament makes any difference'. Finding therefore that their favourite weapon of the rule of law was being turned against them, the opposition resorted to sabotage. The magnates encouraged local resistance to the levy, and in 1639 only 20 per cent. of the tax could be collected. On balance, the judges' decision did the King more harm than good. It seemed, said Clarendon, to leave 'no man anything which he might call his own'; and it prepared his enemies to take drastic steps when the calling of parliament again brought him within reach of their displeasure.

[1] But three more decided for Hampden on the technical ground that they objected to the procedure of collection.

2. *Strafford and the policy of Thorough*

The year 1640 is the real turning-point in the history of England. The overthrow of conciliar government in the first eight months of the Long Parliament deprived the King of the effective use of his discretionary prerogative, and transferred supreme power in the state to the hands of the Commons. Politically, this had long been inevitable, for the balance of economic forces was against the Crown; for all their brave theories, the Stuarts had been steadily on the retreat. The change would be less easy to regret had its social implications not been so tragic. The struggle over enclosures had already revealed what was at stake: against the claim of the landowners that a man might do as he pleased with his own, the Crown had not hesitated to assert the mediaeval doctrine that property was a trust, and that the prosperity of the few must not be founded on the bondage and suffering of the many. The Crown had failed: the economic tide had swamped its efforts to check enclosure. But from the wreck of its social schemes it had succeeded in salvaging the principle that the poor were poor through no fault of their own, and that their care was a charge upon society which it must be forced to perform. Concern for the evicted labourer and the unemployed vagrant was characteristic of the Crown's attitude towards the less fortunate of its subjects. The Catholic idea of the unity of society survived the Reformation, and was only gradually shattered by the Puritan belief that some were born in grace, and that there were others whom no earthly efforts could save. Until 1640 the policy of the Crown, manifested in countless judgments given in the conciliar courts, was to emphasise the responsibilities, as well as the privileges, of property, to maintain the just price, to check engrossing, forestalling and regrating, to curb extortion, and to prevent unscrupulous speculators from exploiting society for their individual profit. The resentment unloosed on the prerogative courts was provoked as much by their social virtues as by the constitutional usurpations with which they were charged. Under the Stuarts, no less than in Tudor and mediaeval times, the intention often outran the performance, and the high ideal was tarnished by political or financial interest. But there was no deviation from the principle. The criterion of a prosperous community was the welfare of all its members; economic efficiency was only a means by which this end could be realised, and not the primary object of being. By its attitude to the vital question of poor relief the victorious oligarchy showed its intention of raising social standards of a different kind.

The twilight of prerogative government in England was illuminated by the career of Thomas Wentworth, Earl of Strafford, one of the noblest figures in the seventeenth-century conflict. The ideal of the system to which Strafford and Laud in their correspondence gave the name of 'Thorough' was a vigorous and unified administration acting impartially in the interests of all. 'For the State indeed', wrote Laud, 'I am for Thorough.' Thorough does not mince matters; it is on the side of discipline and efficiency, and sometimes it is rough with the obstinate and the slow-witted. But it had been an axiom of Tudor government that individual rights must sometimes be sacrificed, and even after 1629 Strafford still hoped to revive the old system. He was ready to admit parliament, suitably chastened and content to resume its traditional relationship with the Crown, to its place in the constitution. But, in the words of his friend George Radcliffe, 'his experience taught him that it was far safer that the King should increase in power, than that the people should gain an advantage over the King. That may turn to the prejudice of particular sufferers, this draws with it the ruin of the whole.' Like Bacon, he claimed an emergency sovereignty for the Crown: the right to set aside the law in the interests of expediency, and to override the complaints of men who 'made the public service an excuse for enriching themselves at the public expense, or the dry, technical arguments of the lawyers which would hinder the accomplishment of schemes for the public good '.[1] The place of parliament was not to hinder, but to offer constructive criticism; its refusal to perform its appointed task had driven Strafford to the service of the Crown. For 'the authority of a King is the keystone which closeth up the arch of order and government'; once 'ravel forth into questions the right of a King and a People', and nothing can follow but confusion. *Stare super vias antiquas*, 'tread the old and wonted boards': in his reverence for tradition and the ancient ways of the constitution, and not in utilitarian theories of popular rights, Strafford found the inspiration which guided his actions.

As President of the Council of the North between 1628 and 1633, he strove to make the court 'a shelter to the poor and innocent from the proud and insolent'. 'He loved justice for justice itself,' said Radcliffe, 'taking great delight to free a poor man from a powerful oppressor.' He forced the gentry to do his bidding. Humble farmers, unable to get justice from the magistrates who were at the same time their judges and their oppressors, obtained their rights in the Council of the North. The magnates were prevented from extending their estates by removing the landmarks of their poorer neighbours; the apprentice laws were enforced; the poor were cared for, out of the pockets of the rich; the statutes regulating wages were observed, at the cost of the profits of the employers; landowners were fined for enclosure or for working their haymakers on Sundays; when the fens were reclaimed, Strafford protected the rights of the original inhabitants, whom the gentry sought to thrust from the more profitable holdings. The magnates and clothiers of Yorkshire did not submit meekly to this régime, but Strafford was determined that the King's law should be obeyed. When a peer defied a sheriff's warrant, Strafford changed his attitude by fetching the artillery from Scarborough; for questioning his authority, Sir David Foulis was imprisoned in the Fleet. At a harsh cost to his popularity and his health, Strafford achieved his objects. The defeat of

[1] Gardiner.

the Crown 'established a system of justice which, at least in the North, amounted to an absolute denial of justice to the poor man. . . . To the wage-earners, and to the poor especially, the disappearance of the Council of the North was pure loss.'[1]

As Lord-Deputy of Ireland Strafford applied the same methods to an even harder task. He found Ireland in the hands of an oligarchy whose sole object was to turn the administration into a source of personal profit. In a few years he freed the Crown's government from the taint of corruption, gave Ireland roads, laws, justice and a fair system of taxation, founded industries, cleared pirates from the coasts; for the first time since the English conquest, Ireland might be a source of strength to the Crown, instead of a permanent drain of men and money and a fertile field for England's enemies. Like Hastings in India, he was often driven to ruthlessness, and dispossessed politicians flocked to England with their complaints of the harsh doings of 'Black Tom Tyrant'. As in the North, his high-handed honesty made dangerous enemies. The administrators in Dublin would not forgive him; the City of London was smarting under a fine from Star Chamber for its failure to fulfil the terms on which it had been granted Coleraine; the Scots were apprehensive for their brethren in Ulster, where Strafford was accused of 'bringing a very Spanish inquisition on our whole Scottish nation'.

Although Strafford was in Ireland from 1633 until 1639, the principles of Thorough were faithfully executed at home. Bishop Juxon, who became Treasurer when Weston died, preserved financial integrity. Poor relief was fairly distributed: 'During the personal government of Charles I we have not only the first thorough execution of the poor law, but a more complete organisation for the help of the weaker classes than at any other period of our history.'[2] Highways and bridges were kept up. (In the next century the roads, whose maintenance had been

[1] R. R. Reid, *The King's Council in the North.*
[2] E. M. Leonard, *The Early History of English Poor Relief.*

a public charge, were farmed to joint-stock companies; the people had to pay tolls to pass about the country, and the poor could not afford to move at all.) Charles's government regulated wages and prices, guarded the nation's supplies of corn and wool, fostered home industries, maintained good relations with wool-growing Spain. To keep the gentry alive to their social responsibilities, Charles sent them from court, and reminded them of their obligations to their less fortunate neighbours. But the gentry were inattentive to their obligations: they wanted their rights, including the right to set aside legislation which hindered them from making money. The case for the Crown need not be overstated; it was not a simple issue of black against white; but after 1640 the policy of paternal concern for the common welfare was abandoned, and it was not resumed until the working-classes were numerous enough and strong enough to force the government to hear of their sufferings and alleviate them.

Except where there was a Strafford to carry it out, the Crown's social policy could not always attain its objects. It broke on the rock of non-co-operation. Charles I had no *Intendants*; he had not even a civil service. In local government he had to depend on unpaid officials who often were the worst offenders against the social legislation which they were required to enforce. Hence the popularity among the poor of the prerogative courts, to which they could bring suits which the common law would judge partially. The Crown supported the losing side: the craftsman, the apprentice, the artisan, the rural labourer, and, always excepting the injustice of monopolies, the consumer. Sheriffs and Justices of the Peace refused to execute the government's instructions. They would be dismissed, and others would replace them, but it was a losing battle. The Crown was committed to a political and social policy which it was unable to enforce on the opposition and self-interest of the gentry of England.

3. *William Laud*

Under the vigorous authority of William Laud the rule of Thorough invaded the realm of conscience. Laud had made his name at Oxford, where, as President of St. John's, he had reformed the University and Colleges, and driven out the strong Calvinist party whose activities had alarmed him. James made use of his learning, and his keen, argumentative brain, in controversies with the Catholics, but he had shrewdly decided that Laud's punctilious, pedantic, fussy mind might irritate the anti-clerical instincts of the people. 'He hath a restless spirit,' said James, 'which cannot see when things are well, but loves to toss and change, and bring matters to a pitch of reformation floating in his own brain.' James had made him Bishop of distant St. David's, but nothing more. Charles, however, discovered in him a zealous, conscientious servant who would heal the Protestant schism in the Church and lay intractable sectaries by the heels. In 1628 Laud became Bishop of London, and made his energies felt outside his diocese; Archbishop Abbot, whose sympathies were Puritan, spent his last years brooding over his misfortune in accidentally shooting a game-keeper, and put up little resistance to Laud's activities. At length, in 1633, Abbot died, and at Canterbury Laud found a wider field opening before him. He planned the reformation of the Church of England; and when that was done, Scotland should be forced into conformity too.

In the heated atmosphere of the early seventeenth century, religious toleration was not the aim of any prominent party; so far, it was only the elusive dream of a handful of scattered and persecuted Independents. In determining, therefore, to compel conformity to the canons, liturgy and usages of the English Church, Laud attempted what Parker and Whitgift had done before him, and what the Presbyterians attempted when he was dead. *Cuius regio*, *eius religio* was a principle which only the Independents questioned. In matters of belief Laud was not intolerant; he would not probe too deeply into men's consciences, so long as, by uniformity in external things, they convinced him that their religion was sound. To those who would not conform he was relentless. A Metropolitical Visitation enabled him to satisfy himself that his discipline was everywhere enforced. He crushed theological discussion, fearing the courses it might take ; prevented Puritan writings ; hunted clergy of Puritan tendencies from their pulpits for disobeying his enactments ; forbade the gentry to keep private chaplains, or corporations to appoint lecturers for preaching duties alone ; harassed conventiclers who conducted services unhallowed by the Prayer Book. He insisted on the use of a proper ceremonial, and ordered that the communion-table should not stand where ' the particular fancy of any humorous person ' might dictate, but that it should be protected from irreverence (some were pleased to use it as a hat-rack) by being railed at the east end of the church. To coerce those who defied him, Laud employed all the resources of the Crown's ecclesiastical supremacy. Clergy were dismissed from their livings, authors, printers, lecturers and their congregations were punished by the Court of High Commission. Hundreds set out for the New World, where they might settle the details of their worship as they pleased.

This is to present Laud's work at its worst. He was not a persecutor ; his latitude in matters of doctrine, as long as it was discreetly expressed, shocked many staunch Anglicans. Moreover, there lay behind his zeal for uniformity something more than the meticulous precision of a tidy mind : the real object than the fastidious precision of a tidy mind : the real object of his attack was slackness and corruption, the real object of the policy to which he dedicated himself was to raise the Church above schisms and disaffections to a place where it could command the devotion of a united people. Laud's energy has won him the name of a man who sought out disobedience and chastised it. His work is better understood if it is realised that the motives which inspired it were defensive. He found the Church's commandments being broken, its ancient beliefs flouted ; to defend it against Puritan encroachments, Laud made a counter-attack, the last bid of the Church of England to hold all men's loyalty to a single faith. He insisted, therefore, on uniformity and ceremonial. 'All that I laboured for in this particular was, that the external worship of God in this Church might be kept up in uniformity and decency and some beauty of holiness.' The beauty of holiness, Laud's finest expression of his faith, had to be protected from the contempt in which the Puritans held the Church. The Puritan maintained, said Thomas Cheshire, that 'there is no more holiness in the church than in his kitchen, nor in the Lord's table than in a dresser-board'. ''Tis superstition nowadays', Laud complained, 'for any man to come with more reverence into a church than a tinker and his bitch come into an ale-house.' An open scorn for the House of God was a means by which many chose to demonstrate the inward worship which was in their hearts. Laud could not thus express himself in contrarieties. 'It is true', he said, 'the inward worship of the heart is the true service of God, and no service acceptable without it; but the external worship of God in His Church is the great witness to the world that our heart stands right in that service of God. . . . Ceremonies are the hedges that fence the substance of religion from all the indignities which profaneness and sacrilege too commonly put upon it.'

Looking back to the Middle Ages, he revived the authority of the Church over social policy and morals. Cardinal Newman claimed for him that he was 'of a stature akin to the elder days of the Church', for his was the policy of Hildebrand and Becket. The ecclesiastical courts took on their old courage. 'Persons of honour and great quality, of the court and the country,' wrote Clarendon, 'were every day cited into the High Commission Court, upon the fame of their incontinence, to their shame and punishment; which sharpened many men's humours against the Bishops.' High Commission was busier in punishing offences against morality than in harassing Puritans. Drunkards, adulterers, clergy guilty of lax habits, were fearlessly summoned and punished; ladies of high estate did penance in a white sheet for their adultery. Many of the suits heard by High Commission were brought voluntarily, by those seeking divorce or complaining of vicious practices. Laud pressed on towards his goal, undismayed by the opposition which thickened about him. He further displeased the Puritans by reissuing James's Book of Sports, which encouraged secular recreations after service on Sundays. The arguments contained in the declaration were appropriately modern. 'For when shall the common people have leave to exercise if not upon the Sundays and holidays? Seeing they must apply their labour, and win their living in all working-days?' Clergy who refused to read the declaration were ejected. In many districts the Puritans broke in upon the games, pulled down maypoles and destroyed the innocent amusements of the villagers. They regarded the Sabbath like 'an image dropped down from Jupiter'; to dance on a Sunday was as grave a crime in their sight as to commit murder. These extreme Puritans would not allow food to be carried to a horse, and condemned even walking as 'vain and profane'. To them Laud gave further offence by spending the money which he received from fines on beautifying the London churches, and Inigo Jones rebuilt part of St. Paul's. This work did not long survive Laud's fall, perishing in the conscientious pillage of the Church by the Saints.

Laud made many enemies. The gentry were affronted by his jurisdiction over their morals, the squire resented the new importance assumed by the parson; even the clergy themselves and many of the officials of the Crown felt that his busy intervention was carried too far. A disgruntled judge, dismissed from his office for trying to suppress the Somerset wakes, complained that England was being 'choked by a pair of lawn-sleeves'. The English are anti-clerical. Even men who endorsed the general tendencies of Laud's policy would have had him go more slowly. His enemies flatly charged him with being a Catholic, with being privy to the Arminian conspiracy to re-unite England with Rome. It was a reasonable suspicion, for Rome had invited him to be a Cardinal. He had refused without hesitation: 'My answer was that somewhat dwelt within me which would not suffer that till Rome were other than it is.' But his insistence on ceremonial, his belief in the sacraments and in the dignity of the priesthood, were linked in the people's mind with the scandalous doings at the court, where the Oratorian Panzani had come on a mission from Rome, and the Queen held a fashionable Mass on Christmas Day. In fact, Laud and the Queen detested each other, and Laud tried to institute proceedings in High Commission against the members of the Catholic mission. But to the staunch Protestant, untroubled by theological niceties, the distinctions between Arminianism and Catholicism were too fine to be appreciated; suspicion of the government's tendencies in religion, more than any other feature of its policy, aroused the people's resentment. The more celebrated victims of Laud's discipline acquired a martyr's halo. Alexander Leighton wrote that Bishops were the 'trumpery of Antichrist . . . bloody beasts . . . knobs and wens of bunchy Popish flesh'. William Prynne abused the stage, although the court was fond of amateur theatricals, and libelled the dignitaries of the Church; the Reverend Henry Burton described Bishops as 'those little toes of Antichrist' and cathedrals as 'so many dens of thieves and cages of filthiness and idolatry'; 'the Church is as full of ceremonies as a dog is of fleas', wrote John Bastwick. Hysterical outbursts of this sort would have to be punished by any government, for authority must protect its officials from libel, and its own dignity from neurotic propaganda. John Lilburne, who was punished for importing revolutionary writings from abroad, was a cross-grained fellow who lived to fall foul of three other governments to whose rule he failed to accommodate himself. Sympathetic crowds gathered to watch these men suffer the pillory and mutilation; elsewhere in Europe their offences would have brought them to the scaffold.

Public sympathy with his victims did not make Laud flinch. He believed that a Church united within itself was the best defence against the pretensions of Rome; and that if there were not unity in the Church, corresponding divisions would appear in the state. He shared Elizabeth's well-grounded fear of the dangers to authority inherent in unrestrained Puritanism. For Puritanism was ' the root of all rebellion and disobedient untractableness, and all schisms and sauciness in the country '. So he was resolved to check its growth by enforcing the law of the land, and by raising the Church to a dignity where all men might reverence it. His methods were harsh and somewhat unimaginative. Personally, he was fussy, quick-tempered and humourless, and he cared too little what men thought of him. He never quite threw off the robes of the don. The Church, too, was unable to bear the weight of the responsibility which he laid upon it ; times had changed since it had been the unquestioned arbiter of the nation's morals. But since the Church turned its back on Laud's ideals, it has never had the same hold on the minds of the English people. It was restored in 1660 as the instrument of successful politicians, and for nearly three hundred years it has been the obedient handmaid of the state. Laud ' ever held it the lowest depths of baseness to frame religion to serve turns '.

4. *The war with Scotland*

Charles's personal government collapsed when Laud, carried away by a dream of religious imperialism, determined to harry the Scots into conformity, as he had harried the English. James had succeeded in imposing on the Scots an episcopal organisation and certain forms of Anglican ritual. These measures had stirred sufficient opposition to warn James not to tamper any farther with the religion of the Scots ; and he had once remarked that if Laud hoped to convert them to English ways, he ' knows not the stomach of that people '. Charles, however, went incautiously. In 1625 he revoked all royal and ecclesiastical lands alienated since 1542 ; thus aligning the nobility with the Presbyterian opponents of the government's policy, for the Act of Revocation was the equivalent of asking the plunderers of the Roman Church to disgorge their loot. In 1633 he was crowned at Holyrood with the pomp and ceremony of the Church of England, and he decreed that henceforth the Scottish ministers should wear the surplice instead of the Geneva gown. In 1635 a new set of canons was forced on the Scots, as if Scotland were ' but a pendicle of the diocese of York ' ; and two years later, to supersede Knox's *Book of Common Order*, came a Prayer Book on the English model. On neither occasion did the government consult the Scottish Bishops, parliament, or General Assembly.

The ghosts of John Knox and Robert the Bruce walked the land. The Scots refused to use a form of service which had been forced upon them by a foreign government, and which was not merely tainted with Popery, ' the skeleton of a Mass-book ', but had ' no warrant of the word of God '. A stool thrown at the preacher at St. Giles's, Edinburgh, banded the Scots in revolt. ' I think our people possessed with a bloody devil ', wrote Baillie. In February, 1638, all classes of the nation united to put their signatures to a National Covenant which pledged them not to rest until the English had withdrawn the hated Prayer Book. The Covenant was the standard of a real Protestant crusade against the policy of Laud and against Strafford's treatment of the Scots in Ulster. At the same time, the Covenanters expressed their continued loyalty to the Crown, and they meant what they said : a contradiction in their aims which they later tried to impose on the English parliament and the Independent army, and which drew them into the royalist and Presbyterian alliance of 1648 and 1660.

Although he had no means of coercing the Scots, Charles chose this occasion to be firm : ' I mean to be obeyed.' The Scottish nobles mustered their feudal levies, and a force of ' Jehovah-drunken ' Covenanters, ' busy preaching, praying, and drilling ', moved towards the Border. They were commanded by a first-class soldier, Alexander Leslie, who had fought in the Swedish armies under Gustavus Adolphus. Charles had no adequate force to send against them. The Northern train-bands, led by nobles who had no enthusiasm for their task, were ragged and ill-equipped, and had nothing to recommend them except their traditional dislike of the Scots. Both sides were ready to discuss terms, and the Treaty of Berwick, in June, 1639, closed the bloodless campaign known as the First Bishops' War. But the Scots soon showed that they did not intend to compromise. They insisted that Charles should abolish episcopacy in Scotland, and surrender his control over parliament and Kirk. Since Charles would not give in, he must fight.

Strafford, who had returned to England, advised Charles to summon parliament and ask for funds to equip an adequate army. He was disappointed if he thought that he could persuade parliament to agree. The resistance of the Scots had dispersed the apathy in which the English had submitted to Charles's personal government, and it had revealed how weak the government was. The leaders of the Commons had kept in touch with one another since 1629,[1] and they came to the Short Parliament in an unyielding temper. Ignoring Charles's request for money for the defence of his kingdom, Pym made a long speech about the violation of liberties by the recent abuses of the prerogative. This speech was decisive : it turned the attention of the members from the menace of the Scots to the more congenial topic of their grievances, which had multiplied during the years in which parliament had not met. They ended by resolving that 'till the liberties of the House and the Kingdom were cleared, they knew not whether they had anything to give or no', and by petitioning that a treaty be made with the Scots, so that their grievances could be fully discussed. They rejected the King's offer to abandon ship-money in return for twelve subsidies, and he dissolved the parliament after a session of only three weeks (May, 1640). The Short Parliament showed Pym that he had a united House behind him.

The country showed itself to be as unresponsive to the national emergency as its representatives at Westminster. Pressed for

[1] In 1630 a company was formed for 'The plantation of Providence, Henrietta, and the Adjacent Islands'. Pym was secretary, and Essex, Warwick, Saye, Brooke, Mandeville and St. John were directors. As Dr. Johnson asked, 'Why is it that we hear the loudest yelps for liberty from the owners of slaves in America?'

funds to meet the Scots, Charles levied a forced loan and ship-money, but the yield was beggarly. Only the clergy responded to his need, Convocation voting him six subsidies. They also attempted to answer the Covenant by issuing canons proclaiming the duty of non-resistance : 'For subjects to bear arms against their King . . . upon any pretence whatsoever, is at least to resist the powers which are ordained of God.' The *etcetera* oath bound all clergy to the defence of the existing establishment. The uncompromising royalism of the leaders of the Church compelled the enemies of the Bishops to be enemies of the Crown.

Short of money—even the supplies voted by the parliament of Ireland disappointed Strafford's expectations — Charles resumed his hopeless struggle against the Scots. France, Spain and the Pope were deaf to his appeal for loans, and a reluctant and mutinous army made its way north. Seven English peers made common cause with the Scots, and invited them into England. In August the Covenanters brushed aside an English force at Newburn, on the Tyne, and poured into the northern counties, where they demanded £850 a day as the price of leaving unmolested the property of the inhabitants and the coal-trade of Newcastle. This policy was shrewdly calculated. To pay them the money they demanded, Charles would be forced to go humbly to parliament and first redress the grievances which it urged. Whereas, if the Scots had attempted to live on the countryside, the northern counties would have risen against the invader and rescued Charles from his difficulties.

Charles sought in vain to find a way out of the trap. A Great Council of peers, summoned to York, appointed sixteen of their number to confer with the Scots, and pledged their personal security for a loan ; but the only advice they could offer was that the King should again carry his difficulties to parliament. At Ripon, in October, he promised to pay the Scots what they demanded.

CHAPTER XV

THE FORMATION OF PARTIES

The Long Parliament's attack on the prerogative. The dispute about religion: Irish rebellion, the Grand Remonstrance. The final division into parties.

1. *The attack on the prerogative*

Like the Reformation Parliament of 1529, the Long Parliament met for the first time on the 3rd of November. It was preceded by the first electioneering campaign in English history. The Scots from the North issued discreet propaganda, assuring the English people that ' we must now stand or fall together. . . . We are brethren '; and Pym, hoisting his unathletic body on to a horse, rode through the country districts exhibiting to the impressed electors Mr. Hampden, the martyr of ship-money. These efforts ' to promote the elections of the puritanical brethren ' succeeded in their intent. Only Wales, Somerset and the barren North returned the candidates favoured by the government; the cloth towns of Yorkshire and the West, the mining districts in the South, the busy, populous counties of East Anglia, decided emphatically against the King. Even in the royal Duchy of Cornwall all but one of the court candidates were defeated.

Unlike its predecessors, the Long Parliament could counter the King's weapon of dissolution; for he depended on parliamentary supply to be able to keep his pledge to the Scots. At last, since it suited them, the Commons voted money for the King's policy; calling it ' a brotherly assistance ', they granted the £25,000 a month which had been demanded. But the

Scots remained in the North, like a gun levelled at Charles's head. There could be ' no fear yet of raising the parliament ', as Baillie said, ' so long as the lads about Newcastle sit still '. A dissolution would set them in motion, and plunge Charles again into a war which he had no means of fighting. For eight months, until the summer of 1641, the Long Parliament passed almost unanimously a series of measures which destroyed for ever conciliar government in England.

Pym's first concern was to clear from his path those servants of the Crown who would thwart his policy. Finch and Secretary Windebank fled abroad, Laud was put in the Tower; while Burton, Bastwick, Prynne, Leighton and Lilburne were released, to assist in the hue and cry after their oppressors. Then Pym launched his attack on Strafford, the one man strong enough to nerve the King to carry the principles of Thorough to their end and strike down the enemies of the Crown. His impeachment broke down, for the charge of treason could not be upheld. St. John remarked that ' it was never accounted either cruelty or foul play to knock foxes and wolves on the head as they can be found, because they be beasts of prey '; and Pym argued that Strafford's several misdemeanours amounted to cumulative treason. But the Lords would not admit the charge that after the dissolution of the Short Parliament Strafford had advised the King to use the Irish army to coerce the English. The impeachment was dropped, but Pym and his plans were not safe so long as Strafford was alive. ' Stone dead hath no fellow ', said Essex. So Pym brought a Bill of Attainder before the Houses, for which it was not necessary to prove treason. The Lords passed it in an atmosphere of hatred and fear, their sense of justice distorted by the revelation of a plot to bring the royalist army from the North to free Strafford and disperse the parliament; by the mob which clamoured round the Houses; and by rumours, ingeniously circulated by Pym, of ' great multitudes of Papists gathering together in Lancashire; then of secret meetings in caves and under ground in Surrey; letters from beyond sea of great provisions of arms making there for the Catholics of England'. At the height of the crisis a member affected to smell gunpowder under the floor of the House, and a rumour went round that the French had seized the Channel Islands. When the Bill was brought to Charles for his assent, the mob circled round Whitehall and shouted for the blood of the Popish Queen. The Constable of the Tower said that, if Charles rejected the Bill, he would butcher Strafford on his own responsibility. With a great and generous gesture Strafford rescued Charles from his dilemma. 'So now, to set your majesty's conscience at liberty,' he wrote from prison, 'I do most humbly beseech your majesty, for the prevention of evils which may happen by your refusal, to pass this bill. . . . To a willing man there is no injury done: and . . . by God's grace, I forgive all the world with calmness and meekness of infinite contentment to my dislodging soul.' On May 12th he went to his death, walking like a conqueror at the head of a victorious army. 'Righteous Judgment—that shall be hereafter.'

Having removed the one man he needed to fear, Pym pressed on his work of destruction. In the name of liberty he attacked the instruments of centralised government. Speed was necessary, before anxiety for the future should open rifts among his supporters, and before the country wearied of paying bribes to the Scots. Already a Triennial Act had provided that not more than three years should pass without the summoning of a parliament; and in May Charles gave his assent to a bill which said that the Long Parliament should not be dissolved without its own consent. In June the Tunnage and Poundage Act declared that recent levies were illegal, and forbade future levies without consent. In July the prerogative courts were swept away. Star Chamber was abolished for its intolerable interference with 'rights and estates'; and with it the Council of the North, the Council of the Marches, the Court of the Duchy of Lancaster, and the Court of Exchequer of the County Palatine of Chester. The destruction of the Court of High Commission brought to an end the prerogative's authority over the Church, and defeated Laud's effort to revive the ecclesiastical jurisdiction of the Middle Ages. Finally, in August, the Commons put a stop to the devices by which the King had maintained himself during their absence. Ship-money was declared to be illegal, the boundaries of the royal forests were fixed at the limits of 1623, and distraint of knighthood was forbidden. The death of Strafford had for the time sapped Charles's resistance; listlessly accepting all the measures which parliament put before him, he signed away his power. In August the Scots army withdrew.

This was the permanent work of the Long Parliament. The storms of the next twenty years blew in many directions, but they left this work always intact. The Restoration restored the office of King, but stripped it of its ancient powers. When James II attempted to recover those powers, the oligarchy combined against him, as it had combined against his father, and re-enacted the settlement of 1641, strengthening it with such safeguards as the intervening years had shown to be necessary. Because Louis XIV threatened to overthrow it with foreign arms, Marlborough humbled him on the battlefields of Europe. Because the only alternative was a Catholic Stuart, in 1714 the oligarchs offered the throne to a squalid German, because he promised to respect their interpretation of the constitution. In 1641 the exceptional powers of the Tudor monarchy were abolished, the courts of common law won their long struggle against rival jurisdictions, and ultimate authority in the state was transferred from the Crown to parliament. In the troubled years that followed, it was to this fruitful settlement that all good constitutionalists, royalists and parliamentarians alike, looked back with the yearning of men from whom the prize of victory had been suddenly snatched.

2. *Disputes about religion*

In the summer of 1641 war was still a year away. Indeed, during the early months of the Long Parliament, war did not seem to be in prospect, for there was no issue on which men were sufficiently divided to fight. In 1641 Charles was in no personal danger. The charge against him had always been that he had allowed himself to be misled by 'evil counsellors'. Now that these were gone, he could have saved his throne by showing that he was willing to abide by the religious and constitutional settlement drawn up by parliament, and by obliging the Queen to dismiss her Jesuit advisers and put a more discreet mask over her participation in rites that were repugnant to most Englishmen. This he would not do. While he was still stunned by Strafford's fall, he had parted from constitutional rights which he would revoke if the tide turned in his favour; but he would not surrender his authority over the Church. Ecclesiastical supremacy belonged to the Crown alone, and not to the Crown-in-parliament. While a unanimous parliament had stripped him of his political powers, he had stood irresolutely aside; but when a divided parliament drew up tentative schemes for a new settlement in religion, he denied its competence to tamper with the organisation of the Church, and attached to himself a party ready to defend his historic rights. In a declaration to the Lords in October, 1641, he said: 'I am constant to the discipline and doctrine of the Church of England established by Queen Elizabeth and my father, and I resolve, by the grace of God, to die in the maintenance of it.' This was the birth of the royalist cause.

On religious questions, on which Charles had irrevocably made up his mind, his opponents were deeply divided. Mostly they were united in disliking toleration, in their faith in a salutary enforcement of the penal laws, and in the common opinion that under Laud's régime the policy of the Church had been intolerably inquisitorial and disfigured by the taint of Popery. They were agreed, too, that supreme authority over the Church should be brought within the control of parliament. Beyond this, however, they could not agree, and conflicting suggestions for the future organisation of the Church were put forward in pamphlets, sermons, petitions and parliamentary debates. Further, there were two minority opinions, both influential in years to come, but in 1641 rejected as unpalatable novelties. The Presbyterian scheme to establish in England a full Genevan orthodoxy, with clerical synods and councils, was supported by the Scots, and was eloquently defended in Milton's pamphlet, *Of Reformation in England*, which was written in the summer of 1641. But Presbyterianism was disliked in England, because its political tendencies were democratic, and because a clerical discipline was unwelcome. 'Instead of every Bishop we put down in a diocese,' protested Digby, 'we shall set up a Pope in every parish.' When in 1643 the parliamentary leaders adopted Presbyterianism, their motive was military necessity; for the second time they had to turn to the Scots for help. The second minority movement, the demand of the Independents for a congregational system, and freedom of worship and conscience for everyone, was universally rejected as blasphemous and anarchic. The Independents, too, found fighting congenial to the spread of their beliefs. They were to win the war for parliament, and their military strength gained them their objects.

The principal source of religious dispute was the fate of the Bishops. Pym, who was the accepted leader of the Long Parliament, at first insisted only that the Church be preserved in an unsullied Protestantism by being placed under the control of laymen responsible to parliament. But when he came to consider details, he accepted the view that episcopacy was dangerous to true religion and incompatible with parliamentary control, and must therefore be abolished. From discussions on this question there emerged a powerful body of opinion which was in favour of a Puritan state Church, as Erastian as Laud's, and combatively intolerant of the objections of Anglicans, sectaries and Catholics.

'They who hated Bishops,' said Falkland, 'hated them worse than the Devil'; whereas 'they who loved them did not love them as well as their dinner'. No one could be found to defend the high pretensions of Arminianism which had culminated in the canons of 1640. But men of conservative temper were provoked to resist Pym's new Erastianism, not because they loved the Bishops, but because they opposed any change in the traditional organisation of the Church. The revision of the Prayer Book distressed them, and they argued with Digby that in 'clipping of these wings of the Prelates by which they have mounted to such insolencies', parliament had done all that was necessary for the healthy reformation of the Church. They pleaded, therefore, that the traditional services of the Church should not be tampered with, and that the 'primitive' office of episcopacy should be retained, now that the indiscretions of recent Bishops had been suitably chastised. The policy of the radicals in the House of Commons drove the moderates to form a party for the defence of the Church of England. Throughout 1641 the extremists ordered the removal of images from the churches, the observation of the Sabbath and the suppression of ceremonial; and they did not hesitate to punish clergy who disobeyed them. Since Laud's restraint was gone, religious self-expression was uncurbed, and each man was free to interpret God's word in his own manner. Tradesmen addicted to religion pointed for their neighbours the paths they should follow, women preachers invaded the pulpits, disbanded soldiers looted the churches, Adamites demonstrated the primitive innocence of man by going naked into the cities. To men disquieted by these extravagances Charles offered a cause which they could follow: a faith in reasonableness and order and the accepted ways of religion.

This divergence in religion broke the unity of the Long Parliament. In February, 1641, the Commons had started to debate a bill founded on the petition of 15,000 Londoners that episcopal government, 'with all its dependencies, roots and branches', be abolished. The bill proposed to make changes in the Prayer Book, and to place ecclesiastical jurisdiction in the hands of nine laymen nominated by parliament, who would undertake a 'godly thorough reformation' of the Church. The bill was resisted, and since the House still had more congenial work to perform, it was dropped. In July the Lords debated a scheme to fetter the authority of the Bishops by appointing for each of them twelve overseers, to be nominated by the King and both Houses. The failure of each of these measures to pass the House which introduced it showed that the enemies of the prerogative could destroy better than they could build. Most of them would have echoed the lament of Oliver Cromwell to the House of Commons: 'I can tell you, sirs, what I would not have; though I cannot, what I would.' [1]

Religion, however, was not the only cause of the war. The conservatives were again attracted to the King's side when the dominant party in the Commons, moving away from the 'fundamentals' of the constitution to which they had appealed in their attack on Charles's personal government, proposed to assume control of the executive power. This was not the purpose for which Coke and Eliot had fought the King, and probably it had not been Pym's purpose when the Long Parliament met. But he was obliged to safeguard what he had won; and if Charles were ever strong enough to recover control of the government, he would undo the work of the Long Parliament, and the blood of its leaders would expiate Strafford's death. Pym's work and his personal safety were endangered by the discontent of the army assembled to fight the Scots in the previous year, by the expressed loyalty of the Covenanters to the Crown, and by the remoter fear of the Catholic army in Ireland. Two facts favoured his purpose: between August and November Charles was in Edinburgh, on a fruitless errand to persuade the Presbyterian Scots to fight for the English Bishops; and the Irish rebellion in October forced parliament to forge its own executive weapons to meet the emergency. Charles's absence, like Louis XVI's ride to Varennes, threw doubt upon his willingness to co-operate in the revised scheme of government, and he was suspected of intriguing with Leslie to overthrow it. While he was away, parliament set up a Council of Defence and governed the country by ordinance.

[1] The remark is a fair comment on Cromwell's career as a whole.

The rebellion in Ulster hastened the drift to war. Here at last was the Queen's plot to extirpate the Protestant religion in the three kingdoms. Stone dead had found a fellow. The usual exaggerations nourished the panic: the rebels massacred not more than five thousand Protestants, but the lowest contemporary estimate numbered the victims at 37,000. There was no army to crush the revolt; and if Charles, who was suspected of having incited the rebels, were granted money to raise one, he might turn it against his enemies at home. Parliament therefore demanded that the army be enlisted and led by men in whom it had confidence, and thus claimed to seize executive power from the King.

The demand converted an episcopalian party into a royalist party. For the defenders of the Church would not concede to their radical opponents control of the executive and an armed force, and they were driven to protect what remained of the King's prerogative. Charles returned from Scotland to find himself at the head of a party, and again pledged himself to defend his religion 'if need be, to the hazard of my life and all that is dear to me'.

Meanwhile, the Grand Remonstrance had emphasised the divisions in parliament. No longer sure of his ground, Pym drew up, in the form of an address to the King, an appeal to the country against the conservative reaction which was imperilling his work and his safety. In reciting once more the misdeeds of the government, and in praising the remedies introduced by the Long Parliament, the Remonstrance recalled to the members their old unity; but the articles which recommended reforms in the Church, and the appointment of ministers 'such as the Parliament may have cause to confide in', defined the issues which divided them. A synod of English and foreign divines was to confer on the 'intended reformation' of the Church. But, in removing the Bishops, the Commons stated that it was 'far from our purpose or desire to let loose the golden reins of discipline and government in the Church, to leave private persons or particular congregations to take up what form of

Divine Service they please '. Laud had been removed to make way for a bondage harsher than Laud's. The moderates preferred to risk another ' despotism ' under the King, rather than to abandon the constitution of Church and state to parliament and parliament's army. The Grand Remonstrance was debated amid hot tempers and drawn swords. When the members at length divided, 159 voted in support of it, and 148 against it (November, 1641). Had it been rejected, Cromwell would have sailed for America the next day. ' So near ', sighed Clarendon, ' was the poor kingdom to its deliverance.'

Charles's answer to the Grand Remonstrance was to take his stand on the known laws of the kingdom and ' the undoubted right of the Crown '. His attitude had won him the support of most of the Lords and a strong party in the Commons. His backing was powerful enough to enable him to resist any radical measures which the extremists might seek to force upon him, and a few months of discretion might have patched together a settlement acceptable to well-intentioned men on both sides. Unfortunately, Charles allowed himself to be jostled out of his caution. Since the Lords refused to deprive the Bishops of their seats, Pym ordered the London mob to intimidate them into keeping to their houses ; and when Charles protested, he answered that he could not dishearten the people by forbidding them to obtain ' their just desires in such a way '. The Queen's repeated intrigues with Roman Catholics abroad, which Charles would have been wise to restrain, gave Pym the opportunity to offend him again. He proposed to impeach the Queen. The plan was impertinent and fantastic, and the Lords would have rejected the impeachment. But Charles lost his head. He ordered the Commons to impeach the five members responsible for the insult ; and when they refused, he went to the House to arrest them. Warned of his coming by Pym's mistress, who was a personal attendant of the Queen, the members had fled by the river.

Charles had forfeited the plea of legality on which he had grounded his actions, and the Commons were able to claim self-defence to justify their own unconstitutional proceedings in the future.

A few days later, on January 10th, 1642, Charles abandoned his capital to his enemies. He moved to Windsor, and presently to York, where a steady stream of supporters came to join him. He left his interests in the prudent hands of Edward Hyde, who in a succession of manifestoes defended the King's policy, and appealed to the sense and justice of the nation against the high-handed and revolutionary demands of the parliamentary party. While parliament further offended conservative opinion by its irregular assumption of executive power, and its abrupt treatment of those who defied it, Charles at York behaved with calculated moderation. After he had rejected parliament's Militia Bill, in March, measures were no longer sent to him for his assent. Parliament's wishes were incorporated in Ordinances of both Houses, which had the force of statutes. Finally, in June, parliament drew up the Nineteen Propositions, which demanded that all issues in dispute should be settled in favour of parliament. It was, in fact, a bid for parliamentary sovereignty: for the Commons were to reform the Church, command the army, appoint councillors and officials, direct foreign policy, and supervise the education and marriage of the King's children. Declining to be a 'mere phantom of a King', Charles rejected a settlement which demanded more of the Crown than was taken in 1689. The Propositions were a virtual declaration of war. Their extravagance injured parliament's cause; for many who had been still hopeful of arriving at a working agreement between the two parties now realised that parliament's terms were not such as the King could accept, and joined him in the defence of his rights.

On June 12th Charles issued Commissions of Array, to summon the county militias. A month later, parliament voted that an army be raised 'for the safety of the King's person, the defence of both Houses of Parliament . . . and the preserving of the true religion, the laws, liberty, and peace of the kingdom'. The members resolved to 'live and die with the

Earl of Essex '. Essex was a dull-witted man, and a poor soldier, but a titled general sanctified the cause of rebellion. In a manifesto parliament accused the King of misgovernment, and claimed to abide by the law which distinguished the nobility and gentry from ' the meaner sort of people, with whom otherwise they would but be fellow-servants '.

The royalists derided the Looking-glass army which parliament proposed to raise :

> 'Tis to preserve his Majesty,
> That we against him fight.

On August 22nd the King raised his standard at Nottingham, calling on his people to protect the constitution and the Church. *Nolumus leges Angliae mutari.*

3. *The two parties*

The English civil war was not fought in the cause of freedom. Indeed, although the King was at war with an influential section of his people, it is scarcely accurate to speak of it as a rebellion against his power or his dignity. The position of the Crown had been defined in 1641, and none but extremists proposed to alter it ; and, so far as freedom was concerned, the lot of the ordinary Englishman was conspicuously more wretched after the war than before it. On the parliamentary side only a handful of zealots, sternly crushed by their leaders, doubted that it was necessary to crush all expressions of democratic or socialist opinion. War broke out because a powerful and coherent ruling class, previously united in pursuing a definite object, had found its unity collapsing under the strain of religious differences which would not heal, and of political differences which naturally followed upon them. Few men welcomed the war,[1] for war seemed to offer no lasting solution of the issues at stake. During the next few years several efforts were made

[1] e.g. the Roundhead Waller wrote to his enemy Hopton on the eve of battle : ' God . . . knows with what a sad sense I go upon this service, and with what a perfect hatred I detest this war without an enemy.'

to arrive at a settlement, but they broke down because parliament put its conditions too high, and because Charles would accept from rebels no terms but their subjection. The struggle dragged on, therefore, until the King was completely beaten in the field; and by that time the original quarrel was almost forgotten in the new disputes which broke out among the conquerors.

Except that the Puritans of East Anglia took up arms for their religion, the private soldiers were not urged into the war by the power of abstract ideas. More forceful impulses were impressment, to which both sides resorted, and the ancient ties of feudalism. Since the war began as an aristocrats' war, it had much of the flavour of the baronial troubles of the Middle Ages, such as the Wars of the Roses or the disturbances under King Stephen. The great families of Sidney, Percy, Russell and Montagu, which fought against the King, were 'overmighty subjects', as their ancestors had been before them. Like party politics in the eighteenth century, the civil war was to a large extent a game of feudal 'follow my leader'. The men of Lancashire, for instance, fought on the royalist side, not because they appreciated the constitutional differences between Pym and Edward Hyde, or the religious scruples which divided Cromwell from Digby, but because the Stanleys were for the Crown. Similarly, the Borderers followed the Duke of Newcastle, and they dispersed when he went abroad after Marston Moor; Lincolnshire divided its allegiance between the Earl of Lindsey and Lord Willoughby of Parham, Warwickshire between the Earl of Northampton and Lord Brooke; Cornwall rallied to the Earl of Hertford, Essex to the Earl of Warwick. Thus there was much fighting that had little connection with the body of the war, as old enemies paid off old scores, and magnates assembled their tenants for a mediaeval affray with a long-hated neighbour. Hence, too, the difficulty experienced by both sides in persuading their levies, who were accustomed to the local character of feudal warfare, to fight outside their own districts.

Except when religion or feudal rivalry sharpened their temper, the people of England took little part in the war, and many were at pains to avoid it. Local pacts of neutrality were made between Cornwall and Devon, and also in Yorkshire and Cheshire; the Clubmen in the West united to protect themselves from both sides. For the farmers and tradesmen soon learned to dislike a struggle which wasted their crops and estates and hampered their business; and if they were inclined towards the end of the war to support the Roundheads, it was because the New Model army refrained from plunder and seemed likelier to be able to end the fighting and restore peace. During the four years of the war there were not more than 140,000 under arms.

When these qualifications have been made, and it is understood that the dominant theme of the war was feudal and aristocratic, and that most Englishmen regarded it with indifference or dislike, it is still possible to make certain distinctions of geography and class between the two parties. Eighty peers and 175 members of the House of Commons joined Charles, and thirty peers and 300 of the Commons remained with Pym. The strength of parliament lay south of a line drawn from Hull to Portsmouth, in the districts which had been the strength of the Yorkists in the fifteenth century, and of the Reformation in the sixteenth: in London and the other big ports, the cloth towns of the West, the mining districts of the South, and in the Eastern counties which provided Mary's martyrs, the Ironsides and the sturdy backbone of New England. The big cities were for parliament, urged to rebellion, said Clarendon, by 'that factious humour which possessed most corporations, and the pride of their wealth'. The King's power lay in the North which despised the busy industry of the South; in uncommercial towns such as Oxford, Chester and York; in the Borders, the Midlands, and Cornwall, whose forty-four members were to be solid in support of Bolingbroke.

The ideal of allegiance to the Lord's anointed drew many to the King's side who would have preferred a peaceful settlement, and had no love for the Bishops, 'for whom this quarrel subsists'. 'I beseech you,' said Verney, 'consider that majesty is sacred. I have eaten the King's bread, and served him near thirty years, and will not do so base a thing as to forsake him.'[1] After Edgehill, when the sword had been drawn against the King, traditional loyalty attracted many to his standard who were undecided on the merits of the quarrel. There came, too, the defenders of the Church. 'O Lord, in Thee have I trusted', prayed a Hampshire vicar; 'let me never be a Roundhead.' With them were landlords who feared the social chaos which a successful rebellion would unloose; the gentry who despised merchants and shopkeepers, with their religion of profit. For, like Hampden in 1637, Charles seemed to the landowners of England to be the defender of their property against unknown dangers. Their suspicion was well grounded. How grave those dangers were, and what shape they would assume, was unrealised in 1642 by the leaders of parliament, who welcomed as their allies men who would fight, not in the cause of parliamentary government, but to establish the Kingdom of God on earth; and others who would regard the defeat of the King as the defeat of all authority, and outrage their masters with a programme of social and political freedom.

[1] Many of the Cavaliers went to war in the spirit of Richard Lovelace. To the Puritan soldier Nehemiah Wharton, such men were 'goddam blades, hatched in hell'.

CHAPTER XVI

THE GREAT REBELLION

Causes of parliament's victory. Progress of the war: the Covenant, Self-denying Ordinance, New Model. Negotiations with the King. The second civil war. The execution of the King.

1. *The reasons for parliament's victory*

If the struggle was to be a long one, all the concrete advantages lay with Pym. In the first place, he was better supplied with money. The large commercial cities, the cloth towns, the ports with their flow of revenue from the customs, were all on the side of parliament; three-quarters of the ship-money tax had been collected from the districts south of the Hull-Bristol line, where parliament's strength was concentrated. The royalist districts, on the other hand, were mainly agricultural. The landowners who supported the King made over their rents to his cause, but in time of war rents were less productive and harder to collect; they were less easily convertible into hard cash than the wealth of the merchants who supported parliament. Although the royalist magnates gave their silver plate to be melted into money, the King never had sufficient to equip his armies. Further, since parliament took over the machinery of government, and ruled by Ordinance, it was able to avail itself of all the regular sources of taxation; and Pym made these sources more productive by levying an excise, and by replacing the old system of subsidies by a monthly assessment, rated according to the fluctuating needs of parliament's military programme. Since the mass of the people was indifferent to the war, this financial strength was a large factor in parliament's victory: the common soldier served the better paymaster. Parliament was able to maintain a navy costing £300,000 a year and an army costing a million; and in 1645 it organised and equipped a professional army which won the war within a year and was master of three kingdoms for fifteen.

Secondly, London was solidly behind Pym. London was more than the capital of the country: it was the heart of the administration, the largest and wealthiest port, the hub of the nation's trade. Alone of the English cities, it had a policy and a character of its own, and often during these years of war and revolution it was to act with the independence of a Greek or Italian city-state. Its train-band, the largest and best equipped in the country, twice played a decisive part in the fighting. 'King Pym' in London was more nearly King of England than the royal fugitive in Oxford; and for this reason the reconquest of London was the central object of Charles's military offensive.

Thirdly, the navy deserted the King. Since the days of Drake and the long, desperate struggle with Catholic Spain, the English seamen had been aggressively Protestant. Devon, which had launched a Catholic rising against Protector Somerset, was made Puritan in a single generation by the example of her great captains. The cry of 'No Popery' united the navy against the King who loved Arminians; and under the leadership of the Earl of Warwick, a man whom sailors could admire, it set the seal on the King's defeat. With a hostile fleet patrolling his coasts, Charles could get no reinforcements from Ireland or the continent; whereas parliament was able to relieve by sea the vital sieges of Hull and Plymouth. If the navy had been loyal, Charles would have won the war in 1643.

2. *Progress of the war*

Since Charles had not the resources to fight a long war, he should have concentrated all his efforts on winning decisive engagements in the early months. Led by his nephew, Prince Rupert, the royalist cavalry were irresistible in the first battles of the war. Unfortunately, however, Rupert had not the self-control to turn a temporary rout into a crushing victory; at Edgehill, where he met the main parliamentary army for the first time, he drove his enemies from the field, but threw away his advantage by an undisciplined pursuit in search of plunder. Essex was therefore able to reach London first, and prepare to defend it against attack. In the following month, November, 1642, Rupert attempted a frontal attack on London, only to find that Essex had double his numbers. The train-bands came out to Turnham Green to defend their city, and Rupert withdrew to Oxford. This check discouraged Charles, and he unwisely abandoned his offensive for the year; in the conventional fashion of mediaeval warfare, he scattered his strength by planting garrisons in all the royalist castles and manor-houses, and settled down to winter in Oxford. Nor was he wise to choose Oxford as his headquarters. It was out of touch with the districts from which royalism recruited its strength; and a fortified outpost in enemy country was not the place from which to execute the threefold attack on London which Charles had planned for the following year.

The plan itself was a good one, and it came near to success. Three royalist armies were to converge on London: Newcastle and his Borderers by way of Yorkshire and East Anglia; Sir Ralph Hopton from the West; and the King himself from Oxford. In the early months of the year all three armies gained a series of victories. Parliament showed its alarm by sending commissioners to Oxford to treat with the King on terms much more favourable to him than those submitted in the Nineteen Propositions of the previous June; but the negotiations broke down because Charles would not abandon his Church. Ultimately, the royalist offensive was wrecked by provincialism. On each of the three fronts the attack was paralysed because in its rear lay a parliamentary stronghold that had not been taken. The Cornishmen would not follow Hopton into Hampshire and

ENGLAND IN THE GREAT REBELLION—I

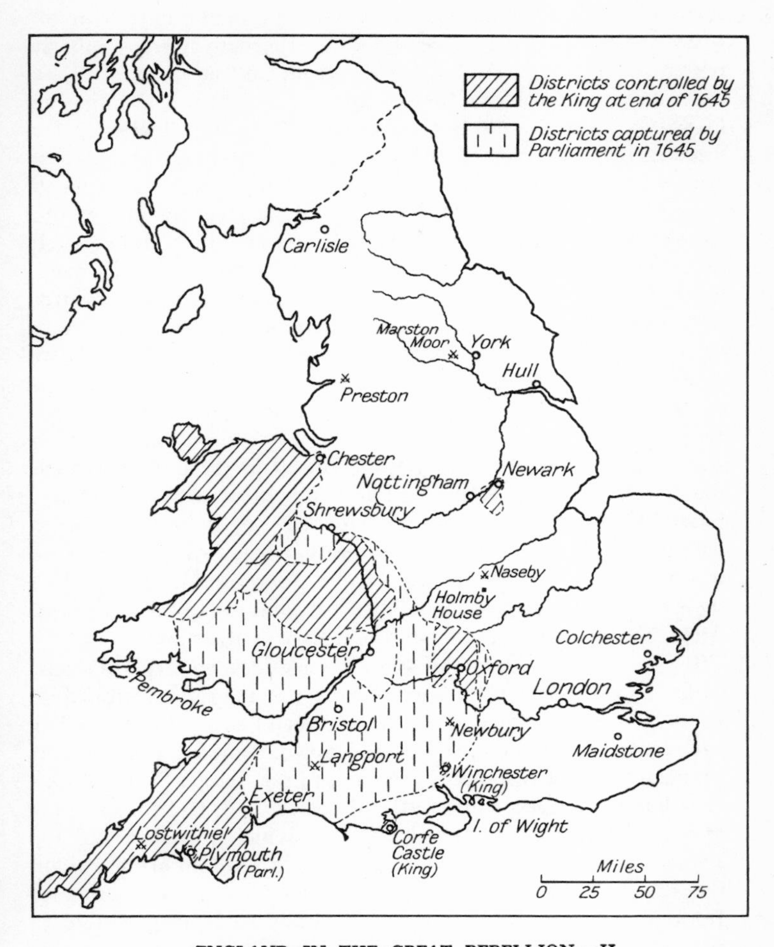

ENGLAND IN THE GREAT REBELLION—II

Kent while the Devon men in Plymouth might cut them off from their homes ; Newcastle's Northerners were similarly frightened of Fairfax's garrison in Hull, and at the first check they drew back across the Humber ; and the Welshmen in Charles's army would not advance so long as Gloucester lay untaken behind them. Precious weeks went by, and the royalist armies came no nearer to their objective. At length, in August, Charles laid siege to Gloucester. Gloucester and Plymouth were the only towns in the West of England which still resisted him ; Plymouth could be victualled and reinforced by the navy, but if Gloucester fell, the main body of his army would be free to invade London. Parliament, therefore, tried a desperate stroke. The relief of Gloucester was preached to the Londoners as a crusade on which their own safety depended ; the shops were closed by order, and Essex led the train-bands across England to raise the siege. As Essex approached, Charles abandoned Gloucester and placed himself in the path by which the Londoners must return. The two armies met at Newbury. Essex held his own in a day of inconclusive fighting, and Charles withdrew in the night ; his ammunition had run short, and he was forced to permit the train-bands to return unmolested to their city. Charles had made his effort, and it had broken down. After Newbury he could not hope to win the war.

By the end of 1643 the King's resources were giving out, while the resistance of his enemies was growing more formidable. In the first place, they had gained a powerful ally. In September parliament subscribed to the Solemn League and Covenant, promising, when the war was over, to undertake a ' reformation of religion . . . according to the Word of God, and the example of the best reformed Churches ' ; for which promise, and for £30,000 a month in cash, the Scots would send an army to help the cause. The war was to be directed by a Committee of Both Kingdoms, the first executive body to be responsible to parliament ; and an assembly of divines was to draw up a plan for the Presbyterian organisation to which parliament had now committed the country. The Scottish alliance was Pym's last service to his party. He died in December; and the House of Commons, which had lost Hampden's calculating brain earlier in the year, was deprived at a critical hour of its ablest leaders. Pym was a self-seeking man, but his party had no one to match his skill as an organiser and a tactician; he had an instinct for facts, and if he had lived, parliament would not in the years to come have blundered so grossly in its dealings with the army and the Independents.

The second cause of the growing strength of the rebels was the army which was being fashioned in the Eastern counties. Parliament had grouped the amateur levies of the counties into three Associations; and the army of the Eastern Association, commanded by the Earl of Manchester, was distinguished by a peculiar fervour and discipline which it derived from the training of a certain Colonel Cromwell. This Cromwell was an ordinary Puritan squire, of a minor branch of a family which had enriched itself by the Reformation. As member for Huntingdon in 1628, and for Cambridge in the Long Parliament, he had made no mark as a politician; but in war he was to find his destiny, and by it he would rise to an uneasy greatness. In the early engagements of the war, at Powick Bridge and Edgehill, he was dismayed by the poor quality and poor spirit of the parliamentary troops. They were 'most of them', he told Hampden, 'old decayed serving-men and tapsters and such kind of fellows'; as Falkland contemptuously remarked, 'tailors or embroiderers or the like'. Such men could not win the war; to beat the Cavaliers, they must have something of the Cavaliers' own spirit, directed by a concentration and singleness of purpose which 'the gentry' were believed to lack. So Colonel Cromwell went home to train the men of his native shires to be the sort of soldiers he saw in his fancy: 'such men', he was to say in later years, 'as had the fear of God before them, and made some conscience of what they did.' The army which he collected was the most remarkable fighting force which England has known. He inspired the Eastern Association, from his 'plain russet-coated captains' down to the humblest trooper, with his own vision of their high destiny. In a few months they were of different calibre from the undisciplined, half-hearted rabbles which followed the King and the other parliamentary leaders. They were regularly paid, and forbidden to plunder; the discipline was severe: 'No man swears but he pays his twelve pence; if he is in drink he is set in the stocks or worse.' Above all, no religious tests were imposed on the men. In deference to the Scots, parliament decreed that all its soldiers must swear an oath of loyalty to the Covenant; but Cromwell, who knew that the first task was to win the war, would accept no conditions which hindered his recruiting. The passion for religious freedom which dignified his strange career was born of the need to get the best soldiers for his army. 'Sir,' he wrote to one of his commanders, 'the State, in choosing men to serve it, takes no notice of their opinions.'

In May, 1643, the Eastern Association won its first victory, in a skirmish at Grantham. Its determined resistance broke the wavering resolution of Newcastle's Borderers, and turned them back across the Humber. By the autumn Cromwell had recovered parliament's hold on Lincolnshire and defeated the royalist advance from the North; and his force was available to help Fairfax to conquer Yorkshire in the following year. Early in 1644 Leslie, now Earl of Leven, led an army of 21,000 Covenanters across the Border, and within a few weeks they joined Fairfax and the Eastern Association in besieging York, to which Newcastle had been compelled to withdraw. Coming with the main royalist army to raise the siege, Rupert was duped into offering battle. On July 2nd the biggest battle of the war was fought at Marston Moor, a few miles from York. After Rupert had swept Fairfax from the field, the men of the Eastern Association won their spurs as the early rout was slowly turned into a victory; 'God made them as stubble to our swords'. The royalists lost their hold on England north of the Trent, but the material consequences of the disaster were less serious than the weary defeatism which henceforward paralysed their cause. Newcastle went abroad, and his personal following abandoned the war ; Rupert had lost all his artillery, and with it his zest for battle ; his cavalry played no important part during the remainder of the war. Deserted by their leaders, the royalist rank-and-file lost heart and ' mouldered away by degrees '.

After this crushing victory parliament should have finished off the war by the end of the year. But parliament too had its military problems. Recruiting by the County Committees failed to raise adequate armies, and the men would not serve outside their own districts ; many soldiers drifted from one side to the other in search of pay and plunder ; Essex and Waller had personal differences, and the commanders as a whole were incompetent and apathetic. Thus parliament failed to drive home its advantage. Essex wandered off into Cornwall, the heart of the royalist country. His army was cut off and he surrendered to Charles at Lostwithiel. His humiliation was less serious than it might have been, because Goring allowed his cavalry to escape, and because the royalists could not afford to keep the prisoners they had taken. Moreover, the Cornishmen again refused to follow the King to London. In October Essex, Waller and Manchester again confronted the King's army at Newbury ; but although they had twice his numbers, they allowed him to withdraw in good order, and had not the strength to pursue him.

A serious breach was opening among the rebels. The parliamentary leaders were committed to Presbyterianism ; accordingly they were planning to reorganise the parishes after the Presbyterian model, and to replace the Prayer Book by a Directory of Public Worship. But to the Independents compulsory Presbyterianism was as unpalatable as compulsory Anglicanism, and the Independents were the best soldiers in parliament's army. As Cromwell boasted, the victory at Marston Moor had been theirs : it ' had all the evidence of an absolute victory obtained by the Lord's blessing upon the godly [1] party principally '. Their value in the field obliged parliament to appease them ;

[1] In the idiom of the time, the ' godly party ' meant the Independent sectaries.

and they argued that, while there was a war to be won, it was madness to impair the military effectiveness of the rebel armies by imposing religious tests, and persecuting soldiers whose consciences were revolted by the Covenant. Further, the Independents were at odds with the leaders of parliament about the very purpose for which the war was being fought. Both sides had drifted into war as the only way out of a deadlock, but they were contending over matters which the sword could never settle. Such men as Essex and Manchester were weary of the struggle, and they wanted peace on the basis of the constitutional arrangements of 1641; they had adopted Presbyterianism, not by conviction, but because it was a cut-and-dried solution of the vexed problem of religion, and one which put the Church under the control of parliament.[1] Early in 1645, therefore, they reopened negotiations with the King at Uxbridge. The terms were severe; the change in the military situation made them harsher than those offered in 1643. Charles was required to transfer to parliament the control of the militia and the appointment of peers, ministers and judges; to take the Covenant and to accept a religious settlement in 'nearest conjunction and uniformity' with that of Scotland; and to consent to the punishment of the men who had offered their lives for his cause. Charles replied that he would always protect the Prayer Book from 'scorn and violence'. 'There are three things I will not part with—the Church, my crown and my friends.' In the face of this refusal the parliamentary leaders had to continue the war; but, as Essex said, it did not suit their purposes to 'beat the King too much'. 'If we beat the King ninety and nine times,' said Manchester, 'yet he is King still, and so will his posterity be after him.' The object of their strategy, therefore, was to avoid clashing with the King's main army, and gradually to wear down his resistance by capturing his garrisons and skirmishing with his reserves; until at length he should be obliged to make an honourable submission and be restored to his throne on terms acceptable to his captors. 'That war would

[1] Further, it would permit them to sell the lands of the Bishops.

never be ended by the sword,' said Manchester, 'but by accommodation.'

But the soldiers and the politicians were beginning to fall out. The propaganda that parliament had put forth at the beginning of the war had deluded many into believing that the defeat of the King would be the dawn of a social and spiritual millennium. These enthusiasts—their contemporaries classed them all as Anabaptists [1]—were beginning to realise that parliament proposed to betray them; they hated the whole of parliament's programme, its Presbyterian intolerance and its negotiations with the tyrant. Cromwell and the officers did not share the social aspirations of their men, but they agreed that the war should be fought to a finish. If Cromwell met the King on the field, he 'would as soon discharge my pistol upon him as at any other private person'. The officers' programme was eventually defined under two heads: they wished to group all the rebel forces into a single regular army under a unified command; and to get rid of the titled commanders who had been useful in the early days of the war to sanctify rebellion, but whose hesitations were now shielding the King from defeat. Cromwell appeared in parliament and taunted Manchester with his 'backwardness to fight' and his unwillingness to press 'to a full victory'. He dropped his charges against Manchester on condition that the parliamentary leaders laid down their commands. Early in 1645 the Self-denying Ordinance decreed that all who had been appointed to military posts by the present parliament should resign their ranks within forty days.[2] At the same time, plans were drawn up for the formation of the first English professional army. The nucleus of the New Model was the remnant of the three armies of Essex, Manchester and Waller. The numbers were brought up to 22,000 by impressment, each county supplying a fixed quota. The men were to

[1] The term Anabaptist was applied indiscriminately to all those drastic reformers whose schemes, whether religious, political or social, alarmed the respectable and propertied classes.

[2] They might, however, be reappointed.

be paid regularly, and in place of the various County Committees there was to be a single commander-in-chief, Sir Thomas Fairfax, with Cromwell as Lieutenant-General. The strength of the New Model was its mobility : it left behind the provincial stagnation which had clogged parliament's operations in the past. The men were professional soldiers, trained and properly equipped, and wherever the King's army lay, they could be led in search of it.

The war was soon over. In June, 1645, the New Model found the King's main army at Naseby and totally destroyed it. Charles lost his infantry, his munitions, his baggage and his tents ; he lost too his private documents, of which his enemies made 'that barbarous use as was agreeable to their natures '.[1] In this triumph Cromwell saw 'none other but the hand of God '. Within a year Fairfax and Cromwell annihilated the scattered troops and fortresses which still adhered to the King. Goring was defeated at Langport, Rupert surrendered Bristol and the towns of the West, Cromwell massacred a Catholic garrison at Basing, Charles himself lost his cavalry at Rowton Heath. The royalist cause finally perished when the magnificent effort of Montrose's Highlanders came to an end at Philiphaugh. In June, 1646, Fairfax in his camp on Headington Hill received the surrender of Oxford.

3. *Rogues fall out*

After the last skirmish of the war, at Stow-on-the-Wold, Sir Jacob Astley sat on a drum on the field of battle and said to his conquerors : 'You have now done your work and may go play, unless you will fall out amongst yourselves.' It was a strange age. The English constitution was to be diverted from the steady stream of its development, and forced for a time into unknown courses. For in the months after the first civil war parliament misused its victory : if it had dealt faithfully with its soldiers, and appeased the Cavaliers by tolerating the Prayer

[1] Clarendon.

Book and pardoning those who had fought for the King, it would have laid on Charles the onus of refusing a peaceful settlement. But, since it declined to satisfy either, it failed to establish its right to be obeyed, and authority passed to him who held the sword. The government of England shifted from the bedrock of custom and convention, and the traditional ways of thought disappeared in a welter of strange experiments, as reformers and innovators, Levellers, Saints and republicans, urged their conflicting counsels of perfection. The lovers of tradition had to bide their time, until at length, as Clarendon hoped, when the enthusiasts had 'reformed their consciences by drinking deep in each other's blood', England should recover 'its old good manners, its old good humour, and its old good nature'.

The King himself was an obstacle to the settlement. At the close of the war neither his person nor his office was in danger: both the politicians and the army officers regarded the monarchy as the corner-stone of the constitution. He was, in fact, the focus of all who wanted peace and order. But even in the extremity of defeat Charles would not abandon his prerogatives and his Church. A less inflexible man would have accepted the position and ended his days in peace and dignity as a constitutional King. But it never occurred to Charles that a King could retire; like his enemies, he had his creed, and he would not forsake it. He saw too that his enemies were divided, and he hoped to turn to his own advantage the differences between parliament, army and Scots. The fact that all three parties in turn sought his co-operation stiffened his conviction that he was indispensable, and betrayed him into the unwisdom of thinking that he was indispensable on his own terms. Finally, his evasions exasperated all who had dealings with him, and in a moment fatal to the future of their cause the army leaders yielded to their troops and consented to his death.

Shortly before the war ended, Charles surrendered to the Scots at Newark, hoping to get better terms from them than from the rebels in England. The Scots were willing to restore him if he would accept the Covenant, but on this issue negotiations broke down. The Queen would have had him accept: for the daughter of Henry IV England was worth a Covenant. But Charles would promise no more than temporary concessions, and early in 1647 the Scots handed him over to parliament: for £400,000 they withdrew their garrisons, abandoned their King and left the country.

Charles could expect little mercy from the victorious parliament. The Propositions submitted to him at Newcastle in 1646 were based on Pym's old plan of reducing the monarchy to a Dogeship: if he would forsake his prerogative, his Church and his friends, he could return to his throne. Charles's replies were obscure and evasive: 'How to make a handsome denying offer is all the difficulty.' It was a favourable moment for evasion, for parliament was estranging itself from its own allies. After a war it is usual for the defeated to suffer: and the Cavaliers duly forfeited some of their estates. But the parliamentary leaders decided that some of the victors should be punished too. Now that the war was won, they determined at the same time to establish Presbyterianism, and to avenge the Self-denying Ordinance, by exterminating the Independent sects. In the closing months of 1646 they brought forward measures to forbid laymen to preach or expound the scriptures, and to punish all who would not submit to the 'lame Erastian Presbytery' which they had set up. It was madness to provoke the Independents; 'these are fine tricks to mock God with', said Cromwell ominously. But it was madder still to proceed to associate the grievances of the Independents with the grievances of the army as a whole. In May, 1647, the army was ordered to disband: a force was to go to Ireland, and some were to remain on garrison duty at home, but the rest were to disperse. There was no longer work for the army to do, but the men would neither go to Ireland nor disband, until they had been promised an indemnity for the past and received their arrears of pay. The infantry were owed for eighteen weeks, the cavalry for forty-three, and parliament wanted them to be content with six weeks' arrears. The common soldier, wanting his pay and an assurance that his deeds would be forgiven, was thus identified with the sectary whose religion was imperilled. To increase the alarm of the Independents, Charles and parliament had reached an agreement. In his final answer to the Propositions of Newcastle he had compromised on the vital issues: he would suffer Presbyterianism for three years and abandon the militia to parliament for ten. On these terms he was to be restored.

The coalition between the royalists and the Presbyterians—it was to produce the second civil war, the Treaty of Newport, and ultimately the Restoration—forced the army into open revolt. For some weeks the officers had struggled to restrain the soldiers' anger at the perfidy of parliament. Cromwell, in particular, had striven to prevent an open breach: 'If that authority falls to nothing', he told his men in the church at Saffron Walden, 'nothing can follow but confusion.' A few weeks later, when the extremists were urging the officers to march on London, he reminded them that 'whatever we get by a treaty will be firm and durable, it will be conveyed to posterity; that which you have by force, I look on it as nothing.' But the schemes of parliament now drove Cromwell to one of those swift, impulsive, and utterly final acts by which he always cut the knot of uncertainty. It was rumoured that parliament was meditating a *coup d'état*: to coerce the Independents into submission with the aid of the Scots, the royalists and the militia of Presbyterian London. Cromwell's reply was decisive. On May 31st he sent Cornet Joyce to fetch the King from Holdenby House, in Northamptonshire, and bring him to the army camp at Newmarket. Parliament's plans centred round the King; without him, they fell to the ground.

It was now the turn of the officers to attempt to make a settlement with Charles. Fairfax had no heart in the quarrel between Independents and Presbyterians; he only wanted fair play for his men. Thus the dominant voices in the officers' council were Cromwell and his son-in-law, Henry Ireton. Cromwell's motives are always hard to fathom, for he tended to solve his problems emotionally. When he was asked what his aims were, he darkly replied that 'no one rises so high as he who knows not whither he is going'. On one point, however, he was convinced: he had fought for liberty of conscience. In 1647 he was a monarchist and he reverenced parliament, but events proved that he would destroy either institution if it denied religious freedom. Ireton was a shrewder man: his mind was lucid and constructive, which Cromwell's was not. He, too, wanted to restore the old constitution, but he was determined to assert for the army an 'equiponderant authority' in securing the objects for which the war had been fought. 'Parliamentary privileges as well as Royal prerogative may be perverted or abused.' Thus the Heads of the Proposals, which Ireton submitted to the King early in August, placed checks on parliament as well as on the Crown. The powers of the prerogative were blunted, but parliament too was to be held within the bounds of a written constitution; the Bishops were to be restored, but with no powers of discipline; the Covenant was not to be enforced; and all but five of the royalists were to be pardoned. Although they were more radical than Clarendon's Restoration of 1660, Ireton's terms were the best ever offered to Charles; and, unlike parliament's various expedients, they were a framework for a permanent plan of government. But their very virtue killed them. Whatever their academic worth, they were too novel and too drastic; in the continuous development of the English constitution there are no fresh starts.

They failed, too, because in his search for an equitable settlement Ireton had not made his proposals sufficiently attractive for any one party. Thus they were repudiated by Charles, by parliament, and by the radicals in the army itself. Charles was certain that he was indispensable. 'You cannot be without me', he told Ireton: 'you will fall to ruin if I do not sustain you.' He dwelt in a fool's paradise, where he saw himself playing off the Heads of Proposals against the Newcastle Propositions, with the programme of the Scots to be brought forward if neither parliament nor army would be reasonable. Parliament, also, rejected Ireton's plan. The army marched to London, and turned certain Presbyterians out of the House. Ireton declared that he would ' purge, and purge, and purge, and never leave purging ' ; he would enlist Frenchmen and Spaniards ' to get the King's business settled '. Even Cromwell, who respected parliament, could see no hope of peace until the irreconcilable Presbyterians were ' put out by the ears '. But parliament would not yield. In September it turned down the Proposals, and resumed its own negotiations with the King.

Lastly, the Proposals brought to a head the swelling dissension between the army and its officers. The soldiers of the New Model had been taught to believe that they were fighting for the immortal cause of social perfection ; their victories had fortified their sense of their high destiny ; they were not men who would lightly be betrayed. In their opinion, Ireton's negotiations with the King contradicted the purposes of the war. Thus the rank-and-file of the army repudiated the programme of the officers : a programme, incidentally, by which the officers would secure all the prizes. For in the soldiers' millennium there was no place for a King or a House of Lords. ' It is very questionable ', said John Wildman, ' whether there be a way left for mercy on that Person ' ; they declined to accept a peace which depended ' upon him that intended our bondage and brought a cruel war upon us '. Throughout the summer and autumn of 1647, in stormy debates at Reading and Putney, the officers wrestled with their turbulent followers, but there was no ground of accommodation. In October the ranks put forth their own programme. Their two pamphlets, *The Case of the Army Truly Stated*, and *The Agreement of the People*, laid down the fundamental rights which no authority should be allowed to usurp. They were largely the work of John Lilburne, an irrepressible Cockney journalist, who was the spokesman of the political extremists, usually known as Levellers. The burden of the Levellers' doctrine was the sovereignty of the people, ' originally and essentially ' the source of all power. The present parliament, therefore, was to be dissolved, and a new one elected by universal manhood suffrage ; all were to be equal before the law ; and there must be complete liberty of conscience, since 'the ways of God's worship are not at all entrusted to us by any human power'. In their discussions with the officers, the Levellers fiercely defended their principles. Colonel Rainborough declared that certain rights, belonging to each individual by the laws of God and nature, were inalienable. 'The poorest he that is in England hath a life to live as the greatest he', and each man should have 'the choice of those who are to make the laws for him to live under'. For 'I do not find anything in the law of God, that a Lord shall choose twenty burgesses and a gentleman but two, and a poor man shall choose none'. Who, the Levellers asked, were the aristocracy? 'What were the Lords of England but William the Conqueror's Colonels? or the Barons but his Majors? or the Knights but his Captains?'

The phantoms of manhood suffrage and the career open to talent disquieted the officers. Democracy, in Cromwell's thinking, was the creed of all poor men and all bad men. Might not their creed, he implored them to consider, 'be but carnal imagination, and carnal reasonings?' The proposed breach with tradition appalled him: for 'would it not be confusion? Would it not be utter confusion?' Ireton was equally distressed, and he was better able to account for his fears. 'All the main thing that I speak for,' he said, 'is because I would have an eye to property.' He voiced the classical argument of Whig political theory: no man should be entitled to vote unless he had a stake in the country. The Englishman's birthright was 'air and place and ground and the freedom of the highways and other things'; but the rulers and the voters should be 'those persons in whom all land lies, and those incorporations in whom all trading lies', those, in short, who had 'a permanent fixed interest in this Kingdom'. The debates dragged on beyond the hope of compromise. At length Cromwell, who dreaded anarchy, could stand it no longer; the agitators were ordered to return to their regiments, and henceforth the affairs of the army were directed solely by the officers: 'a cabinet junta', Lilburne called it, ' of seven or eight self-ended fellows '. But Cromwell's dealings with the King had blasted his credit in the army; and the King's doom was sealed when the officers realised that, in order to unite the army again for the work it had to do, a left-wing programme must be adopted, which had as its foundation the execution of the tyrant.

4. *The second civil war*

On November 11th Charles escaped from the army at Hampton Court. Rumours had come to him that the soldiers were determined that he should die. William Goffe had called on the pure in heart to rise and extirpate that mystery of iniquity, the office of King; Captain Bishop had murmured against ' a compliance to preserve that Man of Blood '; and on the very day of Charles's flight Major Harrison insisted that his position should be discussed by the army council. Men said that Cromwell deliberately allowed Charles to escape. Whether or not this was so, his flight freed Cromwell and the officers from an embarrassing entanglement. Since he had not accepted their terms, they had no further use for him; and Cromwell was now able to persuade himself that he had been dazzled by carnal glories, that the prospect of an Earldom had enticed him from the narrow path of duty, to which he had been recalled by the simple piety of the common soldiers.

Having escaped from the army, Charles now walked to his ruin. He reopened negotiations with parliament, but in the middle of them he came to terms with the Scots. The Scots commissioners visited him in the Isle of Wight and laid their proposals before him: on December 26th he signed the Engagement, in which he agreed to accept Presbyterianism for three years; and in return the Scots would compel the army to disband, and crush the Independent sects. Parliament at once broke off negotiations with the King, and before setting out to war, the army held at Windsor the most famous of its prayer-meetings. The soldiers were ' hardly able to speak a word to each other for weeping'; but between their tears they managed to resolve that 'it was our duty, if ever the Lord brought us back again in peace, to call Charles Stuart, that man of blood, to an account for that blood he had shed'.

The second civil war lasted only a few months. The alliance between royalists and Presbyterians was uneasy, and the mass of the people stood unhappily aside and prepared to accept the arbitrament of war. There were royalist risings in Wales, Kent and Essex; Berwick and Carlisle fell; Lord Inchiquin raised the Irish; a fourth of the navy joined the King. If the Scots had come sooner, there would have been a chance of a royalist victory. As it was, Cromwell had time to subdue the Welsh, and Fairfax to break the back of the resistance in the East: only Pembroke and Colchester were stubborn. When it came, the Scots army was half-hearted and inexperienced; the Highlanders would not fight by the side of Presbyterians, and Leslie's veterans held back because Charles had refused to take the Covenant.[1] Cromwell met Hamilton in August, and in a long, straggling battle between Preston and Warrington he won the greatest of his victories. He was outnumbered by three to one, but he attacked the Scots in detail and completely routed them.

The King's cause was lost. The Presbyterians tried to save themselves and him by again seeking a settlement, but the Newport negotiations collapsed on the old obstacle of religion. Fairfax broke away from the extremists in the army and revived the Heads of Proposals; Charles refused these too. Only the army could make the settlement, and the army was demanding its reward. Its latest victory had been over the Covenant as well as the Church of England, and it was determined to arraign Anglican King and Presbyterian parliament as twin malefactors before the bar of triumphant Independency. Ireton, now disillusioned and ruthless, accepted the constitutional programme of the radicals; his *Remonstrance of the Army* demanded the soldiers' pay, the exclusion of all Presbyterians from the Long

[1] The Kirk banned the expedition.

Parliament, and the trial and death of the King. Cromwell threw off his hesitations. God's constant witnesses against the King were conclusive ; Preston was final proof of His favour. ' He must be a very atheist that does not acknowledge it.' His sense of God's approval, as revealed to him in countless ' Providences ', nerved Cromwell to his drastic work. ' Let us look into Providences ', he said ; ' surely they mean somewhat. They hang so together : have been so constant, so clear, unclouded.' ' Since the Providence of God hath cast this upon us, I cannot but submit to Providence.'

Thus the Independents came to solve by passion and emotion the problem which they could not solve by peaceful settlement. To indulge their instinct for the dramatic, the King must be publicly tried in the name of the people ; the thing should not be done in a corner. Manchester's Earldom had not saved him in 1644, Charles's crown should not save him now ; for earthly authority was ' but dross and dung in comparison with Christ '.[1] ' I tell you,' said Cromwell, ' we will cut off his head with the crown upon it.' But first parliament must be brought to heel : in December Colonel Pride prevented the Presbyterian members from taking their seats. The remnant, a rump of between fifty and sixty members, set up a commission to try the King in the name of the people of England. The show was clumsily staged : the people in the galleries crying ' God save the King ' ; Charles, guarded by soldiers, protesting that the court had no authority to try him ; President Bradshaw, in a shot-proof hat, protesting that it had ; finally, Cromwell, in a mood of ghastly facetiousness, throwing cushions and inking men's faces as he collected signatures for the warrant of death ; and the King led away by the soldiers, crying, ' I am not suffered for to speak. Expect what justice other people will have.' Such things are better done in corners.

On the scaffold, standing by the executioners in their vizors, wigs and false beards, Charles repeated the creed by which he

[1] Cromwell.

had lived. He was being brought to his death, he said, in the cause of the liberty of the people of England 'I must tell you that this liberty and freedom consists in having government, those laws by which their lives and goods may be most their own. It is not their having a share in the government, that is nothing pertaining to them. A subject and a sovereign are clean different things. . . . If I would have given way to have all changed by the power of the sword, I needed not to have come here.' 'This is memorable, that at such time as the King's body was brought out of St. George's hall the sky was serene and clear ; but presently it began to snow, and fell so fast as, by the time they came to the west end of the royal chapel, the black pall was all white (the colour of innocency) being thick covered with snow. So went the white King to his grave, in the forty-eighth year of his age and the twenty-second year and tenth month of his reign.' [1]

[1] Thomas Herbert, *Memoirs.*

CHAPTER XVII

THE INTERREGNUM

Rule of the Rump. The Barebones Parliament. Instrument of Government. Major-Generals. Humble Petition and Advice. Foreign policy.

1. *The rule of the Rump*

In the early months of 1649 the Rump of the Long Parliament passed laws to make England a republic. 'The People are under God, the original of all just power'; and therefore 'whatsoever is enacted or declared for law by the Commons in Parliament assembled, hath the force of law'. It was resolved that the office of King 'is unnecessary, burdensome, and dangerous', and that the House of Lords was 'useless and dangerous, and ought to be abolished'. A Council of State was set up, to perform the work of the vanished Privy Council; a special court of justice executed the republic's enemies; a new treason law defined offences against the state, and made it treason to suggest that the authority of the Commonwealth was usurped or tyrannical, or to challenge the sovereignty of parliament; the press was muzzled by measures which recalled the severity of Star Chamber [1]; finally, all men over the age of eighteen were required to take an Engagement of Fidelity to the Commonwealth.

By these measures the military and sectarian minority of the nation,[2] masquerading as the chosen representatives of the people,

[1] The Long Parliament's censorship of the press had already, in 1644, called forth Milton's *Areopagitica*.

[2] The average attendance in parliament was fifty-six, in the Council of State fifteen.

sought to entrench itself in power. First, however, it had to secure its safety abroad. The regicide government was everywhere detested : its ambassadors were murdered, its ships looted ; there were royalist pirates in the neighbouring islands ; foreign bankers refused loans, merchants would not trade ; the Covenanters were stirring in Scotland, the Catholics in Ireland. There was no imminent danger of invasion, because the Commonwealth's enemies were too divided to act in concert, but the Rump could not embark on its programme of social reform until it had quelled unrest within the three kingdoms. In August, 1649, Cromwell, as commander of the Commonwealth's army, set out to crush the Irish.[1] 'It matters not who be our commander if God be so' ; but he took a salary of £13,000, and set out in princely state, attended by coaches, trumpets and guards. Before he arrived, Ormonde, who commanded the only field-army large enough to have resisted him, was defeated at Rathmines ; his task, therefore, was to capture the towns which were still defended by Catholic or royalist garrisons. Cromwell's doings in Ireland have soiled the honour of one who usually was humane. He has been excused on the ground that he imagined himself to be the avenger of the massacres of 1641, and that he sought, by making a few terrible examples, to avoid bloodshed later on ; but his reports to the Speaker on the taking of Drogheda and Wexford speak with the voice of a man who gloried in the spilling of impious blood. At Drogheda he ordered a steeple to be burned in which eighty men had taken refuge, and he gruesomely recorded the cries of the victims. The governor, Sir Arthur Aston, was battered to death with his own wooden leg. 'I am persuaded that this is a righteous judgment of God upon these barbarous wretches.' At Wexford God's providence again caused the defenders 'to become the prey of the soldier' ; he had intended to spare them, 'yet God would not have it so'. In May, 1650, Cromwell returned to England, leaving Ireton, Ludlow and Fleetwood to complete the conquest of the Irish.

[1] Before he left, a purged and chastened Oxford made him a Doctor of Civil Law.

Bands of fugitives were smoked out of caves and reduced to submission by the pillaging of the countryside. 'These are seals of God's approbation of your great change of government.' When the war was over, rebels and priests were compelled to forfeit their estates ; two-thirds of the land of Ireland was transferred from the natives to Cromwell's soldiers.

Cromwell was recalled to England to deal with the Scots. Montrose had tried to raise the Highlands for the young Charles II, but he was defeated at Carbisdale, and betrayed by Macleod of Assynt. Having lost Montrose, Charles prepared to try his fortune with the Kirk. Being more accommodating in these matters than his father, he took the Covenant, and regretted that the House of Stuart had for so long hindered the work of reformation. The Covenanters were still, and always had been, royalists ; and having found at last a King who would accept their religious programme, they made ready to overthrow the unhallowed republic and restore him to the throne of his fathers. In the summer of 1650 Cromwell marched against them, uneasy in his heart to be making war on those who lately had been his brethren.[1] He sought anxiously to adjust the differences which divided the Kirk from the godly in England : 'I beseech you in the bowels of Christ, think it possible you may be mistaken.' At Dunbar, where the priests made David Leslie abandon an unassailable position, God gave His witness against the Kirk. The Kirk never recovered the prestige it lost by 'the dreadful appearance of God against us at Dunbar after so many public appeals to Him '.[2] 'Surely it's probable ', said Cromwell, 'the Kirk has done their do.' But, for the fourth time in less than fifteen years, a Scottish army crossed the Border. With the King at its head, it marched through Lancashire into the West of England, where in the narrow, winding streets of Worcester the Lord showed His 'crowning mercy ' to the elect of God. Charles escaped, but his followers were sent in batches to Barbados and New England. In Scotland General Monk

[1] Fairfax refused to invade Scotland, and resigned his command.
[2] Alexander Jaffray.

established a form of peace. The Kirk lost its powers of coercion, but the structure of Presbyterian worship was spared; and Scotland, like Ireland, was administered from London, and sent its representatives to the English parliament.

Meanwhile, the Rump had driven its enemies off the sea. Robert Blake, a Puritan soldier, was put in command of the English navy. He forced Prince Rupert's royalist fleet out of its refuge in Ireland, chased him round the Iberian Peninsula into the Mediterranean, and drove him, battered and depleted, into Toulon. Another expedition, under Sir George Ayscue, made the West Indian colonies repent of their royalism, and won their allegiance to the Commonwealth. The statesmen of the Rump then felt themselves strong enough to fight a commercial war against the Dutch.[1] In two years they had doubled the numbers of the English navy, which consisted in 1651 of eighty-two ships. The object of the war, as of the Navigation Act of the previous year, was to recover from the Dutch the carrying-trade which they had seized during the civil wars, and to enforce the right to search Dutch ships. Although it dragged on for three years, when Cromwell ended it, the war was unpopular in England. It was a war made by politicians, with the approval of the merchants of the City. The soldiers disliked it, because they were beginning to mistrust the politicians, and the Saints deplored a war between two Protestant nations; further, it required heavy taxation, which fell on the royalists, and so kept alive that party bitterness which all reasonable men were anxious to forget.

The Rump was bungling the business of government. The rule of a minority had only a minority to support it; and although many Englishmen, like the citizens of Hobbes's *Leviathan*, made their peace with the *de facto* government, the mass of royalists, Catholics, parliament men and Presbyterians, were implacably opposed to the regicide politicians. As well as these traditional enemies, the Rump had to fear the extremists in its own party: those whom Carlyle has called ' the submarine world of Calvin-

[1] For a further discussion of this war, see page 294 *sq*.

istic Sansculottism ', Levellers pleading the rights of the sovereign people, Diggers in quest of a rural communism, Fifth Monarchy Men seeking to establish the reign of Christ on the ruins of human government. Lilburne was unquenchable. He reissued the *Agreement of the People* and attacked the Rump in a pamphlet, *England's New Chains Discovered.* He inspired serious mutinies in the army [1] against the self-seeking of the officers, and when he was finally banished, he kept his cause alive by writing pamphlets abroad. From the Diggers, who established an agricultural community on St. George's Hill, in Surrey, emerged the doctrine that the welfare of the masses was the sole criterion of political action ; to endure, the political revolution must be founded on a social revolution. Their community was broken up, their huts demolished, and their cattle taken from them ; their leaders, Winstanley [2] and Everard, were sternly admonished by the Council of State.

But blank repression was an unstatesmanlike answer to those enthusiasts in the Puritan movement who had fought for Utopian ideals ; ' Magna Carta itself ', as Lilburne said, ' being but a beggarly thing, containing many marks of intolerable bondage.' The Rump inherited a difficult situation, but it took little pains to conciliate its enemies. Elizabeth had met a not dissimilar problem by framing a settlement as comprehensive as possible ; but the Rump, instead of leading the nation towards agreement and peace, tended rather to aggravate existing dissensions. Certainly its members were neither so corrupt nor so inefficient as the army painted them when it turned them out : the work of the Council of State, and of the standing committees which it appointed, was, so far as it went, intelligent and disinterested. No more serious charge can fairly be brought against them than that their task was too big for them ; and that as the first raptures of revolutionary enthusiasm died away, some of them began to find that office was sweet for its own sake. Their worst sins

[1] Crushed by Cromwell and Fairfax at Burford in the spring of 1649.

[2] Winstanley's *Law of Freedom* was the most remarkable document of an age rich in Utopian literature.

were of omission: they did little that was constructive. Thus, although they busied themselves with pulling down cathedrals, closing the theatres, enforcing Sabbath observance, and punishing all kinds of moral wrongdoing from swearing to incest, they shrank from devising any comprehensive plan of ecclesiastical government. Except for Catholics and Prelatists, there was liberty of conscience, but there was no system of worship or discipline to replace the Church or the Presbytery which the Independents had rejected. Similarly, the Rump was urged to reform the laws, but it did not progress beyond setting up a commission to meditate upon the matter.

Thus when the soldiers returned from the wars, strengthened in their certainty of God's favour, they found the government busier with safeguarding its own position than with planting the Kingdom of Heaven among men. They found the Rump fighting a costly war, and paying for it by selling Church lands and harassing the Cavaliers; free speech denied by frightening penalties; the processes of the common law superseded by arbitrary tribunals as ruthless as the old courts of the Crown. Before long they began to murmur. They petitioned for reforms, and were ignored. At length they found that they had 'a strange distaste' for the members of the Rump, for their 'pride and ambition and self-seeking' and their 'design to . . . continue the power in their own hands'. The Independents were dividing into two factions: those who had offices and salaries, and those who had not. The quarrel came to a crisis when the Rump, knowing that an election would drive the Independents from power, began to debate a bill which proposed to keep the present members in their seats for the rest of their lives, with the sole right to co-opt other members of whom they approved. On April 20th, 1653, Cromwell came to the House with a file of musketeers. He listened for a while to the debate; and then, after a passionate speech in which he blended appeals to Heaven with coarse abuse of the members, he closed the doors behind the retreating Rump. 'The spirit was so upon him that he was overruled by it.' In the afternoon the Council of

State, the last remnant of civil power, collapsed before military violence.

Once more Cromwell had solved his difficulties emotionally. He believed in institutions, but in a fit of temper and impatience he had destroyed the two which were the heart of English life. The Rump had fallen into the mistake which Charles and the Long Parliament had made before it: it had counted on overawing the army by the strength of its legal position and the Englishman's reverence for established institutions. Like the King, parliament had thought itself indispensable. In any age but this, both King and parliament would have reckoned rightly, but the soldiers of the Independent army were no ordinary men. Cromwell's career is unintelligible if he is credited with no better motives than personal ambition. In his context he was unquestionably sincere: the cumulative witness of God's many Providences burned into his soul the certainty that he, and the men who fought with him, were of the elect: they were 'God's people',[1] and therefore human society must be modelled to a design of which they could approve. 'The interest of God's people' was the star which constantly guided him; the Self-denying Ordinance, Pride's Purge, the execution of the King, and now the dissolution of the Rump, were all logical steps in his journey. His motive was not his own greatness. Power, with its snares and temptations, frightened him. 'I called not myself to this place,' he said once; 'of that God is witness'; but his conscience told him that he dare not refuse 'the power God had most clearly by His Providence put into my hands'.

The insuperable problem before him was to found the interest of God's people on a more durable basis than the power of the sword. He could not reconcile the benevolent despotism of the godly with the prevailing conviction that government should express the will of the people; and the tolerance and high ideals of the Protectorate were barren of ultimate good, because the people associated them with an intolerable military tyranny. After 1653 even the Independents were split between soldiers

[1] 'People,' he once said, 'that are to God as the apple of His eye.'

and civilians. Thus Cromwell spent the years of the Protectorate trying to restore the two institutions which he had destroyed, for he realised that ' God's cause ' must perish unless he could fix it in the traditional framework of King and parliament. But the one thing which the people of England wanted he could not do : he could not disband the army and call a free parliament, for that would have meant the ruin of the Independent cause. ' I am as much for government by consent as any man, but where shall we find that consent ? '

2. *The Barebones Parliament*

When the Rump had gone, the soldiers were undisputed masters of England. To clothe the nakedness of their despotism, they determined to summon a parliament ; and since they could not face the consequences of a free election, they summoned a body representative of orthodox Puritanism. The Congregational churches were ordered to draw up lists of ' divers persons fearing God, and of approved fidelity and honesty ', and from these lists, together with some additional nominations of their own, the officers made their selection. Acting as Captain-General of the army, Cromwell sent writs to 140 chosen members.

They came together in July, 1653. Their first action was to declare themselves to be a parliament, and their assembly has taken its name from one of its members, Praise-God Barebones, a leather-seller of Fleet Street. It was the first parliament to have representatives from the three kingdoms. In his inaugural address the Captain-General gave expression to the high hopes which their meeting had inspired in him. ' I never looked to see such a day as this—it may be, nor you either—when Jesus Christ should be so owned as he is, at this day and in this work. . . . Indeed, I do think somewhat is at the door.' The Barebones Parliament was the climax of the Puritan movement : when men were summoned to legislate for the country, not because they were men of wealth, or property, or influence, but because they were saintly men, fearing God. Not all of them were fanatics like Harrison and Barebones ; the officers had been careful to include a leavening of commonsense, in the persons of such men as Monk, Ashley, Lambert, Blake and Henry Cromwell. But the moderates were less regular in their attendance than the enthusiasts, who threw themselves into the task of reform with the passionate zeal of men who knew it was their duty to usher into an expectant world ' the long-expected birth of freedom and happiness '. In intention their reforms were excellent. They proposed to chart the ' tortuous, ungodly jungle ' of the law, and rewrite the laws of the land within ' the bigness of a pocket-book '. They passed acts to establish civil marriage and a registry of births, deaths and marriages ; to appoint commissioners for probate, to relieve imprisoned debtors, and to provide for the better custody of lunatics. After a day's debate they abolished the Court of Chancery, whose proceedings had grown irregular, costly and belated.[1] They attacked the abuses of ecclesiastical patronage and the payment of tithes ; and, as a final indiscretion, they began to complain of the excessive cost of the army. These reforms bear the stamp of broad-mindedness and statesmanship ; where the Saints blundered was in destroying what they had not the skill to replace, and in bringing about their devoted heads the wrath of the vested interests. Priests, lawyers and soldiers, a combination strong enough to overturn any government, rose against the men who threatened their livelihood. In December the moderates went to the House early in the morning, before the enthusiasts appeared, and resolved ' to deliver up unto the Lord-General Cromwell the powers they have received from him '.

Cromwell's authority ' was become as boundless and unlimited as before, all things being subjected to arbitrariness, and myself . . . a person having power over the three nations without bound or limit set '. The failure of the godly to rule to the satisfaction of practical men narrowed his spiritual horizons. ' The issue was not answerable to the simplicity and honesty of the design.' His eyes were opened to the evil that is in men, who through

[1] 23,000 cases were waiting to be decided, some of them thirty years old.

sloth and avarice do not wish to live saintly lives. He would never abandon God's people, but henceforward he gradually moved away from the idealists and the doctrinaires, and concerned himself with reviving the ' ancient interests ' and the ancient institutions of England. Henceforth he would have to restrain the fanatics [1] whose spiritual Bolshevism had alarmed the vested interests, and whose zeal imperilled the Puritan cause by shaping it to extravagant and impractical ends. The moral welfare of the people was still his aim : ' that's the question, what's for their good, not what pleases them ', as he had declared as long ago as 1647, when he first began to feel the burden of responsibility which he could not cast off. But he no longer dreamed of seeing the Kingdom of Heaven rise on earth ; and in an hour of disappointed hopes, ' I could not tell what my business was . . . save comparing myself to a good Constable set to keep the peace of the parish '.

3. *The experiments of the Protectorate*

After the failure of their religious experiment, the soldiers devised an expedient of their own. The Instrument of Government was the work of John Lambert, who had taken Ireton's place as the army's constitution-maker.[2] It vested the power of making laws in a ' Single Person ' and a parliament, the Single Person to be Oliver Cromwell, who was to hold the office of Protector for the rest of his life ; and the executive power in the Protector and a Council of fifteen members, also nominated for life. Parliament was to be elected by a franchise reformed in accordance with *The Agreement of the People*, and each parliament must sit for at least five months. The executive was allotted £200,000 for civil administration, and sums sufficient to maintain a navy and an army of 30,000 men. Freedom of worship was granted to all but Papists and Prelatists.[3]

[1] For instance, Harrison was cashiered in 1653, and imprisoned two years later. To the Saints Cromwell became the Bastard of Ashdod.

[2] Ireton died in 1651

[3] A Prelatist believed in the traditional government of the Church by Bishops.

The object of the Instrument was to balance the powers of the executive and legislature, to strike a compromise between the single person and the single House. Cromwell accepted it gladly, because, not although, it limited his arbitrary power: the Protector could veto legislation for only twenty days, he could raise no extraordinary revenue, and the chief officers of state had to be approved by parliament. On the other hand, parliament had no control over the administration or the normal, peace-time revenue; it could not wreck the Protector's government as it had wrecked the King's. But it was not a satisfactory settlement: it merely dressed the power of the sword in what was in effect the apparel of the Elizabethan monarchy. It abandoned alike the dreams of the Saints and the old confidence in the supremacy of parliament. Since the Protector and the members of the Council held their offices for life, there could be no pretence that the ministers were responsible to the representatives of the people. Thus if executive and legislature quarrelled, there was only the power of the sword to settle the dispute between them; and they would quarrel, and never cease to quarrel, until men like Edmund Ludlow had won 'what we fought for: the right to govern ourselves'.

On December 16th, 1653, Cromwell was installed as Lord Protector; thus, said the republican John Carew, he took 'the crown from off the head of Christ and put it on his own'. Parliament was not to assemble until September 3rd, the anniversary of Worcester and Dunbar, and in the intervening months the Protector and his Council devoted themselves to legislation. Their eighty-two Ordinances, which parliament was required to ratify, show Cromwell's quality as a reformer. His administrative measures fulfilled in a more practical form many of the good intentions of the Saints: he eased the plight of debtors, limited the jurisdiction of Chancery and reduced its fees, and took an enlightened interest in education. He pursued, too, that reformation of manners which was one of the essential aims of Puritan government; for 'the mind is the man. If that be kept pure, a man signifies somewhat.' But the purpose nearest his heart was the proper organisation of religion. Implicit in all the declarations of the army were these words from the second *Agreement of the People*[1]: 'That such as profess faith in God by Jesus Christ, however differing in judgment from the doctrine, worship and discipline publicly held forth . . . shall not be restrained from, but shall be protected in the profession of their faith.' Religious toleration was in Cromwell's sight the 'blessedest thing' that his rule could provide; it was dearer to him, and to the men who drew up the Instrument of Government, than any political object. All the varieties of Puritan congregation were allowed, therefore, to think and worship as they pleased; even the Quakers, the strangest and the greatest of the sects, were defended by the Protector from the hostility of priests and magistrates. The Jews were allowed to worship privately; but perhaps this was because they controlled the trade of Iberia and the Levant. Catholics and Anglicans were in theory excluded from this freedom, but in practice they were rarely molested; at least they were not persecuted, and not compelled to attend services which were repugnant to their beliefs. Moreover, Cromwell was wise enough not to endanger his aims by quarrelling with the vested interests. Tithe and patronage were institutions which he could not afford to destroy; but he drew the sting from both by setting up a commission of Triers to test the fitness of candidates presented to livings. Thus bad men could not fill benefices with bad men, and only priests of 'holy and unblameable conversation' could handle the emoluments of the Church. As a corollary, Cromwell appointed Ejectors to visit the parishes, the schools and the Universities, to remove from their offices clergy and teachers who were 'scandalous, ignorant, and insufficient'.

The first parliament of the Protectorate showed Cromwell that his system did not fulfil the wishes of the people. In contrast to his fervent address to the Saints, his speech to the members was sober and practical. He dwelt on the need for a policy

[1] Issued in January, 1649.

of ' healing and settling ', and sought to unite them in a common fear of Levellers and Fifth Monarchy men, whose scandalous and unprofitable ways threatened the safety of the realm. But parliament was irreconcilable; the long battle which it had fought against the Stuarts, who governed by right of God, they would fight again against men who ruled by right of the sword. The members immediately challenged the letter of the constitution by which they sat. Cromwell replied that they might debate and alter the ' circumstantials ' of the constitution, but that its ' fundamentals ' were not to be challenged. In speech more than usually bewildering he stated that to abandon a form of government ' so owned by God, so approved by men, were a thing which I can sooner be willing to be rolled into my grave and buried with infamy than I can give my consent to '. The four ' fundamentals ' from which the army would not depart were the divided sovereignty of legislature and executive; a check on ' perpetual ' parliaments; religious toleration; and the maintenance, independent of the control of parliament, of the army by which that toleration was assured. A block of republicans was excluded from parliament, but the new Rump insisted on amending the constitution: it claimed full sovereignty, and proposed to reduce the numbers of the army. Cromwell knew only one answer to these dissensions. In January, 1655, after it had sat for five lunar months, he dissolved the parliament.

The Presbyterian Edmund Calamy had once told Cromwell that nine of every ten men in the nation were opposed to his policy; and Cromwell had replied: ' What if I should disarm the nine, and put a sword in the tenth man's hands? Would not that do the business? ' Having failed in his attempt to govern by consent, Cromwell fell back on naked force. A royalist rising in the West gave him the excuse to parcel England into eleven districts, each of them under the control of a Major-General and a regiment of soldiers. In such a way William the Conqueror had scattered his captains to hold down a defeated people. Cromwell sent out the Major-Generals partly as a police to keep order among the discontented royalists, and partly to stimulate the magistrates to fulfil the law. Like Richelieu's *Intendants* and the prerogative courts of the Crown, they were to see that the government's word was obeyed in the provinces. They ruled with a heavy hand : their harsh Puritan morality was as much detested as the severity with which they enforced it. The gaols could not accommodate the growing multitude of vagabonds and delinquents, and so many of the offenders were deported to the colonies that *to barbados* entered the language. In an effort to reconcile the taxpayer to these harsh courses, Cromwell reduced the monthly assessment, and met the extra expense by levying a decimation, a further tax of 10 per cent. on the property of royalists. Even when he was ruling by force, his aims were sincere : through the Major-Generals he sought to convert the people more rapidly to a godly way of life. But his means discredited his ends ; the tyranny of the soldiers made Puritan rule abhorrent to thousands who had been ready to accept its essential purpose.

The revenue of the Protectorate was four times that on which Charles had been expected to meet the expenses of government, but the burden of the Spanish war obliged Cromwell to levy extraordinary taxation. By the terms of the Instrument, no additional taxes could be imposed without the consent of parliament. To placate the people, therefore, he recalled the Major-Generals, and tried once more to govern constitutionally. The second parliament of the Protectorate was summoned in September, 1656, but before it met a hundred members were excluded by the Council, and some fifty more stayed away as a protest. The remnant duly voted £400,000 for the war, and set up a high court for the trial and punishment of the Protector's enemies ; then it made an attempt to put an end to martial law, by asking Cromwell to be King. In one respect the plight of England recalled the dangerous days of Elizabeth. The Protector was surrounded by enemies, and the safety of the kingdom depended on his single life ; if he were to die—and the government had just unearthed a Levellers' plot to assassinate him—civil war would break out over his grave, as royalists, Levellers and Presbyterians took up arms to decide how the country should be governed. An obscure member of parliament, John Ashe of Somerset, moved that he be asked to thwart his enemies by adopting the old constitution. In February, 1657, this motion was presented to Cromwell in the form of a Humble Petition and Advice, which requested him to take the crown and revive the Upper House.

The Petition forced upon Cromwell the most difficult decision of his life. 'There is no question that the man was in great agony,' says Clarendon, '. . . and thought it the only way to be safe.' On the one hand he saw the way to permanence: he could rest his work on the secure basis of the old constitution, and leave to his son a legacy of order and good government. In discussions after the battle of Worcester he had urged a settlement 'with somewhat of a monarchical power in it'. The Protectorate was 'somewhat monarchical', and Cromwell lived at Whitehall and wore the purple; but the Protectorate was unknown to the constitution, it was the artificial dress of swordsmen. 'The title is not the question,' said John Thurloe, 'but it's the office, which is known to the laws and this people. . . . Besides, they say the name Protector came in by the sword . . . and will never be the ground of any settlement.' Only by way of the old constitution could Cromwell complete his work of 'healing and settling' the differences which divided the people; any make-shift alternative was 'but a probationer'.

But Cromwell did not take the crown. The officers, self-seekers like Lambert, Desborough and Fleetwood, preferred the Protectorate, for a revival of hereditary monarchy would rob the army of its control over the head of the state. Cromwell knew these men for what they were; it was not their opposition which dissuaded him. The decisive voice was the voice of the common soldier. 'God's people', the men who had fought and won his battles, the best elements in Puritanism, did not wish him to be King; to lay his hands on an earthly crown was to betray the high purposes for which they had striven together.

It was not that he was frightened of the army: he was strong enough to have crushed the objectors and kept it ostensibly loyal. The conflict was in his own heart : he feared that the objections of the common soldiers might be God's witness against his backsliding, against the wickedness of allowing carnal glories to dazzle his vision. At last, after hours of tortured brooding, he surrendered his reason to his conscience : in May he told the members that he could not take the crown. Later in the month, the Petition, adjusted to meet his scruples, passed into law. The Protector was given the right to appoint his successor, and to nominate the members of the new ' Other House ' ; thus he recovered two of the essential powers of the old monarchy. Parliament, too, recovered some of the authority of which the Instrument had deprived it : it had the right to remove the Protector's Councillors, its own members were not to be ejected without the consent of a majority, and it had additional powers in finance.

Thus amended by the Humble Petition and Advice, the constitution of the Protectorate had become in all but name a monarchy. Parliament and Protector were stronger, but the authority of the Council, hitherto the stronghold of the officers, had been weakened : in Lambert's original design it had held the balance between the Protector and the legislature, but the balancing power in the revised constitution was the ' Other House ' ; further, the members of the Council were now responsible to parliament. These changes did not, however, solve Cromwell's problems ; in fact, this sham monarchy was the final admission of his failure. Cromwell was too nearly a King for the republicans to co-operate with him ; the people ' will quake to hear ', said Hazlerig, ' that they are returning to Egypt '. Yet he was not King enough to win over the royalists. The nearer it approached to the pattern of the old constitution, the less justification the Protectorate had for existing, and the narrower became the platform on which it stood. In *Killing No Murder* the Levellers called for the death of the apostate ; in *King Richard III Revived* the unquenchable Prynne decided that he had been better governed under Charles I. Still more ominous were the murmurings in the army. As Cromwell moved back towards the institutions which in his dreams of a golden age he had overthrown, he loosened the ties which bound him to the men who had made him great. When he died, with one foot on the general's saddle and one foot on the throne, he was not the undisputed ruler of the nation, and he was no longer the beloved and trusted leader of the Puritan army.

His last experiment failed as swiftly as the others. Of the forty-two members who sat in the 'Other House' only two were members of the old peerage. The absence of the old nobility and of men of property discredited it: 'they are not a balance, as the old Lords were, as to matters of estate'.[1] Further, the elevation of thirty of Cromwell's closest supporters weakened the government's authority in the lower House, where a block of republicans and Long Parliament men carried on their familiar work of obstruction. Hearing that they were preparing an intrigue with the Saints and the malcontents in the army, Cromwell suddenly drove to the House in a hackney-coach and dispersed the members. 'And I do dissolve this Parliament. And let God be judge between you and me.' Seven months later, on September 3rd, 1658, the greatest of his anniversaries he died. 'Our rest we expect elsewhere: that will be durable.'

4. *Foreign affairs during the Interregnum*

England had been allowed to fight out her domestic quarrels unmolested by foreign interference, because a much greater quarrel had been taking place in Europe. The Thirty Years War had opened with the attempt of the Emperor to carry the Counter-Reformation and the dominion of his House to the shores of the Baltic; but when it came to a close at Westphalia in 1648, the French seemed to have brought to a successful conclusion the long duel which they had been waging against the Hapsburgs since the days of Charles V. But the struggle

[1] Cromwell had intended them to be the 'repairers of breaches and the restorers of paths to dwell in'.

was not yet over. Within a few months of a treaty which had given her Alsace and recognised her sovereign rights to Toul, Metz, and Verdun, France was herself in the grip of civil war; and before the rebellion known as the *Fronde* had been suppressed, the safety of the monarchy had been threatened by a Spanish invasion under the leadership of a French commander.[1] England profited from France's misfortune. For in the dangerous years when the armies of the Commonwealth were engaged with their enemies in the British Isles, the two great Catholic powers were too deeply engrossed in their own quarrel to intervene on behalf of the Stuarts.

Since the timid diplomacy of James I and the repeated humiliations of Buckingham, England had been of little account in European affairs. Whatever criticisms may be brought against the foreign policy of the successive governments of the Commonwealth, it is to their credit that they showed themselves to be more formidable than the Stuarts, and earned the healthy respect, if not the affection, of the continental powers. Europe had been horrified by the execution of the King, but the regicide government rapidly silenced criticism by the quality of its practical achievements: its fleets chased the royalist fugitives into the Mediterranean, chastised Portugal for harbouring its enemies, and harassed the French by unofficial attacks on their commercial shipping. In 1652 the Rump declared war on Holland. The outbreak of this war revealed that the government was in earnest in its attempts to assert and enforce the traditional rights of the English navy. Many long-standing grievances against the Dutch had lately come to a head. For they had not merely shown persistent sympathy with the Stuarts and insulted the Rump's ambassadors: they had taken advantage of the Great Rebellion to seize the carrying-trade from English vessels, they refused to acknowledge the English doctrine of *mare clausum* or to strike the flag to English ships in home waters, and they were accused of infringing the rights of English fisher-

[1] The Prince of Condé, who had broken the power of the Spanish *tercios* at Rocroi in 1643.

men in the North Sea. Men with long memories went on to recall that some thirty years ago English merchants had been treacherously massacred at Amboyna, and the East India Company deprived of the profitable commerce with the Spice Islands.

With the object of recovering the lost carrying-trade the Rump passed the Navigation Act of 1651. It decreed that goods imported into the British Isles from Asia, Africa, and America should be carried in ships belonging to Britain or her colonies ; and that goods brought from a European country should be carried in ships owned by Englishmen or the people of the exporting country. Before these measures could be effectively applied, a final cause of dispute brought the two Republics into war. Maintaining the freedom of the seas, and holding the doctrine that the flag covers the cargo, the Dutch commanders resisted the English claim to search their ships for French goods. Growing exasperation with England's insistence on this right led to a serious skirmish between Blake and Tromp in 1651 ; and in the following year the Dutch decided that they would rather fight than submit to it.

The war brought great hardship to Holland. Seven-eighths of her people depended on sea-borne commerce, and her trade-routes passed by the shores of her enemy. Thus, as the war proceeded, many of her merchantmen dared not put to sea, but lay idle in their harbours ; moreover, their prime duty in acting as convoys to their mercantile marine hampered the Dutch admirals in their efforts to engage the English navy in sufficient strength. On the other hand, the English had a relatively small mercantile marine to protect, and they were able to strike crushing blows at the main Dutch squadrons. Towards the end of 1652 Tromp defeated Blake off Dungeness, and for three triumphant months he sailed the Channel unmolested, but in the end the strategic advantages of the English bore him down. In 1653 he was defeated by Monk and Blake off Portland, and again off Harwich ; and in the summer he lost his life in a gallant attempt to break through the English blockade of the Texel.

Although it won for England the command of the sea, the war

was not popular in England ; for all classes resented the heavy taxation, and the army was jealous both of the politicians who directed it and the sailors who won glory from it. It did not end immediately the Rump was overthrown, because the government of the Saints was anxious to persuade the defeated Dutch to merge their sovereignty with England's and unite in a firm and indissoluble Protestant brotherhood. In April, 1654, however, Cromwell signed a treaty on terms less stringent than those demanded by the idealists. 'You have appealed to the judgment of Heaven,' he told the Dutch. 'The Lord has declared against you.' It pained his conscience to see two Protestant Republics at war with one another when there was God's work to be done in an impious world ; so the Dutch envoys came to Whitehall and joined with the Protector in singing the hundred-and-twenty-third psalm : 'Behold how good and pleasant it is for brethren to dwell together in unity.'

'God's interest in the world is more extensive than all the people of these three nations. God has brought us hither to consider the work we may do in the world as well as at home.' In his own mind Cromwell had no doubts what the foreign policy of the Commonwealth should be : its duty was to put itself at the head of a Protestant crusade to free God's people in all corners of the earth from bondage to the Catholic. But in seeking to order his foreign policy on the basis of religious antagonism, Cromwell failed to appreciate the ambitions of the age in which he lived. After the peace of Westphalia, where it was once more agreed that the religion of the people should be the religion of their sovereign, religious idealism ceased to be even the professed motive of European conflict. When he sought to marshal the Protestant nations in a Holy League, he found them struggling with each other for commercial supremacy and the hegemony of the Baltic ; while at the same time the two great Catholic powers, Spain and France, were too intent upon their own rivalry to serve the discredited cause of the Counter-Reformation. Cromwell, then, was unable to use the awakened strength of

England, as he would have wished, to hammer the infidel. As always, however, his gaze pierced the mists of his spiritual aspirations, and fastened itself on some concrete object: if he could not serve the interest of God's people in the world, at least he could secure some material advantage for England.

Cromwell failed to form his Holy League because the principal Protestant powers, Sweden, Brandenburg, Denmark, and Holland, were divided by personal rivalries which were too acute to be settled at the request of England. He hoped to be able to launch Charles X of Sweden against the Empire as Richelieu had launched Gustavus Adolphus twenty years before. Charles, indeed, was willing enough to play the part which Cromwell had allotted him; but he insisted that he must first consolidate Sweden's position on the shores of the Baltic. His remarkable successes in Poland alarmed Brandenburg and Denmark into making a defensive union against him; and since the Dutch, indifferent to the cause of Protestantism, assiduously attempted to embroil the Baltic powers in the interest of their own commerce, Cromwell was soon obliged to admit that his project had failed. But his diplomatic intervention in the Northern war was not in vain. Two commercial treaties with Sweden opened the Sound to England and made the naval stores of the Baltic more easily available for her shipping. Moreover, when in 1657 Charles was temporarily in difficulties against his enemies, Cromwell forgot the religious ties which united them, and attempted, although unsuccessfully, to exact Bremen as the price of English help.

For a time Cromwell was as unsuccessful in his search for an enemy as in his search for a Protestant ally. Both France and Spain hesitated to take on the rôle of Catholic villain; rather, since they were at grips with each other, they each bid for England's help. It seemed at first that France would be the victim of the Commonwealth's religious zeal. Already French and English seamen were skirmishing at sea; moreover, the rebellious citizens of Bordeaux had shown a flattering interest in the *Agreement of the People*, and the internal difficulties of the government offered Cromwell an opportunity to champion the rights of the unprotected Huguenots. In 1652 Blake scattered a French fleet which was sailing to the relief of Dunkirk, and it was generally expected that the rivalry between the two navies would develop into open war. The French were saved by the breakdown of Cromwell's negotiations with Spain. Before he would lend his support to the Spanish attack on France, he insisted that he should be paid his price ; and in demanding that they should give up Dunkirk,[1] grant religious toleration to English merchants resident in Spain, and allow England to trade with the Spanish-American colonies, he asked a higher price than the Spaniards were prepared to pay.

Spain's refusal to come to terms gave Cromwell the sign which he had been seeking. 'Truly your great enemy is the Spaniard,' he told parliament. 'He is naturally so, by reason of that enmity that is in him against whatsoever is of God.' He decided on the policy which had commended itself to the parliaments of James I : a pirate raid on the Spanish Main. As soon as his mind was made up, he had no difficulty in finding reasons to justify his decision. He declared that the Spaniards had so consistently ill-used English seamen and colonists overseas that the English plantations were in danger of being destroyed. Moreover, the cost of equipping the expedition would be little more than the cost of paying off the fleet or keeping it in idleness ; 'Providence seemed to lead us,' he said to the Council : 'having 160 ships swimming ; most of Europe our enemies.' As a final consideration, was there not 'hope of great profit' ? In fact, Cromwell seems to have been moved by every consideration but that of honour. In the weeks when the expedition was being prepared he was still discussing with the Spanish envoys the possibility of an alliance ; he launched it without any warning or any declaration of war ; and when the Spanish ambassador presented a formal protest from his government, an English manifesto claimed that, in view of the provocation continuously

[1] Captured from France in 1652.

offered by Spain in the West Indies, the raid was a justifiable act of defence.

In conception and execution the expedition recalled the exploits of the Duke of Buckingham. The professional seamen were subordinate in command to the soldiers ; supreme control was distributed among a commission of five ; the force was manned by the dregs of the regiments ; and its object was no more precise than to gain ' an interest in that part of the West Indies in the possession of the Spaniard '. Early in 1655 it landed on Hispaniola, the largest of the islands in the Caribbean ; and, while his men perished of thirst and dysentery, and in their Protestant enthusiasm pelted the Virgin with oranges, of which they had too many, Colonel Venables succeeded in being twice ambushed on the same spot. The expedition withdrew from San Domingo, and occupied Jamaica, which was barely defended. Although the Protector made the most of this barren consolation, Venables and Admiral Penn were imprisoned in the Tower.

Spain now declared war on England, and Blake, who had recently been helping Spain against the Mediterranean pirates, was notified that he had a new enemy. Under Blake the navy had known again the daring and endurance of Elizabethan days. Its contests with Prince Rupert, and the pirates of Tunis and Algiers, had sharpened its weapons and prepared it to face the ancient enemy of English seamen. In the autumn of 1656 Admiral Stayner destroyed the plate fleet off Cadiz, and the Londoners saw thirty-eight carts of treasure drawn in triumph through the streets. In the following spring Blake, who had remained at sea throughout the winter, destroyed another Spanish fleet off the Canaries. This time the Spaniards saved their treasure by moving it inland, but they had no means of shipping it to the continent. The loss of two fleets broke Spain's military resistance : for one army, assembled for the reconquest of Portugal, dispersed for lack of pay, and another was stranded in the Netherlands, unrelieved and unpaid, to face the combined forces of France and England.

For Cromwell had now come to terms with France. A treaty signed in the autumn of 1655 had adjusted the disputes between the two countries, and eighteen months later a further agreement settled the terms of a military alliance. When he had overcome his horror at the massacre by French and Savoyard troops of a Waldensian [1] settlement in the Cottian Alps, and had managed to forget that the Huguenots were still unprotected, Cromwell had agreed to co-operate in a French attack on the Netherlands. His reward was to be Mardyck and Dunkirk; and he still regretted that he was unable to include the Scandinavian powers in his alliance, and attack the Austrian Hapsburgs as well. Mardyck fell, and in June, 1658, the Ironsides earned the respect of the great Turenne at the battle of the Dunes, where they won Dunkirk.

But these glamorous victories did not reconcile the English to a war which they disliked. Even good Puritans opposed it, for 'we are islanders, and our life and soul is trade'. The carrying-trade was captured by neutrals, and, with the navy fighting on the high seas, English merchant shipping was harassed by pirates. Cromwell's foreign policy brought its glories and its permanent advantages. Clarendon declared that his honour stood higher abroad than at home, and there was substance in Thurloe's boast that he 'carried the keys of the continent at his girdle'. Although he was disappointed in his dream of a religious crusade, he pursued his country's interest with an insensitive determination which 'made all the neighbour princes fear him'. Further, the constant naval fighting of the Interregnum revived the pride of English seamanship which had steadily declined since the Armada was beaten. For the first time an English fleet occupied the Mediterranean and realised that the occupation of Gibraltar might be 'both an advantage to our trade and an annoyance to the Spaniard'.

But in other respects Cromwell's policy was disastrous. His zeal to destroy Spain made him the instrument of French

[1] The followers of Peter Waldo of Lyons (fl. 1180), who had anticipated Luther's attack on the priesthood.

ambition. With the ripening strength of France he made war on the decaying power of Spain ; Mazarin duped him as easily as Gondomar had duped James I.[1] Mardyck and Dunkirk were a paltry reward for a war which was so harmful to English trade that the financiers began to desert the Protectorate. Moreover, his frenzied activity overseas hindered the more important work of reaching a settlement at home. His cherished policy of ' healing and settling ' was still-born until he won the confidence of the nation by reducing the forces ; but rather than pay off his men, Cromwell preferred to occupy them in foreign wars. The efficiency of the government, and finally of the forces themselves, was weakened by the cost of these wars. The Protectorate was always insolvent : thus it resorted to decimations and petty tyrannies which made its rule still less acceptable to the nation. Ultimately, this constant lack of money began to take toll of the spirit and competence of the men. Cromwell died opportunely for his fame ; his successors had to count the cost.

Cromwell's enemies declare that his only legacy to his people was a permanent hatred of standing armies. He left Puritanism broken and discredited, for the army, which, united, could have carried on his work, fell in pieces at his death. The wise reforms which emerged during the Interregnum—such as the union of the three kingdoms, the redistribution of seats, and the reform of the franchise—were delayed for generations because they had been prematurely achieved by the sword. Religious toleration, which in the Independents was a humane and generous principle, was to establish itself rather through indifference than through humanity. For the nation rejected Cromwell's rule of Thorough as summarily as it had rejected Strafford's ; it preferred to walk the known paths of the constitution. Thus from the moment when in Pride's Purge they first laid violent hands on institutions

[1] When France and Spain made peace in 1659, Mazarin omitted to stipulate that the English should keep Dunkirk. On the other hand, he undertook that France should not help England against Spain.

which law and custom had sanctified, the Independents condemned themselves to ostracism, and their ideas to destruction. England preferred the government of its fathers to a government founded on first principles ; at the Restoration, Puritan ideals vanished along with the Puritan rulers.

Cromwell had no political theory of his own : his improvised constitutions were plucked from the brains of other men, and except when the omens urged him to destroy, he was a conservative and a traditionalist. His fatal weakness was the impatience of the idealist. When the imperfections of sinful man threatened ' the interest of God's people ', he was too ready to leave the beaten track of the constitution, and reach his goal by short-cuts. He could not wait until ' assiduous preaching ' had convinced the wrongdoer that he was ' mistaken ' ; the sheep must be driven into the fold. In his later years, when he found that the people would not be marshalled by spiritual ' blood and iron ', the idealist in Cromwell increasingly gave place to the squire and the ' good Constable '. It is as the ' good Constable ' who kept the peace in three kingdoms that all Englishmen can respect Cromwell's memory. Dictators are never popular with those who have not come under their spell ; and the religious idiom of the seventeenth century strikes harshly on ears which did not even hear the language the Victorians spoke. But in the cycle of political change revolution always issues in despotism ; and a man who made some conscience of what he did was a worthier man to rule at that time than Presbyterians harshly wedded to the Covenant, or than royalists swept back to power on the tide of reaction. Cromwell did not fear posterity's verdict. ' Let us all not be careful what men will make of these actings.'

CHAPTER XVIII

THE RESTORATION

Collapse of the Protectorate. The Convention. The Restoration settlement. The Clarendon Code. The fall of Clarendon.

1. *The collapse of the Protectorate*

The great Cromwell was dead; but 'this earthquake' Clarendon noted, 'was attended with no signal alteration'. 'There is not a dog wags his tongue,' said Secretary Thurloe, 'so great a calm are we in.' For some weeks men went about their business as though they scarcely realised that Cromwell was gone; his son Richard, his appointed successor, was installed as Protector and as Lord-General of the army, and neither royalist nor republican made a move to prevent him. Richard seemed to inherit his father's power and glory 'without that public hate that visibly attended the other'.[1] But this early calm was deceptive. Cromwell had not bequeathed to his son a settled constitution and a contented people. By his own strength, and his personal prestige in the army, he had imposed on the nation a government which it hated, but where he had dominated he had been unable to reconcile; a Protector less ruthless, and less exalted by a sense of sacred duty, would be at the mercy of factions which only force had held in check. Richard Cromwell did not have to fear only the opposition of those royalists, republicans, Levellers and Saints who had hated his father: he had to contend with disloyalties and divisions in the army itself. Years of meddling in politics had dulled the spirit which on half a dozen great battlefields had united officers and men in the inspiration of a common cause.

[1] Clarendon.

Proud in the possession of wealth and estates, the leaders had estranged themselves from their men by their worldliness and arrogance ; and even the junior officers, jealous and resentful of their superiors, were disposed to listen favourably to the republican doctrines which spread among the common soldiers. Nor was there any real agreement among the leaders. Cromwell's strong hand had stilled their dissensions and damped their political aspirations. Freed from his control, they were freed from a sense of duty, and in a few months of ambition and intrigue they destroyed all that he had striven to accomplish.

The army disliked the new Protector. Richard Cromwell was a simple country gentleman, modest in his tastes and by nature reluctant to be thrust into a place of honour. His father had chosen him, in preference to his abler brother Henry, because as the eldest surviving son he would succeed by the monarchy's ancient principle of primogeniture ; and as a civilian he might reconcile those who objected to the Protectorate because it was founded on military force. But the authority of a civilian was offensive to the pride of the soldiers. Oliver had been Protector because he was Lord-General of the army ; but Richard, who ' never drew sword for the Commonwealth ', was Lord-General only because he was Protector. Thurloe's early optimism melted as he sensed that trouble was brewing in the army, ' as if his Highness were not general of the army, as his father was '. When Richard proposed to dismiss the malcontents and reduce the army's numbers, ' a very eminent spirit of prayer appeared ' among the officers. They asked that the supreme command of the army should be separated from the headship of the state ; that Fleetwood be made commander-in-chief, with sole power to appoint officers ; and that no one should be dismissed from the army except by the verdict of a military court. When Richard refused to consent to proposals which would have made the army a self-governing corporation with constitutional powers equal to his own, the officers ominously continued ' to seek God for a blessing on the affairs of this nation '.

The meeting of parliament, early in 1659, inflamed the old quarrel between civilians and soldiers. Royalists and Presbyterians worked with the old guard of republicans, headed by Vane, Scot, Ludlow and Hazlerig, to ' hang on the wheels of the chariot, that they might not be able to drive so furiously '.[1] They refused to vote the army's arrears of pay and denounced the administration of the officers ; they proposed to investigate recent acts of tyranny, and as a result they started to impeach William Boteler, the most brutal of the Major-Generals. Finally, they bravely answered the army's threats by resolving that the council of officers should not assemble without the consent of the Protector and both Houses of parliament, and that all holders of military command should take an oath to respect the freedom of the Houses. As the regiments once more bore down on London, Richard ordered them to disband ; and Fleetwood, whom Oliver had once called ' a milksop ', retaliated by ordering parliament to dissolve. As had lately been its habit, parliament yielded to force. By summoning his brother from Ireland and Monk from Scotland, Richard could have resisted Fleetwood at the price of civil war ; but ' I will not have a drop of blood spilt for the preservation of my greatness, which is a burden to me '. In May, 1659, he laid down his office and went abroad.

The military Republic had another year of life. To give a constitutional disguise to their actions, the soldiers recalled the Rump of the Long Parliament, and the dying fires of republicanism flickered for the last time as the members resolved to wipe from the constitution the Single Person and the Other House. But parliament would be suffered only so long as it did as it was told, and the tough Long Parliament men, trained in the technique of obstruction, were soon at blows with the army. Soldiers and parliamentarians reached again the deadlock of 1647 ; and this time the soldiers had no King to be used as a weapon in their bargaining and to be made the scapegoat of their failure to bargain successfully. In the summer the

[1] Ludlow.

royalists plunged prematurely and disastrously into rebellion, and restored a temporary unity to their enemies ; speaking in the idiom of his master, General Lambert petitioned the Rump to bow to this renewed evidence of God's favour and mould the constitution according to the wishes of the army. But in October the Rump revoked the commissions of Lambert and seven of the principal officers, and annulled all the acts of the Protectorate which had not been sanctioned by parliament. Once again the army had to intervene ; once again the sitting of the Long Parliament was ' interrupted ', and a Committee of Safety, nominated by the officers, set about drafting a new constitution.

Into these deliberations there broke an authoritative voice from Scotland. At one time a royalist, General Monk had served in turn the King, the parliament, the Rump, the Protector and the Protector's son. Except when he went to sea to fight the Dutch, he had been commander-in-chief of the army in Scotland since 1651 ; and with that army at his back, purged and unshakably loyal, he marched into England early in 1660 to put an end to ' that intolerable slavery of a sword government '. The war had been fought to preserve the Protestant religion, the liberties of the people and the privileges of parliament. These causes had been fought for in vain while the country was at the mercy of an army which made and unmade parliaments, which could govern neither with parliament nor without it, which sacrificed the welfare of the people to the usurped authority of a handful of officers, men raised ' from the meanest mechanics to lord-like inheritances '. Monk was cautious and inscrutable ; when Lambert and the officers had laid down their arms, he would call a free parliament and await the decision of the people. For Cromwell's men, the veterans of Naseby and Dunbar, it was the hour of critical decision : they could follow Lambert and fight once more for their right to frame the constitution by which the state was to be governed ; or they could surrender to Monk, and retire into private life with the pay which they were owed and a pardon for all that they had done. In their decision may be read the overthrow of Cromwell's hopes.

Not like fighters in a noble cause, but like mercenaries serving for pay, they abandoned their ideals and deserted to the man who promised them their wages. Lambert escaped to the Midlands and for the last time raised the banner of the 'good old cause'; but his men would not fight against their old comrades, and he surrendered his sword to the soldiers of the government.

The might of the Independent army having crumbled away at his approach, Monk had still to temper the immoderate enthusiasm of republicans and Presbyterians. The Rump, restored a second time by the anxious and repentant officers, was eager for vengeance on those who had humiliated it; and when Monk ordered it to readmit the members whom Pride had excluded in 1648, the returning Presbyterians exuberantly proclaimed the Covenant and the ecclesiastical arrangements drawn up by the Westminster Assembly. But it was a time for 'healing and settling', not for revenge and the reopening of old differences. Monk told parliament that it must promise the soldiers an indemnity and their pay, and make the necessary preparations for the holding of an election; and at length, its last work performed, on March 16th, 1660, the Long Parliament dissolved itself by its own consent.

While the elections were being held, Hyde issued a manifesto from Breda which promised that the Stuarts too were willing to forgo their revenge: 'That all mention of parties and factions, and all rancour and animosities may be thrown in, and buried like rubbish under the foundation of a peaceful and ordered settlement.' The Declaration promised a complete pardon to the Crown's enemies, 'excepting only such persons as shall hereafter be excepted by Parliament'; arrears of pay for the army; 'a liberty to tender consciences' and to all religious opinions 'which do not disturb the peace of the kingdom'; and a land settlement arranged by parliament. By adding that each of these four provisions should be ratified by parliament, Charles at once proclaimed his attachment to parliamentary government and absolved himself from blame if his promises should not be fulfilled. The sane moderation of Hyde and

Monk bore fruit at the elections to the Convention Parliament. Thurloe was not elected, Hampden's son was defeated in Buckinghamshire; there were few republicans and fewer Saints, and the prevailing temper of both Houses was royalist. The Convention immediately resolved that the government of the kingdom should be by King, Lords and Commons, and that Charles II had been King 'by inherent birthright, and lawful and undoubted succession', since 1649. On May 29th, 1660, his thirtieth birthday, Charles entered London amid the tumultuous acclamation of his people; and he sardonically remarked that since the people were so glad to see him, the blame must be his that he had been away so long.

Cromwell's soldiers assembled for the last time at Blackheath, to be reviewed by the King whom for eleven years they had excluded from his inheritance. The Stuarts had been restored by the action of the only officer in that army who was able to discipline and pay his men. But Monk's services to the constitution did not end when he had persuaded the soldiers to lay down their arms: with the help of Hyde he persuaded the royalists to forbear and to forgive; and by his firm dealings with Presbyterians and fanatics he brought Charles back to England on sane and temperate conditions which it would not be impossible to observe. As he cheated the republicans of their commonwealth, and the Saints of their vision of the Kingdom of Heaven, so he prevented the Presbyterians of the Long Parliament from restoring the monarchy on the terms which they had so often laid before Charles I between 1642 and 1648. On this matter the army had the last word: the returning King should not be forced to take the Covenant, and he should not be the puppet King of the Nineteen Propositions and the Uxbridge negotiations. The restored monarchy was to be the monarchy of 1641.

2. *The Restoration settlement*

In two decades of disturbance and change, the English people had discovered 'fundamentals' of their own. Their recent ordeals had taught them to be anti-democratic, anti-sectarian, anti-militarist and anti-republican ; since the road to Utopia had led them into bondage, they had learned to mistrust paper constitutions and systems of government that were founded on first principles. In 1660 they welcomed back the government which they knew : the old, familiar institutions of Crown and parliament, which were to be administered, as before, by the hereditary King and the hereditary governing class. The first thing to be restored, therefore, was the traditional structure of English society, of the non-military state acknowledging the rule of law. Soldiers with the gift of tongues, Saints who had dreamed of the reign of Christ, all the exponents of the career open to talent, retired into private life and the consolations of conspiracy or commerce ; while the squire and the parson, the lawyer and the magnate, returned to their old duties and their old ways of life, as the hereditary social order of England resumed its broken growth.

The Restoration was made possible because the Independent army voluntarily surrendered the power which it had usurped ; but the making of the settlement was left to the men who had been masters of England when the wars began. When the Convention reaffirmed the acts passed by the Long Parliament to the summer of 1641,[1] the oligarchy consolidated the gains which it had wrung from the Crown. The restored monarchy was not the monarchy of Charles I. A virtual supremacy was vested in parliament, a parliament matured and invigorated by its recent experience of practical administration, and chastened by its failure to control the incontinent allies whom it had raised. The King had the right to appoint his ministers, to veto legislation, to prorogue and dissolve the sessions of parliament ; he was commander-in-chief of the forces ; he held in his hands the conduct of diplomacy, the making of treaties and the waging of war. But his command of the forces was an empty honour when he was deprived of all sources of revenue

[1] Only the Navigation Act survived from the legislative activity of the Commonwealth.

which parliament did not sanction. The Privy Council lost its criminal jurisdiction, its right to issue emergency legislation, and its right to set aside the common law by registering royal proclamations. Thus the Crown had lost the claim to administrative sovereignty which Bacon and Strafford had made for it: the prerogative courts were extinguished for ever; the King could make no laws, raise no taxes, without the consent of an omnipotent parliament.[1] Charles II was too astute to be deceived by the extravagant clamour of loyalty which had greeted his return. The hereditary kingship had passed through the tribulations of martyrdom and exile, and had been miraculously restored to a grateful people; thus the cult of the Divine Right of the royal office reached its zenith in the relief of a nation suddenly delivered from an age of violent and unhallowed experiment. An act for 'the preservation of the King's person and government' defined as treason any attempt to depose him, to levy war against him, or to invite foreigners to invade his dominions; it denied that resistance to the Crown could ever be lawful. But this demonstration of an unshakable allegiance, ostensibly so tender to the security of Kings, had a definite and limited purpose. The theory of Divine Right was no longer the apparel of sovereignty and absolute power; it had reappeared in the negative form of non-resistance, because resistance had been found to issue in war and military tyranny. To protect their lives and estates from the future invasion of sectaries and soldiers, the oligarchs took refuge in the legal maxim that 'the King can do no wrong'. But this did not mean that the King could overstep the limits of the constitution. Although his person was inviolate, the people would take redress from his ministers if he acted unconstitutionally: 'What is done by his ministers unlawfully, there is a remedy against his ministers for it', and the King's authority would not avail to shield them from the vengeance of the law. The principle most firmly impressed on the Restoration settlement was the

[1] The Clarendon Code, which Charles disliked, proved that the King was no longer the effective head of the Church.

principle of the rule of law. The framers of the settlement turned their backs alike on Strafford's *droit administratif* and the Puritan ' Thorough ' of Cromwell, on the illegal extortions of Major-Generals and the Crown's attempt to guide the state by the arbitrary canons of Roman jurisprudence. They entrenched themselves behind the unassailable supremacy of the English common law.[1]

Thus the landed gentry of England settled down to enjoy the fruits of the victory which they had won twenty years before. The dominance and the inclinations of their class soon found expression in the statute-book. The Act of Settlement of 1662 frustrated the good intentions of the Tudor Poor Law by reviving mediaeval villeinage ; it was the fate of the Diggers and their kind to be tied to the soil without the compensating protection of the lord and the custom of the manor. Export bounties on corn brought the landlords new wealth ; savage Game Laws protected their amusements from the interference of the destitute ; in 1711 a high property qualification attempted to make the House of Commons the preserve of landowners. But the gentry did not enter with the same zest into the performance of their duties. In local government and the administration of justice they had rich opportunities to rise to those ideals of efficient and disinterested service which Strafford had set before them. But the rule of law imposes no obligations which its letter does not specify. Where the prerogative courts had set their own standards of the national interest, the gentry were content to discharge their bare legal obligations, and to discharge them in the interest of themselves. For two hundred years they were free to pursue their irresponsible course, going at intervals to Westminster to make the laws, and returning home to administer them to the disadvantage of their less illustrious neighbours.

[1] The gentry further protected themselves by placing the local militias in the hands of the Lords-Lieutenant of the counties, who appointed the commanders and chose the men. The propertied classes therefore had at their disposal an armed force to resist alike the Crown and the sects, and it was this force which defeated James II.

Except in the important matter of religion, the details of the settlement were drafted by the Convention Parliament, which sat from April to December, 1660. Its chief task was to express in legal form the promises made by the King at Breda. In the first place, unmindful of the generous impulses which the prospect of a Restoration had aroused in them, the members gave way to human instincts of revenge. Twenty-six of the regicides were still alive; thirteen of them, exempted by parliament from the amnesty which the King had offered, came to the block at Charing Cross and died with their faces towards Whitehall.[1] The oligarchy further retrieved its self-respect by decreeing that Cromwell, Ireton, Bradshaw, Pride and Pym should be removed from their tombs in Westminster Abbey. Their bodies were hanged for a day at Tyburn and buried at the foot of the gallows. The land question, however, was less easily solved. Cavaliers who had forfeited their estates by fighting for the King, who had followed him into exile, or sold their lands to bear the crippling taxation of the Protectorate, naturally expected to come into their own again. But no revolution can be wholly undone, least of all in its land settlement; and there were several reasons why the Cavaliers should be thwarted in their legitimate expectations. The Stuarts had been restored by the consent of a nation which had come to regret that they had ever been sent away. Thus the rebels, who argued that their repentance entitled them to remain in possession of their new estates, had to be compensated for their help in restoring the monarchy. The strength of the landed interest in the Convention was too formidable to be ignored. Moreover, much of the property taken from the Cavaliers had been bought by speculators, who had divided and re-sold it; it could not be returned to its former owners without injustice to the present occupiers. So the government decided to compromise. The Crown and the Church resumed the public lands of which they had been deprived, and all confiscated estates were restored to their original owners; but the royalists

[1] The younger Vane, who was not a regicide, was executed in 1662.

were forbidden to recover property which they had voluntarily sold, even if they had sold it in order to pay Cromwell's decimations. The Cavaliers complained bitterly of a settlement which made ' the enemies to the Constitution masters, in effect, of the booty of three nations '.[1] But the government could not please everyone, and it acted wisely in identifying its rule with a general security of property.

The Convention's last work was to settle the details of the King's revenue. Since Clarendon ' had no mind to put the King out of the necessity of having recourse to his parliament ', the Convention granted Charles an income which should enable him in normal times to ' live of his own ', but would oblige him to rely for extraordinary expenditure on the co-operation of parliament. This income was fixed at £1,200,000 ; which was £300,000 more than Charles I had collected during the last years of his personal government, but £1,000,000 less than the average annual expenditure of the Protectorate. The money was to be provided from the revenue from the Crown lands ; from the Crown's hereditary feudal dues, which were commuted for a fixed sum [2] ; and from the yield of the customs. The Convention made these arrangements in good faith, but its financial settlement broke down because during the first dozen years of Charles's reign the yield fell about £400,000 short of the estimated figure ; and the additional imposition of a hearth tax, an unpopular expedient borrowed from the French, did not make up the deficiency. The Crown, then, was perpetually short of money. Charles did what he could. He paid into the Treasury his wife's dowry and the proceeds of the sale of Dunkirk ; he mortgaged and sold his estates ; he farmed the collection of the taxes, and raised money by pledging the taxes in advance, at a ruinous rate of interest. But there was no adequate machinery of credit to relieve him from his embarrassment. His payments fell into arrears, the services deteriorated,

[1] Roger L'Estrange.

[2] This sum was raised by an excise. Thus the landowners, on whom the feudal dues had hitherto fallen, were relieved of a substantial burden.

the Crown lands, imperfectly administered, grew less productive ; finally, in 1672, he was obliged to repudiate his debts. The Commons, on the other hand, tightened their control of the Crown's finances. In 1665 they insisted on appropriating the money which they voted for the Dutch war ; in the following year they set up commissioners to audit the King's accounts. Their financial supremacy was completed when Convocation surrendered its right to assess the taxes to be levied on the clergy.[1] The settlement of 1660 failed largely because the King was prevented by his poverty from playing the part assigned to him by the constitution. Nor can his poverty be explained away by the Whig legend that his court was unduly extravagant ; the strictest economy would not have made him solvent. Moreover, the prestige of a monarchy is as deeply rooted in its foibles as in its services to the nation ; a King who had been humiliated and banished had almost a duty to revive, as well as he knew how, the traditional splendours of his royal office. The Restoration settlement was unworkable, and therefore impermanent, because it made parliament master of the King's finances, without recognising its consequent authority over his policy.

3. *The Clarendon Code*

The Convention Parliament dispersed without having settled the most important question of all : whether men might henceforth be permitted to worship God in their own way. The King, who was a Deist, favoured a comprehensive settlement, to embrace all varieties of religious thinking which were compatible with the safety of the state. His Declaration on Ecclesiastical Affairs, which he issued in the autumn of 1660, invited parliament to withdraw the penal laws, to modify ceremonial in deference to squeamish consciences, and, by the principles of Bishop Ussher's 'Model', to limit the authority of the Bishops by synods of Presbyters. To Charles's practical mind

[1] For the importance of Convocation's right to assess its own taxes, see, e.g., its action in 1640.

religion was not worth fighting about ; and finer minds than his thought, with Andrew Marvell, ' the cause too good to have been fought for '. But the English people were not ready for toleration. The Convention debated Ussher's plan, but the members lost themselves in the discussion of detail : they argued over fast days and Sabbath observance and measures to expose the people to what the King called the ' disease of sermons '. When they dissolved, they had agreed only to reject the King's plan for comprehension. In 1661 a conference of twelve Bishops and twelve Presbyterians met at the Savoy Palace, but they reached no agreement ; their controversies only showed how wide and deep was the schism in the Protestant faith.

The divines had had the opportunity to end their religious differences in compromise and harmony ; the decision was now to be taken out of their hands. Before the Savoy Conference broke up in unspiritual acrimony, the Cavalier Parliament had assembled. The nation had gone to the polls nerve-strained and anxious. The carefree atmosphere of the King's home-coming had quickly evaporated, and sober men watched with alarm the unabated vigour of the sects, While the pulpits echoed the heavy thunder of Puritan oratory, and Quakers were ' blowing the bellows of rebellion among the ignorant ', there were anxious rumours from the West, where ' Jack Presbyter stands a-tiptoe ', and whispers of plots to bring the Dutch and the armies of the Kirk to save ' the good old cause ' in the hour of its defeat. A trifle gave substance to these forebodings. Thomas Venner, a bottler of wines, sent fifty men through the streets of London to proclaim the reign of King Jesus. Venner himself was captured in an ale-house near Cripplegate, and the King's guards easily rounded up his little army, but the harm was done. Panic-stricken magistrates put four thousand Quakers behind bars in order to relieve the state of its imminent peril. In this frightened temper the nation elected the Cavalier Parliament ; only fifty Puritans were returned to it.

The squires came to Westminster determined to scatter to

the winds the menace of Anabaptist conspiracy. To 'expel the poison of sin and rebellion', they enacted the measures which bear the name of the bewildered Clarendon. Their Corporation Act, 1661, required all holders of municipal office to renounce the Covenant, receive the sacraments of the Church of England, and take an oath of non-resistance. By this comprehensive measure they protected themselves from Presbyterians, Catholics and republicans, and strengthened their hand in parliamentary elections by confining municipal office to royalist Anglicans. In the following year an Act of Uniformity required the clergy to give 'unfeigned assent and consent to all and everything contained' in the Prayer Book of Queen Elizabeth, and two thousand Puritan clergymen gave up their livings. Finding that these ejected clergy evaded the intentions of the law by holding unofficial services among their former congregations, parliament passed in 1664 the Conventicle Act, which forbade more than five persons to meet for any form of worship which was not prescribed by the Prayer Book. 'Never was there a more merciful bill,' decided Henry Coventry, 'that punishes, neither with blood nor banishment, a people that has punished us with both these.' The Cavaliers rounded off their savage code with the Five Mile Act of 1665. It insisted again that all holders of office must swear that they would not 'at any time endeavour any alteration of Government either in Church or State'; and it forbade Nonconformist ministers to preach, to teach in schools, or to come within five miles of a corporate town.

In a sense the Clarendon Code was no more than a logical retribution. The Presbyterians had broken the unity of Elizabeth's Church, by urging that it was too comprehensive, and they had darkened the hour of their victory by declaring that intolerance was a duty which they owed to their God. The Church of England hearkened to their teaching. It narrowed its boundaries, as they had demanded, and made them the victims of their own doctrine of intolerance; finally, it forbade them to serve the King whom they had excluded from his inheritance. But the chief importance of the Clarendon Code was social: the whole temper of the Restoration settlement bore witness to the boundless strength of the governing class which had resumed its old functions, no longer hampered in its ambitions by the discretionary powers of the Crown. The central doctrine of the Puritan creed, that all men are equal with one another, conflicted with the interests of a squirearchy that in its tradition and its organisation was still semi-feudal. The unwelcome victory of the Independents had revealed to the landowners that the formula 'no Bishop, no King'[1] had a corollary, equally true, which bore uncomfortably on their own interests: 'no parson, no squire'. Thus their championship of the Church of England did not reflect zeal for its doctrines so much as concern to preserve their own social security. The Puritan gentry, some of them wealthy and honoured before the revolution, and some but lately enriched by the property bought from Cavaliers, had to decide between their religion and their worldly interest. Few of them hesitated: they stilled their consciences, and kept their estates by conforming to the law.

The King tried to stem the tide of persecution. In 1662 he suspended the Act of Uniformity for three months, and later in the year his Declaration of Indulgence attempted to shelter the Dissenters from the fury of the law. But times had changed since Elizabeth had warned her parliaments off the discussion of religion. Bishop Sheldon rebuked Charles for inviting 'God's heavy wrath and indignation', and the Commons flatly rejected his plea for toleration, which they described as a scheme for 'establishing schism by law'. Yet this was what they were themselves in the course of doing. The Anglican Church, whose exclusiveness they had buttressed with the majesty of the law, was not the Church of England which Laud had striven to build; the limiting word 'Anglican' proclaimed that it fell short of his ideal of a Church which should embrace all Protestants in a common form of worship.

[1] The Presbyterians failed to master England largely because they did not appreciate the truth of this maxim.

The Bishops and the sectaries had alike been too zealous : the spirit of the Restoration was anti-clerical, and the Church was restored by secular politicians in the interest of their own secular purposes. Anglicanism was the sect which parliament, having rejected the ideal of comprehension, chose to patronise ; and the Tory squires put on the mantle of Defenders of the Faith against an infidel court and the dangers of militant Puritanism. The Church had become an instrument of political faction ; and a Church whose loyalties were reflected in the accommodating conscience of the Vicar of Bray was ill equipped for the spiritual guidance of the nation. In some of the Bishops, in Morley at Winchester, Cosin at Durham, Rainbowe at Carlisle, there lingered a sense of Christian duty born in earlier times. But for the most part the divines of the Church of England were content to spend their powers in arid controversy ; and the country parson fulfilled his ministry by reading to his flock the sermons of the great masters of theology, while he devoted all his tact to the higher task of being chaplain and companion to the squire who had appointed him. Outside the large towns, the people, who had had of late a surfeit of religious teaching, were no more inclined to seek inspiration than their pastors to provide it. Before the close of the century an Archbishop was heard to defend his calling largely on the ground that he had been struck by ' the wisdom of being religious '.[1]

Even while it was abandoning its spiritual ideals, the Anglican Church was not being entirely successful in its political mission. The Clarendon Code accomplished its main object, of breaking the back of Puritanism as a political force. As magistrates the Anglican squires relentlessly enforced the laws which they had made, and organised Puritanism, like the Stuarts' plan of government, fell before the strength of the Commons and the Justices of the Peace. But the Puritan spirit did not die. As they were forced to abandon their vision of a Church and state moulded by their principles, the sects gradually forsook the

[1] Tillotson, Archbishop of Canterbury, 1691–4.

extravagant notions which had persuaded them to strangle the social life of the people ; it was no longer superstition to deck one's house with holly at Christmas ; it was no longer Popery to eat a mince-pie. But persecution did not extinguish them. No longer hampered by their unpopular connection with the Scots, and deserted by the leaders who had adopted their movement for political ends, they settled down to practise those habits of thrift and self-restraint which have henceforth distinguished the English middle class. In every town and village the rivalry of 'Church' and 'Chapel' reminds us that the Clarendon Code failed in half its purpose. The self-conscious roysterings of the Cavaliers, the scurrilous gaiety of the court and the Restoration theatre, touched only the surface of the nation's life. Beneath it a middle class bearing indelibly the mark of Puritan influence went quietly on with its work ; its purpose strengthened by daily reading of the Bible and daily participation in family prayers, its worldly labours rewarded by the conscientious shopkeeping by which it avoided the abhorrent sin of idleness. These qualities captured for Englishmen the markets of the world and brought them an empire which they also knew how to govern.

Within a generation of the making of the Clarendon Code, the changing spirit of the age had relieved the Dissenters of many of their sufferings. Toleration did not come heroically, in Cromwell's way. It did not come because Chillingworth and Jeremy Taylor had pleaded for it, nor because Milton had nobly urged that truth was powerful in itself to defeat falsehood. It came because in an age of deflated passion men could muster no convincing arguments against it.[1] As religion fell from the heights of revelation to the flat levels of common sense, the scepticism of Selden was at last heard above the voices of the Covenanters whom he had chastised ; and intolerance began to seem unpractical and absurd to an age unfamiliar with the spiritual struggles of which it was born. As the century

[1] Although its coming was delayed because the Clarendon Code gave the Tories a vested interest in intolerance.

advanced, men no longer sought religious sanctions for what they did. Already Thomas Hobbes had justified obedience to the state by arguments of fear and calculation; presently Locke would base political obligation on reason and the laws of nature, sanctions which would have been incomprehensible to Cromwell and James I. But the age of Newton and Boyle and the Royal Society measured life by the standards of practical efficiency. Even its architecture pointed to the decay of religious zeal. There was no splendour or mystery in Wren's churches; they were firm and dignified, but they did not recapture the spirit which pervaded the old Gothic cathedrals, that in them the worshipper might approach the unknown.

The new England, therefore, grew impatient of religious intolerance. Catholics must be persecuted, for their plottings threatened the safety of the state; but the Protestant Dissenters had lately shown themselves to be loyal and sober citizens. The arguments of the economists supported the gibes of free-thinkers, for the commercial prosperity of Holland was believed to depend in part on religious toleration. In the end the Dissenters won their freedom when the old Puritan gentry returned to lead the men whom they had deserted. For the Anglican Church was not impregnable. The Whig party drew its legions from the Nonconformist tradesmen scattered through the cities, and its leaders from the renegade Presbyterians who in 1661 had uttered their lukewarm allegiance to the Church and the Crown. Toleration was to be the Dissenters' reward for faithful service to their old masters.

4. *The fall of Clarendon*

In 1667 Charles dropped the pilot who had brought him home. In the days of the personal government of Charles I, Edward Hyde, an earnest barrister of the Middle Temple, had stoutly opposed a policy which all lawyers had thought to be unconstitutional and despotic. In the Long Parliament he had struck down the instruments of this tyranny: he had helped to prepare the impeachment of Strafford, and to frame the legislation which removed the prerogative courts. But the Grand Remonstrance had found him equally ready to protect the constitution from those who menaced it from the other side, and from that time he devotedly served the House of Stuart. At York he drew up the manifestos in which the Crown defended its policy; during the rebellion he acted for the King in the various negotiations with parliament; and after the battle of Worcester he followed his new master to the continent. During the weary years of waiting, his firm confidence that loyal Englishmen would 'see good days again' was a tonic to the exiled court; and when that time came, he was able to assure Monk that the returning King would bury the past and defer to the will of his parliament. Finally, as Lord Chancellor, and honoured with the Earldom of Clarendon, he supervised the making of the settlement; not always approving of what was done, but always watchful that the government should not strain the loyalty of the people.

In happier days, however, Charles began to find him an irksome minister. Clarendon was proud, testy, and by his own confession 'uncounsellable'; he was quick to make enemies, and slow to reconcile them. As his old friends, Nicholas, Ormonde, Southampton, died or left the ministry, he found himself surrounded by opportunists and intriguers, a tribe whom he disdained as 'men of no conscience'. The wits at court mocked his heavy ways; landless Cavaliers never forgave him for not restoring their estates—'upon all occasions', ran a clause in his impeachment, 'he discouraged the poor and suffering Royalists'; the new men who came to parliament through the many by-elections [1] were hostile to the statesman of a former age. The nation, too, had its grievances against him, and made him the scapegoat of all the misfortunes of recent years. Men said that Dunkirk had been sold to the French to provide Clarendon with money to build himself a palace; that he had married Charles to a barren Queen so that

[1] By 1667 there were 129 new members.

he might one day be father-in-law to a King [1]; and in particular, they blamed him for the indignities suffered from the Dutch in a war which he hated and opposed.

But these trivial animosities would not have brought him down if the King had wished to retain him; he fell because his constitutional theories were obsolete. Clarendon was the last of the Elizabethans. He still reverenced 'the good old frame of government', an antiquated theory of the constitution in which parliament made the law, the courts interpreted it, and an efficient Privy Council administered it in the interest of the nation. The Council was the guardian of the 'regalities' and 'mysteries' of royal power; 'the body of it is the most sacred and hath the greatest authority in the government of the state, next to the person of the King himself'. The function of parliament, in Clarendon's theory of government, was to vote money and to make the laws. It had the right to criticise the administration, and in the last resort it might uphold the sanctity of the law by impeaching ministers who broke it; but it had no right to dictate to the King the ministers he should appoint, or the policy he should carry out. These conceptions necessarily brought Clarendon into conflict with the champions of parliament, and drove him into a position which he could not successfully defend against the Commons' ascendancy in finance. 'Since Queen Elizabeth did her business in '88 without calling a parliament', he attempted to run the Dutch war and negotiate the peace without parliament's advice; parliament sat for only fourteen months between 1663 and 1667. But the war exposed the poverty of the Crown, and the Commons rebuked and frustrated Clarendon's policy by resolving to appropriate and audit the King's finances. One of the charges brought against him when he fell was that he would not admit that 'the House of Commons was the fittest judge of the necessities and grievances of the people'.

[1] His daughter Anne had married James, Duke of York. In 1662 Charles married Catherine of Braganza, who failed to bear him any children.

The theories which stirred parliament to angry defence of its rights were also embarrassing to the King. Charles, as his victim admitted, ' did not naturally love old men ' ; he resented Clarendon's fatherly addresses on the levity of his court, and was inclined to blame him because his Declaration of Indulgence had miscarried. He was finally driven to dismiss him when he saw that Clarendon's methods had ended in a constitutional deadlock. For the Privy Council was no longer able to bear the weight of authority which Clarendon had laid upon it. It was a cumbrous body with about fifty members ; in full session its work was mainly declaratory, and the important work of administration was performed by smaller committees. Charles preferred to evade the unwieldy Council, and to carry on his government through the various heads of departments—the two Secretaries of State, the officials of the Treasury and the navy, and the Secretary at War—who met in an informal cabinet. These men were in close touch with parliament, and were willing to obtain its approval for the government's actions. Charles knew that without this approval he was helpless ; parliament's control of the purse enabled it to wreck any policy which it disliked. With Clarendon he found it impossible ' to do those things with Parliament that must be done ', for Clarendon's indifference to the rights and prejudices of the Commons had exposed the Crown to attack and humiliation.

A court intrigue, engineered by the King's mistresses and the rising politicians of the future, drove Clarendon to his fall. With him perished the Tudor constitution which he had hoped to restore : the division of duties among a Crown, Council and parliament which were united in purpose. In the eighteenth century the yet unborn conventions of party and the cabinet would allow the aristocracy to revive in its essentials the Tudor plan of government, but the unsuccessful attempts in 1679 and 1701 to restore the old authority of the Privy Council pointed to the fundamental causes of Clarendon's fall. ' The good old frame of government ' was broken, and Clarendon sadly left an England which he did not understand. ' The King is a suitor to you,' he had said to the Convention in 1660, '. . . that you will join with him in restoring the whole nation to its primitive temper and integrity, its old good manners, its old good humour, and its old good nature.' It was his great service to England that he grounded the Restoration on law and mercy, and that he prevented a royalist reign of terror in 1661, by persuading the revengeful Cavaliers 'to learn that excellent art of forgetfulness'. In 1667 he retired in exile to the continent, to enrich both history and literature by setting down the things which he had seen.

CHAPTER XIX

THE REIGN OF CHARLES II

The Cabal. Foreign policy: the Treaty of Dover. Danby and parliament. The Whigs and Exclusion. The Tory triumph.

1. *The Cabal and the Treaty of Dover*

The Cabal seems most infamous when it is least understood. For Charles II was not a tyrant. The men who knew him have left a portrait of a man pleasant, easy-going and fond of his comforts; a superbly skilful politician when he was driven to act, but mostly too lazy to bestir himself. Burnet records that he admired, and casually envied, the boundless authority of the King of France, but that he 'would not give himself the trouble of laying or managing it'. Halifax said that no man of equal ability was ever so lazy in asserting himself: 'He chose rather to be eclipsed than to be troubled: he loved too much to lie on his own down-bed of ease.' [1] Pepys would find him indulging in the 'bewitching kind of pleasure called sauntering', or neglecting his business for the fascinations of 'a little fantastical gentleman called Cupid', while he 'employed his lips about the court'. If Charles had the inclination to be a tyrant, he had neither the energy nor the persistence to disarm the deep-seated suspicions of his people. If tyranny was his object, the time for it was in 1660, when the more enthusiastic royalists urged him to keep the army in being and govern by the Cromwellian prerogative of the sword. But Charles desired no more

[1] Cf. Ailesbury, Charles's intimate friend: 'In fine, his heart was set to live at ease'.

than to preserve the freedom of action which the constitution allowed him. Burnet shrewdly calculated that ' he did not wish to be like a Grand Signior, with some mutes about him and bags of bowstrings to strangle men as he had a mind to it ; but he did not think he was a King as long as a company of fellows were looking into all his actions, and examining his ministers as well as his accounts '.

Charles did not delude himself : he knew that he could never enjoy the prerogatives of his father. But he was determined to carry out a policy of his own, with the help of ministers who were content to do as he bade them. Similarly, he would not, if he could avoid it, accept the dictation of parliament ; and when he remarked that ' a King of England that is not slave to five hundred Kings is King enough ', he fairly summarised the political programme which Whig historians have found so wicked. By a coincidence, the initial letters of the names of five of the ministers through whom he directed his policy spelt the word Cabal, but to contemporaries the word had not the sinister significance with which posterity has coloured it. Besides Clifford, Arlington, Buckingham, Ashley and Lauderdale, Charles had other servants who were in various ways useful to him, such as Arundell, Trevor, Bridgeman, Dering and Henry Coventry ; but since their names made up no convenient pattern, they have been less often remembered. Moreover, the Cabal should not be regarded as a ministry in the modern sense of the word. The members had few links with one another : they were bound only in their common service of the King. Since Charles was determined to preserve his personal independence—after Clarendon he did not intend to have another ' first minister ' —he took none of them fully into his confidence ; therefore they could not hope to be effective as a combination. They further hampered themselves by giving way to jealousy and personal rivalries : four of them disliked Lauderdale, four of them mistrusted Ashley, and there was a steady feud between Buckingham and Arlington. In fact, the ministers of the Cabal were fit servants for a master who himself was not inflexible in his principles. Clifford, the only honest man among them, was fierce and narrow; Lauderdale, who was naturally a bully, had once been a Covenanter, and he had betrayed Montrose; Arlington's unblushing opportunism was soon to allow him to negotiate an alliance with a nation to which he had lately declared his undying enmity. Ashley and Buckingham had had still more varied careers. Ashley entered the civil war as a royalist, but he was shrewd enough to change sides in 1644; he retired from politics during the dangerous years after the war, but in 1653 he emerged to take his seat in the Barebones Parliament. He sat in all the parliaments of the Protectorate, but in 1660 he assured Monk of his support, and was in high favour at the Restoration. For the present he was content to be a King's Friend, but no man could count on his allegiance or his word; his darkest crimes still lay in the future. Buckingham, the son of Charles I's beloved Steenie, had lost his estates and gone into exile with the unrepentant royalists. In 1657, however, he had made his peace with the government, and returned to England to marry the daughter of Fairfax; and these new attachments had not prevented him from discovering in 1660 that he was still a devoted servant of the House of Stuart.

But these unscrupulous men, free-lances in the world of politics, had certain objects in common: they were eager to promote the nation's trade, they hated the Dutch, and they were in favour of toleration. These objects were interdependent, since the Dutch were commercial rivals, and practical men were beginning to urge that toleration was 'good for trade'. The purpose of the Cabal was to put these principles into action, and it was natural that the King should choose ministers who were ready to support him in a policy conceived in the national interest. Where they miscalculated was in thinking that the Cavalier Parliament would support it too. For Charles did not intend to defy parliament as Clarendon had done. Parliament was prorogued for several months while the Cabal's policy was being prepared, and again while it was executed; for it was the undoubted right of the Crown to frame the national policy and to carry it out. But Charles hoped that parliament could be persuaded to support a policy of which it was to be invited to bear the cost. He counted on his ministers to break down the opposition: on Ashley's downright oratory, on Arlington's capacity for intrigue, on Buckingham's miscellaneous band of personal followers and the block of voters who came from his Yorkshire estates. It was a hopeless quest. There were indeed members who supported the government's policy on its merits, and time-servers who would vote for the King's ministers on any issue. But the temper of the Cavalier Parliament was hostile to everything the Cabal represented. The landowners were opposed to war, for war meant standing armies and taxes to be levied on their estates; and they resisted any pandering to the commercial interest which raised merchants and financiers to a wealth and eminence equal to their own. They hated France, where 'thin cheeks, canvas clothing and wooden shoes' were symbols of the people's bondage; they did not waver in their rooted fear of Popery; and if time was beginning to mellow their hatred of the Puritan sects, Colonel Strangways came up from Dorset to remind them 'what principles brought the King to the block', and to revive among them 'a bitter venom against the fanatics'; so that in 1670 they re-enacted the Conventicle Act, which was 'attended with a great shout at its passing'.

Here were prejudices which the ministry could not hope to break down. Not one of the Cabal was a sound Anglican: Clifford and Arlington were Catholics, Lauderdale a Covenanter, Buckingham a patron of Independents, Ashley a rationalist who detested the Anglican monopoly because it hampered the development of commerce. It was not within the power of these men to win the support of country gentlemen who added to their other prejudices a mistrust of all policies manufactured by the court. In effect, therefore, Charles was the leader of the opposition to the dominant party in the Commons; and even his supporters fell from him when they discovered that, instead of taking parliament fully into his confidence, he had made a secret agreement with a foreign King.

The Cabal was brought low by the failure of its foreign policy. Charles's plan was to join England with France in a war to exterminate the Dutch ; and during the war to achieve the third of his objects by bringing forward measures for the relief of Dissenters. The policy was well chosen for a nation which was beginning to be conscious of its economic strength. The Rump had pointed the way, and Restoration England made haste to follow it : in the reign of Charles II men realised the possibilities of an overseas empire in which each colony was an economic unit in a system controlled by the mother country. The renewal in 1660 of the Rump's Navigation Act showed that the new government proposed to use all the resources of the state in the cause of commercial expansion.[1] It imposed the tariffs and passed the protectionist measures which contemporary economic opinion demanded ; and, in order to keep itself properly informed on economic questions, it set up various committees for trade and plantations which in 1696 were organised as a permanent Board of Trade. The purpose of the Navigation Laws was not merely to encourage shipping and ship-building : they were designed to promote the welfare of England and her colonies by pooling the resources of the old world and the new. The colonies were compelled to export only to England commodities which were not produced at home ; these ' enumerated commodities ' included sugar, tobacco, raw cotton and indigo, and, later, rice and naval stores. Similarly, if they wished to import the produce of Europe, they had to fetch it from England, whither it had been brought in English ships. The new zeal for imperial planning was expressed in 1663 in the foundation of Carolina. Its founders did not design it to be, like most of the American colonies, a settlement for religious refugees ; they hoped that it would supply them with the silks, fruits and oils which at that time England was obliged to import from the Mediterranean. Under the stimulus of colonial expansion, English merchants entered on happy days. It is

[1] The comparative peace of Charles's reign permitted the nation to amass capital and invest it shrewdly in colonial settlements.

significant of the new trend in commercial ideas that the older companies, those which had been founded to trade with Europe, rapidly declined. The Muscovy Company, the Merchant Adventurers, once the proud rivals of the Hanseatic League, the Eastland Company, which handled the trade of the Baltic, found that their great days were past. The companies which flourished were those which traded over the high seas. The Levant Company brought home the rich products of Asia; the East India Company, driven from the Spice Islands by the unscrupulous rivalry of the Dutch, settled its factories on the Indian mainland [1] and sent to England valuable cargoes of calico and silk; the African Company recovered the slave-trade with the West Indies; the Hudson's Bay Company was founded in 1670 to carry on a lucrative trade in the furs which were bought from the Indian trappers.

In all their enterprises, however, the English merchants were hampered by the ubiquitous energy of the Dutch. The Rump's hostility had yielded to Cromwell's desire to live in peace with all his Protestant brethren, but at the Restoration complaints broke out anew that the Dutch were ruining English trade. In 1661 a Council for Trade and Plantations reported that they made war on natives and unjustly confiscated British shipping; three years later another committee declared that the Dutch were 'the chief authors' of the heavy losses lately suffered by the East India Company. In 1665 the continuous friction, which Cromwell's peace had not relieved, brought the two countries into war. Its objects were entirely commercial; Clarendon denounced it as 'a bare-faced war', and laid the blame on the African Company and the City financiers, who used the resources of the state to protect their investments. The plague and the fire paralysed England's efforts, and in 1667 de Ruyter sailed up the Medway and burned the ships which lay in dock at Chatham; but the Dutch were equally unable to sustain the war, and in the same year they agreed to concede to England

[1] Charles gave the Company Bombay, which the Queen had brought in her dowry.

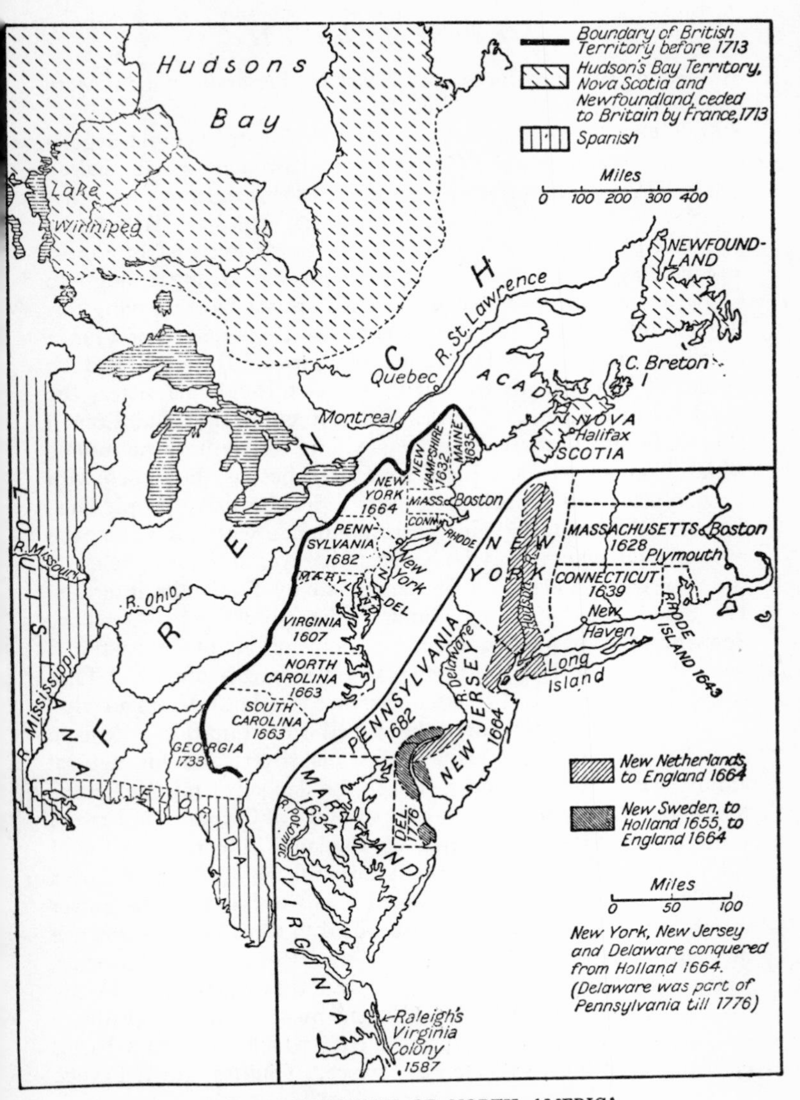

THE COLONISATION OF NORTH AMERICA

the important provinces of New Netherlands which were renamed New York and New Jersey.

In 1668 Charles changed sides. Sir William Temple negotiated an alliance with Holland and Sweden which halted Louis XIV in his path of conquest. But this did not mean that Charles had altered his main purpose. He had earned the goodwill of parliament by ministering to its mistrust of Louis, and he had shown Louis that England was strong enough to be reckoned with, and that her friendship was worth paying for. But his intention all the time was to use the strength of France to help him to drive Dutch competition off the seas, and he immediately began to treat with Louis through his sister, the Duchess of Orleans. Charles did not enter into the French alliance simply because Louis was willing to pay him the money which his own people refused him ; nor because he hoped with French arms and French gold to drive a submissive people back into the Roman faith ; his correspondence with his sister, the only person whom he wholly trusted, reveals that he believed the war with Holland to be demanded by England's interests. He hated the 'stinking Dutch', the 'butterboxes', whose doctrine of *mare liberum* defied the conventions of international law. He never forgave them for burning his ships : 'That country,' he wrote to Minette, 'has used us both very scurvily.' Charles's patriotism cannot be called into question ; it is a sounder criticism that his love for his sister, and his natural affinity with France, blinded him to the danger of raising France too high. Under the vigorous imperialism of Colbert, the French were becoming serious rivals of England in commercial and colonial expansion ; and, like Cromwell before him, Charles may be charged with having helped Louis to build up the power which at the turn of the century seemed to threaten the existence of England and the Protestant religion. By that time, however, Louis was master of the harbours and the trade-routes of the Spanish Empire, and the English had made themselves vulnerable by changing their King ; events which in 1670 Charles need not have been expected to foresee. Charles joined France partly in self-defence: to forestall the Dutch, who were angling for the same alliance as himself. 'France will have us or Holland always with her,' he said, 'and if we take them not, Holland will have them.' When he learned that De Witt had proposed to Louis that France and Holland should partition the Spanish Empire, he was obliged to hurry. But in all his dealings with France his first care was England's supremacy at sea: in the treaties he persuaded Louis to suspend ship-building, and stipulated that the naval operations against Holland should be conducted by the English. In the reign of Charles II England pursued the 'westwards' policy which the Rump had preferred to the 'continental' designs of former ages, which Cromwell had continued almost by accident, and which the genius of Chatham was to crown with victory in the eighteenth century. It is arguable that this policy was no less careful of England's interest than the wars which protected the House of Orange, and the anxious diplomacy which was lavished on the beggarly Electorate.

The most serious accusation men brought against Charles was that his foreign policy was the mask of a Popish Plot. In May, 1670, Clifford, Arlington, and Lord Arundell of Wardour signed a secret treaty with the French at Dover. It settled the details of the offensive alliance against the Dutch: as well as an army, France was to provide £225,000 a year; England's reward was to be the Zeeland Islands, and any colonial possessions which she might seize. But that was not all. Louis was to pay Charles £150,000 to declare himself a Catholic, and to lend him 6,000 soldiers if the English should rebel. What Charles and Louis intended by these secret clauses, it is impossible to tell; history records only their actions, and not their private thoughts. By the letter of an unfulfilled treaty Charles stands convicted of a plot to revert to a religion which his people hated, and to crush their resentment with foreign arms. But his actions suggest that he was more anxious to get Louis' money than to fulfil his side of the bargain. Although he generously pictured Louis glowing with an 'inward content of mind' when his conversion should be announced, he found a series of excuses to postpone the day; when war broke out, he was still unconverted, and the matter was dropped. Charles and Louis were practical men. It is not conceivable that, on the threshold of a war which was important for both of them, Charles really intended to shatter the unity of his people by reverting to Rome, or Louis to send six thousand of his precious soldiers in pursuit of the intangible satisfaction of a religious conversion. Louis doubtless felt that his money was well spent if he could be sure of England's co-operation in his war; and Charles did no more than issue in 1672 a Declaration of Indulgence for Tender Consciences, which suspended the penal laws, and permitted Protestant Dissenters to worship in public and Catholics in private. When parliament protested, he withdrew it; a quiet life in England was worth more than a Mass.

The policy which has provoked so much controversy completely failed in action. Ashley's reiterated '*delenda est Carthago*' induced the Commons to vote money for the extinction of the old enemy; and at the end of 1670 Buckingham negotiated a second and public Treaty of Dover, from which the Catholic clauses were omitted. While Louis prepared his alliances in Europe, Sir George Downing was sent to the Hague to irritate the Dutch. But the war, which began in 1672, was not a success. The Dutch overthrew their republican leaders and once more called on the House of Orange to save them in the hour of need. As Turenne's armies came upon them, they cut the dykes and flooded their country in the path of the invader; while at sea the great de Ruyter kept his fleet in being and saved his country. For England had not the resources for a long war. Already, in order to get his navy to sea, Charles had been obliged to suspend the payment of interest on the government's debts; and while de Ruyter's actions in Southwold Bay and the Texel were frustrating the allies' hopes of an immediate invasion, the English parliament was coming to the rescue of the Dutch. Parliament met early in 1673, full of angry suspicions. The government should not have a penny for its war until grievances had been redressed. Charles withdrew his Declaration of Indulgence, and surrendered his suspending power, but the Commons wanted more : in March they smashed the government's designs in pieces by passing the Test Act,[1] which required all servants of the state to accept the sacraments of the Church of England and to take an oath that they disbelieved in the Roman doctrine of transubstantiation. The blow struck home : Clifford and the Duke of York resigned their posts. Summoned again in the autumn, the Commons resumed the 'great baiting' where they had left off : they had many more complaints to make before they would consider granting supplies. Charles knew when he was beaten. His ministry was broken : Clifford was gone, Shaftesbury[2] had joined the opposition, Arlington was threatened with impeachment. His war policy had collapsed because he had no money to carry it on. So in 1674 he gracefully accepted the inevitable : surrendering to the prejudices of the Cavalier Parliament, he left Louis to fight his war alone.

2. *The ministry of Danby*

After the collapse of the Cabal Charles chose his ministers from men who were in greater sympathy with the humours of his parliament. Recent experience had exposed the true worth of the extravagant professions of loyalty with which the Cavaliers had greeted the Restoration : in practice, the famous parliaments of the previous generation had not been more jealous of the prerogative than the body which men had supposed to be more royalist than the King.[3] Charles kept it because he knew that he would not find a better ; but he had learned that he must appoint ministers who respected it, shared its prejudices, and knew how to handle it.

He found an admirable instrument for his purpose in the

[1] In assenting to the Test Act, Charles virtually surrendered the Crown's supremacy in the Church.

[2] Ashley was made Earl of Shaftesbury in 1672.

[3] The loyal Finch considered some of its measures to be 'introductive to a commonwealth'.

Earl of Danby, whom he appointed to succeed Clifford as Lord Treasurer. Danby laid before Crown and parliament a programme in which each would profit if it made appropriate concessions to the other. True alike to the Cavalier tradition and to the vintage Toryism of the future, he rested his policy on the King's prerogative and the Church of England. For his part, Charles must 'show his steadiness to the Church'; and since in 1674 staunch Anglicanism implied a hatred of Catholic France, he must be won to the foreign policy of his subjects. In return, Danby undertook to revive the parliamentary co-operation which the loyal enthusiasm of 1661 had seemed to promise. If Charles would meet the Commons in foreign policy and religion, the Commons might be persuaded to relieve the Crown of its financial embarrassments.

Danby's programme promised to save the Restoration settlement by improvising from it a workable system of government. He did, indeed, achieve partial success. By means of bribery he won a substantial block of members to the side of the government, and with their help he rescued Charles from debt. In 1675 he brought the revenue up to £1,400,000, paid off the expenses of the war, and restored the Crown's credit by resuming the payments which had been suspended in 1672. His antagonism to France bore fruit when in 1677 the marriage of Princess Mary, daughter of the Duke of York, to William of Orange forged a personal link between England and Holland; and his foreign policy seemed to stand on the threshold of success when in 1677, and again in 1678, parliament voted supplies for a war against the French. But Danby's triumphs were few and intermittent. Final and complete success eluded him because three men cleverer and more persistent than he—Charles, Shaftesbury, and Louis XIV—did not wish him to succeed.

In the first place, Charles was not a suitable King for the brand of Tory sentiment from which Danby tried to profit. The Tories were most at ease in their professions of non-resistance when they were serving a King who was content to fall in with their policy. But the time had not yet arrived when Charles was ready to be a Tory mascot ; he was still determined to protect his policy from parliamentary interference. He was grateful to Danby for making him solvent, but he resented the mood in which the money was granted. When parliament petitioned for an alliance with Holland for the purpose of bringing France within the boundaries fixed by the Peace of the Pyrenees in 1659, he again refused to admit that its financial supremacy entitled it to usurp the Crown's prerogative in foreign affairs. The collapse of his policy in 1673 had not shaken his personal preference for an alliance with Louis, and he had no intention of allowing Danby and the Cavaliers to hustle him into a war of which he disapproved. He was willing, however, to feign enthusiasm for parliament's policy if this pretence would persuade the Commons to vote him supplies for a war which he did not intend to fight ; and he gladly consented to such hostile demonstrations as Mary's marriage, since they punished Louis for his intrigues with Shaftesbury, and strengthened his hand for future negotiations with France. Thus between 1675 and 1678 Charles was able to evade the control of parliament and conduct a foreign policy of his own. He silenced parliament by twice proroguing it for fifteen months, and he bound Danby to his service by the convention that a minister's first duty was to his sovereign. So powerful was this convention that the helpless Danby found himself acting as Charles's emissary in pledging England to a policy of neutrality, even while he was publicly seeking parliament's support for war.

Danby not only failed to persuade the King : he failed, even by corruption, to unite parliament in support of his policy. Shaftesbury and Buckingham had not forgiven the master who had deceived them in the secret Treaty of Dover. Revenge and ambition inspired them to frustrate Danby's attempt to base the government on exclusive Anglicanism and an excessive tenderness to the King's prerogative. For Shaftesbury was the first man to shake off the spell of 1661, to argue that the political future of England was not of necessity bound up with the interests of the Anglican squirearchy ; in the financiers, the merchants, and the Nonconformist shopkeepers, he saw the elements of a party which with aristocratic leadership would be strong enough to end the Cavaliers' long enjoyment of power. His main purpose was to dissolve the Cavalier Parliament, so that the strength of the moneyed interests in the boroughs might elect a House of Commons more favourable to his designs. But only the King could dissolve parliament, and for the present Shaftesbury had to be content with the negative satisfaction of wrecking Danby's policy. He did not fear to attack the tenderest of Cavalier prejudices, proclaiming his alliance with the Dissenters and asserting the rights of parliament against the efforts of corrupt ministers to bind it to the service of the Crown. In time his persistence skilfully divided his enemies. He prevented the passing of the Non-Resisting Bill, by which Danby sought to impose on all members and officials an undertaking to abide by the existing constitution of Church and state ; by reviving the old shibboleth that the King should ' live of his own ', he managed to keep Charles short of money ; and through the Englishman's dread of standing armies, he disappointed Danby's hopes of war. The fear of standing armies was an emotion which overcame all distinctions of party or principle. Thus the members who clamoured for war were easily stirred to suspect the King's real intentions. ' These red-coats ', they concluded, ' may fight against Magna Carta ' ; and therefore ' drums ought not to be beat here ; nor red-coats to be about the Parliament, *in terrorem populi* '. Although they wanted a war, they could not trust the soldiers who were to fight it.

Shaftesbury found a willing ally in the King of France. Louis would lay his hand on any weapon which would prevent the English army from interfering with his campaign in Flanders : sometimes he paid Charles to keep parliament prorogued ; he even managed to bribe the Dutch ambassadors to hold up the negotiations with England ; and when these resources failed him, he bribed the opposition to harass the ministry in parliament. A succession of skilful envoys—Courtin, Barillon, Ruvigny—moved among the members and scattered French gold where it would serve French designs: Shaftesbury and Russell were ready to be factious without being paid for it, but Buckingham, Algernon Sidney and Hampden's son followed their King in being pensioners of France. In the summer of 1678 Louis brought his war to a close at Nymuegen. He had added Franche Comté to his territories, and he had defeated both the efforts of Danby to check him by force, and of Charles to act as a salaried mediator between France and her enemies.

3. *Oates and Exclusion*

Deceived by his master, and stampeded out of his designs by a determined opposition in parliament, Danby was in a hopeless position; by 1678 his ministry, like that of Clarendon and the Cabal before him, had come to a deadlock, and he was wandering aimlessly among the ruins of his policy. At this point chance threw the game into Shaftesbury's hands. In August, 1678, Charles was informed that two strange men, Titus Oates and Israel Tonge, were spreading rumours of a Catholic plot against the safety of the state. Oates was the son of a Baptist preacher who had been an army chaplain. He had been expelled from Merchant Taylor's School, from a naval chaplaincy, and from a Jesuit College,[1] and he had already been in prison for perjury. Before the Jesuits threw him out, he had picked up in the colleges at Valladolid and St. Omer enough information to give colour to the extraordinary stories he began to tell when, in the guise of a Doctor of Divinity of Salamanca, he returned to England in 1678. He spoke of a Papist conspiracy to fire the City, massacre Protestants, kill the King, and establish the Duke of York on a throne supported by the bayonets of Ireland and France. There were no half-measures in Oates's lying. His accusations, drawn up in eighty-one sections, not merely gave the

[1] He had not, however, been expelled from Trinity, Cambridge.

details of the plot, but named the conspirators and the work which each was to perform.

'It is a stupendous thing,' as Secretary Coventry observed, 'to think what vast concerns are like to depend upon the evidence of one young man who hath twice changed his religion.'[1] In many ways the mind of Restoration England was sane and practical, but it had not yet learned to think clearly about Popery. To a generation living on its nerves Oates said nothing that was not credible ; indeed, his tales confirmed the gloomy suspicions of recent years. If the Papists had, as men believed, set fire to London once, they would do it again. It did not matter that Charles summoned Oates before the Council and twice convicted him of lying : sane men were helpless before the storm of fear and anger. Some monks had been heard singing a *Te Deum*, a store of cutlasses had been discovered underground ; so Lady Shaftesbury carried a pistol in her muff, cannon were brought to Whitehall, and guards ceaselessly patrolled the cellars at Westminster. To swell the panic, fortune three times favoured Oates's impudence. First, his accusations chanced to unearth evidence of the real Popish Plot, the designs which matured when James II was King : searchers discovered the correspondence of Edward Coleman, secretary to the Duchess of York, with the courts of France and Rome. Secondly, the strangled body of Sir Edmund Godfrey, a popular magistrate to whom Oates declared that he had entrusted the proofs of his accusations, was found in a ditch by Primrose Hill. It was inevitable that men should believe that the Papists had killed him to suppress the evidence of their guilt. Finally, a former ambassador to the Court of St. Germain chose this heated moment to reveal Charles's recent negotiations with Louis, and the part which Danby had so unwillingly played in them. Montagu's treachery was a crushing blow to those who hoped that the panic would be quickly past, for it implicated the Crown and its ministers in the Popish Plot. Danby pleaded in vain that he had been only the impersonal instrument of his master's wishes ; to save him

[1] Oates had once been an Anglican parson.

from impeachment, Charles parted at last from the Cavalier Parliament.

Shaftesbury did not waste the opportunity for which he had waited so long. Panic blotted out all party distinctions: Cavalier sentiment disappeared in the nation's mistrust of the policy of the court. Thus at the elections in the spring of 1679 Shaftesbury's 'country party' was returned in overwhelming strength; men saw Godfrey's admonitory ghost at their shoulder as they went to the polls, and only the 'heathens' of Cornwall remained loyal to the court. With Cavalier loyalty thus led astray by wrath, Charles made ready to fight his lonely battle for the prerogative. He knew already what he had to face: for in the previous November, during the final session of the Cavalier Parliament, Shaftesbury's satellites had formally proposed the exclusion of the Duke of York. Charles had suffered much: in his conflicts with parliament he had seen his prerogative whittled down, and had submitted to what he could not prevent; but he refused to submit to a scheme which damaged both the principle of hereditary kingship and the honour of his House. He refused to allow the monarchy to be converted into an elective office whose tenure rested on the capricious approbation of parliament. One easy solution lay before him: he might divorce his barren Queen, and marry again in the hope of begetting an heir. But with unexpected chivalry he declared that he would not 'see an innocent woman abused'. York was his brother and his heir, and York should succeed him.

Halifax likened Charles's tactics to the deceptive pliancy of a feather-bed, which yields to blows but is never broken. So long as passion ran high, he let it take its course. He sent his brother out of the country; when parliament attainted Danby, he did not again try to protect him; he stood aside while Oates gathered in his dreadful harvest. Shaftesbury's little band of pensioned perjurers, lately joined by William Bedloe, a horse-thief from Chepstow, swore away the lives of about thirty-five innocent men: 'Let the blood lie on them that condemn them,' said

Charles, ' for God knows I sign with tears in my eyes.' On two points Charles stood firm : he vetoed a measure to deprive him of his command of the militia ; and when the Queen was accused of a plot to poison him, he furiously compelled Oates to drop his charges. For the most part, however, he ' let the laws take their course ', confident that time would soften hatreds, and that eventually his people would be sane again. In his struggle to protect the hereditary kingship, one great man stood always by his side. In the *Character of a Trimmer* the Marquis of Halifax has written down the articles of his political faith. To a violent, nerve-ridden age he brought the cool mind and the moderating counsel of a *Politique.* He loved neither despots nor demagogues ; and against the anarchy of despotism and faction he appealed to the law, ' not the King's laws, nor the Parliament's laws, but the Laws of England '. For ' Our Trimmer thinketh that the King and Kingdom ought to be one creature, not to be separated in their political capacity ; and when either of them undertake to act a part, it is like the crawling of worms after they are cut in pieces '.

While Charles bargained with Louis for money to carry on his government, he fretted Shaftesbury with ingenious delays. To gain time, he fell in with a doctrinaire scheme fathered by Sir William Temple. In April, 1679, the Privy Council was replaced by a new Council, only half of whose thirty members were members of the ministry ; it being hoped that this body, by which all business was to be transacted, would be able to hold the balance between the ministers and parliament. The scheme failed, but it sheltered Charles from too frequent clashes with a House of Commons dominated by Shaftesbury. In July, after it had read an Exclusion Bill for the second time, he dissolved this parliament ; and when the autumn elections returned a second Whig parliament as uncompromising as the first, he prorogued it for a year before it met. In the meantime, he was offering a programme of his own which good Cavaliers, when they had shaken off their panic, might find easy to accept : he agreed that if York became King, his power should be limited. In effect, he revived the proposals which the Long Parliament had vainly submitted to his father between 1642 and 1648. In November, 1678, he promised that he would assent to measures ' to make you safe in the reign of my successor ', and to ' establish a firm security for the Protestant religion '. In 1679 his ministers made concrete proposals : parliament should control appointments in Church and state. In 1681 he was to go so far as to offer to make Mary and Anne regents, so long as their father held the hereditary title. The government's policy of ' limitation ' reconciled the two fundamentals of Cavalier politics, respect for the King and respect for the established Church. To recover the allegiance of the Cavaliers, Charles abandoned his hope of toleration, and meekly entered the Anglican fold. He vowed that he would ' maintain the Church as it is now established, and not be of a religion that can make all things lawful, as Presbytery can '. The exclusion crisis taught him what he had been slow to learn : that the wise old formula, ' No Bishop, no King ' was still as true as it ever was. ' I will not be for lessening ' the Church, he said ; ' for if I do, I know that I less my Crown, for we must march together.'

The tide turned slowly in favour of the King. In July, 1679, when the Queen's physician was acquitted of a plot to poison Charles, Oates was for the first time baulked of a victim ; and when he failed to bring down the judge who had conducted the trial, judges and juries found again the courage which they had lost. Shaftesbury began to grow anxious. The success of his designs depended on an artificial panic which was already waning ; and between May, 1679, and October of the following year, no parliament sat to translate his programme into law. Unlike Charles, he would not compromise : he rejected the expedient of ' limitation ', which, said Richard Hampden, was like ' binding Samson with withes '. He preferred to keep alive the fear of Popery by a campaign of organised violence. In Aldersgate, among the rabble which had once served Pym, the Green Ribbon Club deliberately prolonged the reign of terror. The King was attacked in lewd songs and libellous pamphlets ;

letters found in a meal tub were proclaimed to be fresh evidence of the irrepressible wickedness of all who adhered to the Catholic faith; a band of cattle-stealers was brought from Ireland to reveal the black intrigues of the Irish clergy. In an attempt to intimidate Charles into summoning parliament, Shaftesbury organised a series of petitions, from which were born the famous names of Whig and Tory. The 'petitioners' were nicknamed Whigamores, after the sour faces of the Scottish Covenanters; and the courtiers who 'abhorred' the petitions were called Tories, after the bands of Popish robbers who dwelt in the Irish mountains.

By way of violence Shaftesbury hurried to his own destruction, as Charles had intended that he should. His greatest mistake was to adopt as his candidate for the throne Charles's illegitimate son, the Duke of Monmouth. If James was unfit to be King, the lawful heir—and, therefore, the only candidate for an honest man—was his Protestant daughter Mary, with or without her husband, the Prince of Orange. When Shaftesbury adopted Monmouth, a weak man, popular but unstable, he exposed his real aims: he would challenge the indefeasible, hereditary right of the House of Stuart, in order to set on the throne the chosen puppet of Whig politicians. He did not better his case by asserting that Charles and Lucy Walters[1] had been legally married, and that the proof of it was stored in a Black Box which had been stolen by the Pope. His mistake was final. In fear of the overmighty subject all the 'trimmers' joined the King.

4. *The Tory triumph*

When parliament met at last, in October, 1680, the Tories could not arrest the triumphant progress of an Exclusion Bill through the House of Commons; but when it was brought to the Lords, Halifax rose fifteen times in a single afternoon to defend the hereditary succession. 'So much the weight of one

[1] Monmouth's father may have been Robert Sidney.

brave man can do': the Bill was rejected by 63 votes to 30. To placate the furious Commons, the peers sent the aged Viscount Stafford to the block,[1] but it was Shaftesbury's last success. In January Charles dissolved parliament, in the face of a threat that the 'brisk boys' would storm the Palace; for he judged that the time had come when he could appeal to the country against the violence of the Whigs.

The elections once more returned an overwhelming majority of members pledged to exclusion; but this result did not reflect the will of the nation, so much as Shaftesbury's skill in electioneering, and the oddity of the electoral system. The counties returned eighty members, the boroughs more than four hundred; the Whigs won the election because their strength lay in the towns. Charles ordered the parliament to meet in Oxford, ever the 'retreat of Kings in time of war and pestilence',[2] where Shaftesbury's City mob would be unable to terrorise the members. The Whigs bore down on Oxford like an army, each lord attended by his retainers, and Monmouth assuming the dignities proper to a King. In his speech to parliament Charles went to the limits of concession; and when the Whigs again refused to accept anything less than exclusion, he prepared to strike his blow. 'I will never yield,' he said, 'and I will not be intimidated. . . . I have reason and law in my favour; well-minded people are on my side.' So was the King of France. Fearing that the success of exclusion might bring William of Orange to the English throne, Barillon gave his master's promise to pay Charles money to rule without parliament. On the next day, only a week after it had met, parliament was dissolved. Their 'loud sighs' and 'dreadful faces' told of the dismay and astonishment of the Whigs, who believed that they had at last brought the King to the point of surrender. But their protests were not more serious than 'the distractions and dejections of routed armies'. Taken by surprise in the hour of apparent victory,

[1] He had been charged by Oates and imprisoned in 1678.

[2] The court occupied Merton, Christ Church and Corpus. The Whigs went to Balliol.

they had no plan; although Shaftesbury tried to rally them to resist, their nerve failed them, and they hurriedly took to their horses and their homes.

Charles had won. Throughout the long crisis he had surrendered only two minor points: henceforth the dissolution of parliament would not terminate the process of an impeachment; and in 1679 parliament passed an act to revise the procedure of *Habeas Corpus.* Otherwise, Charles had kept his prerogative intact; and in the end he had not merely saved the hereditary succession, but he had saved it free of the conditions which he had been prepared to accept. But his victory was won at a price. Henceforth he would have to abandon toleration and the French alliance, and conform to the Tory prejudices which he had formerly sought to evade. In 1681 he asked parliament to 'make the laws of the land your rule, because I am resolved they shall be mine'; at last he would be a constitutional King. For in reality the Crown's success in 1681 was less a victory for the royal prerogative than the victory of the Tory party. Charles saved the succession by identifying it with property, the law, and the Anglican Church, against Shaftesbury's alliance of aristocrats, Dissenters, and merchants, the alliance which had fought the King in 1642 and which seemed to be ready to fight him again. In his extremity Charles had admitted the right of subjects to impose limitations on the Crown; and he was not rescued from it until the imminence of civil war reminded the Tories that it was by an alliance with the court that they had shattered their enemies in 1661. No King, no Bishop; and therefore no Anglican monopoly of power. Shaftesbury overreached himself, and drove the moderates [1] to the side of his natural enemies, by adopting an obvious puppet as his Pretender, and by showing that he would risk a war to gain his ends. As Sir Edward Seymour had told the Commons in 1680, 'when you seclude the Duke for religion, you make a war for religion'; Louis would take up the cause of the banished Prince, and exclusion could not be maintained without a standing army.

[1] i.e. men who had broken the Cabal and mistrusted Danby.

At the threat of war the nation rejected both the bastard and the King-maker.

Between 1681 and 1685 no parliament was summoned, and there were the misleading appearances of a royal despotism. The crisis had again shown the Tories that their political interests were best served by the doctrine of non-resistance ; that the attempt to exclude the Duke of York had been also an attempt to exclude themselves from the seats of power. It was natural, therefore, that in their relief that the danger had been withdrawn they should somewhat overstate their principle. A spate of poems, plays and pamphlets proclaimed the sacred duty of obedience. While Tory controversialists sought to prove that their enemies were really republicans, Dryden's allegorical poem *Absalom and Achitophel* exposed the motives of the defeated exclusionists ; in his *Observator* Roger L'Estrange, a journalist of genius, assailed even the 'trimmers' for the lukewarmness of their allegiance ; among a profusion of loyal addresses, the University of Oxford condemned the theory that government depended on a compact between the King and his subjects, and the men of Devon besought the King 'never to trust this generation of men more, whose religion had its birth in rebellion and is as inconsistent with monarchy as light with darkness'.

But the value of these protestations was no more than academic. 'In their cups,' wrote Burnet, 'the old vigour and the swaggerings of the Cavaliers seemed to be revived' ; but the misfortunes of James were to prove the unwisdom of putting too heavy a strain on the doctrine of non-resistance. Although Filmer's historic defence of Divine Right was at length published, nearly thirty years after its author was dead, no Tory was prepared to accept its theories literally. The real business of the Tories in these years was to avenge the past by completing the rout of their enemies, and to safeguard the future by arming themselves against further surprise. Charles's last ministry was the first in English history to be drawn exclusively from a single party. It contained, it is true, Halifax, who did not partake of the enthusiasms of the triumphant squires; and Ormonde and Nottingham, who represented the old-fashioned Toryism of Clarendon and were suspicious even of Tory faction. But the bulk of the court party, led by Rochester and Clarendon, sons of the old Chancellor, were determined to use their power to break the strength of Shaftesbury's following.

In 1683 a Whig conspiracy gave the Tories the opportunity to take the revenge from which Charles and Halifax had so far restrained them. Frantically urging his friends to acts of violence, Shaftesbury saved his own skin by taking refuge in Holland. Two old Cromwellian soldiers, Rumbold and Rumsey, obeyed him too well: they planned to assassinate the King at the Rye House as he returned from Newmarket. Of the Whig leaders involved in the plot, Russell and Algernon Sidney died on the scaffold, and Essex cut his throat in prison. Meanwhile, the Tories were busy in driving their enemies from public life. The detailed severity of the Clarendon Code damped the rising hopes of the Nonconformists; loyal churchmen replaced Whig Justices and Lords-Lieutenant; in London a royalist Lord Mayor secured the return of Tory sheriffs who would answer for the goodwill of the City juries.

In a short time, therefore, the principal institutions and social groups in the country were absorbed into the government's system. The great trading companies would have preferred the Whigs, but were ready to submit to a government that did not neglect their interests; the established Church was already a part of the Tory machine; Nonconformity had as yet no political coherence; the Universities were extravagant in their loyalty; and the Inns of Court furnished no *noblesse de robe* like that which distracted the monarchy in France. Finally, the Tories expelled the Whigs from their last stronghold, the municipal corporations. By their judicial powers, and in particular by their control over borough elections, the corporations were able to obstruct the policy of governments of which they disapproved. These privileges depended, however, on charters which had been granted by the Crown, and what the

Crown had granted, it might lawfully revoke. Evesham and Norwich were the first to fall; and in 1683 the City of London itself, 'the Republic at the King's side', was forced by the procedure of *Quo Warranto* to surrender its charter. When London had fallen, no provincial city could hope to resist; as Jeffreys went about his work, the corporations hastened to yield their charters at his approach. Their surrender completed the victory of the Crown,[1] which was now master both of municipal government and of parliamentary elections in the towns. Although Halifax urged that one be called, no parliament met during these years; probably because, now that Charles had deferred to their prejudices, the Tory gentlemen found no business sufficiently pressing to justify the tedious and costly journey to London. But the effectiveness of their machinery was triumphantly tested in the first parliament of James II, in which there were only forty members who were hostile to the court. An eventful reign thus drew quietly to its close, with the Tories entrenched in an impregnable citadel from which they could not be removed unless they consented to surrender it themselves. To their own surprise, this was exactly what they were going to do. For in 1685 Charles II died, and England was delivered to '*la sottise de mon frère*'.

[1] Danby's unsuccessful Non-Resisting Bill of 1675 was now a reality.

CHAPTER XX

THE SECOND REVOLUTION

The follies of James. The Revolution. The settlement.

1. '*Capax imperii nisi imperasset*'

As a French historian has written of the Emperor Napoleon III, '*le grand malheur de cet homme fut de regner*'.[1] Before he came to the throne, James II had shown himself to be a highly competent bureaucrat. As Governor of the Royal African Company, and later of the Hudson's Bay Company, he had been jealous of his people's rights and had stimulated their growing interest in overseas expansion; as Lord High Admiral, he had fought bravely and not unsuccessfully against the Dutch, and with Pepys he had thrown himself with enthusiasm into the duties of naval administration. But, although he was a good administrator, he had not a shred of the political sense which fits a man to hold a post of discretion. He lacked Charles's easy humour and suppleness of mind; instead, he had inherited his father's austere inflexibility, his awkwardness in human contacts, his inability to gauge men's reaction to his doings. His resignation in 1673 had proved the firmness of his conscience, his unwavering determination during the crisis of exclusion had revealed his courage; but neither of these setbacks had taught him wisdom. He came to his throne apparently unaware how nearly he had lost it, his brain echoing the soothing phrases of Tory loyalty, but forgetful that a politician as resourceful as his brother had been obliged to bow to Tory prejudice.

Charles himself had had little confidence in James's wisdom.

[1] P. de la Gorce, *Le Second Empire.*

' When I am dead and gone ', he once remarked, ' I know not what my brother will do : I am much afraid that when he comes to wear the crown he will be obliged to travel again.' Yet few English Kings have come to so secure a throne. The court, the local magistracy, the town corporations, and potentially the House of Commons, were recruited from a party which admitted the principle of the Divine Right of Kings, and did not challenge the Crown's prerogatives to appoint ministers, officers and judges, to summon and dissolve parliaments, to control expenditure, and within reasonable limits to exercise a dispensing power. Something, it is true, was demanded in return : the King must acknowledge parliament's supremacy in legislation and finance, and in framing his policy both at home and abroad he must respect the principles of the Anglican Church. James had only to avoid offending Tory susceptibilities and the Tories would, in their own interests, protect him from the Whig doctrine that the King was a public servant holding his office by the goodwill of the nation. Moreover, his enthusiasm for the navy, colonial development, and the growth of trade, was likely to win him the favour of the Whigs, whose political principles were always liable to be adjusted to correspond with the figures in their trading accounts.

It was only by his own fault, therefore, that James failed to be a successful and respected King. His undoing was his obstinate devotion to the Catholic religion. Halifax marvelled to see how ' the Old Lady Rome ' still had power to fascinate the hearts of men : ' so far from handsome, yet so imperious ; so painted, yet so pretending ; after having abused, deposed and murdered so many of her lovers, she still findeth others glad and proud of their new chains. She sitteth in her shop and selleth at dear rates her rattles and her hobby-horses, while the deluded world still continueth to furnish her with customers.' Unguided by the lessons of the recent past, James determined to make England Catholic again : if not to overthrow the established Church, at least to withdraw the penal laws and to raise Catholics to high offices in the army and the state. He chose an unlucky moment for his designs. In 1685 Louis XIV revoked the Edict of Nantes.

and thousands of Huguenots fled in terror from his *dragonnades* ; before the English had recovered from the shock which Oates had given them, these refugees were the living witness of a Popish Plot as terrible as any which Oates had imagined. When, therefore, James failed to carry out his plans by constitutional means, he fell back on the unfettered exercise of his prerogative. The challenge alike to the Protestant religion and to the constitutional gains which they had secured in 1641, united the oligarchs of England to destroy James as they had destroyed his father.

The reign opened with a necessary formality : Oates was fined and pilloried, whipped from Aldgate to Newgate and from Newgate to Tyburn, and finally thrown in prison.[1] Then, in May, 1685, James met his first parliament. The government used all its influence, and the new borough constitutions did their work : the King was greeted by solid ranks of Cavaliers, more firmly royalist than in 1661, since the recent crisis had taught them that royalism was an expedient doctrine. The Commons voted James an income of nearly £2,000,000 for the rest of his reign, but the course of the debates should have warned him that there were some matters in which their loyalty should not be strained too far : they insisted, for instance, that the laws against Dissenters should be enforced, and they asked James to define his attitude to France.

Their discussions were interrupted, however, by anxious rumours of rebellion. The Earl of Argyll, whose family had a tradition of disloyalty as unbroken as that of the Russells in England, tried to raise the Lowlands against the government. He was easily caught ; the real danger came from Monmouth's rising in the Western counties. Monmouth was handsome and attractive, and he was known to be a Protestant, but his rebellion was not wholly dynastic. A series of bad harvests had im-

[1] In 1688 the martyr was released and granted a pension. He became a Nonconformist minister, and was dismissed for embezzling the funds of his chapel.

poverished the yeomen and the peasants, and the cloth towns of the West were losing their trade to the competition of the Yorkshire Ridings. Thus the army which fought at Sedgemoor was recruited from unemployed labourers who seized on this clumsy hope of bettering their fortunes. After the battle the government took an inhuman revenge. While Jeffreys condemned hundreds of the helpless peasants to transportation, Colonel Kirke and his 'Lambs' put into practice the devices which they had learned in the garrison at Tangier: as music played a dance of death, the victims' stomachs were smeared with pitch and fired. A wiser tactician than James would have spared even Monmouth's life; for with Monmouth dead, Orange would have the undivided support of all the advocates of exclusion.

When parliament reassembled, in November, James declared that he must have 'a well-disciplined standing force' as a precaution against future rebellion. The members, who had been badly frightened, offered £700,000 for the upkeep of an army, but first they wished to know why there were Catholics in the army which had returned from the West, and why there was a Catholic chapel in the camp on Hounslow Heath. James's reply openly declared his intentions: he admitted that he had appointed Catholic officers, and asked parliament to legalise the appointments by repealing the Test Act. Whereat there was a 'great dejection of countenance'. James had asked of Tory loyalty more than it could give. Even before he came to the throne, Bishop Morley had warned him that 'if ever he depended upon the doctrine of non-resistance, he would find himself deceived'; and when he asked them to give up the Test Act, which they regarded as their stoutest dyke against the overwhelming flood of Popery, he dissolved the alliance with the Tories which was the firmest prop of his throne.

Parliament was prorogued in the same November, and although it was not dissolved until the summer of 1687, it never met again. Henceforth James was 'for rougher methods'.[1] Since parliament and the Tories had failed him, he would accomplish his

[1] Burnet.

objects by means of his prerogative ; and when, as he hoped, his policy of toleration had won the Dissenters to his side, a more complaisant parliament might repeal the Test Act and allow him once more to behave as a constitutional King. In June, 1686, the judges gave a decision which enabled him to fill all the offices of state with Catholics. In the case of Godden *v.* Hales they decided, with only one dissentient, that, as ' the laws are his laws ', the King had the right to evade statutes by the exercise of his dispensing power. Legally the decision was correct, but it meant that all the statutory defences against Popery were ineffective against a King who had the will to destroy them. On the strength of it, James filled his ministry with Catholics. Halifax had already gone, for defending the Test Act ; and even Clarendon and Rochester, High Churchmen though they were, could not hold their places under a Catholic King. For his inner council, or cabinet, James relied on the Earl of Tyrconnel, Lord-Lieutenant and commander of the Irish army ; Nicholas Butler, a convert from Protestantism ; Father Petre, his confessor ; Henry Jermyn, once chamberlain to Henrietta Maria ; and the Earl of Sunderland, a man of no religion, who had already been both a courtier and an exclusionist. The Catholic Strickland was appointed to command the fleet, and provoked a mutiny by ordering a public Mass ; four Catholic lords, Powis, Arundell, Dover and Bellasyse, entered the Privy Council ; the Catholics Melfort and Perth controlled the government of Scotland. Catholics flocked into offices high and low, in the army, in the corporations, as lawyers, mayors and Justices of the Peace. A nuncio came from Rome ; there was a Catholic chapel at Whitehall, a Jesuit school at the Savoy ; the Dominicans and Benedictines opened friaries, Catholic priests celebrated Mass all over the country.

This was only a beginning. To achieve his purpose, James had to bring his attack against the very heart of Anglicanism : the corporations, the magistracy, the universities, and finally the Church itself. In 1686 he set up a Court of Ecclesiastical Commission. In order to evade the law of 1641, it had authority over ecclesiastics only, and it was established on the plea that the

King needed such a court to perform his duties as Head of the Church ; its real purpose, however, was to force the clergy into obedience to the King,[1] and its first action was to suspend the Bishop of London for refusing to carry out his master's orders. Then James began to invade the privileges of the universities. At Cambridge, the Vice-Chancellor was suspended for refusing to give a degree to a Benedictine monk. At Oxford, the Catholic Bishop Parker made conversions among the Fellows and the students, the Master of University College celebrated Mass in his College chapel, and the King used his dispensing power to appoint a Catholic as Dean of Christ Church. Finally, the Fellows of Magdalen were ejected in a body for electing their own President in preference to a Catholic whom the King ordered them to choose.

In 1687 James decided to test the success of his policy by summoning a new parliament. As a first step he offered a substantial bribe to the Dissenters : a Declaration of Indulgence, issued in April, safeguarded the Anglican establishment and the holders of monastic property, but it suspended the penal laws and gave Catholics and Dissenters freedom to practise their religion. Further to prepare his ground, James attempted both to counter the influence of the Tories in the country districts and to drive them from their new stronghold in the borough corporations. Like Shaftesbury, he set himself to break the Anglican monopoly of power : 'The whole machine was phanatick ; and the design was, to compass a phanatick Parliament.' In the towns 'Regulators' were appointed to purge the corporations and admit Catholics and Dissenters to the franchise ; and in the counties the Lords-Lieutenant were urged to bring pressure on the Justices to pledge themselves to support the repeal of tests, and to procure the election of candidates who supported the King's programme.

But the 'phanatick machine' refused to work. In the first place, the Dissenters hesitated to be rescued by the prerogative

[1] Thus the weapon used by the Tudors against Rome was finally used by a Catholic King against the Church of England.

which their fathers had fought to reduce. Halifax had no love for the Dissenters' religion, which he regarded as 'a disease that hath seized upon their minds'; but in two of the most influential pamphlets ever written, the *Letter to a Dissenter* and *The Anatomy of an Equivalent*, he earnestly implored them to harden their hearts against a Catholic bearing gifts. This freedom which they were promised was but the prelude to a harsher bondage: for 'these new friends did not make you their choice but their refuge. . . . The other day you were sons of Belial, now you are angels of light.' Let them, therefore, be mistrustful of this coming together of 'liberty and infallibility . . . the two most contrary things that are in the world.'

Secondly, while the Dissenters were ready to sacrifice the promise of immediate toleration for the prospect of toleration constitutionally granted by parliament in a remoter future, the Tory party abandoned its alliance with the Crown. James had loosened the two strongest props of his throne, the landed gentry and the Anglican Church; by threatening the rights of parliament and the integrity of the Protestant religion, he had reawakened the prejudices which had overwhelmed the Cabal in 1674. Whatever may have lain beyond it, his goal of toleration was a worthy one. Burnet spoke of liberty of conscience as 'one of the rights of human nature'; it was the ideal of the great Quaker William Penn; Locke justified it by appealing to human reason; in happier circumstances no one cherished it more dearly than Halifax. James failed because he associated the cause of toleration with armed Popery and unconstitutional government; and because that cause was distasteful to the men whose social and political interests were bound up with an exclusive and persecuting Anglicanism.[1] Thus his attempt to sway the elections collapsed before the obstinacy of the gentry. The Lords-Lieutenant and the magistrates were undeterred by threats that they would be dismissed: they resolutely refused to 'pre-ingage.' Seymour united the magnates of the West;

[1] Cf. Newcastle: 'There is no gentlemen but such as go to Church and hear Common prayer.'

in London the Tory Mayor and aldermen lost their posts ; with the loyal families of Astley, Stanley, Bertie and Finch, the Tory leaders deserted the Crown.

Sufficient evidence of his people's displeasure came to James to persuade him that the time was not yet ripe for summoning his parliament. Believing, however, that the Dissenters would support him if they knew what he had offered them, he determined to advertise his clemency : in May, 1688, he reissued his Declaration of Indulgence, with orders that it should be read on two successive Sundays in every church in the kingdom. Thus he drove the clergy into a dilemma from which they could not escape : either they must betray the principles of their Church, or they must resist their King. At length Archbishop Sancroft and six of the Bishops petitioned the King to revoke his order, on the ground that his use of the dispensing power had three times been declared illegal by parliament. James decided to take a strong line : by humiliating the leaders of the Church, he would show that he was not to be trifled with. Thus, while troops of Irish Catholics swelled the army at Hounslow, he proclaimed the petition to be ' a standard of rebellion,' and ordered the Bishops to be charged with seditious libel. On June 30th they were acquitted, and ' there was a most wonderful shout, that one would have thought the Hall had cracked ' ; it was an ill day for the monarchy when Presbyterian London was provoked to make heroes of Bishops.

2. *The Revolution*

On the day that the Bishops were acquitted, another seven met in Shrewsbury's house in London, and sent a formal invitation to William of Orange to land in England. For the past year several English politicians had been cautiously sounding William's attitude. In April, 1688, Admiral Russell went to the Hague ' to put upon the Prince to explain himself what he intended to do.' William was equally cautious. To the rights of the religious and constitutional conflict in England he was indifferent ; he thought only of the greater conflict in Europe, where the Dutch were defending their existence against Louis XIV. If, as King of England, he could draw his new people into the struggle, Louis might be defeated ; on the other hand, he could not afford to risk time or men or money in forcing himself on a country where he was not welcome. At first, therefore, he contented himself with declaring that, although religious tests should be maintained, he was in favour of a measure of toleration for Protestant Dissenters ; and even when James embedded himself more deeply in his stupidities, William would go no farther than to say that he would be ready to sail in the autumn if the ' most valued ' men in England assured him of their support.

In England opposition was slow to form. Discontent was general, but it is a long step from discontent to revolution ; the savagery of 1685 had made its mark upon the nation, and the formidable array on Hounslow Heath discouraged recklessness. But in June, 1688, a son was born to Mary of Modena, James's Catholic Queen.[1] Men saw before them an endless succession of Catholic Kings ; they might no longer reflect that the rigours which they suffered from James would vanish when his Protestant daughters succeeded him. The protest of the Bishops made rebellion possible, for the doctrine of non-resistance had been abandoned by the men who most strenuously upheld it ; their acquittal showed that the King could be defied. James had already lost the support of parliament, the universities and the gentry ; the Dissenters were deaf to his offers ; finally, the Church and the judges had deserted him, and even his soldiers had shown their sympathy with the Bishops. Three weeks after the birth of a Catholic heir had made revolution necessary, the trial of the Bishops showed that it was likely to succeed.

The seven men who invited William to sail represented no single party and no single interest ; Whig and Tory forgot their differences in the face of James's attack on their religion and their

[1] His first wife, Anne Hyde, died in 1671, leaving him two daughters, Mary and Anne. He married Mary of Modena in 1673.

political power. Devonshire, Russell and Henry Sidney were Whigs ; Danby and Bishop Compton were Tories ; Shrewsbury and Lumley, both converts from Rome, had both held office under James and his brother. Their invitation was cold and cautious ; success has made them heroes, but at the time they were just conspirators who might be caught. They gave William the guarantee which he needed : that ' nineteen parts out of twenty of the people ' would welcome his coming. If, therefore, ' upon a due consideration of all the circumstances, Your Highness shall think fit to venture upon the attempt . . . we, who subscribe this, will not fail to attend Your Highness upon your landing '. Warned by Louis of his danger, James tried to save his throne. He restored the magistrates whom he had dismissed, abolished his Ecclesiastical Court, and admitted the exiled Fellows back to Magdalen ; London was given a Presbyterian Mayor, the fleet was put under the command of a Protestant ; James even gave back all the municipal charters which had been annulled since 1679. But his repentance came too late, and no one could believe that it was sincere ; the English had learned to mistrust Stuarts who offered them concessions as plums are dangled before children. His offers of help rejected by James, Louis took his armies to the Rhine, and William was free to sail.

The Protestant winds carried him safely past the English fleet, and he landed at Torbay on November 5th. Even now James's cause was not lost. He had a loyal navy ; his army of 40,000 men was nearly three times as large as William's. But his greatest strength lay in the orderliness and conservatism of his people, in their reluctance to settle their quarrels by force. Whatever he had done in the past, the bulk of the nation still preferred him to the foreigner ; tradition, law, and national prejudice were on his side. If, therefore, he had, like William, promised to summon a freely elected parliament, and to abide by its decisions ; and if he had proved his sincerity by dismissing Catholics from his service, and particularly from his army ; then he would have won to his cause thousands who had scorned his promises before William had landed. For his cause grew stronger as the prospect of war drew nearer ; the anointed King could have saved himself from the Pretender if, like Charles II, he had appealed to the overwhelming majority of his people who preferred a peaceful settlement. But James did not give his supporters a lead ; he stubbornly refused to negotiate as long as there was a foreign army in the country. His indecision lost him his throne. While William lingered at Exeter, as ready to take to his ships as to advance on London, the magnates raised the militias against the Crown, and the courtiers and the leaders of the army deserted the King who had deserted them. For what, asked Rochester, ' can the most loyal and dutiful body in the world do, without a head ? ' James did not even fight. He might still have appealed to national sentiment against the foreign army which had invaded English soil, with Dutchmen, negroes, Swiss and Germans in its ranks ; and if he had stood his ground, it is unlikely that William would have risked his precious soldiers in a war which he could not be certain of winning. Instead, James solved the problem in the simplest way. He agreed to negotiate, when the cause of ' expedients ' was already lost ; and when this effort failed, he fled. By Christmas he was in France.

James's flight made it inevitable that William should be invited to be King. For with the county militias in arms, James's soldiers wandering unpaid about the country, and angry mobs burning Catholic houses and looting Catholic chapels, his Dutch troops were the only guarantee of order. A body of peers set up a provisional government in London, put the civil and military administration of the country in William's charge, and hastily issued writs for the summoning of a parliament. In this Convention, which met at the end of the year, the Tories vainly sought a constitutional formula which should reconcile their recent actions with their theory of non-resistance. Since James had fled, they could not again take refuge in ' limitation ' ; and they failed to carry a proposal to offer the crown to Mary and appoint William as her Regent. William joined with the Whigs in rejecting this solution. He had come to win England's resources for his war with France, and he refused to be made 'his wife's gentleman usher'; [1] unless he were offered the crown in full sovereignty with Mary, he would return to Holland and 'meddle no more in their affairs'. The perils of the interregnum enabled him to dictate his terms: if he withdrew his troops, the country would fall into anarchy and be almost defenceless against James and the armies of France. Thus the same necessity which had obliged the Tories to offer William temporary authority in December obliged them in February to make him their King. They had to agree that James had 'abdicated', that 'the throne is thereby vacant', and that William and Mary were the only suitable candidates to fill it.

3. *The settlement*

The Revolution of 1688 is important in the history of political thought for having vindicated the Whig theory of the constitution. In order to 'justify to the world the people of England', John Locke described in his *Essay of Civil Government* the theory of government which permitted Kings to be deposed. For convenience and efficiency society delegates power to an executive, whose duty is to preserve and respect their lives, their liberty and their estates. So long as the executive abides by this fundamental contract, it must be obeyed; but a government which violates the contract forfeits the allegiance of the people and may be removed. For revolution is the safeguard of law. Thus the nation had arrived at the utilitarian conception of monarchy which Selden had proclaimed a generation earlier. 'Never King dropped out of the clouds. . . . A King is a thing men have made for their own sakes, for quietness' sake. Just as in a Family one man is appointed to buy the meat. If every man should buy, or if there were many buyers, they would never agree.' The Whig theory was established without the shedding of blood because James's abdication tacitly admitted that it was true; if James had stood his ground, it would have been less easily

[1] Halifax.

asserted against the Tory theory that, although a bad King might be fettered and controlled, the principle of a hereditary and indefeasible succession was sacrosanct.

In constitutional details, however, the Revolution brought little change. James was the real revolutionary, for it was he who challenged the existing order ; the magnates who resisted him were merely restoring society as they knew it. James had refused to accept as final the Crown's defeat in 1641. First he tried to turn to the advantage of the Crown the Tory victory of 1681 ; then he made overtures to the tradesmen and Dissenters who were the nucleus of the Whigs. No one doubted that his object was to increase his own power and to force on the country an unpopular religion. Thus ' No Popery ' became the battle-cry of liberty in a wider sense. Whig and Tory combined to restrain the Crown within its constitutional limits, and to reassert the supremacy of parliament and the aristocracy ; the essence of their settlement was the restoration by parliament of the vested rights of property and religion which James had threatened.

The basis of the settlement was a Declaration of Rights which was drawn up by the Convention in December, 1688, and passed into law in the following year. The Declaration was prepared within a week, at a time when the country had no settled government. Thus it was not a moment for the elaboration of constitutional fancies, and the Declaration was no more than a rough and ready summary of the conditions which William and Mary must promise to observe before they could be offered the throne. First it enumerated the illegal actions of James : his standing army, his Ecclesiastical Court, the packing of parliament, the corruption of justice, his use of the suspending and dispensing power. The rest of its provisions were largely declaratory of existing law. It asserted freedom of speech in parliament and the subject's right to petition the King ; it forbade tampering with parliamentary elections ; it denounced ecclesiastical courts as ' illegal and pernicious ' ; the suspending power was forbidden altogether, and the dispensing power ' as it hath been assumed and exercised of late ' ; finally, the King was forbidden to levy excessive bail or excessive fines, to raise money ' by pretence of prerogative ', and to assemble an army in time of peace without the consent of parliament. The Bill of Rights made only two innovations. First, all subjects were required to take an oath of allegiance to William and Mary. Secondly, the throne must be occupied by a Protestant : the succession was vested in the heirs of Mary, in Anne and her heirs, and finally in William's heirs by another wife. England had reversed the principle of ' *cuius regio, eius religio* ' ; James had fallen, as Mary Stuart had died, for being a Catholic claimant to the English throne.

The framers of the Bill of Rights were largely content, therefore, with asserting the law as it existed ; they left the future to work out its own remedies for problems which they were reluctant to face. Thus, although they took steps to ensure that the King should be a Protestant, they avoided the pressing question of toleration ; they left the King free to appoint his own ministers, and did not insist that they should be responsible to parliament ; judges still held office during the King's pleasure ; the Crown's income was not fixed ; beyond a resolution that ' for redress of all grievances and for the amending, strengthening and preserving of the laws parliaments ought to be held frequently ', nothing was done to compel the King to summon regular meetings of parliament. These questions remained to be settled by practice, not by theory ; the Interregnum had bred an abiding mistrust of paper constitutions. After the Revolution, therefore, the Crown found itself in possession of considerable powers : certainly of greater powers than had been allowed to Charles I in the proposals submitted by the Long Parliament. The King was master of the royal household, of the colonies, the navy, and, in time of war, of the army ; he could choose his own ministers and conduct his own foreign policy. But in practice these powers were to be limited by the constant interference of a sovereign parliament. The importance of the Revolution of 1688 lies, not in the constitutional provisions which accompanied it, but in the sense that the King and his people had found a new relationship. The King had lost his indefeasible title to his throne ; he was the first servant of the sovereign people, and if he disobeyed his masters, he would be removed from his post.

In 1689, then, the King became a salaried official with definite tasks to perform. Henceforth the theory of Divine Right reflected only the common opinion that the Crown was necessary to the nation ; as Bolingbroke observed, the ' legal reverence ' due to the King became ' national and not personal '. During the reigns of William and Anne a series of laws and constitutional conventions restricted the Crown's power of independent action, and forced it to yield more frequently to the will of the sovereign legislature. The most important of these checks on the Crown's freedom of action was parliament's control of finance. William was granted a permanent income of £1,200,000, which, even when it was increased by temporary grants from the customs, was quite inadequate for his wartime needs. He was obliged, therefore, to make a concession which his predecessors had always resisted : he surrendered to parliament the right to control the expenditure of the money which it had voted. In 1690–1 the Commons appointed commissioners to audit the King's accounts and to supervise the expenditure of the taxes ; indeed, after 1697 parliament took full financial responsibility for the fighting services, which were no longer a charge on the royal revenue. Parliament even ventured to interfere with the use which William made of the hereditary domains of the Crown : he was compelled to revoke the grant of estates in Denbighshire which he had made to the Dutch Earl of Portland. He was forbidden, too, to distribute among his foreign favourites the lands confiscated from Irish rebels between 1689 and 1691.

By passing the Appropriation Act and the Mutiny Act, by which the government maintained discipline in the army, for periods of one year only, the Commons forced William to summon regular parliaments ; and the Triennial Act of 1694, which ordered a new election to be held at least every three years, prevented him from clinging for an indefinite time to a parliament whose subservience he had purchased by corruption. Parliament further established its supremacy by means of the ancient weapon of impeachment ; by setting up committees of members which took the direction of policy out of the hands of the ministers ; by a succession of Place Acts which excluded the King's servants from parliament ; and by the device of ' tacking ' controversial measures on to the routine bills which the King had to sign in order to carry on the government. The royal veto was not used after 1707 ; the Act of Settlement enacted that after the death of Anne the judges should hold office ' *quamdiu se bene gesserint* ', and could not be dismissed except by an address from both Houses ; the press was freed of the government's censorship when the Licensing Act expired in 1695 and was not renewed ; a Treasons Act in 1696 provided that a charge of treason must be upheld by at least two independent witnesses. The climax of parliament's authority over the executive was reached in the provisions of the Act of Settlement, in which the power of an alien King was restricted by a parliament in which none of his servants might sit, and by a Privy Council whose members must be Englishmen and were to be individually and jointly responsible for all the acts of the government.

By these means the King was made to realise that when he promised in his Coronation Oath to govern ' according to the statutes in Parliament ', and to preserve the Church ' as by law established ', he was swearing no idle vow. Moreover, his power would probably have been even more drastically reduced if the country had not been involved in two long and serious wars. William managed to save something of his royal authority because he was the nation's leader in the struggle with France. Success in this war was vital to William himself as a Dutchman ; but it was equally vital to the politicians who had brought him to the throne, since Louis had taken up the cause of the exiled James. Thus the nation could not afford to weaken its military strength by indulging in constitutional quarrels, and both William and his parliamentary opponents were ready to compromise for the sake of effective action abroad. During the French war there was, for the first time for a hundred years, a substantial harmony between an executive and a legislature united once more in a common purpose ; and in the eighteenth century, when the development of the cabinet and the party system settled the relationship between parliament and the ministry, this harmony was to become permanent. But the attack which parliament made on William between 1697 and 1701, in the interval between the two wars, hinted at the indignities which the Crown might have been made to suffer if the national emergency had not compelled the enemies of the prerogative to hold their hand.

The defeat of the Tories' King meant the defeat of the Tory monopoly of religion, for the Whigs were committed to reward the Dissenters for having resisted the blandishments of James. In order to unite the nation for the war against France, William was in favour of religious comprehension ; but national unity could not be achieved unless the Tories too were in some measure placated for the breakdown of their exclusive Anglicanism. Thus the religious settlement of the Revolution was a compromise between liberty and exclusiveness. The Tories were strong enough in the Convention Parliament to prevent the repeal of any of the penal statutes ; but they could not prevent the passing in 1689 of the Toleration Act, which granted freedom of worship to all who accepted thirty-four of the Thirty-nine Articles, made a declaration against Rome, and were prepared to acknowledge the Dutch King as head of the English Church. In effect, this measure relieved all but Papists and Unitarians [1] from the Conventicle and Uniformity Acts ; Dissenters might worship in their own assemblies and set up their own schools. But religious belief still involved civil penalties : the Test and Corporation Acts were still in force, and the Dissenters were still debarred from holding municipal office and from taking civil or military employment under the state.

Although the misnamed Toleration Act thus relieved them only partially from their disabilities, the lot of the Dissenters steadily improved. The war saved them from the persecution of Tory magistrates ; and when the leaders of the Church refused to take

[1] Quakers were allowed to make an affirmation.

the oath of allegiance to William,[1] the government appointed Latitudinarian, or Low Church, Bishops, who were willing to leave the Dissenters unmolested. In their days of power in the reign of Anne the Tories attempted to recover, by the Schism Act and the Act against Occasional Conformity, the monopoly which had been invaded, but the Whigs were loyal to their allies,[2] and the spread of Deism chilled the enthusiasms by which religious persecution is made possible. High Churchmen like Nottingham, who sighed for the rigid Anglicanism of a former age, ceased to be representative of Tory opinion ; the bulk of the party were content to accept as their leader Robert Harley, who had once been a Presbyterian.

[1] The 'Non-Jurors' included six of the seven Bishops who had resisted James.

[2] Addison's Tory Foxhunter complained that 'there is scarce a Presbyterian in the whole county except the Bishop'.

CHAPTER XXI

THE DEFENCE OF THE SETTLEMENT

Settlement of Scotland and Ireland. The King's war. Spanish Succession: the Whig war, the Tory peace. The Peace of Utrecht.

1. *The settlement of Great Britain*

In Scotland James's offers of toleration were received more warmly than in England. Since the Restoration, the Covenanters had had to endure the hated rule and discipline of Anglican Bishops, and they were ready to accept even the measure of relief which a Catholic King offered them. It did not, of course, persuade them to defend him in 1688; James's Catholic adherents put up a feeble resistance, and in Scotland the Revolution was principally an occasion for Covenanting mobs to fall to the ever-congenial sport of raiding Papist chapels and Bishops' palaces. But the Presbyterians were determined not to let their opportunity pass: the Convention Parliament, which offered William and Mary the throne of Scotland, presented them also with a 'Claim of Right', asserting that episcopacy was 'a great and intolerable grievance', and should be abolished. William's position was too precarious for him to insist fully on his rights. The inevitable Jacobite rising was easily subdued after Graham of Claverhouse had died in the hour of victory at Killiecrankie; but William, harassed by a serious rebellion in Ireland and anxious to take his part in the war against France, surrendered several of his prerogatives to the insistence of the Scots. With the fall of the Bishops the Crown lost its authority over the Scottish Church; and when it was denied the right to appoint the members of the Lords of the Articles, it lost too its control over the Scottish parliament.

Thus the House of Orange won recognition in Scotland only at a price: the Scots refused to have their religion and their policy dictated to them by ministers appointed in London. When the Act of Settlement vested the succession in the Electress of Hanover and her heirs, the Scots made a further and more serious gesture of independence. In 1703 the parliament at Edinburgh asserted in a General Security Act its right to choose Anne's successor in Scotland, if she should die without issue; and to ensure that the Act should be executed, the whole of the able-bodied population was to be formed into a national militia. Since the union of the crowns was the only link between the two peoples, it seemed that the growing friction between them must end in separation. The Scots had many causes of grievance against their neighbours. The Highlanders had neither forgiven nor forgotten the massacre of Glencoe, when Campbell of Glenlyon had murdered thirty-eight Macdonalds who were his hosts; the Presbyterians could not feel that the Kirk was permanently safe from Tory vengeance; and the whole nation was resentful because in commerce the English government persisted in treating Scotland as a foreign country. Prohibitive tariffs excluded Scottish goods from English markets, and the Navigation Acts forbade the Scots to share in the wealth of the colonies. Nor had the Scots been successful in their attempts to develop a colonial trade on their own initiative: a Scottish East India Company was being ruined by the jealousy of the English merchants, and a Scottish settlement on the Isthmus of Darien had collapsed because neither the English government nor its colonists in America would protect it from Spanish attack.

When the fury of the ruined investors was directed against the English connection, the rulers of England at length saw merit in the wise proposals of James I. If the Scots were to revive the 'auld alliance' with France, the Stuarts might be restored to England by the armies of Louis XIV; the safest escape from this danger was to approach the adjustable differences in a spirit of compromise, and to unite the two nations under a single government. The negotiations were long and delicate, for on both sides of the Border there were parties hostile to reconciliation on any terms; but in 1707 an Act of Union was finally piloted through the Scottish parliament. England and Scotland were to form the United Kingdom of Great Britain, and the succession to the throne was to be fixed by the provisions of the Act of Settlement. The Edinburgh parliament was to exist no longer, but forty-five commoners and sixteen elected peers were to represent their country at Westminster. So far the balance of advantage lay with England, but the English negotiators made substantial concessions to Scottish independence: England abandoned her commercial exclusiveness, and admitted the Scots to complete freedom of trade; the Scots were exempted from paying some of the taxes levied on Englishmen, and the government made a contribution of £398,085, partly to defray Scotland's national debt, and partly to compensate the investors in the Darien enterprise; finally, the Scots were allowed to preserve their own religion and their own legal institutions.

The Act of Union was a triumph of statesmanship and moderation—although it would be possible to applaud English statesmanship still more enthusiastically if the Act had been carried a hundred years earlier. The union was at first unpopular, while Covenanters, Anglicans, Jacobites and merchants feared that they had strengthened their rivals to their own irretrievable ruin; but fears and resentments soon passed away as the peoples of both countries settled down to a political and economic partnership which has enriched them both. Particularly, perhaps, has it enriched the Scots. 'Till the Union made them acquainted with English manners', remarked Dr. Johnson, 'the culture of their lands was unskilful and their domestic life unformed.'

In Ireland, however, the influence of old, unreasonable hatreds shaped a settlement which was barren of mercy or statesmanship.

In the years before the Revolution the wise and tolerant rule of Ormonde had sheltered the Irish from the full ferocity of the penal laws ; and then the policy of James and his Deputy, the Earl of Tyrconnel, had persuaded them that the time had come when they would be delivered from their Protestant masters. When the English rebelled against James, Tyrconnel kept his hold on Ireland. The native Catholics rose against the Protestants, and drove them to take refuge in Londonderry and Enniskillen ; a Catholic parliament decreed liberty of conscience, revoked all grants of land made to foreigners or Protestants since 1641, threw the English colonies open to Irish trade, and denied the English parliament any authority in Ireland. In March, 1689, a French fleet brought James II to Ireland to open his campaign for the recovery of his throne.

Thus William's first task was to crush the Catholic rebellion in Ireland ; before he could send his armies to the continent, he must meet Louis' attempt to attack him in his rear. By the end of 1690 the English had recovered Ireland as far as the Shannon : Londonderry was relieved after a siege of more than a hundred days, the garrison of Enniskillen defeated the Catholics at Newtown Butler ; after William's victory at the Battle of the Boyne, James fled again to France, and the capture of Dublin, Waterford, Cork and Kinsale deprived the French of their easiest landing-places. In 1691 the Dutch general Ginkel took Athlone, and occupied Galway after a victory at Aughrim. Finally, the Irish surrendered their last stronghold, at Limerick, on condition that the garrison should be allowed to go to France, and that Catholics in Ireland should have the same privileges which they had enjoyed under the lenient rule of Charles II.

Once Ireland had been subdued, the English government proceeded to break its word. Catholics were excluded from parliament and public life ; they were not allowed to possess arms, to buy land, to live within a corporate town, to own a horse worth more than five pounds, or to educate their children in any but Protestant schools. While the peasant paid his tithe to the Anglican Bishop, the law forbade him to celebrate Catholic holidays or to make pilgrimages to his holy shrines. Meanwhile, the merchants and manufacturers of England protected their interests by stifling Irish trade. While most of Ireland's available wealth poured into England in payments to absentee landlords and clerics, the people were forbidden to export cattle to England, or to send raw wool to the continent, where the European manufacturers were ready to pay high prices for it ; Irish shipping was hindered by the Navigation Acts ; finally, in 1699, the Irish were ordered to export their cloth only to England, where it could scarcely hope to surmount the formidable tariff by which the English manufacturers protected their home-made product. The most that can be said for the government's policy is that the enslavement of Ireland was effective. When Jacobite rebellions shook the Hanoverians on their English throne, the Irish did not dare to stir ; and while Scots and Englishmen grew rich and prosperous, most of the Irish starved.

2. '*King William's War*'

In 1686 the Emperor and the states of Germany had united in the League of Augsburg to resist the victorious aggression of Louis XIV. Three years later Holland and England joined the League, Spain and Savoy followed them, and the principal nations of Europe were knit into a Grand Alliance to protect themselves from France. As the war went on, and the English fleet and armies achieved no success to justify the heavy taxation which maintained them, Tory opinion turned against the continental commitments in which William had involved the country. The war was denounced as 'the King's war' ; William was accused of spending English money and English lives in a quarrel which affected him as Prince of Orange, but not as King of England. The landowners might grumble at the taxes, but it was vital to their interests that Louis should not overrun Holland and the Spanish Netherlands. The war was really

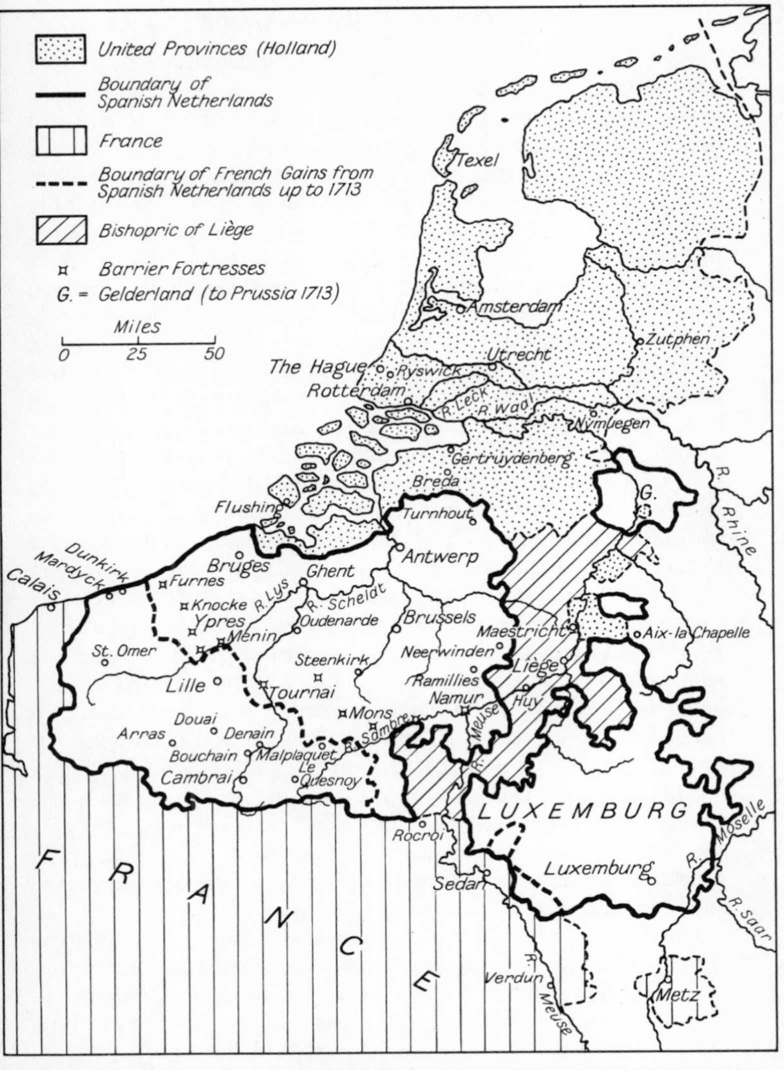

THE NETHERLANDS IN THE TIME OF WILLIAM III AND MARLBOROUGH

the war of English succession ; for if William were defeated on the continent, the French would be able to restore James to his lawful throne. As in the days of Elizabeth, England was still unable to resist an armada that sailed from Antwerp or the Texel.

England opened the war on the defensive, for the French were both sending help to the rebels in Ireland, and planning an invasion of England itself. In 1690 Louis equipped a large fleet under the command of Admiral Tourville. The Earl of Torrington, commanding the English and Dutch contingents, reluctantly gave battle off Beachy Head ; although he was undeniably defeated, and subsequently disgraced, he managed to keep his fleet in being. Thus Marshal Humières, who was waiting in Picardy with a large army, dared not risk the Channel crossing, and Tourville had to be content with a raid on Teignmouth. The day after Torrington's defeat in the Channel, William's victory on the Boyne turned the tide in Ireland ; and two years later Russell recovered the command of the sea by defeating a French and Jacobite expedition off Cape La Hogue. The battle dispelled the immediate fear of invasion and freed the navy from the more pressing anxieties of defence. Its work during the rest of the war, however, was undistinguished. It occupied itself mainly in skirmishes with the French privateers who preyed on English commerce, but its raids on their strongholds in Dunkirk, St. Malo and Dieppe had little effect ; it failed in 1693 to prevent Tourville catching and destroying the Smyrna convoy off Lagos ; and in 1694 it bungled an attack on Brest, partly because John Churchill elected to warn the French commander of its approach. Russell was the only English seaman to increase his reputation : in 1694–5 he heartened his Spanish allies by wintering in the Mediterranean and saving Barcelona from the French.

On land the war was fought on many fronts : in the Netherlands, on the Danube and the Rhine, in North Italy and Spain. English action was confined to the Netherlands, where an unexciting war of trenches and sieges dragged on through nine campaigns. Like his famous ancestor, William was an indifferent soldier, but a brave and tenacious leader. After a generation of peace the English had to learn again the very rudiments of war, and their inexperience drew out the best of William's qualities: during long years of defeat and disappointment he held together his wavering alliance, and turned his raw and unwilling recruits into the veterans who followed Marlborough to victory. As a soldier William was no match for his great opponent, the Marshal Duke of Luxemburg. One by one the towns of Flanders fell to the French advance; when William tried to resist it, he was routed in 1692 at Steenkirk and in the following year at Neerwinden. But in 1694, the sixth year of the war, the allies recovered the fortress of Huy. Luxemburg died in 1695, and Louis measured the loss of the French nation by creating eleven new Marshals to replace him; thereafter the English began to hold their own. In his greatest military achievement William reconquered Namur, and the French advance was checked.

Louis had been almost as successful on other fronts, but his treasury could not bear the strain of constant fighting in all corners of Europe. He wished, too, to devote all his ingenuity and resources to seizing a greater prize which lay within his reach. So in 1697 he made peace on terms which his enemies could welcome. In the Treaty of Ryswick he surrendered all that he had won since 1678, with the exception of Strasburg; he allowed the Dutch to safeguard their freedom by garrisoning the frontier fortresses in the Netherlands; and in recognising William as King of England, he promised that France would not give aid to England's enemies.

The treaty fulfilled the purposes for which England had entered the war: Holland was safe from Louis, and the English throne from James II. But the chief importance of the war was that it caused the government to adopt financial expedients which have been the basis of the nation's economy ever since. The total cost of the war was £40,000,000.[1] This sum was too large to be met either by the ordinary revenues of the Crown

[1] The interest on the debt exceeded the revenue of Charles II in 1660.

or by increased taxation, and in 1692 Charles Montagu, an enterprising Whig financier, suggested that a group of City merchants should lend the government a million pounds on the security of life-annuities to be paid out of future taxation. The payment of the interest thus became a permanent charge on the government, and an additional excise was imposed to guarantee the interest for ninety-nine years. In 1694 this device was carried a stage farther. The Whig financiers undertook to raise a sum of £1,200,000 and lend it to the government at 8 per cent. ; the subscribers formed themselves into a joint-stock bank which was known as the Bank of England. The Tories complained that Whig business men drew interest from the taxes contributed by the landowners,[1] but by the creation of a permanent national debt the government had at last solved the problem of raising a revenue adequate to its needs. Indeed, the Tories tried to counter the influence of the City financiers by setting up a Land Bank of their own, but they failed to raise the £2,564,000 which they had promised.

The foundation of the Bank immediately affected the course of the war. While Louis was paying 20 per cent. on his loans, the English government could borrow at low interest. The Bank raised the money for the campaign which recovered Namur, and it carried the country through a crisis caused by the over-issue of paper money ; in 1696 it was able to benefit the nation by calling in a debased coinage and issuing coins with milled edges which could not be 'clipped'. Finally, the creation of a permanent debt was fatal to the Jacobite cause. The government's creditors believed, not without reason, that if the Stuarts were restored, they would repudiate the debts of the usurper. Thus the financiers, whose power in the state was undermining the influence of the Tory landowners, were irretrievably committed to the exclusion of the Jacobites. Like the Reformation, the Revolution settlement had become a vested interest.

[1] A land tax of four shillings in the pound was a principal source of revenue.

3. *Spanish Succession*

Louis had made peace in 1697 because a greater contest lay before him. Charles II of Spain was dying, and with him the Spanish Hapsburgs would become extinct. By the influence of family ties the Spanish Empire would probably pass to the Austrian branch of the Hapsburgs, but Louis hoped to unite the rest of Europe to protest against so vast a disturbance of the balance of power,[1] and to persuade his neighbours by a display of magnanimity that part of the Spanish dominions would be safe in the keeping of France. Accordingly he abandoned his renewed plans for an invasion of England and acknowledged William's claim, and sought the goodwill of Spain by restoring Luxemburg, Catalonia and the French conquests in the Netherlands. For his part, William was anxious for peace, and he calculated that he could best serve Dutch and English interests by ensuring that neither Austria nor France should inherit the whole of the Spanish Empire. In 1698, therefore, England, Holland and France signed a secret Treaty of Partition. Naples, Sicily, Guipuscoa, and the Spanish ports in Tuscany were to go to the Dauphin; Milan and Luxemburg to the Archduke Charles, younger son of the Emperor; and Spain, the Netherlands and the Spanish colonies to the Electoral Prince of Bavaria, who was descended from Charles II's sister. The arrangement was a fair one, and William had done his part by insisting that only the outlying provinces of the Spanish Empire should fall to the Bourbons. In 1699, however, the Bavarian Prince died, and the partitioners had to start their work again. A second Partition Treaty allotted Spain, the Netherlands and the colonies to the Austrian Archduke, and added Milan to the portion of the Dauphin.

But the problem was not to be solved so easily. The Emperor, freed by the Peace of Carlowitz from the menace of the Turks, refused to accept a settlement about which he had not been consulted. Moreover, from his death-bed Charles II made a

[1] It would revive the Empire of Charles V.

spirited attempt to keep his Empire intact: he made a will leaving the whole of his dominions to Louis' grandson, the Duke of Anjou; and if Anjou would not accept them, they were to pass intact to the Archduke Charles. In 1700 Charles II died. Greed overcame Louis' caution: he broke his pledges to William, and proclaimed his grandson to be Philip V of Spain.

William would never have been able by his own efforts to persuade the English to oppose this settlement. Reassured by Louis' promise that the thrones of France and Spain should never be united, parliament preferred Charles II's will to William's treaties. The truculent Tory opposition fell upon the ministers who had allowed the King to conduct his own diplomacy; and the most that parliament would concede was a promise that if Louis invaded Holland an English army should go to its defence under the terms of the treaty of 1677. But if William could not make England aware of its danger, Louis could. The real author of the new Grand Alliance of 1701 was the King of France: by three gestures of calculated stupidity he stopped the Commons short in their pastime of baiting William, and won them to the policy for which they had lately rebuked their government. Suspicion was first awakened by the hostile movements of the French troops, who occupied Cologne and the Milanese, and began to expel the Dutch garrisons from the Netherlands. Then Louis and Philip closed their harbours to all imports from Great Britain; henceforth France was to enjoy special privileges in the trade of the Spanish Empire. At this moment James II died; and as a final act of folly Louis chose to proclaim his son, James Edward, as King of England. Louis' obvious intention to make effective the Bourbon alliance of France and Spain stirred the English from their apathy; William's 'Dutch' interests had again become English and European. While the outraged shopkeepers sought to free their trade from Louis' prohibitions, the magnates once more sank their differences in the common need to defend their settlement against foreign interference. The revocation of the

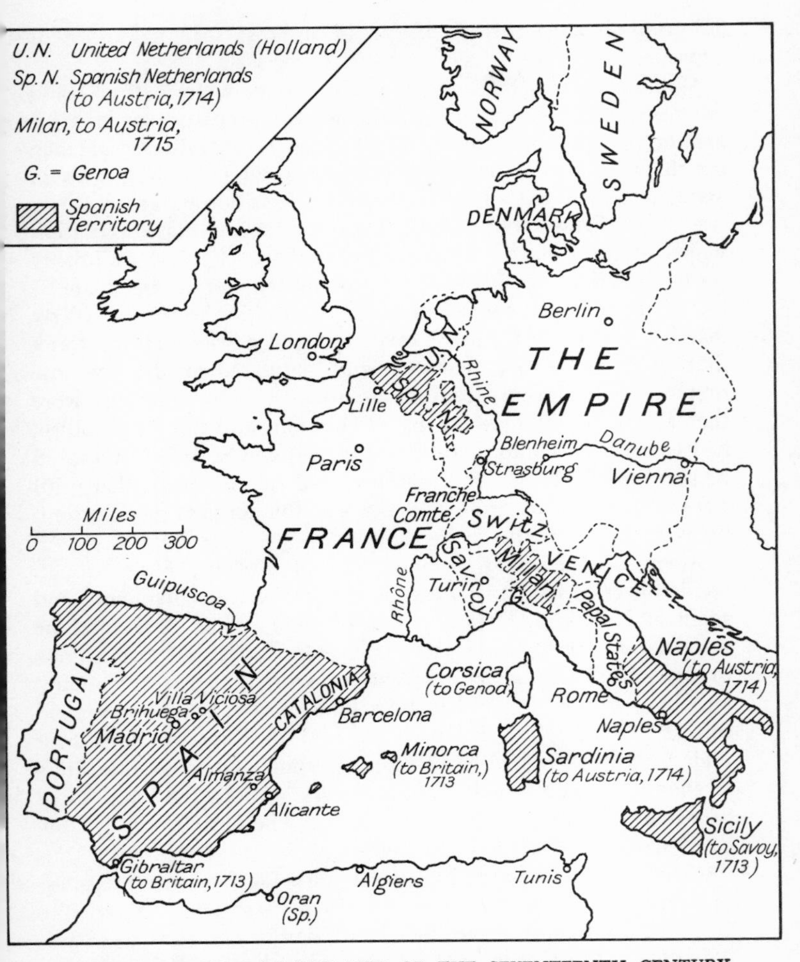

WESTERN EUROPE AT THE END OF THE SEVENTEENTH CENTURY

Edict of Nantes turned a war of interest into a Protestant crusade.

William's last service to his cause was to re-form the Grand Alliance; he died in 1702 while he was preparing to lead his armies to the continent. His place as commander was taken by the man whom he had selected: John Churchill, who in 1702 became Duke of Marlborough. Marlborough's greatness was more firmly founded than the somewhat easy reputation which attaches itself to successful soldiers. He was childishly mean, but that was his affair;[1] his loyalty was always suspect, but he lived in an age when political loyalties were not clearly marked and when frequent crises obliged a wise man to think first of himself. In character and temperament he was the first of the eighteenth-century aristocrats. His emotions were the servant of his reason; by calculation, and not by impulse, he saw what he could justifiably attempt, and what he attempted he accomplished. So well did his head rule his heart that until 1711, when he had prolonged the war for his own glorification, he was never on the losing side.

Alone of the great commanders of history, Marlborough seems never to have made a serious mistake. At Blenheim, and again at Ramillies, his early attacks were beaten back, and he won his victory by daring to change his tactics and dispositions in the confusion of battle. But he was more than a great general: an allied commander had to be a man of tact as well as a good soldier. Although the Dutch made him Captain-General of their forces, he had to endure the constant and irresolute interference of the unskilled 'field deputies' whom they appointed to watch over their armies in the field. The Dutch were waging a defensive war for the protection of their own territories; thus they viewed with alarm his march into Germany in 1704, his projected invasions of France, or his plan to take his army to Italy in 1706 and leave the Netherlands comparatively undefended. More than once Marlborough had to abandon some bold enterprise because the Dutch would not take their men

[1] And not Lord Macaulay's.

beyond the barrier fortresses. To add to his difficulties, he had to keep his eye on the political situation in England, where the Tories were always trying to lower his influence; and by courtesy, patience and good humour to weld his jealous and scattered allies into an effective fighting combination. It was not enough to win victories in the field; between his campaigns he hurried to London, The Hague, and the capitals of Germany, to interview diplomats, cajole politicians and encourage unsuccessful generals. Although most of his own fighting was done in the Netherlands, he attempted to co-ordinate every detail of the allied campaign, from the Emperor's operations on the Rhine to the English expeditions in the Mediterranean. Apart from all the other qualities which his task demanded, for a man in his fifties his conduct of the war was an astonishing feat of physical endurance.

As before, the maritime powers and the Emperor were the core of the Grand Alliance. The outbreak of war brought them several minor allies: some of the German states, notably Hanover, Brandenburg, the Elector Palatine, and Münster; the Catalans, who rose against the rule of the Bourbon; and the *Camisards*, the Huguenots of the Cevennes, who fought for their persecuted religion. In 1703, when the war was going ill, they won Portugal, an important ally on the flank of Spain; and they found the Duke of Savoy ready, as always, to sell his mountain passes to the highest bidder. Against this combination Louis failed to revive the traditional French alliance with the Turks, but he succeeded in rousing the Hungarians against the Emperor, and the important co-operation of the Elector of Bavaria allowed his armies to threaten Vienna from the heart of Germany.

The critical months of the war came at the end of 1708. By that time Louis had been beaten to his knees: his treasury was empty, his people were starving, and his despotism was breaking under the strain of defeat on every front. Marlborough's victories at Donauwörth and Blenheim had saved Vienna from invasion, and cleared the French from Germany; from that time the Bourbons had steadily fallen back before the pressure of the allies. At Ramillies and Oudenarde Marlborough had freed the Netherlands from the French, and he was relentlessly capturing the fortresses which guarded the road to Paris; Eugene's great victory at Turin had saved North Italy from the French and brought the Emperor to Milan; the Hungarians had been subdued; the English fleet had won a footing in Spain, and in Gibraltar, Sardinia and Minorca possessed bases for a sustained attack.

In 1706 Louis made proposals for peace in which he surrendered all the vital issues for which the allies had entered the war; his terms were refused, because the allies hoped to better them by continuing on their triumphant way. In the autumn of 1708 he renewed his offers: he agreed to abandon his grandson's claims in Spain, to expel the Pretender, to allow the Dutch to garrison the barrier fortresses, and to destroy the fortifications of Strasburg and Dunkirk. The allies greeted these offers with counter-proposals which suggested that they were happy for the war to continue, in the confidence that they were strong enough to compel Louis to submit to whatever they pleased to demand. The Emperor demanded Alsace; the Duke of Savoy insisted on extending his frontiers; and, led by the English Whigs, the allies required Louis to lend them active help in driving his grandson from Spain.

The English had entered the war to protect their interests; in 1709 they continued it in order to establish an Austrian Archduke on the throne of Spain. The government allowed itself to be carried away by the fascination of Marlborough's new strategy: by his plan to march on France from the Netherlands, Italy and the Rhine, while Spain was attacked from Portugal, Catalonia, and the naval bases in the Mediterranean. The allies paid the price of over-confidence: they had undertaken more than they could carry through. First, their new programme made a serious breach in the Grand Alliance. The Dutch, who never departed from the strictly defensive objects for which they were fighting, were unwilling to assist the

Emperor to realise his ambitions in Spain. Thus England had to forestall Louis by conceding them what they asked : a treaty was made in October, 1709, which allowed them to garrison as many as fifteen barrier fortresses, and to impose a tariff to the disadvantage of English and Austrian merchants. Secondly, the allies should already have learned that the conquest of Spain was beyond their power. In 1706 their armies had brought Charles for a few weeks to Madrid, but the French and the Spaniards had driven him out. The proud Castilians had no love for Philip as a Bourbon, but they fought for him as the symbol of the unity of their Empire ; in 1707 the Duke of Berwick, a natural son of James II, routed the allies at Almanza, and a few months later only Barcelona and Alicante still resisted the Bourbons.

The allies chose to neglect the lesson of Almanza, which should have been decisive. After 1708 none of their campaigns was successful. The threat of invasion, and the humiliating terms which had been offered to their King, spurred the French to a gallant defence of their freedom. At Malplaquet Marlborough won the last of his victories, but he left 22,000 of his men on the field. Elsewhere the allies failed : the French recovered Alicante ; an Austrian invasion was defeated in Franche Comté, and Berwick repulsed an attack from Piedmont. In 1710 Charles came again to Madrid, but he was driven out by French victories at Brihuega and Villa Viciosa ; at the beginning of 1711 the allies were so far from fulfilling their aims that only the Catalans denied the authority of Philip.

At the end of 1710 the Queen dismissed her Whig ministers, and called in the Tories to end a war which no longer served the interests of England. The fighting still continued, and Marlborough broke through the lines of *Ne Plus Ultra* and took Bouchain, but in 1711 the sudden death of his brother left Charles the ruler of the Hapsburg Empire. His accession strengthened the arguments of the peace party, who were able to underline the absurdity of fighting to add Spain to territories already so vast. Before the end of the year England signed the preliminaries of peace, and in 1712 a peace conference sat at The Hague even while the Dutch and the Austrians obstinately continued the war. With Marlborough dismissed and England bent on peace, the allies had to abandon their efforts; a heavy defeat at Denain, and the loss of Douai, Le Quesnoy and Bouchain, prompted them to end the war before further French successes encouraged Louis to stiffen his terms. Treaties were formally signed at Utrecht in the spring of 1713. England was ceded Nova Scotia, the Hudson's Bay Territory, Newfoundland, Gibraltar and Minorca; Louis abandoned the Pretender, and promised to destroy the fortifications of Dunkirk; and the English were granted the slave-trade with America and the right to send one ship a year to Portobello. Savoy received the Kingdom of Sicily, and Prussia was granted Spanish Gelderland; the Dutch had their barrier fortresses, though not so many as in 1709, and won some commercial privileges from the French. The Emperor satisfied his dignity by prolonging his efforts for another year, but at Rastadt in 1714 he accepted the terms which Louis and the Tories had arranged for him three years before: he received the Netherlands, the Milanese, Naples and Sardinia.

The settlement made at Utrecht has been criticised on two grounds: that the government shamelessly abandoned its allies, and that it concluded a glorious war on terms too lenient to the defeated. *Albion perfide* needed to have no regrets in abandoning the Dutch, the Emperor and the German Princes, who were strong enough to protect their interests; but she left her Portuguese ally almost unrewarded, she did not insist on an amnesty for the *Camisards*, and she allowed the Catalans to be reluctantly absorbed by Castile. The second charge, however, was unfounded: from the English point of view Utrecht was a good peace. The Tories gained all the essential objects of the war, and more besides. The expulsion of the Bourbons from Spain had not been one of England's original aims; and even if it had been, the unexpected accession of Charles to the Empire would have obliged wise men to abandon it. England had saved the Protestant succession, and her acquisitions in America and the Mediterranean had brought the commerce of the world within her grasp. Indeed, the Tories tried to end the tariff war with France, but their commercial treaty was defeated by the jealousy of the merchants ; thus for another seventy years the two countries refused to accept from each other even the goods which they could not produce themselves. Finally, the threat of a Bourbon hegemony in Europe had been faced and broken. Bankrupt and dispirited, France was no longer '*la grande nation*' ; Bolingbroke could justly tell Torcy that 'we are no longer afraid of you'. Holland had been saved, the independence of Spain was assured by the provision that her crown should not be united with France ; and if the French attempted in the future to extend their frontiers, they would find the Prussians facing them on the Lower Rhine, the Austrians on the Upper Rhine and in Italy, and the Dutch fortresses in the Netherlands. France was encircled by a barrier which only Napoleon was able to break.

CHAPTER XXII

THE GROWTH OF PARTIES

Whig and Tory. Parties under William. The Whig war and the Tory peace. The Tories and the succession.

1. *Whig and Tory*

English parties were born when the House of Commons divided over the Grand Remonstrance. In 1660 they had combined again to overthrow the army and the sects, and in 1688 to overthrow the King, but such issues as the Clarendon Code and the Exclusion Bill had emphasised the essential differences of interest and principle which divided the leaders of English society. As soon as William was established on his throne, the temporary unity of 1688–9 fell apart, and the two great parties once more faced each other in a struggle for control of the state.

The essence of Toryism was still respect for the Crown and reverence for the Anglican Church. Its principles, wrote Bolingbroke, were 'divine hereditary and indefeasible right, lineal succession, passive obedience, prerogative, non-resistance, slavery, nay and sometimes popery too'. Religion had been the fundamental issue in 1641, and it was still the essential test of party allegiance in 1690: in the manors and rectories from which the Tory party drew its personnel and its strength, thousands of loyal Anglicans instinctively recognised that if there were no parson, there would be no squire. Addison's Tory Foxhunter 'had scarce any other notion of religion, but that it consisted in hating Presbyterians', and although the Tory inn-keeper had no time to go to church, he 'had headed a mob at the pulling down of two or three meeting-houses'. The second fundamental of Toryism, the doctrine of non-resistance, had been permanently damaged in 1688 : the Tories had resisted the Crown and sacrificed the hereditary succession. Expediency had obliged them to accept William, at the expense of their principles. A sovereign who was prepared to favour their prejudices could still be sure of their support, and they made a brave show of reverence to Anne, who was the grand-daughter of Clarendon and a staunch upholder of the Church. In practice, however, the Tories acknowledged the Whig conception of utilitarian monarchy. Most of them were loyal to the Protestant succession, and feared the Stuarts more than they disliked the Whigs.

In Bolingbroke's analysis, ' the bulk of the landed interest ' were Tory : those ' possessors of the soil ', who in Swift's opinion were ' the best judges of what is for the advantage of the kingdom '. In the reigns of William and Anne the Tories were the party of peace, but that was only an accident of the struggle for office ; under Charles II they had been equally emphatic for war. But the feud of landowner and tradesman was deep and permanent ; next to religion, it was the most important issue of party conflict. The Foxhunter believed that ' trade would be the ruin of the English nation ', for it was trade and an expanding empire which had brought merchants and financiers to an influence which belonged by tradition to the landed interest. The Tory squires lamented in vain against the City financiers whose strength lay in the Bank of England and the national debt : England had become a land of shopkeepers.

The Whig party was made up, according to Swift, who disliked it, of ' heterogeneous, inconsistent parts '. It was strong among the Puritan yeomanry ; William's Low Church Bishops gave it a small majority in the Lords ; and its military aggressiveness commanded the loyalty of the army. Its chief strength, however, was founded on the Dissenters and free-thinkers whom it protected from the wrath of the Anglican Church ; and since the Dissenters throve on commerce, it had the support of the trading and financial classes. The Whigs, wrote Bolingbroke, were ' the remains of a party, formed against the ill-designs of the

Court under King Charles II, nursed into strength and applied to contrary uses by King William III, and yet still so weak as to lean on the Presbyterians, on the bank and other corporations, on the Dutch and other allies '. Their principles he defined as ' the power and majesty of the people, an original contract, the authority and independency of parliaments, liberty, resistance, exclusion, abdication, deposition '. But these seemingly popular principles did not imply any democratic aspirations. The Whig leaders were aristocrats, with a leaning, when fortune favoured them, to the excesses of the overmighty subject ; they were as prompt as the Tories to fall upon anything that smacked of Levelling, equality or the career open to talent.

In 1689 Englishmen did not expect to find in party government a solution of the outstanding constitutional problem of the seventeenth century, the problem of ministerial responsibility. Theoretically, the party system is indefensible. No single party has a monopoly of wisdom or honesty ; it should not, therefore, expect to have a monopoly of office. The statesmen who still respected the constitution—Halifax, Danby, Harley, Godolphin —tried to protect the Crown from party domination. ' The best party ', wrote Halifax, ' is but a kind of a conspiracy against the rest of the nation ' ; and ' I cannot forbear to put in a caveat against men tied to a party. Such a man can hardly be called a free agent, and for that reason is very unfit to be trusted with the people's liberty after he hath given up his own.' These suspicions were justified by Bolingbroke's confession of the spirit in which the Tories came to power in 1710. ' The principal spring of our actions was to have the government of the state in our hands ; our principal views were the conservation of this power, great employments to ourselves, and great opportunities . . . of hurting those who stood in opposition to us . . . and to fill the employments of the Kingdom, down to the meanest, with Tories.' Their enemies were equally unscrupulous : the Act of Settlement, which excluded office-holders from parliament and attempted to revive the authority of the Privy Council, was in effect a condemnation of the factious policy of the Whig Junto.

But neither an act of parliament nor the concern of conservative statesmen could stay the growth of party government. The constitution allowed the King to choose his own ministers and, beyond insisting that they should be Protestant, did not attempt to guide his choice. William therefore tried to select his ministers from both parties and to make professional competence, rather than party allegiance, the criterion of office. But the policy of 'men, not measures' failed in practice; 'mixed' ministries proved to be almost unworkable. Ministers of different political opinions did not easily work together, and were more inclined to serve their party than to support the King; moreover, ministers of one party were attacked in parliament by the adherents of the other, and debates in the Houses passed beyond the government's control. In the years after the Treaty of Ryswick a ministry consisting of Whigs and Dutchmen was helpless against a Commons dominated by the Tories. Eventually, therefore, in spite of the obstinate resistance of William and Anne, the Crown had to fall in with a suggestion first submitted by Sunderland: that government would be more easily carried on if the ministry were selected from the party which had a majority in the House of Commons.

Although the King was thus unable to do without parties, parties could not do without the King. The Crown was the source of all honour in the state: it distributed salaries, sinecures and pensions, it appointed the members of the royal household and the officials of state, it controlled promotion in the army, the navy, the colonies and the Church, and it could secure the election of a solid block of members to parliament.[1] Thus no party could succeed unless it stood in favour at court and could wield in its interests the vast 'patronage' of the Crown. The long triumph of the Whigs in the eighteenth century was founded on the goodwill and co-operation of the first two Hanoverian

[1] Governments supported by the Crown rarely lost an election. In fact, elections tended to follow, rather than precede, ministerial changes.

Kings; and when George III descended into the political arena, he showed what vast authority the Crown might still possess if the King were a good parliamentarian. In their humbler way, both William and Anne used their power to protect the country from the worst results of party despotism. William saved the Tories from a Whig vengeance in 1690, and the Whigs from the Tories in 1701; Anne thwarted a Tory attempt to revive religious intolerance during the crisis of a war, dismissed the Whigs when they prolonged that war for selfish motives, and on her death-bed saved the Protestant succession from the conspiracies of the Tory extremists. Thus they anticipated what has become the chief constitutional function of the Crown: to intervene in politics only when party factiousness jeopardises the national interests. William IV used his prerogative to carry the Reform Bill in 1832; it was used again in 1911, when the Crown assisted the Liberals to cripple the House of Lords.

2. *Parties under William*

Early in his reign William showed that he would not permit the unity of his people to be distracted by party bitterness. In 1690 the Whigs attempted to turn to their advantage their majority in the Convention: they introduced a Corporation Bill, to exclude from municipal office for seven years the men who had advised and carried through the surrender of the borough charters under Charles II. William therefore dismissed the Convention, and in the new parliament he carried an Act of Grace which gave a comprehensive pardon for all political offences. Until 1694 William governed through a 'mixed' ministry which, under the leadership of Danby,[1] had at first a predominantly Tory flavour. But he found the Tories unsatisfactory instruments for the conduct of a war: they were jealous of the Dutch favourites—Portland, Keppel, Athlone—to whom alone he gave his real confidence, but as war ministers they

[1] Danby was made Marquis of Carmarthen in 1689 and Duke of Leeds in 1694.

were half-hearted and unsuccessful, and their followers in the Commons complained of the heavy taxation. Further, the death of Mary in 1694 weakened Tory allegiance to the Crown. Since the Tories had failed him, William was obliged to call in the Whigs, who had already undertaken to finance his war and were willing to conduct it with enthusiasm and efficiency. Somers and Trenchard entered the ministry in 1693, Shrewsbury, Montagu and Russell in the following year ; Godolphin was the only Tory to survive, for his financial skill made him indispensable.

When William called in the Whigs, he sacrificed much of his independence : he needed Whig money and Whig votes, and he had to pay the price in subservience to the all-powerful Junto. The Whig leaders, the Junto of Wharton, Somers, Montagu and Russell, mobilised the party of magnates and merchants which Pym and Manchester had created, and forced it on the helpless King by the sheer weight of its financial and political influence. It performed considerable services for the nation : it financed and won the war, withdrew a debased coinage, and solved for ever the problem of raising an adequate revenue ; it passed a Treasons Act and abandoned the censorship of the press ; and when the Jacobites plotted William's death in 1696, the Whigs displayed the country's firmness for the Protestant succession by organising a National Association to protect him, and by enacting that parliament should sit for a further six months when he was dead. Some of their actions, however, were dictated by less exalted motives of vengeance and personal profit. They tried to impeach Danby, the leader of their enemies ; they tried to make their National Association a test for the holding of office ; they used the weapon of attainder against a Jacobite conspirator, because his confessions were damaging to certain members of the ministry ; and in the interest of the moneyed classes they wrecked the Scottish Darien Company and ruined the Irish woollen trade.

With the coming of peace the power of the Junto began to decline. They weakened themselves by personal divisions, and in particular by their mistrust of Sunderland's influence with the King ; when the war was over, their financial resources were less important to the Crown ; and they were harassed by a growing party in the Commons whom their high-handedness had driven into opposition. The leader of this opposition was Robert Harley, formerly a Presbyterian and a Whig. Gathering about him the Tory minority and the malcontent Whigs, Harley assembled a party which, although it bore the label of Tory, departed from many of the traditions of Cavalier politics. It was founded less on principle than on opportunism : its purpose was to assert the independence of parliament against the Junto and its exorbitant influence at the court. Thus in its methods and objects it recalled the country party which Shaftesbury had formed in the days when the court had been the preserve of the Cavaliers. Many of these objects it would forget when the turn of the tide brought it into office ; but the permanent importance of Harley's work was that he put himself at the head of a new and combative Toryism which rejected the Jacobite intrigues of the Non-Jurors and accepted the sovereignty of parliament. Although Nottingham still embodied the Cavalier tradition, and the Foxhunter had ' always been for passive obedience, and shall be always for opposing a prince who makes use of ministers that are of another opinion ', the aim of the Tories would henceforth be to bind the executive to the will of parliament. The autocracy of the Junto forced the Tories to accept the principles of the Revolution.

The elections of 1698 recovered for the country party the majority which they had lost in 1695. If William had been prepared to accept the party system, he would have called the Tories into office and saved himself some of the humiliation which followed ; but apart from various changes in personnel, he kept his Whig ministry in power. The Commons fell ruthlessly upon the prerogative. Reviving the old cry against a standing army, they compelled the King to send away his Dutch Guards, and reduced the numbers of the army to 7,000 men ; they carried a bill to investigate the grants of Irish land to Dutch favourites, and vested the land in parliamentary trustees ; they challenged the King's prerogative in the conduct of foreign policy, and arraigned the ministers who had assisted him to draw up the Partition Treaties with France. Finally, the death of the Duke of Gloucester, Anne's last surviving child, gave conservatives of all denominations the opportunity to express in a statute their alarm at the heavy expenses of government, the military enterprises of a foreign King, and the high-handedness of ministers.

The chief business of the Act of Settlement was to protect the Protestant succession in a new emergency. Since neither Mary nor Anne left an heir to the throne, the statesman of the Revolution had to look elsewhere for a suitable candidate. They chose the Princess Sophia, Dowager Electress of Hanover,[1] who was a descendant of the marriage between Elizabeth Stuart and the Elector Palatine ; and they decided to improve the occasion by passing measures for ' better securing the rights and liberties of the subject '. As originally devised, the Act of Settlement provided that, after the death of Anne, no war should be undertaken without the consent of parliament ; that the sovereign should not leave the country without his subjects' approval ; that no foreigner should sit in the Council or parliament, hold office in the army or the state, or receive grants of land from the Crown. The Act made a last attempt to assert the authority of the Privy Council over the informal cabinet of ministers whom the King chose to consult ; for the Commons had lately found it difficult to bring responsibility home to culpable or unpopular ministers. They decided, therefore, that all matters cognizable by the Council should be transacted there, and that all its members should affix their signatures to resolutions of which they approved. A final blow at the government was a provision that judges should no longer hold office during the King's pleasure, and that no man who held a pension or an office of profit under the Crown should be eligible to sit in parliament.

[1] As well as James II's son, the Catholic Duchess of Savoy had a superior claim.

Thus Sophia and her descendants were to be made to pay for the unpopularity of William and the Junto. The constitutional clauses of the Act of Settlement were the greatest triumph of the phalanx of country gentlemen, traditionally conservative and suspicious, who came to every parliament in a spirit of hostility to the court. But their work was merely obstructive ; if their proposals had remained on the statute-book, no ministry would have been able to function. By 1714 most of their provisions had been repealed, for the Tories discovered, when they came to power, that the measures which they had passed in opposition would deprive them of the lawful perquisites of office. It was impossible, too, to revive the authority of the Privy Council. The cabinet provided a necessary link between the legislature and the government, and the constant criticism of a vigorous opposition guaranteed that power would not be abused.

3. *The Whig war and the Tory peace*

The follies committed by Louis in 1701 spared William from further parliamentary attack. The justices and freeholders of Kent petitioned the Commons to suspend their factious wrangling and vote supplies for the defence of the country ; and although the Commons asserted their offended majesty by voting the petition to be an outrage, and ordering the arrest of its authors, William correctly judged that it expressed the will of the people. Accordingly he dissolved the parliament which had been elected earlier in the year, and appealed to the nation. The new parliament was still predominantly Tory, but the members were pledged to war and the support of the King.

For the next three years the war was directed by another ' mixed ' ministry, an uneasy coalition of Whigs and Tories whose Tory members—Rochester, Seymour, Harley, Nottingham—found their position becoming steadily more embarrassing. They were able to abandon the anti-monarchical rôle which they had adopted when the King was at the mercy of the Junto, but they had to work in circumstances essentially uncongenial to them. As before, they were not the party to conduct a war. War meant standing armies, which they hated; and it was necessarily to the profit of the 'usurers and stockjobbers' who had already entrenched their power in the Bank of England and an everlasting debt. Thus the Tories lost ground by their half-hearted co-operation in the work of the Grand Alliance. Their suggestion that England's share should be confined to naval and colonial enterprises was unimpressive after Blenheim had justified military operations on the continent; and their only reply to Blenheim was to lavish exaggerated praises on Admiral Rooke for his successful defence of Gibraltar, and on the Earl of Peterborough for his capture of Barcelona. Their campaign was quite ineffective: they failed to prevent parliament from voting supplies for further enterprises in Europe. Moreover, it lost them the support of Marlborough and Godolphin, who had been regarded hitherto as moderate Tories. Marlborough was not a party man. 'All parties are alike', he said, 'unreasonable and unjust'; he vowed that he would have as his friends only 'such as will support the Queen and the government'. But at that time the Queen's government meant the Duke of Marlborough's war, and he was thrown into the arms of the men whose interest in the war was wholehearted.

The Tories completed their ruin by choosing this moment to revive religious differences. The Dissenters had fallen into the practice of evading the Clarendon Code by occasionally taking the sacraments of the Church of England. Three times the Tories sought to stop this gap in the Anglican fortress by introducing a bill against Occasional Conformity; and each time their enemies accused them of trying to weaken the nation in the hour of military emergency. In 1705 the coalition broke up. Although Anne's personal preference was for the Tories, the Duchess of Marlborough was her intimate friend; and she was forced to yield to the argument that the war would be more efficiently conducted by a ministry which was united in its aims. So she reluctantly entrusted her government to the new Whig Junto, led by Somers, Orford,[1] Wharton, Halifax [2] and the third Earl of Sunderland. In 1708 a threat of collective resignation persuaded Harley to give up his office, and the ministry became exclusively Whig.

Once more, however, Harley showed himself to be a skilful leader of opposition. He hired Defoe and Swift to use their literary gifts to ridicule the government ; through the commonplace Mrs. Masham he countered the Duchess of Marlborough's influence over the Queen ; and once more he stirred the animosities of the independent country gentlemen against a government controlled and abused by the triumphant Whigs. His enemies played into his hands by protracting the war. After 1708 the war did not serve the nation's interest ; it was continued for the glorification of Whig generals, and for the reward of the 'moneyed men . . . whose perpetual harvest is war, and whose beneficial way of traffic must very much decline by a peace '.[3] The people grew tired of paying taxes for these somewhat limited purposes, and came to look on the Queen as another Royal Martyr in the hands of an army and an unscrupulous parliament. Anne herself was anxious to escape from the dominance of the Whigs : 'Whoever of the Whigs thinks I am to be hectored or frightened into a compliance is mightily mistaken in me.' In 1710 the ministry attempted to impeach an ineffectual divine, named Sacheverell, for a sermon in which he revived the doctrine of non-resistance and denounced the Whigs as enemies of the Church. The affair provoked an agitation quite beyond its merits ; and Anne learned from a spate of pamphlets and the demonstrations of the London mob that she might safely dismiss her ministers.

The nation upheld her decision. At the elections the Crown made skilful use of its influence, and the Tories were returned in overwhelming numbers to negotiate a peace. The Whigs tried to save themselves by appealing to the Dutch and the

[1] Formerly Admiral Russell. [2] Formerly Charles Montagu.
[3] Swift, *Conduct of the Allies.*

Austrians, and Eugene came to England to urge the government to continue the war. In the Lords the Whigs found unexpected allies : in return for passing the Act against Occasional Conformity, they persuaded Nottingham and the High Churchmen to vote against the peace. But they could not fight against a party which had the Crown on its side. Anne exercised her prerogative to create twelve peers to carry the peace in the Upper House, and the Whigs were left to console themselves with Wharton's mocking enquiry whether the twelve would register their votes singly or through a foreman.

4. *The Tories and the succession*

Once they had carried the peace, the Tories had to taste the disadvantages of divided purposes and divided leadership. Two men, Harley, now Earl of Oxford, and Henry St. John, Viscount Bolingbroke, struggled to win the leadership of the party and to guide its destiny according to their individual inclinations and temperament. Harley was an experienced politician, cautious and accommodating, and taught by his own successes as leader of an opposition how easily a ministry might abuse its power and provoke the formidable resentment of the country gentlemen. Harley, in fact, was not altogether a party man. He believed that the Crown, and not a party junto, should be ' the centre of power and union ' ; even a Tory majority alarmed him, and he was so overwhelmed by the exuberance of his own supporters in 1710–11 that he vainly implored some of the Whig ministers to remain in office. His rival Bolingbroke was less experienced and less discreet ; he had a good mind, but his character was too unstable, and his nerve too irresolute, to fit him for the leadership of a great party in the critical years which lay ahead. Bolingbroke betrayed the Tories into a policy which was to exclude them from power, and almost to end their independent existence, for nearly half a century.

In the October Club Bolingbroke put himself at the head of the Tory extremists who were impatient of Harley's moderation.

In their opinion, 1681 was come again: the Tory majority should be used to identify the state once more with the interests of the Anglican Church and the landed classes, and to eradicate such temporary features of the Revolution as toleration, the influence of the moneyed men, standing armies and a permanent debt. The Act against Occasional Conformity was a start in this direction, and Bolingbroke's faction followed it with a measure to impose a high property qualification on members of parliament; with a Stamp Act, which enabled the government to silence its critics by means of a heavy duty on journals and pamphlets; and with an act to check the immigration of foreign refugees, who would occupy themselves in trade and give their votes to the Whigs.

The elections of 1713 strengthened Bolingbroke's majority, and encouraged the October Club to begin to play a dangerous and fatal game. Bolingbroke knew that his time was short: his attempt to revive the old, intolerant Toryism, divested of the half-hearted malcontents whom Harley had recruited from the Whigs, depended on the life of the Queen. The Whigs had been assiduous at the court of Hanover, and when Anne was dead the Tories could expect little favour from her successor. Bolingbroke was an opportunist and a man without principles: there can be no doubt that he would have repealed the Act of Settlement if he had been able to persuade parliament and the nation to support him. But the Jacobite cause had two fatal weaknesses: the government's creditors feared that they would lose their money, and the Pretender was an obstinate Catholic. When the Tories approached him, he damaged his chances beyond repair by promising nothing better than a 'reasonable security' for the Protestant religion. It is unlikely, therefore, that Bolingbroke contemplated a scheme so hopeless and irresponsible as a restoration of the Stuarts and an attack on the Protestant succession. His object, as he later confessed, was to fill every important office in the kingdom with Tories, in the hope that the new King would not venture to remove them. He hoped that the Tory monopoly of office, 'joined to the advantages of our numbers and our property ', would make the party ' too considerable not to make our terms in all events which might happen afterwards : concerning which, to speak truly, I think few or none of us had very settled resolutions '. The Tory conspiracy had no precise aims, for Bolingbroke was an opportunist who liked to wait on events ; but its general purpose was to occupy the vital strongholds in the Church, the army and the state in such overwhelming strength that the Hanoverians would be forced to keep the Tories in office.

In 1714 Bolingbroke won the Anglican diehards to his side by passing the Schism Act, which decreed that only members of the Church of England might teach or keep a school. Meanwhile, he persuaded the Queen to appoint his followers to all the important military posts ; and he won his last success when he bullied her into dismissing the temporising Harley from his office. Five days later Anne was dead ; but in her last hours she confounded Bolingbroke's hopes by selecting as Harley's successor in the Treasury, not Bolingbroke, but the ' trimming ' Duke of Shrewsbury. Bolingbroke had gone too far. His real motives were misunderstood, and his policy was interpreted as an attempt to restore the Stuarts. The Whigs defeated him over the Council-table by urging the Queen to come to the defence of her Church. In the crisis his nerve failed him and he fled to Europe ; without enthusiasm and without resistance the people watched the arrival of the Elector of Hanover, the unimpressive token of their resolve that only Protestants should rule in England.

In 1727, when the second Hanoverian King succeeded quietly to his father's throne, the statesmen of England could feel that what they had won by their Revolution was theirs to enjoy in a calm and settled future. They had defended their constitutional settlement against the attack of France, and they had crushed a Jacobite rising ; they had survived a financial crisis and the fury of thousands of ruined gamblers ; the Riot Act was in some measure a guarantee of order, the Septennial Act of a parliament which bribery could cajole into acquiescence. In this unfamiliar security they had leisure to ask themselves what the country had gained from the struggles of the past two hundred years.

In 1485 England was an unimportant island lying off the northern coast of Europe, notable on the continent only for the ferocity and persistence with which its inhabitants periodically poured across the Channel into France. The Tudors found this island in the grip of profitless dissensions which had broken its peace, hindered its commerce, and destroyed its ruling class. They brought to it the strong hand of an orderly, peaceful government; they encouraged its people to take to the sea and carry their commerce to distant lands; under their guidance the country threw off the dominion of the Pope, chose its own religion, and defended its independence against the Counter-Reformation and the strength of Hapsburg Spain. In all this the Crown was the leader and the servant of the nation; and the Tudors showed the people how to be strong enough to want to undertake the responsibilities of government for themselves. In the struggle which followed only one result was possible. The tasks of administration had become too complex for one man and his chosen servants to perform; the gentry of England were rich and enterprising, and they had been matured by the service which the Tudors had asked of them. Thus, for the sake of efficiency, supreme power in the state had to pass from the Crown to the political and economic leaders of the nation. In the long and bitter struggle men called on false gods to sanction what they did: when power is being grasped by a ruthless oligarchy, freedom is an incongruous label to attach to the process. By the opening years of the eighteenth century the work was done. An indisputably Protestant England had discovered the wisdom and humanity of religious toleration; commercial settlements in five continents heralded England's bid for the markets of the world; and an unassailable government, in which the King was a puppet and a figurehead, had the power to arm and discipline the people of a united commonwealth for the destined pursuit of imperial and economic glories.

When so much was gained in the way of material efficiency, it may seem irrelevant to point to what was lost. The landowners and plutocrats who had established their claim to be the new rulers of England had too little sense of the obligations which their eminence required of them. Whatever may be the faults of an autocratic monarchy, the King must always realise that his interest and the nation's are one ; when the monarchy had been humbled, a distinction began to appear between the interests of the nation and the personal interests of the ruling classes. The idle pretence that the members of the government were the chosen representatives of the people was unavailing in a country whose rulers argued that poverty was an affliction which God had inexorably chosen to lay upon most of His children ; the sovereignty of the people was a theory which the oligarchy followed only so far as it excused their own usurpation of an authority which had formerly been exercised in the interests of the nation as a whole. The unanswerable charge against the new rulers of England is that they forgot that power carried with it responsibilities as well as rewards. Beneath the fastidious civilisation which was the pride of the eighteenth century lay the helplessness of a diseased and ignorant rabble ; on the other side of a Gainsborough portrait is painted a picture of Hogarth's London.

APPENDICES

ENCLOSURES IN ENGLAND, 1485-1607

The map on page 67 is based on an analysis by E. F. Gay (*Quarterly Journal of Economics* (1903), vol. XVII, no. 4) of the commissioners' returns in the only two Inquisitions of which any substantial records are known to exist: those of 1517–19 and 1607. The first of these has been published in *The Domesday of Inclosures*, edited by I. S. Leadam (1897), and covers twenty-three counties; the second, preserved in the Record Office, is confined to six counties, but these are all in the Midlands, where enclosing activity was greatest. The returns are summarised in the following table. Each commission is taken to cover a retrospective period of some thirty years, leaving a space of sixty years between them. On the assumption that in these sixty years the rate of enclosing was at least equal to that of the earlier period, Gay doubles the known acreage, or for the counties included in both earlier and later returns he takes the sum of the two. To complete the gaps in the 1607 return he repeats the figures for 1517, and obtains the following conjectural results. The purely inferred totals are shown in italics.

It is obvious that figures arrived at in this way are only hypothetical, and they must not be made to carry too much weight. Nevertheless they probably bring us nearer to the facts than the allusions and complaints which are scattered through contemporary literature.

County	Enclosures (acres)				Percentage of County area enclosed
	1485–1517	1518–1577	1578–1607	Total	
Hunts.	7,677½	15,355	7,677½	30,710	13·17
Northants.	14,081½	41,417	27,335½	82,834	13·02
Oxon.	11,831	23,662	11,831	47,324	9·90
Beds.	4,137	14,141	10,004	28,282	9·37
Bucks.	9,921	16,998½	7,077½	33,997	7·12
Leics.	5,780½	18,071	12,290½	36,142	6·81
Middlesex	2,236½	4,473	2,236½	8,946	6·08
Berks.	6,392	12,784	6,392	25,568	5·57
Warwick	9,694	15,067	5,373	30,134	5·23
Notts.	4,470	8,940	4,470	17,880	3·33
Norfolk	9,334	18,668	9,334	37,336	2·86
Rutland	531	1,062	531	2,124	2·19
Gloucs.	3,681½	7,363	3,681½	14,726	1·84
Lincoln	4,866½	9,733	4,866½	19,466	1·15
Cambs.	1,402	2,804	1,402	5,608	1·02
Hereford	1,185	2,370	1,185	4,740	0·88
Salop	1,859	3,718	1,859	7,436	0·87
Yorks., N.R.	2,503	5,006	2,503	10,012	0·74
Yorks., E.R.	1,384	2,768	1,384	5,536	0·74
Essex	1,248	2,496	1,248	4,992	0·51
Yorks., W.R.	1,837	3,674	1,837	7,348	0·42
Hants.	1,035	2,070	1,035	4,140	0·39
Derby	620	1,240	620	2,480	0·38
Staffs.	538	1,076	538	2,152	0·29
Somerset	660	1,320	660	2,640	0·25
Cheshire	65½	131	65½	262	0·04

LISTS OF CONTEMPORARY RULERS

1. *The Papacy*

1484 Innocent VIII
1492 Alexander VI (Borgia)
1503 Pius III
1503 Julius II
1513 Leo X (Medici)
1522 Adrian VI
1523 Clement VII (Medici)
1534 Paul III (Farnese) (*d.* 1549)
1550 Julius III
1555 Marcellus II
1555 Paul IV (Caraffa)
1559 Pius IV (Medici) (*d.* 1565)
1566 Pius V
1572 Gregory XIII
1585 Sixtus V
1590 Urban VII
1590 Gregory XIV
1591 Innocent IX (*d.* 1591)
1592 Clement VIII
1605 Leo XI
1605 Paul V
1621 Gregory XV
1623 Urban VIII
1644 Innocent X
1655 Alexander VII
1667 Clement IX (*d.* 1669)
1670 Clement X
1676 Innocent XI
1689 Alexander VIII
1691 Innocent XII
1700 Clement XI (*d.* 1721)

2. *The Holy Roman Empire*

1493 Maximilian I
1519 Charles V
1558 Ferdinand I
1564 Maximilian II
1576 Rudolf II
1612 Matthias
1619 Ferdinand II
1637 Ferdinand III
1658 Leopold I
1705 Joseph I
1711 Charles VI (*d.* 1740)

(All of the House of Hapsburg)

3. *France*

Valois :
1483 Charles VIII
1498 Louis XII
1515 Francis I
1547 Henry II
1559 Francis II
1560 Charles IX
1574 Henry III
Bourbon :
1589 Henry IV
1610 Louis XIII
1643 Louis XIV (*d.* 1715)

4. *Spain*

Ferdinand of Aragon (1479–1516) *m.* Isabella of Castile (1474–1504)
1516 Charles I (Emperor Charles V, 1519)
1556 Philip II
1598 Philip III
1621 Philip IV
1665 Charles II
1700 Philip V of Bourbon (*d.* 1746)

5. *Scotland*

1488 James IV
1513 James V
1542 Mary
1567 James VI (James I of England)

GENEALOGIES

1. THE HOUSE OF TUDOR

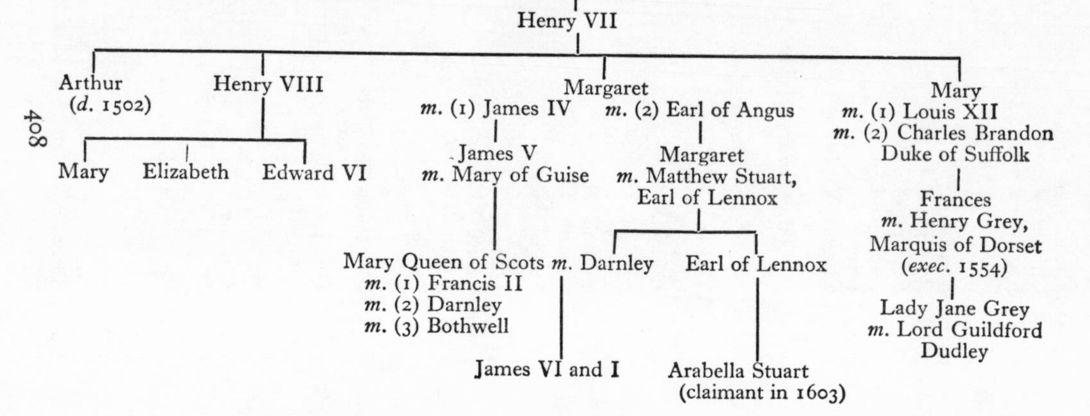

2. THE YORKIST CLAIMANTS TO THE THRONE

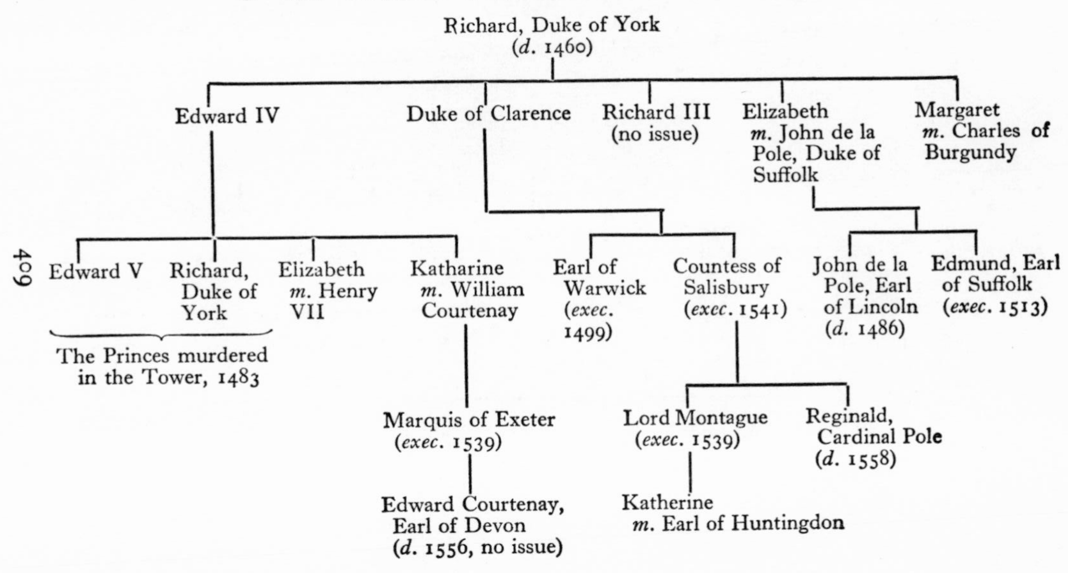

3. THE ENGLISH SUCCESSION

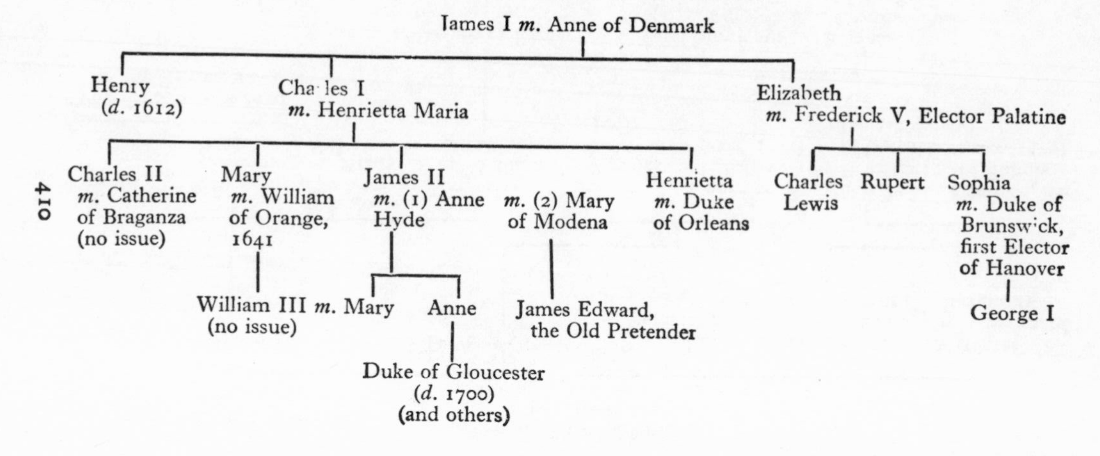

4. THE SPANISH SUCCESSION

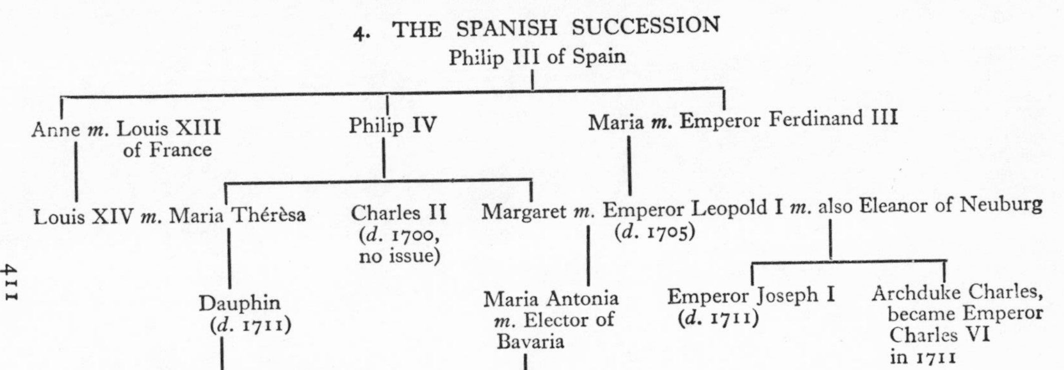

SELECT LIST FOR FURTHER READING

1. GENERAL

(*a*) *Political*

The Cambridge Modern History

The Political History of England (Longman): the volumes by H. A. L. Fisher, A. F. Pollard, F. C. Montague, R. Lodge, I. S. Leadam

The Oxford History of England: J. D. Mackie, *The Earlier Tudors*; J. B. Black, *The Reign of Elizabeth*; G. Davies, *The Early Stuarts*; G. N. Clark, *The Later Stuarts*

A History of England (Methuen): G. R. Elton, *England under the Tudors*; G. M. Trevelyan, *England under the Stuarts*

The Pelican History of England: S. T. Bindoff, *Tudor England*; M. Ashley, *England in the Seventeenth Century*

Lord Acton: *Lectures in Modern History*

A. F. Pollard: *Factors in Modern History*

J. R. Seeley: *The Growth of British Policy*

E. Wingfield-Stratford: *History of English Civilisation*

(*b*) *Constitutional*

W. Anson: *Law and Custom of the Constitution*

G. R. Elton: *The Tudor Revolution in Government*

D. L. Keir: *Constitutional History of Modern Britain*

F. W. Maitland: *Constitutional History of England*

J. E. Neale: *The Elizabethan House of Commons*
Elizabeth I and her Parliaments

K. M. Pickthorn: *Early Tudor Government*

J. R. Tanner: *English Constitutional Conflicts in the Seventeenth Century*

(Documents) G. W. Prothero: *Statutes and Constitutional Documents, 1558–1625*; S. R. Gardiner: *Constitutional Documents, 1625–60*; C. Grant Robertson: *Select Statutes, Cases and Documents*; J. R. Tanner: *Tudor Constitutional Documents. Constitutional Documents of the Reign of James I.*

(*c*) *Social and Economic*

M. St.C. Byrne: *Elizabethan Life in Town and Country*
J. H. Clapham: *Concise Economic History of Britain*
G. N. Clark: *The Wealth of England*
W. Cunningham: *Growth of English Industry and Commerce*
H. E. Egerton: *Short History of British Colonial Policy*
Life in Shakespeare's England (ed. J. Dover Wilson)
E. Lipson: *Economic History of England*
D. Mathew: *The Social Structure of Caroline England*
C. R. N. Routh: *They Saw it Happen, 1485–1688*
J. R. Seeley: *The Expansion of England*
Shakespeare's England (ed. C. T. Onions)
Social England (ed. H. D. Traill and J. S. Mann)
R. H. Tawney: *Religion and the Rise of Capitalism*
G. M. Trevelyan: *English Social History*
H. R. Trevor-Roper: *The Gentry, 1540–1640*
J. A. Williamson: *Short History of British Expansion*

(*d*) *The Church*

G. W. O. Addleshaw and F. Etchells: *The Architectural Setting of Anglican Worship*
G. Baskerville: *English Monks and the Suppression of the Monasteries*
R. S. Bosher: *The Making of the Restoration Settlement*
G. Constant: *The Reformation in England*
History of the English Church: 1509–58, by J. Gairdner; 1558–1625, by W. H. Frere; 1625–1714, by W. H. Hutton
P. Hughes: *The Reformation in England*
W. K. Jordan: *The Development of Religious Toleration in England*
M. M. Knappen: *Tudor Puritanism*
R. A. Knox: *Enthusiasm*
H. Maynard Smith: *Pre-Reformation England. Henry VIII and the Reformation*
T. M. Parker: *The English Reformation to 1558*
F. M. Powicke: *The Reformation in England*
E. G. Rupp: *The English Protestant Tradition*
A. F. Scott Pearson: *Thomas Cartwright and Elizabethan Puritanism*
F. Seebohm: *The Oxford Reformers*
J. V. P. Thompson: *Supreme Governor*

(*e*) *Literature and Thought*

J. W. Allen: *History of Political Thought in the Sixteenth Century. English Political Thought, 1603–60*
F. LeV. Baumer: *The Early Tudor Theory of Kingship*

Select List for Further Reading

J. Bowle: *Western Political Thought*
H. Craig: *The Enchanted Glass*
L. Einstein: *Tudor Ideals*
J. N. Figgis: *The Divine Right of Kings*
G. P. Gooch: *English Political Thought from Bacon to Halifax. English Democratic Ideas in the Seventeenth Century*
H. Grierson: *Cross Currents in English Literature of the Seventeenth Century*
H. J. Laski: *English Political Thought from Locke to Bentham*
C. S. Lewis: *English Literature in the Sixteenth Century*
C. Morris: *Political Thought in England from Tyndale to Hooker*
M. M. Reese: *Shakespeare: his World and his Work*
G. H. Sabine: *History of Political Theory*
E. M. W. Tillyard: *The Elizabethan World Picture*
C. V. Wedgwood: *Seventeenth Century English Literature*
B. Willey: *The Seventeenth Century Background*
A. S. P. Woodhouse: *Puritanism and Liberty*

2. THE TUDOR PERIOD

F. Bacon: *History of the Reign of Henry VII*
A. Browning: *The Age of Elizabeth*
R. W. Chambers: *Sir Thomas More*
C. G. Cruickshank: *Elizabeth's Army*
J. A. Froude: *History of England*
K. Garvin: *The Great Tudors*
G. Mattingly: *Catherine of Aragon*
C. Morris: *The Tudors*
E. Muir: *John Knox*
J. E. Neale: *Queen Elizabeth*
A. F. Pollard: *Wolsey. Henry VIII. Thomas Cranmer and the English Reformation. England under Protector Somerset*
H. F. M. Prescott: *Mary Tudor*
D. B. Quinn: *Raleigh and the British Empire*
C. Read: *The Tudors. Mr Secretary Walsingham and the Policy of Elizabeth. Mr Secretary Cecil and Queen Elizabeth*
A. L. Rowse: *The England of Elizabeth. The Expansion of Elizabethan England. Tudor Cornwall. Sir Richard Grenville*
R. H. Tawney: *The Agrarian Problem in the Sixteenth Century*
E. G. R. Taylor: *Tudor Geography*
E. Waugh: *Edmund Campion*
C. H. Williams: *Making of the Tudor Despotism*
J. A. Williamson: *The Tudor Age. Maritime Enterprise, 1485–1558. The Age of Drake. Hawkins of Plymouth*

3. THE STUART PERIOD

C. D. Bowen : *The Lion and the Throne: Life and Times of Sir Edward Coke*
A. Browning : *Danby*
D. Brunton and D. H. Pennington : *The Members of the Long Parliament*
G. Burnet : *History of my Own Time*
A. Bryant : *Charles II. Pepys*
J. Buchan : *Montrose. Oliver Cromwell*
T. Carlyle : *Letters and Speeches of Oliver Cromwell*
W. S. Churchill : *Life and Times of Marlborough*
Lord Clarendon : *History of the Great Rebellion*
I. Deane Jones : *The English Revolution*
K. G. Feiling : *History of the Tory Party. British Foreign Policy, 1660–72*
C. H. Firth : *Oliver Cromwell. Cromwell's Army*
S. R. Gardiner : *History of England, 1603–42. The Great Civil War. Commonwealth and Protectorate*
C. H. Hartmann : *Charles II and Madame. Clifford of the Cabal.*
T. B. Macaulay : *History of England*
W. McElwee : *England's Precedence*
D. Mathew : *The Jacobean Age. The Age of Charles I*
D. Ogg : *England in the Reign of Charles II. England in the Reigns of James II and William III*
D. Nichol Smith : *Characters of the Seventeenth Century*
J. Summerson : *Sir Christopher Wren*
R. H. Tawney : *Business and Politics under James I*
H. D. Traill : *Shaftesbury*
G. M. Trevelyan : *England under Queen Anne*
H. R. Trevor-Roper : *Archbishop Laud*
C. V. Wedgwood : *Strafford. The King's Peace. The King's War*
B. H. G. Wormald : *Clarendon*
G. M. Young : *Charles I and Cromwell*

4. CONTEMPORARY WRITINGS

More : *Utopia*
Machiavelli : *Prince*
Latimer : *Sermons*
Foxe : *Book of Martyrs*
Hakluyt : *Voyages*
Spenser : *Faerie Queen*, book I
Hooker : *Ecclesiastical Polity*

Select List for Further Reading

Bacon: *Essays. New Atlantis*, etc.
Selden: *Table Talk*
George Herbert: *The Temple*
Fuller: *Holy and Profane State*
Butler: *Hudibras*
Lucy Hutchinson: *Memoirs of the Life of Colonel Hutchinson*
Walton: *The Compleat Angler*
Hobbes: *Leviathan*
Milton: *Areopagitica*, and other prose works
Harrington: *The Commonwealth of Oceana*
Pepys: *Diary*
Evelyn: *Diary*
Halifax: *Works* (ed. Raleigh)
Bunyan: *The Pilgrim's Progress*
Dryden: *Absalom and Achitophel*
Locke: *Two Treatises on Civil Government. Letters on Toleration*
Swift: *Conduct of the Allies. Public Spirit of the Whigs. Tale of a Tub*
Defoe: *Shortest Way with Dissenters. Tour through Britain*
Addison: *The Tory Foxhunter*, and other essays
The Spectator

INDEX

Dates printed after rulers are the dates in which they held office.

Abbot, George, Archbishop of Canterbury (1562–1633), 231
Abergavenny, George Neville, Baron of (1471–1535), 32
Absalom and Achitophel (1681), 347
Addison, Joseph (1672–1719), quoted, 367 n., 386–7, 392
Addled Parliament (1614), 191
Adrian VI, Pope (1522–1523), 42
Aerschot, 129
Africa, 119, 294
African Company, Royal (1662), 330, 350
Agreement of the People
1647: 271, 286, 298
1649: 281, 288
Ailesbury, Thomas Bruce, Earl of (1655–1741), quoted, 325 n.
Akbar, Great Mogul (1556–1605), 170
A Lasco, John (1499–1560), 79
Albany, John Stuart, Duke of (1481–1536), 24, 39
Alençon, Duke of, *see* Anjou
Alexander VI, Pope (1492–1503), 119
Algiers, 299
Alicante, 383
Allen, William, Cardinal (1532–1594), 142
Almanza, 383
Alsace, 294, 382
Alva, Fernando Alvarez de Toledo, Duke of (1508–1582), 96, 115, 123–7
Amboyna, 295
Anatomy of an Equivalent (1688), 356
Ancrum Moor, 58
Andrewes, Lancelot, Bishop of Winchester (1555–1626), 179, 214
Angus, Archibald Douglas, Earl of (1489–1557), 111, 176
Anjou, 22
Anjou, Francis of Valois, Duke of, formerly Duke of Alençon (1556–1584), 108, 126, 130 n., 132, 160; woos Elizabeth, 130–1
Anjou, Henry of Valois, Duke of, *see* Henry III
Anjou, Philip of Bourbon, Duke of, *see* Philip V
Annates, 51, 93
Annates, Act of (1532), 51
Anne, Queen (1702–1714), 358 n., 363–5, 367, 369, 393; and parties in England, 387, 389–90, 395–7; and the succession, 390, 398–9; quoted, 396
Anne of Cleves, Queen (1515–1557), 56
Anne of Denmark, Queen (1574–1619), 162
Antwerp, 106, 119, 127, 129, 132–4, 138, 374
Appeals, Act in Restraint of (1533), 52
Appello Caesarem (1625), 210
Apprentices, Statute of (1563), 72

Index

Appropriation Act (1689), 364
Arches, Court of, 36
Areopagitica (1644), 277 n.
Argyll, Archibald Campbell, Earl of (d. 1685), 352
Arlington, Henry Bennet, Earl of (1618–1685), 326–8, 333, 335
Armada, Spanish, 122, 132, 135–8, 140
Arminianism, 179, 214–5, 217, 219–20, 234–5, 245, 256
Arminius (James Hermanzoon) (1560–1609), 214
Arques, 139
Arran, James Hamilton, Earl of (1530–1609), 107, 109–10
Arthur, Prince of Wales (1486–1502), 17–18, 22–3, 47
Artois, 42
Arundel, Henry Fitzalan, Earl of (1511–1580), 104
Arundel, Thom s Howard, Earl of (1586–1646), 211
Arundell, Henry (Baron Arundell of Wardour, 1606–1694), 326, 333, 354
Ashe, John, 291
Ashley, Baron, *see* Shaftesbury
Asia, 294, 330
Astley, Sir Jacob (1579–1652), quoted, 266
Aston, Sir Arthur (d. 1649), 278
Athlone, 371
Athlone, Godert de Ginkel, Earl of (1630–1703), 371, 390
Audience, Court of, 36
Aughrim, 371
Augsburg, 93
Augsburg, League of (1686), 372
Austria, and war of Spanish succession, 377–85, 396
Autolycus, 70
Avignon, 49
Axel, 134
Ayscue, Sir George (d. 1671), 280
Azores, 131

Babington, Anthony (1561–1586), 135
Bacon, Francis, Baron Verulam (1561–1626), 66, 156, 168, 177, 184, 190–1, 200, 204, 227, 310; compared with Coke, 194–6; quoted, 13–14, 19–20, 24, 195, 200
Baillie, Robert (1599–1662), quoted, 237, 241
Balliol College, 345 n.
Baltic Sea, 296–7, 330
Bancroft, Richard, Archbishop of Canterbury (1544–1610), 180, 183, 193
Bank of England, 376, 387, 395
Barbados, 279, 290
Barbary pirates, 224
Barcelona, 374, 383, 395
Barcelona, Treaty of (1529), 44
Bardolph, 71
Barebones Parliament (1653), 284–5, 327
Barebones, Praise-God (1596–1679), 284–5
Barillon, Paul de, Marquis de Branges, 339, 345
Barrow, Henry (*c.* 1550–1593), 148 n., 151
Basilicon Doron (1599), 158
Basing, 266
Bastwick, John (1593–1654), 235, 241; quoted, 235
Bate, John, 185–6
Bavaria, Joseph Ferdinand, Electoral Prince of (1692–1699), 377
Bavaria, Maximilian Emmanuel, Elector of (1679–1726), 381
Baxter, Richard (1615–1691), 76
Beachy Head, 374
Beaton, David, Archbishop of St. Andrews (1494–1546), 58–9, 105
Beaufort, Lady Margaret (1443–1509), 12, 27
Bedloe, William (1650–1680), 341
Bellasyse, John, Baron (1614–1689), 354
Bemerton, 157
Bengal, 170

Index

Berwick, 225, 274
Berwick, James Fitzjames, Duke of (1670–1734), 383
Berwick, Treaty of (1639), 238
Bible, English
1539 : 56–7
1611 : 156, 180–1, 181 n.
Bilbao, 135
Bill of Rights (1689), 362–3
Bishop, George, quoted, 273
Bishops' Book (1537), 55
Bishops' Wars (1639–1640), 237–9
Blackfriars, 44, 48
Blackheath, 18, 308
Black Rubric, 85, 100
Blake, Robert (1599–1657), 280, 285, 295, 298–9
Blenheim, 280–1, 395
Blois, Treaty of (1572), 125–6
Board of Trade, 77, 329
Bohemia, 195
Boleyn, Anne, Queen (1507–1536), 47, 50–2, 98
Bolingbroke, Henry St. John, Viscount (1678–1751), 253, 388 ; and the succession, 397–9 ; quoted, 364, 385–8, 398–9
Bologna, 28
Bombay, 330 n.
Bond of Association (1584), 134, 136
Bonner, Edmund, Bishop of London (1500–1569), 89, 98
Book of Advertisements (1566), 49
Book of Common Order (1564), 237
Book of Homilies (1562), 101
Book of Martyrs (1563), 93
Book of Rates (1608), 186
Book of Sports (1633), 234
Bordeaux, 20, 297
Bosworth, 11
Boteler, William, 305
Bothwell, James Hepburn, Earl of (1536–1578), 113
Bouchain, 383–4
Boulogne, 58, 84
Bourbon, Charles, Cardinal of, Archbishop of Rouen (d. 1590), 133, 139
Boyle, Robert (1627–1691), 320
Boyne, river, 371, 374
Brabant, 133
Bracton, Henry de (d. 1268), 194
Bradshaw, John (1602–1659), 275, 312
Brandenburg, 297, 381 ; *see also* Prussia
Bray, Sir Reginald (d. 1503), 15
Brazil, 119
Breda, Declaration of (1660), 307, 312
Bremen, 297
Brest, 374
Bridgeman, Sir Orlando (1606–1674), 326
Bridport, 21
Brihuega, 383
Brill, 125, 134
Bristol, 255, 266
Bristol, John Digby, Earl of (1580–1654), 212
Brittany, 22
Brittany, Anne of (1477–1514), 22
Brooke, Robert Greville, Baron (1608–1643), 238 n., 252
Broughton, 225
Browne, Robert (1550–1633), 148 n., 151
Bruges, 42
Brussels, 106, 118, 123
Bryan, C. J., 64
Bucer, Martin (1491–1551), 79, 86 ; quoted, 86
Buckingham, Edward Stafford, Duke of (1478–1521), 17, 32, 46 n.
Buckingham, George Villiers, Duke of (1592–1628), 161–2, 192, 202–5, 208–9, 218, 221, 224, 294, 299, 327 ; character, 189–90, 210–11 ; war with Spain, 210–11 ; war with France, 208, 212–13, 219 ; attacked in parliament, 211–12, 216–17
Buckingham, George Villiers, Duke of (1628–1687), 326–8, 334, 337, 339

Buckinghamshire, 183, 308
Bunyan, John (1628–1688), 155–6; quoted, 75
Burford, 281 n.
Burghley, William Cecil, Baron (1520–1598), 103, 132, 138, 149–50; quoted, 172
Burgundy, 22
Burnet, Gilbert, Bishop of Salisbury (1643–1715), quoted, 325–6, 347, 353, 356
Burton, Henry (1578–1648), 235, 241; quoted, 235
Butler, Nicholas, 354
Bye Plot (1603), 176

Cabal, members of, 326–7; objects, 327–9; failure, 334–5, 339, 356
Cadiz, 137, 140, 210, 299
Cairo, 170
Calais, 26, 54, 84, 88, 105, 108–9; loss of, 95–6, 104
Calamy, Edmund (1635–1685), 289
Calvin, John (1509–1564), 79, 85, 93, 96, 106, 155; *see also* Puritanism
Cambrai, Peace of (1529), 44
Cambridge, 261
Cambridge University, 79, 148, 148 n., 150, 339 n., 354
Camisards, 381, 384
Campbell, Archibald, Duke of Argyll (1651–1703), 369
Campeggio, Lorenzo, Cardinal (1464–1539), 44, 48
Campion, Edmund (1540–1581), 143–4; quoted, 143
Canaries, 299
Canterbury, 79
Cape Verde Islands, 135
Caraffa, Cardinal, *see* Paul IV
Carberry Hill, 113
Carbisdale, 279
Carew, John (d. 1660) quoted, 287
Caribbean Sea, 119–20, 135, 140, 196, 201, 299
Carlisle, 274
Carlowitz, Treaty of (1699), 377
Carlyle, Thomas (1795–1881), quoted 160, 280
Carmarthen, 94
Carolina, 329
Cartagena, 135
Cartwright, Thomas (1535–1603), 148–9
Case of the Army Truly Stated (1647), 271
Casimir, John, Count Palatine (1543–1592), 130
Casket Letters, 114
Castellio, Sebastian (1515–1563), quoted, 96
Castile, 383–4
Catalonia, 377, 381–4
Cateau-Cambrésis, Treaty of (1559), 105, 118
Catesby, Robert (1573–1605), 181
Catherine of Aragon, Queen (1485–1536), 13, 19 n., 22–4, 40, 46, 90, 98; her "divorce", 43–4, 47–8, 50–2
Catherine of Braganza, Queen (1638–1705), 313, 321, 322 n., 330 n., 341–2
Catherine Howard, Queen (1522–1542), 56–7
Catherine de Medici, Queen of France (1519–1589), 125–6, 133; aims of, 108–9
Catholic League (1576, 1585), 125, 133, 139
Catholics, English, treatment of: under Elizabeth, 99–101, 141–5; under James I, 171, 176, 181–2, 199, 202–3; under Charles I, 199 n., 208–9, 211, 214, 234–5; during the Interregnum, 282, 286, 288; under Charles II, 316, 328, 334; under James II, 351, 353–7, 360; after 1688, 366
Cavalier Parliament (1661–1679): religious settlement, 315–8; and Clarendon, 321–3; and the Cabal, 328, 334–5; and France, 328, 334–9; and Danby, 335–40

Cavendish, George (1500–1561), quoted 33
Cecil, Robert, *see* Salisbury
Cecil, William, *see* Burghley
Cerdagne, 23
Cevennes, 381
Champel, 93
Chancery, Court of, 31–3, 36, 45, 52, 183, 200, 285, 285 n., 287
Chantries, dissolution of (1547), 70, 80
Character of a Trimmer (1685), 342
Charles I (1625–1649), Chapters XIII–XVI; 24, 175, 196, 203–5, 283, 292; character, 206–8, 267; religious policy, 157, 215, 244, 246, 248; social policy, 69, 73–4, 222, 226–7, 229–30; financial measures, 209–10, 213, 216–20, 222–6, 243, 255, 290, 313; and Spanish marriage, 197–9, 202; and Spanish war, 208–11, 222; and French war, 212–13, 219, 222; and Petition of Right, 216–17; personal government, Chapter XIV, 69, 73–4; and the Scots, 236–9, 247, 267–8, 273–4; submits to parliament, 240–3; forms a party, 244, 247–50, 253–4; and the Great Rebellion, 255–66; negotiations with parliament, 257, 264, 267–9, 271, 273–4; negotiations with the army, 267, 269–71, 273–4; trial and death, 275–6; quoted, 206–7, 212–3, 215, 219–21, 237, 244, 248–50, 264, 268, 270, 275–6
Charles II (1660–1685), Chapters XVIII–XIX; 76, 279, 350–1, 360, 371, 388; his restoration, 307–8; character, 325; religious policy, 310 n., 314–15, 317, 329, 332–5; political objects, 323, 325–8, 337, 341; financial difficulties, 313–14, 332, 334, 336; and Clarendon, 320–3; and the Cabal, 326–9, 334–5; and Danby, 336–7, 339–41; and Exclusion, 341–7; and the Tories, 336–7, 346–7; and France, 332–5, 337, 339–40, 342; and Holland, 329, 332–5; quoted, 315, 326, 332–3, 341–43, 345–6, 349, 351
Charles I of Spain (1516–1556), Emperor Charles V (1519–1558), 54, 123, 293; and Wolsey, 37–45; elected Emperor, 39–40; and Mary Tudor, 90, 92
Charles II of Spain (1665–1700), 377–8
Charles VIII of France (1483–1498), 22–3, 37
Charles IX of France (1560–1574), 108, 111
Charles X of Sweden (1654–1660), 297
Charles, Archduke, later Emperor Charles VI (1711–1740), 377–78, 382–4
Charles of Styria, Archduke, 111
Chatham, 330
Chatham, Earl of (1708–1778), 333
Chepstow, 341
Cheshire, 253
Cheshire, Thomas, quoted 233
Chester, 253
Chesterton, 62
Chillingworth William (1602–1644), 319
Christ Church, 345 n., 355
Christian IV of Denmark (1588–1648), 209, 213
Cimarron Indians, 120
Claim of Right (1690), 368
Clarendon, Edward Hyde, Earl of (1609–1674), 190, 250, 252, 270, 300, 316, 326, 330, 339, 348, 387; and the Restoration, 307–8, 313, 321, 323; political theories, 322–3, 348; fall of, 320–3, quoted, 222–3, 225, 233, 249, 253, 266–7, 291, 303, 313, 321, 322–4, 330

Clarendon, Henry Hyde, Earl of (1638–1700), 348, 354
Clarendon Code, 75–6, 310 n., 316–20, 348, 386, 395; social and political effects, 317–19
Clement VII, Pope (1523–1534), 42–5; and the "divorce", 43–4, 47–8, 51
Cleves, 197
Clifford, Thomas, Baron Clifford of Chudleigh (1630–1673), 326–8, 333, 335–6
Clubmen, 253
Cobham, Henry Brooke, Baron (d. 1619), 176
Coke, Sir Edward (1552–1634), 191, 200, 216–17, 222, 247; and James I, 192–5; compared with Bacon, 194–6; quoted, 192–3, 195, 216–17
Colbert, Jean Baptiste, Marquis de Seignelay (1619–1683), 332
Colchester, 274
Coleman, Edward (d. 1678), 340
Coleraine, 229
Colet, John (1467–1519), 27, 48
Coligny, Gaspard de, Admiral of France (1519–1572), 108, 125–26, 130
Cologne, 378
Colvill, Robert (b. 1605), 185
Complaint of Roderik Mors (1543), (by Henry Brinkelow), 65
Compton, Henry, Bishop of London (1632–1713), 359
Condé, Louis de Bourbon, Prince of (1530–1569), 111
Condé, Louis de Bourbon, Prince of (1621–1686), 294 n.
Conduct of the Allies (1711), 396
Congregation, Lords of the, 106
Congregationalists, *see* Independents
Constable of France, Charles, Duke of Bourbon (1490–1527), 42
Constantinople, 170
Conventicle Act
1593: 151
1664: 316, 328, 366
Convention Parliament (1660), 308–9, 312–15, 324
Convention Parliament (1688–1690), 360, 362, 366, 390
Convention Parliament (Scottish), (1690), 368
Convocation, 34, 37, 51–2, 99, 116, 147, 180, 239, 314, 314 n.
Cork, 371
Cornwall, 13, 18, 81, 140, 240, 252–3, 257, 263, 341
Coronation Oath, 365
Corporation Act (1661), 316, 366
Corporation Bill (1690), 390
Corpus Christi College, Oxford 345 n.
Cosin, John, Bishop of Durham (1594–1672), 318
Council of Blood, 96
Counter-Reformation, 97, 102, 122, 125–7, 130, 132, 135, 147, 167–8, 198, 293; in England, 141–5
County Palatine of Chester, Court of, 242
Courtenay, Edward, Earl of Devonshire (1526–1556), 89–91
Courtin, Honoré de, Seigneur de Chantereine (1622–1685), 339
Coventry, 72
Coventry, Henry (1619–1686), 326; quoted, 316, 340
Cowell, Dr. John (1554–1611), 186; quoted, 186
Cox, Richard, Bishop of Ely (1500–1581), 148 n.
Cranfield, Lionel, Earl of Middlesex (1575–1645), 190–2, 203–205, 218, 224
Cranmer, Thomas, Archbishop of Canterbury (1489–1556), 51–52, 56–7, 94; his Prayer Books, 80–1, 85–6; quoted, 56 n., 86
Cromwell, Henry (1628–1674), 285, 304–5

Cromwell, Oliver (1599–1658), Chapter XVI–XVII; 74, 116, 247 n., 249, 252, 303–4, 306 312, 320, 330, 332–3; character, 269, 283, 302; religious policy, 262, 270, 288, 301, 319; political aims, 269–70, 272, 283–4, 286; military achievements, 262–3, 266, 274, 278–9, 281 n., 300; social reforms, 287–8, 290; and the Eastern Association, 261–2; and the Long Parliament, 265, 269–71; and the King, 269–70, 273, 275; and the Levellers, 271–3, 289; becomes Protector, 286–7; quarrels with the parliaments of the Interregnum, 282–3, 289, 293; offered the crown, 291–2; aims of his foreign policy, 296–7; and Holland, 280, 296–7; and France, 297–301; and Spain, 297–301; his achievement, 300–3; quoted, 247, 261–3, 265–6, 268–72, 275, 278–9, 283, 283 n., 284–9, 291, 293, 293 n., 296, 298–300, 302, 305
Cromwell, Richard (1626–1712), 303–5; quoted, 305
Cromwell, Thomas, Earl of Essex (1485–1540), 53–6, 94

Dacre, Leonard (d. 1573), 115
Dacre, Thomas, Lord, of the North, 42
D'Albret, Jean, King of Navarre (1483–1512), 28
Danby, Sir Robert, C. J., 64
Danby, Thomas Osborne, Earl of (1631–1712), 349 n., 359, 388, 390, 390 n., 391; and Charles II, 336–7, 339–41; and the Cavalier Parliament, 335–9; and France, 336–7; quoted, 336
Dante, Alighieri (1265–1321), 164
Danube, river, 374
Darien, 120, 369–70, 391
Darleton, 62
Darnel, Sir Thomas (d. 1640), 213
Darnley, Henry Stuart, Earl of (1545–1567), 111–14, 162
Davison, William (1541–1608), 136
Day, George, Bishop of Chichester (1501–1556), 89
Declaration of Indulgence
1662: 317, 323
1672: 334–5
1687: 355
1688: 357
Defensor Pacis (1324), 168
Defoe, Daniel (1661–1731), 396; quoted, 77
De Feria, Gomez Suarez de Figueroa, Count, 98; quoted, 102 n.
De Haeretico Comburendo (1401), 79, 92
De la Gorce, Pierre, quoted, 350
Delft, 133
Delhi, 170
De Monarchia (1311), 164
Denain, 384
Denbigh, William Feilding, Earl of (d. 1643), 213
Denbighshire, 364
Dendermonde, 133
Denmark, 20, 45, 209, 297
Deptford, 129
Dering, Sir Edward, 326
De Ruyter, Michael Adriaanzoon (1607–1676), 330, 334
Desborough, John (1608–1680), 291
Deserted Village (1770), 69
De Spes, Don Gueran, 115, 123–5, 142
Devonshire, 81, 253, 256, 260, 347
Devonshire, William Cavendish, Duke of (1640–1707), 359
D'Ewes, Sir Simonds (1602–1650), quoted, 220
De Witt, Jan (1625–1672), 333
Dieppe, 374

Digby, George, Earl of Bristol (1612–1677), 252; quoted, 245–6
Diggers, 74, 281, 311
Digges, Sir Dudley (1583–1639), 211
Directory of Public Worship (1645), 263
Dissenters, *see* Puritanism
Divine Right of Kings: history of the theory, 164–8; and James I, 163–4, 204, 207; and Charles I, 207–8, 267; after 1660, 310, 347, 351, 364
Doesburg, 134
Dogberry, 70
Don Antonio, Prior of Crato (1531–1595), 140
Donauwörth, 381
Don Carlos, Prince of Spain (1545–1568), 111
Don John of Austria (1545–1578), 129, 129 n.
Doria, Andrea (1468–1560), 43–4
Dorset, 328
Dorset, Thomas Grey, Marquis of (1477–1530), 17, 28, 32
Dort, Synod of (1618–1619), 214
Douai, 142–3, 384
Dover, 204
Dover, Henry Jermyn, Baron (1636–1708), 354
Dover, Treaties of (1670), 333–4, 337
Downing, Sir George (1623–1684), 334
Drake, Sir Francis (1540-1596), 134, 140, 210–11, 256; in 1572: 120; in 1577: 129; in 1585: 135; in 1587: 136–7
Drogheda, 278
Dryden, John (1631–1700), 347
Dublin, 13, 24, 229, 371
Duchy of Lancaster, Court of, 242
Dudley, Edmund (1462–1510), 15, 19, 27, 83
Dudley, Lord Guildford (d. 1554), 87, 91
Dudley, Robert, *see* Leicester
Dunbar, 279, 287, 306
Dunes, battle of the, 300
Dungeness, 295
Dunkirk, 224, 298, 298 n., 300–1, 301 n., 313, 321, 374, 382, 384
Dunstable, 52

Eastern Association (1643), 261–2
East India Company (1600), 295, 330, 330 n.
East Indies, 170, 295
Eastland Company (1579), 330
Ecclesiasticae Disciplinae Explicatio (1574), 149
Ecclesiastical Commission, Court of, 354–5, 359, 362
Edgehill, 254, 257, 261
Edict of Nantes, revocation of (1685), 351–2, 380
Edinburgh, 58, 106, 237, 247, 369–70
Edinburgh, Treaty of (1560), 107, 110
Edmund, 156
Edward IV (1470–1483), 12, 19, 23, 32, 46, 64
Edward VI (1547–1553), Chapter V; 55, 57–9
Elbe, 213
Eliot, Sir John (1592–1632), 191, 211, 216, 218–20, 247; quoted, 179, 216, 219
Elizabeth I, Queen (1558–1603), Chapter VI–IX; 52, 86, 90–1, 95, 159, 161, 173–4, 181, 204 n., 281; character, 97, 102–4, 122, 160; social policy, 66–8, 71–3; religious settlement, 81, 96–101, 105, 146; treatment of Catholics, 99–100, 141–5; treatment of Puritans, 145–53, 177, 236; aims of her foreign policy, 102–3, 122–3, 127; and Mary: expels French from Scotland, 105–7; refuses Mary the succession, 110–12;

keeps Mary in England, 113–117, 125, 127, 136; and Spain: causes of dispute, 119–24, 127; truce in 1573, 126–7; at war, 132, 134, 136–140, 172; and Netherlands, 103, 122–3; sends an army, 134, 138–9; and France: aids Huguenots, 107–9; treaty of Blois, 125–6; aids Henry IV, 138–9; quoted, 97, 97 n. 98, 102–4, 111–12, 114, 127, 133–4, 148–9, 171–3
Elizabeth of Bohemia (1596–1662), 197–8, 201, 393
Elizabeth of Valois, Queen of Spain (1546–1568), 105, 118, 139
Elizabeth of York, Queen (1465–1503), 12, 19 n.
Ellesmere, Sir Thomas Egerton, Baron, quoted, 178
Emden, 119
Empson, Sir Richard (d. 1510), 15, 19, 27
Enclosures, Chapter IV; 33, 223, 226; unpopularity of, 61–3, 65–6; condemned by the government, 63–4; government's failure to check, 64–9; defended, 63, 66, 68–9
Engagement (1647), 273–4
England's New Chains Discovered (1649), 281
Enniskillen, 371
Epping Forest, 223
Erasmus, Desiderius (1467–1536), 27, 35, 48
Essay of Civil Government (1690), 361
Essex, 223, 252, 274
Essex, Arthur Capel, Earl of (1631–1683), 348
Essex, Robert Devereux, Earl of (1567–1601), 140, 153, 161
Essex, Robert Devereux, Earl of (1591–1646), 238 n., 251, 257, 260, 263–5; quoted, 241, 264
Etaples, Treaty of (1492), 23
Eugene, Prince of Savoy-Carignan (1663–1736), 382, 397
Everard, William, 281
Exclusion, 341–7, 386
Excommunication, Bull of (1570), 101, 120, 124, 141–2, 145
Exeter, 360
Exeter, Henry Courtenay, Marquis of (1496–1538), 46, 55

Fable of the Bees (1714), 77
Fagius, Paul (1504–1549), 79
Fairfax, Ferdinando, Baron (1584–1648), 260
Fairfax, Thomas, Baron (1612–71), 262, 266, 269, 274, 279 n., 281 n., 327
Falkland, Lucius Cary, Viscount (1610–1643), quoted, 245, 261
Falstaff, 70
Fawkes, Guido (1570–1606), 181
Felton, John (1595–1628), 218–19
Ferdinand I, Emperor (1558–1564), 118
Ferdinand II, Emperor (1619–1637), 198–9, 293
Ferdinand II of Aragon (1479–1516), V of Castile, 13, 22–3, 28–9, 39, 47
Ferrar, Robert, Bishop of St. David's (1500–1555), 94
Field of Cloth of Gold (1520), 40
Filmer, Sir Robert (d. 1653), 347
Finch, Heneage, Earl of Nottingham (1621–1682), quoted 335 n.
Finch, Sir John (1584–1660), 225, 241; quoted, 225
Fisher, John, Bishop of Rochester (1459–1535), 54
Five Mile Act (1665), 316
Flanders, 133, 338, 375; wool trade with, 20–1, 23, 40, 45, 50, 54–5, 61, 91, 119–20, 124–7; *see also* Netherlands
Flanders, Philip, Count of (1478–1506), 20, 23
Fleet prison, 183, 200, 228

Fleetwood, Charles (d. 1692), 278, 291, 304–5
Flodden, 29
Florence, 20, 28, 40, 44
Floyd, Edward (d. 1648), 200–1, 218
Flushing, 134, 204
Forest of Dean, 223
Form of Apology and Satisfaction (1604), 183–4
Fortescue, Sir John (1394–1476), 167, 194
Fortrey, Samuel (1622–1681), quoted, 69
Forty-two Articles (1553), 86, 101
Fotheringay Castle, 136
Foulis, Sir David (d. 1642), 228
Fox, Richard, Bishop of Winchester (1448–1528), 15, 29; quoted, 39 n.
Foxe, John (1516–1587), 93; quoted, 94
France
  and Henry VII, 21–4
  and Henry VIII, 28–9, 37–44, 54–5, 58–9
  and Edward VI, 83–4
  and Mary, 95–6
  and Elizabeth, Chapter VII–VIII; Fr. party driven from Scotland, 105–7; religious wars in, 107–9, 125; treaty of Blois, 125–6; and Netherlands revolt, 125–6, 130–2; war of French succession, 132–4, 138–9
  and James I, 196–7, 204
  and Charles I, 208–9, 211, 239; war with, 212–3, 219, 222
  during the Interregnum, 293–8; alliance with Cromwell, 299–301
  and Charles II, 328–9, 336–9, 340, 342, 345–6, 351; treaties of Dover, 332–5
  and James II, 352, 359
  and William III, 358–9, 361, 365–6, 368–9, 371
  and the Spanish succession, 377–385, 391, 395–7
Franche Comté, 339, 383
Francis I of France (1515–1547), 38–44, 54; quoted, 148
Francis II of France (1559–1560), 83, 91, 105, 107–9
Frankfort, 98
Frederick V, Elector Palatine (1610–1623), 197–9, 201, 393
Frith, Mary (1592–1659), 70
Fronde (1648–1652), 294
Fuentarrabia, 42

Gainsborough, Thomas (1727–1788), 401
Galway, 371
Gardiner, S. R. (1829–1902), quoted, 228
Gardiner, Stephen, Bishop of Winchester (1483–1555), 57, 89–90, 93–4, 168
Gascony, 22
Gelderland, 384
Gelt, river, 116
Gembloux, 129
General Security Act (1703), 369
Geneva, 79, 98, 146
Genoa, 28, 40, 44, 124
George I (1714–1727), 243, 399
George II (1727–1760), 399
George III (1760–1820), 390
Ghent, 133
Gibraltar, 300, 382, 384, 395
Ginkel, *see* Athlone
Giustiniani, Sebastian, quoted, 31–2, 38
Giving Alms no Charity (1704), 77
Glastonbury, 79
Glencoe, 369
Gloucester, 94, 260
Gloucester, William, Duke of (1689–1700), 393
Godden v. Hales (1686), 354
Godolphin, Sidney, Earl of Godolphin (1645–1712), 388, 391, 395
Goffe, William (d. 1679), 273
Golden Hind, 129
Gondomar, Diego Sarmiento de Acuna, Count of (1567–1626), 189, 191, 197–9, 301

Index

Goodwin, Sir Francis, 183
Goring, George, Baron (1608–1657), 263, 266
Gorleston, 60
Grace, Act of (1690), 390
Graham, John, of Claverhouse, Viscount Dundee (1649–1689), 368
Grand Alliance, 372, 378–85, 395
Grand Design, 196
Grand Remonstrance (1641), 248–249, 321, 386
Grantham, 262
Gravelines, 40
Gregory XIII, Pope (1572–1585), 126, 143–4
Green Ribbon Club, 343
Greenwich, 52 ; monastery of, 93
Greenwood, John (d. 1593), 148 n.
Gresham, Sir Thomas (1519–1579), 103, 106 ; quoted, 107
Grey, Lady Jane (1537–1554), 87, 91
Grindal, Edmund, Archbishop of Canterbury (1519–1583), 148 n., 149–50
Grotius, Hugo (1583–1645), 214, 224 n.
Guienne, 22, 28, 40
Guildford, Sir Richard (1455–1506), 15
Guinea, 119
Guipuscoa, 28, 377
Guise, Francis, Duke of (1519–1563), 95, 104
Guise, Henry, Duke of (1550–1588), 162
Guise, house of, 104–5, 107–9, 118, 132 ; alliance with Spain, 130–1, 133, 138–9 ; *see also* Mary of Guise
Guisnes, 95
Gunpowder-Plot (1605), 181–2, 197
Gustavus Adolphus of Sweden (1611–1632), 237, 297

Habeas Corpus Act (1679), 346
Hague, The, 334, 357, 381, 384
Hakewill, William (1574–1655), 191
Hales, John (d. 1571), quoted, 62, 65
Halifax, George Savile, Marquis of (1633–1695), 347–9, 354, 356, 388 ; and exclusion, 341–2, 344 ; quoted, 1, 325, 342, 351, 356, 361, 388
Hamilton, James Hamilton, Duke of (1606–1649), 274
Hamlet, 168
Hampden, John (1594–1643), 179, 254, 261 ; and ship-money, 225, 240 ; quoted, 179
Hampden, Richard (1631–1695), 308, 339 ; quoted, 343
Hampshire, 257
Hampton Court, 273
Hampton Court Conference (1604), 178, 180–1, 183
Hanover, 381
Hanseatic League, 20, 170, 330
Harley, Robert, Earl of Oxford (1661–1724), 367, 388, 392, 394, 396 ; and Bolingbroke, 397–9 ; quoted, 397
Harrison, Thomas (1606–1660), 273, 285, 286 n.
Harwich, 295
Hastings, George, Earl of Huntingdon (1488–1545), 32
Hatton, Sir Christopher (1540–1591), 120
Hawkins, Sir John (1532–1595), 119–20, 211
Hawkins, William (d. 1589), 119
Hazlerig, Sir Arthur (d. 1661), 305 ; quoted, 292
Headington, 266
Heads of the Proposals (1647), 270–1, 274
Heath, Nicholas, Archbishop of York (1501–1578), 89
Henrietta, Duchess of Orleans ("Minette") (1644–1670), 332
Henrietta, Maria, Queen (1609–1669), 208, 212, 214, 235, 242, 244, 248–9, 268

Henry VII (1485–1509), Chapter I, 32 ; character and aims, 14, 25 ; claim to the throne, 11–12 ; risings against, 12–13, 18 ; methods of government, 14–17 ; financial policy, 18–21 ; foreign policy, 21–4 ; his achievement, 11, 24–5 ; quoted, 13
Henry VIII (1509–1547), Chapter II–III ; 17, 23, 79–81, 83, 86–7, 90, 93, 97–9, 156, 167, 173 ; character, 26–7, 57, 59 ; foreign policy, 28–9, 37, 45, 58–9 ; dismisses Wolsey, 44–45 ; and the " divorce ", 43–4, 47–8, 51–2 ; breach with Rome, 50–2 ; dissolves the monasteries, 52–4 ; defines doctrine, 55–7 ; and Ireland, 26, 57 ; and Scotland, 58–9 ; quoted, 29–30, 47, 55, 79
Henry II of France (1547–1559), 39, 105, 108
Henry III of France (1574–1589), 108, 125, 132–3
Henry IV of France (1589–1610), 126, 132–4, 138–9, 171, 188, 196, 208
Henry, Prince of Wales (1594–1612), 158, 188, 197, 206
Herbert, George (1593–1633), 101 n., 157
Herbert, Sir Thomas (1606–1682), quoted, 276
Hertford, Earl of, *see* Somerset
Hertford, William Seymour, Marquis of (1588–1660), 252
High Commission, Court of, 150, 153, 232–4, 242
Hispaniola, 299
Hobbes, Thomas (1588–1679), 280, 320
Hogarth, William (1697–1764), 401
Holdenby House, 269
Holland
  and James I, 197, 203–4
  and Charles I, 209–10, 214, 224
Holland
  during the Interregnum, 297 ; first Dutch War, 280, 294–6
  and Charles II, 320, 329, 336–8, 348 ; commercial rivalry, 327, 330–2 ; second Dutch War, 314, 322, 330–1 ; third Dutch War, 333–5
  and James II, 358
  and William III, 372–6
  and Spanish succession, 377–85, 396
  See also Netherlands
Holles, Denzil, Baron Holles of Ifield (1599–1680), quoted, 213
Holy League
  1509 : 28–9
  1526 : 43–4, 48
Holyrood Palace, 110, 237
Hooker, Richard (1554–1600), 157, 179, 214 ; quoted, 157
Hooper, John, Bishop of Gloucester (1475–1555), 81, 85, 94
Hopton, Ralph, Baron (1598–1662), 251 n., 257
Hounslow Heath, 353, 357–8
Hudson's Bay Company (1670), 330, 350
Hudson's Bay Territory, 384
Huguenots, 298, 300, 352 ; and Elizabeth, 103, 107–9, 115, 125–6, 130, 132, 138 ; and Charles I, 208–9, 212–3
Hull, 253, 255–6, 260
Humble Petition and Advice (1657), 291–2
Humières, Louis de Crevant, Duke of, 374
Hungary, 45, 381–2
Hunsdon, Henry Carey, Baron (1524–1596), 115
Huntingdon, 261
Huy, 375
Hyde, Anne, Duchess of York (1637–1671), 322 n., 343, 358 n.
Hyde, Edward, *see* Clarendon

Index

Iachimo, 156
Iago, 156
Iceland, 20
Inchiquin, Murrough O'Brien, Earl of (1614–1674), 274
Independents, 251, 261, 273, 282–284, 301–2, 307, 309, 317; religious policy, 151–2, 154, 231, 245, 288, 301; breach with Long Parliament, 263–5, 268–71; demand the death of the King, 271, 273–5
Infanta of Spain, Princess Maria Althea, 198, 202, 208
Innocent VIII, Pope (1484–1492), 23
Inquisition, 90, 96, 123, 141, 170, 182
Instrument of Government (1653), 286–8, 290, 292
Ipswich, 35
Ireland: under Henry VII, 13, 24; under Henry VIII, 26, 57; under Elizabeth, 133, 140, 143, 153, 171, 173; under Charles I, 229, 237, 247–8, 268, 274; during the Interregnum, 278–80; under Charles II, 371; under William III, 364, 368, 370–2, 391
Ireton, Henry (1611–1651), 269–272, 274, 278, 286 n., 312; quoted, 270–2
Ironsides, 253, 300
Isle of Wight, 58, 64, 273
Italy, 22–3, 374; wars of Henry VIII and Wolsey, 28–9, 37–45, 50; and Spanish succession, 380, 382–4
Ivan IV, the Terrible, Czar (1533–1584), 170
Ivry, 139

Jaffray, Alexander (1614–1673), quoted, 279
Jamaica, 299
James I (1603–1625), James VI of Scotland (1567–1625), Chapters X–XII; 68, 73, 112–13, 133, 136, 140, 153, 207, 209, 214, 224, 231, 234, 236, 294, 301, 320, 369; character, 158–162, 174–5; conceptions of monarchy, 158–9, 163–4, 192; his difficulties in 1603, 170–4; financial problems, 173–4, 185–7, 191–2; his favourites, 161–2, 189–90; and the Puritans, 161, 176–80, 183; and the Catholics, 171, 176, 181–2; and Coke, 192–5; breach with parliament in 1621, 201–2; and Scotland, 158, 160, 184–5, 187; aims of his foreign policy, 182, 196–7; and Spain, 182, 190, 201, seeks Spanish marriage, 197–9, 202, at war, 203–4; quoted, 158–60, 162–4, 175, 175 n., 178, 180, 182–5, 187, 193, 198, 201–3, 231, 236
James II (1685–1688), Chapter XX; 243, 311 n., 322 n., 335–6, 339–44, 346–7, 349, 368, 371, 374–5, 378, 383; character and aims, 350–1; religious policy, 351, 353–7, 362; and William of Orange, 359–61; causes of his fall, 352, 358, 362–3; quoted, 357
James IV of Scotland (1488–1513), 13, 24, 29
James V of Scotland (1513–1542), 46, 54, 58, 105
James Edward, Prince, the Old Pretender (1688–1766), 358, 378, 382, 384, 393 n., 398; quoted, 398
Japan, 170
Jeffreys, George, Baron (1648–1689), 349, 353
Jermyn, Henry, *see* Dover
Jesuits, 141, 143–4, 176, 244, 339, 354
Jewel, John, Bishop of Salisbury (1522–1571), 103; quoted, 142, 168

Jews, 288
Joanna of Castile (1479–1555), 19 n., 23
John, Prince of Asturias (d. 1497), 23 n.
Johnson, Samuel (1709–1784), quoted, 238 n., 370
Joinville, Treaty of (1585), 133
Jones, Inigo (1573–1652), 234
Joseph I, Emperor (1705–1711), 382–3
Joyce, George, 269
Juliers, 197
Julius II, Pope (1503–1513), 28, 47, 52
Juxon, William, Archbishop of Canterbury (1582–1663), 229

Kent, 44, 90, 260, 274, 394
Keppel, Arnold Joost van, Earl of Albemarle (1669–1718), 390
Ket, Robert (d. 1549), 65, 81–2
Kildare, Gerald Fitzgerald, Earl of (d. 1513), 24
Killiecrankie, 368
Killing No Murder (1657), 292
King John, 194
King Lear, 71
King Richard III Revived (1657), 292
King's Book (1543), 56, 81
Kinsale, 371
Kirke, Percy (1646–1691), 353
Kitchin, Anthony, Bishop of Llandaff (1477–1563), 100
Knewstubs, John (1544–1624), 178
Knollys, Sir Francis (1514–1596), 149
Knox, John (1505–1572), 85, 103, 106, 110, 112, 237; quoted, 106, 110

Lagos, 374
La Hogue, 374
Lambert, John (1619–1683), 285–286, 291–2, 306–7
Lancashire, 241, 252, 279
Landriano, 44
Langport, 266
Langside, 113
La Rochelle, 124, 209, 212–3, 219
Latimer, Hugh, Bishop of Winchester (1485–1555), 14, 168; quoted, 61, 65, 82
Laud, William, Archbishop of Canterbury (1573–1645), 215, 227, 241, 245–6, 249; character, 231–2, 236; religious policy, 231–6, 244, 317; and Scotland, 236–7
Lauderdale, John Maitland, Duke of (1616–1682), 326–8
Law of Freedom (1652), 281 n.
Laws of Ecclesiastical Polity (1594), 157
Le Havre, 108–9
Leicester Abbey, 45
Leicester, Robert Dudley, Earl of (1532–1588), 104, 111, 115, 120, 134, 148, 160–1
Leighton, Alexander (1568–1649), 235, 241; quoted, 235
Leith, 106
Leo X, Pope (1513–1522), 30, 34, 39–42
Leonard, E. M., quoted, 229
Leopold I, Emperor (1658–1705), 372, 377, 381–2
Lepanto, 125, 129
Le Quesnoy, 384
Leslie, Alexander, Earl of Leven (1580–1661), 237, 247, 262, 274
Leslie, David, Baron Newark (1601–1682), 279
L'Estrange, Sir Roger (1616–1674), 347; quoted, 313
Letter to a Dissenter (1686), 356
Levant, 20, 170, 288
Levant Company (1581), 330
Levellers, 271–3, 281, 289-90, 292, 303, 388
Leviathan (1651), 280
Leyden, 214
Licensing Act, 365
Lilburne, John (1614–1657), 235, 241, 271, 281; quoted, 272, 281

Lima, 129
Limerick, 371
Linacre, Thomas (1460–1524), **27**
Lincoln, John de la Pole, Earl of (1464–1487), 13
Lincolnshire, 54, 252, 262
Lindsey, Robert Bertie, Earl of (1582–1642), 219, 252
Livery and Maintenance, Act of (1487), 15–16, 70
Lochleven Castle, 113–14
Locke, John (1632–1704), **77**, **320**, 356, 361 ; quoted, 361
Lollards, 34, 49
London, 11, 21, 72, 74, 90, 124, 159, 229, 269, 315, 348–9, 357, 359, 381 ; during the Great Rebellion, 253, 256–7, 260
London, Treaty of (1518), 39
Londonderry, 371
Long Parliament (1640–1660), Chapter XV–XVI ; 277 n., 283 ; attack on the prerogative, 240–3, 309 ; divided on religious questions, 244–9 ; declares war, 250–1 ; quarrel with the Independents, 263–5, 268–71 ; negotiations with the King, 257, 264, 267–9, 271, 273–4, 343, 363 ; purged, 275 ; restored and dissolved, 307 ; *see also* Rump
Lostwithiel, 263
Louis XI of France (1461–1483), 22
Louis XII of France (1498–1515), 24, 29–30, 38
Louis XIII of France (1610–1643), 204, 208, 212
Louis XIV of France (1643–1715), 209, 243, 345–6, 351, 358–9, 365, 369, 371, 394 ; and Charles II, 332–5, 337, 339–340, 342, 345 ; and Danby, 336–9 ; war with William III, 372–6 ; and Spain, 332–3, 377–85
Louis, Dauphin of France (d. 1711), 377
Louvain, 129
Lovelace, Richard (1618–1658), 254 n.
Lovell, Francis, Viscount (1454–1487), 12–13
Ludlow, Edmund (1617–1692), 278, 305 ; quoted, 287, 305
Lumley, Richard, Earl of Scarborough (d. 1721), 359
Luther, Martin (1483–1546), **42**, 48–50, 85 ; quoted, 55
Luxemburg, 377
Luxemburg, Francis, Duke of (1628–1695), 375

Macaulay, Thomas Babington, Baron (1800–1859), 380 n.
Macdonalds of Glencoe, 369
Machiavelli, Niccolo (1469–1527), 156
Macleod, Neil, eleventh of Assynt (1628–1697), 279
Madrid, 202, 209, 383
Mad Tom, 71
Magdalen College, 355, 359
Magnus Intercursus (1496), **20**
Main Plot (1603), 176
Maitland, William, of Lethington (1528–1573), 110
Major-Generals, rule of (1655–1656), 289–90
Malines, 106
Malplaquet, 383
Manchester, Edward Montagu, Earl of (1602–1671), 238 n., 261, 263–5, 275, 391 ; quoted, 264–5
Mandeville, Bernard (1670–1733), quoted, 77
Mandeville, Viscount, *see* Manchester
Mansell, Sir Robert (1573–1656), 224
Mansfeld, Count Ernest von (1580–1626), 204, 209
Manwaring, Roger, Bishop of St. David's (1590–1653), 215, 217 ; quoted, 215
Marches, Council of, **17**, **33**, **66**, 242

Mardyck, 300–1
Mare Clausum (1635), 224
Mare Liberum (1609), 224
Margaret of Burgundy (1446–1503), 12–13
Margaret of Austria, Duchess of Savoy (1480–1530), 23 n.
Marignano, 38
Marlborough, John Churchill, Duke of (1650–1722), 243, 374–5, 395; estimate of, 380–1; and Spanish succession, 380–4; quoted, 395
Marlborough, Sarah Churchill, Duchess of (1660–1744), 395–396
Marsiglio of Padua (1278–1343), 164, 168
Marston Moor, 252, 262–3
Martin Marprelate Tracts (1588–1589), 151, 179
Martyr, Peter (Pietro Martire Vermigli, 1500–1562), 79; quoted, 80
Marvell, Andrew (1621–1678), quoted, 315
Mary I, Queen (1553–1558), Chapter VI; 39–40, 46, 68, 86–7, 97–8, 146, 197; character, 88–9; marriage, 90–1, 118; religious policy, 90, 92–4; quoted, 91
Mary II, Queen (1688–1694), 336–7, 343–4, 358 n., 360–3, 368, 391
Mary of Burgundy (1457-1482), 123
Mary of Guise (1515–1560), 58, 105–6
Mary of Modena, Queen (1658–1718), 340, 358, 358 n.
Mary, Queen of Scots (1542–1587), 58–9, 83, 91, 158, 162, 363; character, 110; rules in Scotland, 109–13; claims English throne, 110–12; flees to England, 113–14; detained in England, 114–15; centre of Catholic and Spanish plots, 115–17, 123–4, 129, 133–6, 142; executed, 135–6
Masham, Abigail, Lady (d. 1734), 396
Massacre of St. Bartholomew (1572), 125–6
Matthew's Bible (1537), 94
Maurice, Prince of Nassau (1567–1625), 139
Maximilian I, Emperor (1493–1519), 23, 23 n., 29, 39, 123
Mazarin, Jules, Cardinal (1602–1661), 301, 301 n.
Medina del Campo, Treaty of (1489), 22
Medina Sidonia, Alfonso Perez de Guzman, Duke of (1550–1615), 137; quoted, 137
Mediterranean Sea, 280, 294, 299–300, 329, 374, 381–2, 385
Melford, John Drummond, Earl of (1649–1714), 354
Mendoza, Bernardino de, 129, 133; quoted, 131
Merchant Adventurers (1505), 20, 170, 330
Merton College, 345 n.
Metropolitical Visitation (1633–1637), 231
Metz, 294
Milan, 28, 38–42, 377–8, 382, 384
Mildmay, Sir Walter (1520–1589), 149
Millenary Petition (1603), 176–7, 179–80
Milton, John (1608–1674), 245, 277 n., 319; quoted, 177
Minorca, 382, 384
Mitchell, Sir Francis, 200
Mompesson, Sir Giles (1584–1651), 200
Monasteries, dissolution of (1536, 1539), 52–4, 70, 92, 156
Monk, George, Duke of Albermarle (1608–1670), 279–80, 285, 295, 305, 321, 327; and the Restoration, 306–8; quoted, 306

Monopolies : under Elizabeth, 153, 174 ; under James I, 191, 200, 203, 223 ; under Charles I, 223–4, 230
Monmouth, James Scott, Duke of (1649–1685), 344, 344 n., 345, 347 ; rebellion, 352–3
Montagu, Charles, Earl of Halifax (1661–1715), 376, 391, 396
Montagu, Ralph, Duke of Montagu (1638–1709), 340
Montagu, Richard, Bishop of Chichester (1577–1641), 210, 215, 219 ; quoted, 215
Montague, Sir Henry Pole, Baron (1492–1538), 46, 55
Montrose, James Graham, Marquis of (1612–1650), 266, 279, 327
Moors, 107
More, Sir Thomas (1478–1535), 27, 35, 48, 54, 170 ; quoted, 61
Morlaix, 42
Morley, George, Bishop of Winchester (1597–1684), 318 ; quoted, 353
Morton, John, Archbishop of Canterbury (1420–1500), 15, 19
Morton, James Douglas, Earl of (1525–1581), 127, 133
Mountjoy, William Blount, Baron (d. 1534), 27
Mousehold Heath, 82
Münster, 381
Murray, James Stuart, Earl of (1531–1570), 113–15
Muscovy Company (1555), 330
Mutiny Act (1689), 364

Namur, 375–6
Naples, 38–9, 44, 95, 377, 384
Naseby, 266, 306
National Association (1696), 391
National Covenant (1638), 237, 239, 247
Navarre, 28, 39
Navarre, Henry of, *see* Henry IV
Navigation Act, 20
  1651 : 280, 295, 309 n.
  1660 : 329, 369, 372
Neerwinden, 375
Neile, Richard, Archbishop of York (1562–1640), 193
Ne Plus Ultra, lines of, 383
Netherlands, 39–40, 91, 299–300 ; war of independence, 103, 115, 122–34, 138–9 ; and wars of William III, 372–6 ; and Spanish succession, 378–385 ; *see also* Flanders, Holland
Newark, 176, 267
Newburn-on-Tyne, 239
Newbury, 260, 263
Newcastle, 239, 241
Newcastle, William Cavendish, Duke of (1592–1676), 252, 257, 260, 262
Newcastle, John Holles, Duke of (1662–1711), quoted 356 n.
Newcastle, Propositions of (1646), 268–70
New England, 253, 279
New Forest, 223
Newfoundland, 384
New Jersey, 331–2
Newman, John Henry, Cardinal (1801–1890), quoted, 233
Newmarket, 269, 348
New Model Army, 253, 256, 265–6, 271
New Netherlands, 331–2
Newport, Treaty of (1648), 269, 274
Newton, Sir Isaac (1642–1727), 320
Newtown Butler, 371
New York, 331–2
Nicholas, Sir Edward (1593–1669), 321
Nineteen Propositions (1642), 250, 308
Nombre de Dios, 120
Non-Jurors, 366–7, 367 n., 392
Non-Resisting Bill (1675), 338, 349 n.
Norfolk, 65, 87

Norfolk, Thomas Howard, Earl of Surrey, second Duke of (1443–1524), 15, 29
Norfolk, Thomas Howard, Earl of Surrey, third Duke of (1473–1554), 32, 42, 46, 56–8, 84, 89
Norfolk, Thomas Howard, fourth Duke of (1536–1572), 115–16
North, Council of the, 33, 66, 228–9, 242
Northampton, 149
Northampton, Spencer Compton, Earl of (1601–1643), 252
Northern Earls, Rebellion of (1569–1570), 115–16, 120, 124, 142
Northumberland, John Dudley, Duke of (1502–1553), 82, 173; character, 83–4; and enclosures, 63, 66, 82, 84; religious policy, 84–7, 94; succession plot, 86–7
Northumberland, Henry Percy, Earl of (1478–1527), 32
Northumberland, Thomas Percy, Earl of (1528–1572), 115
Norwich, 21, 72, 349
Notre Dame, 213
Nottingham, 251
Nottingham, Charles Howard, Earl of (1536–1624), 224
Nottingham, Daniel Finch, Earl of (1647–1730), 348, 367, 392, 394, 397
Nova Scotia, 384
Novgorod, 170
Nun of Kent, Elizabeth Barton (1506–1534), 54
Nymuegen, Treaty of (1678), 339

Oates, Titus (1649–1705), 339–41, 339 n., 343, 352, 352 n.
Observator (1681–1687), 347
Occasional Conformity, measures against, 367, 395, 397–8
October Club, 397–8
Of Reformation in England (1641), 245
Oldenbarneveldt, Johan von (1547–1619), 214
On True Obedience (1535), 168
Orinoco, river, 197
Ormonde, James Butler, Duke of (1610–1688), 278, 321, 348, 371
Oudenarde, 381
Oxford, 12, 94; during the Great Rebellion, 253, 256–7, 266
Oxford, John de Vere, Earl of (1443–1513), 15
Oxford Parliament (1681), 345–6
Oxford University, 29, 35, 79, 231, 278 n., 347, 355
Oxfordshire, 66

Pace, Richard (1482–1536), 27
Pacific, 120, 129
Palatinate, 198–9, 201, 203, 381
Panama, 120
Panzani, Gregorio, 235
Paris, 42, 106–7, 126, 382
Parker, Matthew, Archbishop of Canterbury (1504–1575), 100–101, 103, 147, 149, 231
Parker, Samuel, Bishop of Oxford (1640–1688), 355
Parma, Alexander Farnese, Duke of (1545–1592), 129, 129 n., 130, 132–4, 137–9
Parsons, Robert (1546–1610), 144, 181
Partition Treaties (1698–1699), 377–8, 393
Paul IV, Pope (1555–1559), 95
Pavia, 42
Pecquiny, Treaty of (1475), 23
Pembroke, 274
Penn, Sir William, admiral (1621–1670), 299
Penn, William (1644–1718), 356
Penry, John (1559–1593), 148 n.
Pepys, Samuel (1633–1673), 350; quoted, 325
Persia, 170
Perth, 106
Perth, James Drummond, Earl of (1648–1716), 354

Index

Peru, 120, 174
Pescara, Ferdinando d' Avalos, Marquis of (1490–1525), 43
Peterborough, Charles Mordaunt, Earl of (1658–1735), 395
Peter's Pence, 52
Petition of Right (1628), 194–5, 216–18
Petre, Edward (1631–1699), 354
Petty, Sir William (1623–1687), quoted, 75
Phelips, Sir Robert (1586–1638), 191, 200, 209
Philip II of Spain (1556–1598), Chapter VIII; 40, 112; and Mary Tudor, 90–5; proposes marriage to Elizabeth, 104–5, 118; plots against Elizabeth, 115–17, 123–4, 133–5, 142; causes of quarrel with England, 119–24, 127, 135; and the Netherlands, 122, 126–7, 129, 133, 135, 138–9; alliance with the Guises, 130–1, 133, 138–9; at war with England, 136–7, 139–40
Philip V of Spain (1700–1746), 378, 382–3
Philiphaugh, 266
Picardy, 40, 374
Pickering, Sir William (1516–1575), 104
Piedmont, 382
Pilgrimage of Grace (1536–1537), 54, 65
Pilkington, James, Bishop of Durham (1520–1576), 148 n.; quoted, 147
Pinkie, 83
Pisa, 20
Pistor, Tristram, quoted, 152
Pius IV, Pope (1559–1566), 112
Pius V, Pope (1566–1572), 115
Plymouth, 119, 124, 211, 256, 260
Pole, Reginald, Archbishop of Canterbury (1500–1558), 90, 92–5, 99
Politiques, 109, 134
Poor relief: Tudor poor laws, 71–3, 311; in the seventeenth century, 73–7, 229, 311; attitude of Puritans to, 75–7
Portland, 295
Portland, William Bentinck, Earl of (1634–1709), 364, 390
Portobello, 384
Portsmouth, 253
Portugal, 119, 131, 140, 294, 299, 381–2, 384
'*Post-nati*', 184–5
Powick Bridge, 261
Powis, William Herbert, Marquis of (1617–1696), 354
Poynings, Sir Edward (1459–1521), 15, 24
Praemunire, Statute of (1353), 49, 51
Prayer Book
  1549: 80–1
  1552: 85–6, 89
  1559: 99, 150, 180, 316
  efforts to revise, 149, 152, 177, 246, 248, 263–4
Presbyterianism: under Elizabeth, 148–9, 151–2; under James I, 178–9; under Charles I, in Scotland 236–8, in the Long Parliament 245, 248–9, and the Covenant 260, 263–4, 268–9, 271, 273–5; during the Interregnum, 279–80, 305, 307–8; under Charles II, 315–16, 317 n., 320; after 1688, 367, 367 n., 368–9; *see also* Puritanism
Preston, 274–5
Pride, Thomas (d. 1658), 275, 312
Pride's Purge (1648), 275, 283, 301, 307
Proclamations, Statute of (1539), 55, 79
Prophesyings, 149–50, 152, 178
Provence, 22
Proverbs, Book of, 62, 155, 164
Providence Company (1630), 238 n.
Provisors, Statute of (1351), 49
Prussia, 384–5

Prynne, William (1600–1669), 235, 241, 292
Puritanism: the Puritan creed, 153–157, 214, 226, 233–5, 319; attitude to poverty, 75–7; opposition to ritual, 146–7; permanent effects of, 155–7, 318–19; under Elizabeth, 150–3; under James I, 176–80, 204; under Charles I, 214–15, 232–6, 252; during the Interregnum, 283–5, 288, 290; under Charles II, 302, 315–320, 328; under James II, 354–7; after 1688, 366–7, 387–8, 395; *see also* Independents, Presbyterianism, Prophesyings
Putney, 271
Pym, John (1584–1643), 191, 201, 215, 238, 238 n., 240, 247, 252–3, 255–6, 260–1, 268, 312, 343, 391; attack on the prerogative, 241–3, 248–9; religious policy, 245–6, 248; quoted, 249
Pyrenees, Peace of (1659), 301 n., 337

Quakers, 288, 315, 366
Quo Warranto, 349

Radcliffe, Sir George (1593–1657), quoted, 227–8
Ragenell, 62
Ragusa, 124
Rainborough, Thomas (d. 1648), 272; quoted, 272
Rainborough, William (d. 1642), 225
Rainbowe, Edward, Bishop of Carlisle (1608–1684), 318
Raleigh, Sir Walter (1552–1618), 138, 168, 172, 176, 188–9, 197–8; quoted, 68, 173
Ramillies, 380, 382
Rammekens, 134
Rastadt, Treaty of (1714), 384
Rathmines, 278
Reading, 271
Reformation Parliament (1529–1536), 50–2, 219, 240
Reform Bill (1832), 390
Reid, R. R., quoted, 229
Remonstrance of the Army (1648), 274
Renard, Simon, 90–3, 95
Renée of Valois, Duchess of Ferrara (1510–1575), 48
Requescens y Zuniga, Don Luis de (d. 1576), 127, 129
Requests, Court of, 17, 32–3, 64, 82
Revocation, Act of (1625), 236
Reynolds, John (1549–1607), 178
Rhé, Isle of, 212
Rhine, river, 359, 374, 381–2, 385
Rich, Sir Nathaniel (1585–1636), quoted, 209
Richard II (1377–1399), 166–7; quoted, 167
Richard II, 168
Richard of York (1472–1483), 13
Richelieu, Armand-Jean du Plessis, Cardinal, Duke of (1585–1642), 212–13, 219, 290, 297
Richmond, Sir Henry Fitzroy, Duke of (1519–1536), 33, 47
Ridley, Nicholas, Bishop of London (1500–1555), 85, 94
Ridolfi, Roberto (1531–1612), 116, 120, 124, 142
Riga, 20
Riot Act (1715), 399
Ripon, 239
Rizzio, David (1533–1566), 112, 114, 159
Rochester, Laurence Hyde, Earl of (1641–1711), 348, 354, 394; quoted, 360
Rockingham Forest, 223
Rocroi, 294 n.
Rogers, John (1500–1555), 94
Roll^, John (1598–1648), 219
Romanov, Michael, Czar (1613–1645), 197
Rome, 39, 43–4, 48, 143
Rooke, Sir George (1650–1709), 395

Root and Branch Bill (1641), 246–7
Roussillon, 23
Rowton Heath, 266
Royal Society, 320
Rudyerd, Sir Benjamin (1572–1658), quoted, 220
Rumbold, Richard (1622–1685), 348
Rump (of the Long Parliament): rule of, 277–82; dissolved, 282; restored, 305–7; foreign policy, 280, 294–6, 329–330, 333
Rumsey, John, 348
Rupert, Prince (1619–1682), 257, 262–3, 266, 280, 299
Russell, Edward, Earl of Orford (1653–1727), 357, 359, 374, 391, 396
Russell, William, Lord (1639–1683), 339, 348
Russia, 20, 197
Ruvigny, Henry de Massue de, Marquis of (1648–1720), 339
Rye House Plot (1683), 348
Ryswick, Treaty of (1697), 375, 389

Sacheverell, Henry (1674–1724), 396
Saffron Walden, 269
St. Albans, Abbey of, 30
St. Andrews, 106
St. John, Oliver (1598–1673), 238 n.; quoted, 241
St. Leger, Sir Anthony (1496–1559), 57
St. Malo, 374
St. Margaret's, 191
St. Omer, 339
St. Paul, quoted, 70 n.
St. Paul's, 34, 234
Salamanca, 339
Salisbury, Robert Cecil, Earl of (1563–1612), 161, 185–6, 188, 190, 204; quoted, 68
Salisbury, Margaret Pole, Countess of (1473–1541), 55
Sallee, 225
Sancroft, William, Archbishop of Canterbury (1617–1693), 357
San Domingo, 135, 299
Sandys, Edwin, Archbishop of York (1516–1588), 148 n.
Sandys Sir Edwin (1561–1629), 191
San Felipe, 137
San Juan d'Ulloa, 120, 124
Santiago (Cape Verde Islands), 135
Santiago (Chile), 129
Sardinia, 382, 384
Savoy, 300, 372
Savoy Conference (1661), 315
Savoy, Emmanuel Philibert, Duke of (1553–1580), 95
Savoy, Victor Amadeus II, Duke of (1675–1730), 381–2, 384
Savoy, Anna Maria, Duchess of (1669–1728), 393 n.
Saye and Sele, William Fiennes, Viscount (1582–1662), 225, 238 n.
Scarborough, 228
Scheldt, river, 127
Schism Act (1714), 367, 399
Scone, 166
Scot, Thomas (d. 1660), 305
Scotland
  under Henry VII, 13, 24
  under Henry VIII, 29, 39, 42, 57–9
  under Edward VI, 78, 83–4
  under Elizabeth, 127, 133, 136; French party expelled, 105–7; Mary Stuart in, 109–113; Mary expelled, 113
  under James I, 160, 184–5, 187, 236
  under Charles I, 231, 236–9; Scottish army in England, 239–43; during Great Rebellion, 260, 262–3, 274; negotiations with Charles, 247, 267–8, 273
  during the Interregnum, 278–280, 306
  after 1660, 368–70, 391; Act of Union, 370

Sedgemoor, 353
Selden, John (1584–1654), 33, 224 319, 361; quoted, 361
Self-Denying Ordinance (1645), 265, 268, 283
Seminary priests, 142–3
Septennial Act (1716), 399
Servetus, Miguel (1511–1553), 93
Settlement, Act of (1701), 365, 369–70, 388, 393–4, 398
Settlement, Law of (1662), 74–5, 311
Seville, 143
Seymour, Sir Edward (1633–1708), 356, 394; quoted, 346
Seymour, Francis, Baron Seymour of Trowbridge (1590–1664), quoted, 203
Seymour, Thomas, Baron Seymour of Sudeley (1508–1549), 82
Sforza, Massimiliano, Duke of Milan (1512–1515), 38
Shaftesbury, Anthony Ashley Cooper, Earl of (1621–1683), 285, 348, 355, 392; and Cabal., 326–8, 334–5; and Danby, 336–9; and the Whig party, 337–8, 341; and Exclusion, 339–47; quoted, 334
Shaftesbury, Mary, Countess of, 340
Shakespeare, William (1564–1616), 155–6, 168, 194; quoted 70, 168, 204
Shannon, river, 371
Sheldon, Gilbert, Archbishop of Canterbury (1598–1677), quoted, 317
Ship-money, 213, 224–5, 238–9, 243
Shirley, Sir Thomas (1542–1612), 183
Short Parliament (1640), 238, 241
Shrewsbury, Charles Talbot, Duke of (1660–1718), 357, 359, 391, 399
Shrewsbury, George Talbot, Earl of (1468–1538), 15
Sibthorpe, Robert (d. 1662), quoted, 215
Sicily, 377, 384
Sidney, Algernon (1622–1683), 339, 348
Sidney, Henry, Earl of Romney (1641–1704), 359
Sidney, Robert, 344 n.
Simnel, Lambert (*c.* 1475–*c.* 1535), 12–13
Sion, monastery of, 93
Six Articles
  1539: 55, 56 n., 79, 81
  1583: 150
Slave trade, 119–20, 384
Smith, Sir Thomas (1513–1577), 32 n.; quoted, 32
Smithfield, 94, 96, 182
Smithfield, monastery of, 93
Smyrna, 374
Solemn League and Covenant (1643), 260, 262, 264, 267–8, 270, 274, 279, 302, 307–8, 316
Solway Moss, 58
Somers, John, Baron (1651–1716), 391, 396
Somerset, 234, 240, 291
Somerset, Robert Carr, Earl of (1590–1645), 159, 161–2, 189
Somerset, Edward Seymour, Duke of (1506–1552), 58, 256; character and aims, 78–9, 83; and enclosures, 65, 81–2; religious policy, 79–82; and Scotland, 78, 83, 105
Sophia, Electress of Hanover (1630–1714), 369, 393–4
South America, Spanish colonies in, 39, 64, 91, 119–21, 170, 196, 298, 377–8
Southampton, 124
Southampton, Thomas Wriothesley, Earl of (1607–1667), 321
Southwold Bay, 334
Spain
  and Henry VII, 22–3
  and Henry VIII, 28–9, 37–45, 54–5
  and Mary Tudor, 90–2, 95

Spain
 and Elizabeth, Chapter VIII; 97, 106, 115–16; causes of quarrel, 119–24, 127, 135; at war, 134, 136–40
 and James I, 182, 190, 196, 201–2; marriage project, 197–199; at war, 203–4
 and Charles I, 208–11, 222, 239
 during the Interregnum, 294, 296–7; at war, 290, 298–301; and William III, 372, 374
 war of succession, 377–85
Spenser, Edmund (1552–1599), 156
Spice Islands, 295, 330
Spinola, Ambrogio de, Marquis of (1571–1630), 204
Stade, 213
Stafford, Humphrey, 12
Stafford, William Howard, Viscount (1614–1680), 345, 345 n.
Stamp Act (1712), 398
Star Chamber, Court of, 32, 45, 64, 136 164, 229, 277; Act of 1487, 17; abolished, 242
Stayner, Sir Richard (d. 1662), 299
Steele, Richard (1629–1692), quoted, 75–6
Steenkirk, 375
Stirling, 106, 113
Stoke, 13
Stow-on-the-Wold, 266
Strafford, Thomas Wentworth, Earl of (1593–1641), 190–1, 219, 238–9, 244, 301, 310–11, 321; ideals of government, 195, 226–30; joins the King, 218; and the Council of the North, 228–9; and Ireland, 229, 237, 239; arrest and execution, 241–3; quoted, 228, 242
Strangways, Giles, 328; quoted, 328
Strasburg, 375, 382
Strickland, Sir Roger (1640–1717), 354
Strickland, Walter, 149
Strode, William (1599–1645), 220
Stuart, Lady Arabella (1575–1615), 176
Stuart, Esmé Duke of Lennox (1542–1583), 133, 162
Stubbs, John (1543–1591), 131; quoted, 131
Stubbs, Philip (fl. 1580), quoted, 66
Stubbs, William, Bishop of Oxford (1825–1901), quoted, 31
Suffolk, Charles Brandon, Duke of (1484–1545), 42, 46, 87; quoted, 48
Suffolk, John de la Pole, Duke of (1442–1491), 12
Sully, Maximilien de Béthune, Duke of (1559–1641), 196
Sunderland, Robert Spencer, second Earl of (1640–1702), 354, 389, 391
Sunderland, Charles Spencer, third Earl of (1674–1722), 396
Supremacy, Act of
 1534: 52, 92
 1559: 99
Surrey, 59, 241, 281
Surrey, Henry Howard, Earl of (1517–1547), 57, 170
Surrey, Earls of, *see* Norfolk
Sweden, 297, 332
Swift, Jonathan (1667–1745), 396; quoted, 387, 396
Swiss (army), 38
Swiss reformers, 81, 84–6

Tangier, 353
Taylor, Jeremy, Bishop of Down and Connor (1613–1667), 319
Teignmouth, 374
Temple, Sir William (1628–1699), 332, 342
Ten Articles (1536), 55–6
Test Act (1673), 335, 353–4, 366
Teviotdale, 161, 189
Texel, island, 295, 334, 374
Thérouanne, 28
Thirty-nine Articles (1563), **101**, 150, 366

Thirty Years War (1618–1648), 196, 198–204, 293
'Thorough', 226–30, 301
Three Resolutions (1629), 220–1
Throckmorton, Francis (1554–1584), 133
Throckmorton, Sir Nicholas (1515–1571), 106
Thurloe, John (1616–1668), 304, 308; quoted, 291, 300, 303–4
Tilbury, 137
Tillotson, John, Archbishop of Canterbury (1630–1694), quoted, 318
Tirlemont, 129
Toleration Act (1689), 366
Tonge, Israel (1621–1680), 339
Torbay, 359
Torcy, Jean-Baptiste Colbert, Marquis of, 385
Torrington, Arthur Herbert, Earl of (1647–1716), 374
Tory party: origin of the name, 344; composition, 386–7, 392; political principles, 336–337, 343, 351, 360–2, 386–7, 392; religious principles, 317–318, 319 n., 336–7, 386, 390, 395, 398–9; and Exclusion, 346–7; first Tory ministry, 347–9; and James II, 353, 355–6; and the Revolution, 358–62; and the French wars, 373, 381, 383, 387, 390–1, 395–7; and the succession, 397–9
Toul, 294
Toulon, 280
Tournai, 13, 28
Tourville, Anne-Hilarion de Costentin, Count of (1642–1701), 374
Tradesman's Calling, The (1684), 75–6
Travers, Walter (1548–1635), 148 n., 149
Treason Act: of Henry VIII, 54–5, 79, 84; of the Rump, 277; of 1696, 365, 391
Trenchard, Sir John (1640–1695), 391
Trent, Council of, 118, 133, 141, 180
Trevor, Sir John (1626–1672), 326
Trew Law of Free Monarchies (1603), 163
Triennial Act
1641: 242
1694: 364
Tripoli, 107
Tromp, Martin Harpetzoon van (1597–1653), 295
Tudor, Edmund, Earl of Richmond (1430–1456), 12
Tudor, Jasper, Duke of Bedford (1431–1495), 12
Tudor, Margaret, Queen of Scotland (1489–1541), 18, 24, 46, 105, 111–12, 176
Tudor, Mary, Queen of France (1496–1533), 24, 29, 38, 87
Tudor, Owen (d. 1461), 11
'Tudor Despotism', nature of, 169–72, 174, 184, 323, 400
Tunis, 299
Tunnage and Poundage, 210, 213, 217–20, 222
Tunnage and Poundage Act (1641), 218, 242
Tunstall, Cuthbert, Bishop of Durham (1474–1559), 27, 81, 83, 89
Turenne, Henry de la Tour d'Auvergne, Viscount of (1611–1675), 300, 334
Turin, 382
Turks, 125, 224, 377, 381
Turnham Green, 257
Turnhout, 139
Tuscany, 377
Tyburn, 143, 312, 352
Tyndale, William (1484–1536), 181; quoted, 61
Tyrconnel, Richard Talbot, Earl of (1630–1691), 354, 371

Udall, John (1560–1592), 148 n., 151

Ulster, 229, 237, **248**
'Undertakers', 191
Unemployment, problem of, 70–1; Tudor measures, 71–3; *see also* poor relief
Uniformity, Act of
1549: 80
1552: 85
1559: 99
1662: 316–17, 366
Union, Act of (1707), **370**
Unitarians, 366
Urban VIII, Pope (1623–1644), 239
Ussher, James, Archbishop of Armagh (1581–1656), **314–5**
Utopia (1516), 61
Utrecht, Peace of (1711–1713), 384–5, 397
Uxbridge, Treaty of (1645), 264, 308

Valentine, Benjamin (d. 1652), 220
Valladolid, 143, 339
Valparaiso, 129
Vane, Sir Henry, the younger (1613–1662), 305, 312 n.
Venables, Robert (1612–1687), 299
Venice, 20, 28, 124
Venner Thomas (d. 1661), 315
Verdun, 294
Vere, Sir Francis (1560–1609), 139
Verney, Sir Edmund (1590–1642), 202; quoted, 254
Vervins, Peace of (1598), **139**
Vienna, 381
Vigo, 135
Villa Viciosa, 383

Waldensians, 300
Waldo, Peter (fl. 1180), 300 n.
Wales, 26, 57, 240, 260, 274
Waller, Sir William (1597–1668), 263, 265; quoted, 251 n.
Walloons, 79
Walsingham, Sir Francis (1530–1590), 103, 120, 125, 134–5, 148 n., 149; quoted, 130
Walters, Lucy (1630–1658), 344
Waltham Forest, 223
Warbeck, Perkin (1474–1499), **13**, 23
Warham, William, Archbishop of Canterbury (1450–1532), 30, 37, 52
Warrington, 274
Warwick, Edward Plantagenet, Earl of (1475–1499), 12–13, 47
Warwick, John Dudley, Earl of, *see* Northumberland
Warwick, Ambrose Dudley, Earl of (1528–1590), 109
Warwick, Robert Rich, Earl of (1587–1658), 238 n., 252, 256
Warwickshire, 252
Waterford, 371
Watson, William (1559–1603), 176, 182
Wentworth, Peter (1530–1596), 149; quoted, 149
Wentworth, Sir Thomas, *see* Strafford
West Indies, 280, 299, 330
Westminster, 74, 114
Westminster Abbey, 191, **312**
Westminster Assembly (1643), **307**
Westminster, Colloquy of (1559), 99
Westminster, monastery of, 93, 98
Westmorland, Charles Neville, Earl of (1543–1601), 115
Weston, Richard, Earl of Portland (1577–1635), 219, 222, 229
Westphalia, Peace of (1648), 293, 296
Wexford, 278
Wharton, Nehemiah, quoted, 254 n.
Wharton, Thomas, Marquis of (1648–1715), 391, 396–7
Whig party: origin of the name, 344; composition, 320, 338, 362, 387–8, 391; political principles, 351, 361, 364, 388; financial policy, 375–6, 395; and Exclusion, 341–6; and the Revolution, 358–62; and the French wars, 376, 382, 390–1, 396–7; the Junto, 389, 391–2, 394, 396

Whitehall, 242, 291, 295, 312, 340, 354
Whitgift, John, Archbishop of Canterbury (1530–1604), 103, 150–2, 178, 231; quoted, 150
Wildman, Sir John (1621–1693), quoted, 271
William III (1688–1702), 336, 344–5, 353; and James II, 357–61; and the English throne, 360–3; powers of, 363–6, 389–90; and parties in England, 386–7, 388–94; financial problems, 364, 375–376; and France, 358–9, 361, 365–6, 368, 371; French war, 372–6; and Spanish succession, 377–80; and Scotland, 368–70; and Ireland, 368, 370–2; quoted, 358, 361
William IV (1830–1837), 390
William of Ockham (1300–1349), 164
William of Orange (1533–1584), 103, 127, 129–30, 132–3, 139, 374
Willoughby, Francis, Baron Willoughby of Parham (1613–1666), 252
Wimbledon, Sir Edward Cecil, Viscount (1572–1638), 210–11
Winchcombe, Richard Kidderminster, Abbot of (d. 1531), 34
Winchester, 91
Windebank, Sir Francis (1582–1646), 241
Windsor, 250, 273
Winstanley, Gerrard, 281, 281 n.
Winter, Sir William (d. 1589), 106
Winwood, Sir Ralph (1563–1617), 191
Wolsey, Thomas, Archbishop of York (1475–1530), Chapter II; 23; character and influence, 29–31, 45; administration of justice, 31–3, 36; and enclosures, 33, 64; and the Church, 33–7, 50–1; foreign policy, 29, 37–44, 48, 118; and the 'divorce', 43–4, 48; failure and fall, 44–5, 48; quoted, 31, 43, 48
Worcester, 279, 287, 291, 321
Worms, Diet of (1521), 42
Wotton, Sir Henry (1568–1639), quoted, 190
Wren, Sir Christopher (1632–1723), 320
Wyatt, Sir Thomas (1503–1542), 170
Wyatt, Sir Thomas (1521–1554), 90
Wycliffe, John (1320–1384), 48–9

York, 12, 45, 72, 114, 239, 250, 253, 262, 321
Yorkshire, 228, 240, 253, 257, 262, 328
Young, Thomas, Archbishop of York (1507–1568), 148 n.

Zeeland Islands, 333
Zutphen, 134
Zwinglianism, 85, 100–1